IN THE
BLOODY
RAILROAD CUT
AT
GETTYSBURG

Old Railroad Cut in which the 2d Mississippi with its colors were captured.

THE UNFINISHED RAILROAD CUT

This photo was taken in the late 1860s or 1870s before tracks were laid in the railroad cut. The charge of the 6th Wisconsin occurred in the immediate foreground.

IN THE
BLOODY
RAILROAD CUT
AT
GETTYSBURG

By
Lance J. Herdegen
and
William J. K. Beaudot

Morningside
1990

ISBN: 089029-535-X

Morningside House, Inc.
260 Oak Street, Dayton, Ohio 45410

BOMC offers recordings and compact discs, cassettes
and records. For information and catalog write to
BOMR, Camp Hill, PA 17012.

With thanks to the forbearance and support of my family, Michelle, Corinne, Andre and Renee Beaudot, and Jean.

William J. K. Beaudot

TATTERED BANNER
The National Flag carried by the 6th Wisconsin in the Charge on the Railroad Cut.

vi

For my father, a teller of first-rate stories himself, and for Bonnie, Lisa, Jill, Jennifer and Nicole, but most of all, with love and admiration, for Shirley.

Lance J. Herdegen

CAPTURED FLAG

The Captured Flag of the 2nd Mississippi. This photo was taken when the flag was
brought to Milwaukee when the 6th Wisconsin returned on veteran furlough in 1864.

CONTENTS

PHOTOGRAPHS

CENTER PAGES

MAPS

FRANCIS A. WALLAR
Postwar photo
Captured a Rebel Flag

xiv

FOREWORD

The great story of Gettysburg is well known to Civil War readers. That great story is made up of a number of "little stories," particular incidents that were unusually dramatic. A few of the particular, dramatic incidents were also decisive in terms of the outcome of the battle. One of these was the successful assault on the railroad cut by the Sixth Wisconsin Volunteers and the Iron Brigade Guard on the first day of the battle.

It is fair to say that this early action at the railroad cut preserved the First Corps' line along McPherson's Ridge at the outset of the three-day battle. The preservation of that line set up the rest of the fighting on the first day. Although defeated on that day, the First and Eleventh Corps punished the Confederates severely and delayed them so that the high ground south of the town was saved for the Union. It was from this high ground that the Federal army decisively defeated the Army of Northern Virginia on the second two days of the battle. Had the First Corps been driven from McPherson's Ridge on the morning of July 1, 1863, the events that afternoon and on July 2 and July 3 would surely have taken a different course, a course destructive to the Federals.

The early action on the railroad cut is therefore entitled to an in-depth description. Lance J. Herdegen and William J. K. Beaudot have carefully examined this action. Having researched the event with a depth and scope that is truly remarkable, and that includes the observations of a number of participants, they have put the story together in a detailed, fast-moving account. Excellently written, the book also tells us a great deal about what the Civil War was really like. It is a valuable contribution to our knowledge of Gettysburg and our understanding of the war as a whole.

Alan T. Nolan
October 13, 1989
Indianapolis, Indiana

CAPT. RUFUS R. DAWES
He Raised the Lemonweir Minute Men

ACKNOWLEDGEMENTS

In writing any book that deals with history—especially Civil War history—any writer or writers, as in this case, find themselves quickly in debt to a number of people. It was simply overwhelming to discover how many folks will come forward to help in the gathering of elusive letters, newspaper accounts and forgotten photographs. Without putting a measure on their contributions, the authors would like to thank a number of them individually.

Anyone writing on the most famous brigade of the Army of the Potomac must first consult Alan T. Nolan's *The Iron Brigade*, a study of such fine scholarship and written in such a first-rate fashion that it still ranks today as the most comprehensive book on the subject. Alan, a very old friend, was always a source of inspiration, advice and information. Alan D. Gaff, another fine writer in his own right, also provided valuable information. He is without peer as a researcher on Iron Brigade matters, as his own book, *Brave Men's Tears*, bears witness. Certainly, it is somehow fitting these Indianans came forward more than 125 years later to stand with Wisconsin men as this book about an Iron Brigade regiment came together.

The authors also would like to salute Howard Michael Madaus for his overall assistance and his individual contribution of an appendix on the Iron Brigade uniform. A nationally recognized Civil War scholar and author, Howard, a curator at the Milwaukee Public Museum, is an old comrade and friend, and, to steal a description from Jerome A. Watrous, "No private in the old brigade fired his musket faster or carried a larger knapsack."

We must also cite a number of folks with personal ties to the 6th Wisconsin, Robert A. Sullivan and his wife, Pat, of La Crosse, Wisconsin; James Fitz Sullivan of New Port Richey, Florida; Bryan and Michael Haynes of St. Louis; William Washburn of Chicago. The Sullivans of La Crosse were extremely helpful in filling out details and providing photos of James Patrick Sullivan, the famous "Mickey of Company K." Pat Sullivan, especially, was tireless in adding to the Sullivan story, while Mickey's son, James F. Sullivan, is much the "bright-eyed boy" that so characterized his father. Bryan and Michael Haynes, whose kinsman include the dauntless Rufus R. Dawes, provided material from the Dawes Family, whose ancestors figured in so much American history. Bryan and Michael shared a campfire, stood fire on the skirmish line with the modern-day "Calico boys," and, we are sure, the "old general" would have been proud. Mr. Washburn came forward with a photo and additional information on his grandfather, Jerome A. Watrous, who wrote so much on the old regiment. We thank them all.

Others who contributed in a major fashion included Marc Storch and Craig Johnson, true Badgers even though they now live in Maryland; that front-rank member of the "Bohemian Brigade," Dick Martin, editor of the *Kenosha News*; Merton Eberlein of Mauston, Wisconsin; those tireless protectors of Wisconsin's Civil War battle flags, Richard Zeitlein and Lynnette Wolfe of the GAR Memorial Hall at Madison; fellow members of the Milwaukee Civil War Round Table; our comrades in the modern-day 6th Wisconsin Volunteers, especially Michael Lauer of Detroit, and Dr. Lon Kiem and Larry Lefler of Nebraska; David Vermilion of the Dawes Arboretum at Newark, Ohio; Jerry Coates of Washington, D.C.; William A. Bolgrien of Beloit; Gary D. Remy of Madison; Mary Slough and Tom Tomczak of the Milwaukee Public Library, and so many others. Of course, a special thanks to Bob and Mary Younger of the Morningside Bookshop, who provide so much fine reading for Civil War buffs.

Lance J. Herdegen, William J. K. Beaudot
December 1, 1989, Milwaukee, Wisconsin

INTRODUCTION

No sooner had the armies left the battlefield at Gettysburg, Pennsylvania, that July of 1863, than the war correspondents, military officials, historians, participants and others began writing about what was and is the greatest battle ever fought in the Western Hemisphere. No single military event in American history has been the subject of so much controversy. As a result, there is an overwhelming quantity of published material on Gettysburg from various writers and participants explaining what happened and why. Even President Abraham Lincoln, in his November, 1863, visit to dedicate a soldier cemetery, tried to put Gettysburg in perspective, and, in one fashion, he was the most successful. "The brave men, living and dead, who struggled here, have consecrated it far above our poor power to add or detract," said Lincoln in his two-minute speech. "The world will little note, nor long remember what we say here, but it can never forget what they did here."

Some of those "brave men" were the "Calico Boys" of the 6th Wisconsin Volunteer Infantry of the Iron Brigade, soldiers such as James P. Sullivan, a farmer-turned-volunteer who carried a canteen of fresh milk into the battle; New York State-born Loyd Harris, who led a make-shift unit called the "Iron Brigade Guard;" Rufus R. Dawes of Marietta, Ohio, who commanded the Wisconsin regiment, and brothers Frank and Sam Wallar, late of Bad Ax County, Wisconsin, two of the toughest soldiers in the Army of the Potomac. They left Wisconsin two years earlier along with friends and neighbors to preserve a Union of states. In 1863, they went to a place called Gettysburg and fought in the epic battle of the Civil War. In the very opening of the infantry fighting on July 1, 1863, the 6th Wisconsin double-quicked a half-mile to charge a Confederate brigade in an unfinished railroad cut west of the town. They captured 225 prisoners and the flag of the 2nd Mississippi Infantry.

The successful attack had far-reaching consequences. In his "Official Report" of the Iron Brigade at Gettysburg, written in 1878, William Dudley, a 19th Indiana officer who lost a leg fighting with his regiment, explained why the charge of the 6th Wisconsin was significant. The Iron Brigade had been successful in its attack on Archer's Confederate Brigade in McPherson's Woods, but the second Union Brigade of Wadsworth's small Division, commanded by Lysander Cutler, had "met with reverses" and was retreating. "[T]he whole line was thus threatened with disaster, when the gallant 6th Wisconsin of the Iron Brigade struck the flank of the victorious enemy and turned disaster into victory, thereby saving not only Cutler's brigade, but relieving our own and by consequence the division and corps," said Dudley. "By this brilliant achievement the Rebels were kept at respectful distance until the afternoon, our lines perfected by the arrival of the remainder of the [I] corps, and the stubborn resistance to the advance of the Rebel army made, which rendered the occupation of the Culp's and Cemetery hills and Round Top line by the remainder of the army, and their decisive victory thereon of July 2d and 3rd possible. Thus much is due to the truth of history." A 6th Wisconsin soldier put it plainer: "If the First corps had not held back three times their number, on the 1st [of July], the Confederates would have had Cemetery Ridge, Culp's Hill and the Round tops and there would have been no battle of Gettysburg. A just history will never deny that."

What the 6th Wisconsin accomplished that Wednesday morning at Gettysburg became a key factor in the Union success in the opening phase of the battle, and it was one of the few instances during the three days of fighting an individual regiment (others include the 1st Minnesota and the 20th Maine) had a significant impact on the outcome of the battle. But 6th Wisconsin men always believed what they had done was overlooked in the thousands of accounts of the battle, most of them produced by Eastern writers and Eastern officers. Never successful in their attempts to set the record straight, 6th Wisconsin survivors always believed they never received the credit due them. Twenty years after the great battle, Private Sullivan was already writing, with obvious bitterness, that the furious charge of his small regiment into the flank of a Confederate brigade had been all but forgotten. And there was further proof of all this as late as June, 1988, at the great 125th anniversary reenactment of Gettysburg. The sponsors and organizers decided to re-create the McPherson's Ridge fighting as the highlight of the First Day. Given the number of participants, it was determined only two of the five Iron Brigade regiments would be re-formed. The regiments selected were the

24th Michigan and 19th Indiana. Overlooked were the 2nd and 7th Wisconsin and, of course, the 6th Wisconsin. Even the commercial video tape of the reenactment mistakenly credited the charge against the advancing Confederate brigade of Joseph R. Davis to the "left regiments of Cutler's Brigade" and not to the 6th Wisconsin.

This then is not a recounting of the battle of Gettysburg or even of the first morning's fighting. It is the story of one Union regiment and what it did at Gettysburg, and, perhaps more important, how the soldiers remembered it. The story is based on dozens of first-hand accounts that have never before been used. These tell the story of a *significant* regiment that accomplished a *signficant* success that was a *significant* factor in the Union victory. The 6th Wisconsin men fought, not with their famous Iron Brigade that morning, but alone and unattached.

Of those 20 minutes of fighting, the 6th Wisconsin men left a remarkable record. Only little of what they wrote, however, has been used in the hundreds of books on Gettysburg since 1863. Dozens of their accounts were preserved, thanks to Jerome A. Watrous, who joined the regiment as a private at Appleton, Wisconsin, and later became editor of a Milwaukee society weekly newspaper called *The Milwaukee Sunday Telegraph*. For two decades Watrous reported on the old-soldier reunions and filled his columns with hundreds of interviews and recollections, most involving his beloved 6th Wisconsin. He always saw himself and his comrades in heroic light, and if, as he admitted in a letter to his former commander, Rufus R. Dawes, he sometimes "romanced" an incident or two, the record he left of the 6th Wisconsin is unmatched for any other regiment of the Civil War. While these accounts by the Wisconsin men answer some of the lingering questions about what happened the morning of July 1, 1863, they have been overlooked the past century.

Here then is the story of the forgotten charge of the 6th Wisconsin Infantry on an unfinished railroad cut at Gettysburg as left by J. P. Sullivan, R. R. Dawes, Frank and Sam Wallar, Bill Remington, George Fairfield, Loyd Harris and dozens of the "Calico Boys." Thus much is due to the truth of history, as William Dudley wrote a century ago.

Lance J. Herdegen, William J. K. Beaudot
May, 1989, Milwaukee, Wisconsin

JAMES P. SULLIVAN
"Mickey of Company K"

22

CHAPTER ONE

There are hats in the closets, old; ugly to view,
  Of very slight value, they may be to you;
But the wealth of the Astors, should not buy them to-day,
  With their letters of honor, old Company "K."
                                        — By "Mickey"

Mickey of Company K

The train carrying J. P. "Mickey" Sullivan back into the war rolled through a troubled countryside that February in 1863. After two years of bloody fighting, the Federal armies were stalled on both fronts; casualty lists were growing, and the Northern war spirit was just about played out. Nothing had been resolved despite the thousands of deaths, and there was now open talk at the home front against the war taxes and the draft, and the calls for peace at any price were louder and more strident. To a common soldier, it was all troubling those short, gray winter days; the road ahead forbidding and unsure. And if the locomotive's whistle seemed sad and mournful as the train rolled through Illinois, Indiana and then Ohio, perhaps it was because no one, even James Patrick Sullivan, could predict where it all was heading.

The young Irishman, a farmer, had been caught up in the war from the start. He had enlisted in a company raised in his home county in Wisconsin in 1861 and was sent to the war front at Washington. In his third battle, at South Mountain in Maryland, the rebels shot him in the right foot, putting him out of the army. He returned home in time for the Christmas holiday only to find things changed in the 18 months since he had left to be a soldier. It was all disconcerting, Sullivan remembered, for the war was touching even his home state with the women complaining about high prices, the men growling over tight money and the only young men in evidence banged-up soldiers or those dodging the war. The home folks had welcomed him, set him down, then

23

solemnly asked how it was, this soldiering; but they had not really listened when he tried to tell them, almost as if they were in one war and he another. His friends and relatives had made a big commotion about his battle wound, yet somehow, the Irishman wrote 20 years later of those strange weeks at home in the middle of the war, it was troubling, this pulling himself up to a full table and sleeping in a soft bed while the boys in his old company were off in Virginia breaking teeth on hardtack and sleeping on the ground. Uneasy and restless, Sullivan visited here and there; then one day he packed his traps, said his good-byes and went to Madison to look up the recruiting officer. He was not able to explain it then or when he wrote about it in middle age: he just knew he had to go back and see the thing through.

At Washington, he caught the steamer *John Brooks* to Belle Plain near Fredericksburg, where the Army of the Potomac had established a sprawling wintering place. The young Irishman made his way down the gangplank into a dock area tangled with boxed supplies, tents, munitions and wagons and marked by the cluttered, yet used-up look of a place where an army had spent too much time. Farther out, he could see the camps spread out on the bare hillsides, most of the trees long gone for firewood or construction, smoke curling from the sentry posts and the chimneys of the thousands of soldier huts. He was returning to an army beset with internal intrigue and frustrated by its defeats. In the west, the Union army was stalled in a bid to capture Vicksburg on the Mississippi. In the East, the Army of the Potomac was reorganizing from the December, 1862, bloodbath at Fredericksburg.

The roadway Sullivan followed was corduroyed with pine logs that caused difficulty for even teamsters and army mules, but, after a time, he located his 6th Wisconsin Infantry two miles below Belle Plain on the side of a steep knoll along the broad Potomac River. It was a pleasant enough camp with a fine view. The Badger soldiers, handy with ax and saw, had constructed substantial huts to wait out the winter. There was even a large log building for meetings as well as public performances by the young officers of the various regiments.

Sullivan's arrival set off a great "helloing" in the Wisconsin bivouac. Heads in broad-brimmed black hats poked out of tent doors on the company street, and there were muffled shouts inside the shebangs as the boys came spilling out, pulling on coats and wrapping blankets around their shoulders. They gathered around Sullivan, all grins, questions and handshakes. Last heard, the Irishman had been discharged from the army on a one-fifth disability pension. Yes, he had been back in Wisconsin the past weeks, but things were all different there with the war and all, Sullivan explained, trying to answer several questions at once, and then he dropped what the boys in the army camps in those days called called a "Big Thing": he was on his way to report to regimental headquarters because he had re-enlisted in the Old 6th for another nine months of shouldering a musket to put down the Rebellion. That triggered another uproar, and had the boys in Company K, his old neighbors, friends and comrades, shaking their heads in wonder and amusement. But it was good to have him back. Army life always seemed a little slow without Mickey.

Sullivan was a great camp favorite, a "slight, bright-eyed boy" who was "full of mischief," with a sharp glint in his friendly blue eyes. He "never lost a fight, never neglected a duty," one comrade said, and he was known far and wide as "Mickey of Company K." It was hard not to like the young Irishman. He was the kind of soldier an officer was proud to have on a firing line but kept a wary eye on in a winter camp. Sullivan had a decidedly "Western" outlook on soldiering, with the conviction he was as good as any man, shoulder straps notwithstanding. The Irish cockiness was there, along with a quick intelligence and a strong Wisconsin conviction in the enduring virtue of Common Sense. He was quick to point out the failings of his officers, and there was humor in what he wrote later of his soldier days as well as black Irish anger. Said one friend and admirer: "A hundred men wore the star of generals who did not dare or do as much in the war as J. P. Sullivan."

The farmer boy had been one of the earliest to sign the rolls to defend the Union when the volunteer company was assembled by Captain Rufus R. Dawes at Mauston in Juneau County in 1861, but he had earned his way out of the army with a bad case of shell-shock and two wounds in his first two years of soldiering.[1] The first time he ended up in an army hospital it caused a brigade uproar. On Washington's Birthday, 1862, the regiments had been formed in "a semicircle in close column" before the broad portico

1. U.S. Pension Office, James P. Sullivan file, affidavit of April 18, 1891.

of the Arlington House, near the nation's capitol, for a reading of the General's Farewell Address. Brigadier General Rufus King, the *Milwaukee Sentinel* editor-turned-soldier, had a few patriotic remarks, then the columns were deployed and battalion volleys of blank cartridges fired in honor of the day.[2] At the first crash of the muskets, Sullivan was knocked out of the line. Some private in the 7th Wisconsin behind the 6th had, unfortunately, failed to withdraw his ramrod after loading and the twirling steel shaft had whacked Sullivan in the back. The worried Company K boys gathered around the downed Irishman had raised angry fists, and there was muttering, loud enough to be heard in the other regiment, about a certain damned fool. So, Sullivan was in an army hospital for a day or two, but was soon back in ranks, a little worse for the wear. The incident did not improve already strained relations between the two regiments.[3]

The brigade's first battle came in late August as it was being tramped here and there during the opening of the Second Bull Run campaign. The soldiers were marching along a roadway near the old Bull Run battlefield when "Stonewall" Jackson's men came out of a woods. It was a savage baptism of fire for the Westerners in the dusk light on the farm fields owned by the Brawner family. The 2nd Wisconsin went in first, then another regiment, and finally Wisconsin's 6th. Sullivan recalled:

> It was about 80 rods across the field to a strip of woods. We had never been engaged at close quarters before, and the experience was new to all of us. I don't know how the others felt, but I am free to confess that I felt a queer choking sensation about the throat, but someone in the rear rank awkwardly stepped on my heel and I instantly forgot all about the choking feeling and turned on him, angrily, to demand if there was not room for him to march without skinning my heel; and we were jawing and fussing until the colonel shouted halt . . . [and he] gave the command: "6th Regiment, Ready! Aim-Aim Low, Fire!" and our regiment delivered one of

2. Rufus R. Dawes, *Service With The Sixth Wisconsin Volunteers*, (Marietta, Ohio, 1890), pp. 35-36. This book was reprinted by the Morningside Bookshop of Dayton, Ohio, in 1984.
3. Jerome A. Watrous, "The Old Brigade," *Milwaukee Sunday Telegraph*, September 27, 1885; U.S. Pension Office, Sullivan file.

the volleys by regiment for which it was noted. Every gun cracked at once . . .

The Western regiments stood their ground in that fight and Sullivan escaped unhurt. Two days later, in the battle of Second Bull Run, he was left dazed and deaf by an artillery barrage, but "shellshock" was not a disability recognized during the 19th century, so Sullivan was returned to ranks, probably to the good-natured jibes of his comrades.

The Union humiliation at Second Bull Run left the boys in the ranks "defeated, disgusted, dispirited, but not despairing," he wrote much later about that period; noting "Gallant little Hugh Talty" put it plain: "Arrah, if the big ginerals wus worth a cint, we'd show thim rebels what diligant hands we were at fightin'." With Robert E. Lee's army raiding into Maryland and General John Pope a failure at Second Bull Run, George B. McClellan had been restored to partial command. "Most of our men were jubilant in consequence, but [Sullivan tentmate Erastus] Smith and myself, who had no inclination to throw up our hats for anybody unless he had done something to deserve it. We reserved our cheers for future use."

A few days later, the 6th Wisconsin and the rest of the brigade marched in haste for Rockville, Maryland, in an attempt to intercept one of Lee's northward-reaching columns. Sullivan recalled:

> The day was very warm, and the clouds of dust nearly suffocating, and we marched all day with only the shortest possible halts and no stoppage for coffee, and in the afternoon the men who were completely worn out, began to straggle and fall out in squads. I marched until 3 o'clock and, seeing no prospect of coffee or any let up in the pace we were going, I assumed command of myself and gave orders to halt and lay down, which I did, and using my knapsack for a pillow I tried to get a little rest.

After a time, along came General Ambrose Burnside on "a powerful black horse," forcing the stragglers along "by attempting to ride over" those who were lying down. Burnside was known throughout the army for his magnificent mustache, a thick thatch of hair that covered his upper lip and flowed along the jaw. He was a Regular Army officer, and his star was rising in the Army of the

27

Potomac. Burnside was out of sorts that day, Sullivan said, and ordered the resting private to get up and go on; "but I paid no attention to it, as I considered I did not belong to his command and he was not my 'boss,' and with an exclamation that he'd make me leave there, he spurred his horse towards me."

General or not, all "the fighting blood of my race . . . rose up at the thought of being ridden over like a dog, and I sprang to my feet and cocking my gun, which had been loaded the day before on picket, brought it to a ready, determined to let the result be what it would, to kill him right there," Sullivan said. "Whether he was struck with shame at the thought of riding down a tired and worn out boy, or that he saw death in my look, he stopped." Burnside asked what regiment Sullivan belonged to and was given an answer. "You are one of the Western men," Burnside said, and it was more to himself than the high private. The general conferred briefly with a staff officer, gave Sullivan a long, steady look and told him to hurry along, and the officers rode off without looking back, or at least that is the way the farmer boy-turned-soldier remembered it all 20 years later.

After another hour or so of rest, Sullivan gathered himself up and stopped at a neighboring farm where he "bought a canteen of fresh milk and a batch of biscuits." He hurried up the roadway and soon overtook several of the Juneau County boys of Company K. They were in about the same fix. "We went along, gaining addition to our number and apples, potatoes, chickens and other additions to our larder, and at dusk we took possession of a small grove and had coffee with milk in it and biscuits, roast potatoes, apples and burned chicken to our hearts' content," the Irishman recalled. "Early next morning, refreshed and vigorous, we started and soon overtook the command bivouacked in a field close to the road, where it had halted for the simple reason that there was no longer any one to march."

A few days later, the 6th Wisconsin was fighting along the National Road at South Mountain when Sullivan's Irish luck ran out. He and the Company K boys were on the skirmish line in a field filled with large boulders. Despite the heavy fire and having to move uphill, the advance was steady. "Part of the men would fire and then rush forward while the others covered them and fired at the rebels, and then the rear line would pass through to the front," Sullivan wrote later. Here and there, behind a boulder,

28

three or four of the men would gather and hold it until the enemy was driven out of range. "The utmost enthusiasm prevailed," he recalled, "and our fellows were as cool and collected as if at target practice, and, in fact, on more than one occasion . . . one would ask the other to watch his shot and see where he hit."

Sullivan was working up the hill with his "comrades in battle," Privates George Chamberlain of Mauston, Ephraim Cornish of Lindina and Corporal Franklin Wilcox of Lemonweir. It was sundown and the light was fading. The four had taken shelter behind a big boulder, two firing from one side and two from the other. Sullivan and Chamberlain were working together. The boyish Chamberlain had left a circus to enlist at Mauston, and the boys generally agreed he had had a hard life and joined the army for relief.[4] Sullivan said he and Chamberlain were the "stray waifs" of Company K and had "to suffer for all the misdeeds or mistakes, no matter by whom committed." They had been companions "in many an hour's knapsack drill or extra tour of guard, given sometimes for our own offenses and sometimes for the offenses of others." It was a common remark around camp, he recalled, that if Rufus R. Dawes "would stub his toe he'd put Mickey and Chamberlain on knapsack drill," and "consequently we were inseparable companions and fast friends."

Mickey was having more trouble than just ducking rebel bullets that late afternoon at South Mountain. He had the mumps and his cheeks had "reached a respectable rotundity," even to the point Lieutenant Lyman Upham, who the boys called "Lyme" behind his back, and who had come into the company from Mauston's rival city of New Lisbon, had given him a silk handkerchief to tie around his face. Sullivan had taken it off and stuffed it in his pocket because it bothered his shooting. Chamberlain, the circus boy, and puffy-cheeked Sullivan, the farmer, made an unlikely pair of soldiers, each popping up to shoot, then ducking down to load, both talking at the same time and looking for the flash of rebel muskets in the gathering darkness.

Then a "heavy line of battle" rose up on their right and fired a volley, filling the air with bullets that splattered off the rocks and thunked around them. "When that crash came, either a bullet split in pieces against the stone or a fragment of the boulder hit

4. Rufus R. Dawes, *Mauston Star*, January 8, 1885; *Milwaukee Sunday Telegraph*, August 24, 1884.

29

me on the sore jaw," Sullivan remembered, "causing exquisite pain, and I was undetermined whether to run away or swear . . ." Somewhere in the shadows, Cornish said with a groan, "Mickey, Chamberlain is killed and I'm wounded." There was another "crashing volley" and Sullivan felt "a stinging, burning sensation in my right foot followed by the most excruciating pain . . ." He jumped up and saw Wilcox "topple over wounded." It was time to get out, and, using his musket for a crutch, Sullivan hopped downhill "a good deal faster than I had come up." He passed through the ranks of Company C of his regiment as it advanced, catching the eye of Sergeant Edward A. Whaley, who looked him over and checked his wound, then told the young Irishman he'd "better get to the rear." Whaley saw him off before turning to catch up with his own company. The sergeant would also catch a rebel bullet before the day was finished.[5]

"In the darkness the sides of the mountain seemed in a blaze of flame," Sullivan said:

> The lines of combatants did not appear more than three or four rods apart, but ours was steadily advancing. The pain in my foot and angry "zip, zip whing" of the bullets prevented me from dwelling long on the sight, and I made the best of time down to the turnpike which was lit up by the flashes of a couple of Battery B's [4th U.S. Artillery] guns which were firing as guns never fired before. The two pieces made an almost continual roar and they were being pushed forward by hand at every discharge. The gap in the mountain seemed all aflame and the noise and uproar and cheers and yells were terrific.

A few hundred yards more and Sullivan was out of it, hobbling along with scores of other wounded soldiers coming off the hill. He came upon a body of cavalry halted in the road. He asked, "What regiment?" and was told "McClellan's body guard." Further on, the wounded private found a Company K man, Emory Mitchell of Quincy, assisting several injured men. Mitchell, who had been kept out of the fight because of a "bad hernia," sat Sullivan

5. *Roster of Wisconsin Volunteers, War of the Rebellion, 1861-1865*, Vol. I (Madison, 1886), p. 505.

down, took the sleeve of his extra shirt and Lieutenant Upham's silk handkerchief, wet both from a canteen, rolled the two together and wrapped the wounded foot. The two sat for a time, listening to the battle, Mitchell remarking with some satisfaction "our fellows" were "giving 'em Wisconsin hell" and that "we had some generals now." There was fresh coffee, then Mitchell fixed a gum blanket for the wounded Sullivan to sleep on with his own knapsack for Sullivan's pillow. "I lay down and slept some," Sullivan said. "But Mitchell said I kept him awake all night twitching my injured foot."

The next morning the injured were taken to a field hospital in a barnyard, where a doctor dressed Sullivan's wound and tried to extract the ball, which had wedged between the bones. Finally, the doctor gave up, saying he was sending the young soldier to another hospital. After a time, as Sullivan waited for transport, an attendant came around offering him some brandy. ". . . But I told him I'd rather take another wound sooner, [so the hospital orderly] . . . drank it himself." It was a hard war for hospital attendants as well.

Sullivan was taken to a hospital at nearby Frederick, Maryland, where the Sisters of Charity (those "white winged angels of mercy") served as nurses. But that too was filled with wounded, and he was ambulanced to Washington, to the makeshift hospital in the House of Representatives chamber, where surgeons removed the ball as well as the second toe of his right foot. By December, he was getting around again in good fashion, and on the 18th, Sullivan was ordered to report to a board, and "after some scientific stares through their eye-glasses and some scientific talk about 'cuspal,' and 'flexious' and a good deal more unintelligible jargon," he was ordered back to his ward. Three days later, directed to the hospital office, he was told he was discharged from service, handed final statements and advised to go home. "[When] I said I didn't want any discharge, I was told that I did not belong to the hospital any longer and must leave," he recalled. Not having been paid in six months, Sullivan found himself on the streets of Washington, flat broke except for carfare borrowed from a 56th Pennsylvania soldier to get him downtown to the paymaster's office. But the pay office was locked, a card on the door: "Closed for want of funds." It was, Sullivan remembered, "a fine fix to be in; turned loose in a strange city, crippled, unknown, no money, and a

31

thousand miles from home." Several others were in the same circumstance, and finally they learned of "a patriot, who, for patriotic considerations and a discount of 10 per cent, would cash our papers, provided we accepted state currency, and considering that his patriotism and state currency were better than none," the boys "closed on his offer," Sullivan remembered.[6] So, it was out of the war and home to Wisconsin.

Born in Ireland in 1841, Sullivan had come to the Wisconsin Territory with his parents in the early 1840s. The family resided briefly in Fort Winnebago Township in Portage County, then moved west into Bad Ax County which was formed in 1851. The population of the new county (the name was changed to Vernon in 1863) more than doubled from about 4,800 in 1855 to 11,000 in 1860, but, despite the new folks, it was still hard country on a raw frontier. Sometime prior to 1860, Sullivan left the home of eight brothers and sisters to work as a farm laborer. He had enlisted formally at Mauston on June 21st, his 20th birthday.[7]

It was all changed at home that winter of 1862-63 because of the war, Sullivan found:

> There was no company there; only discharged invalids that had killed half the rebel army, and men who were growling about the draft, the army, and the scarcity of money; and women that were growling worse because they had to pay forty and fifty cents a yard for calico and twenty-five cents for a spool of thread. There was no change to be had, and every business man and merchant had cards printed good for so many cents. . . .

He lasted six weeks before traveling to Middleton near Madison to see the recruiting officer. "Could I enlist?" he asked. "Anything owning a name could enlist," said the soldier, and, Sullivan wrote 25 years later, "knowing that there was a first-class chance to get killed in the 6th within that time, I enlisted for nine months or sooner 'killed.' "

6. James P. Sullivan, "The Battle of Gainesville," *Milwaukee Sunday Telegraph*, November 4, 1883; James P. Sullivan, "A Private's Story," *Milwaukee Sunday Telegraph*, May 13, 1888. The 1888 account contains Sullivan's recollections of his encounter with Burnside, South Mountain, his hospitalization, return to Wisconsin and re-enlistment.
7. U.S. Census, 1840, 1860. Sullivan was listed as a farmer laborer at Wonewoc in 1860.

The first fight of his second enlistment came even before he left Camp Randall in Madison. It seemed there was a "young gawk" who "fancied himself able to butt a locomotive off the track," and, having enlisted in a Western regiment, was "offensive in his talk" about soldiers in Eastern armies, especially those in the Army of the Potomac. Words were exchanged, then Sullivan "admonished" the "young gawk" with an "Iron Brigade rap between the eyes, and at it we went, and that time the Army of the Potomac came out victorious," he recollected with the satisfaction of a man reporting a job well done.

Finally, he was on the train East with several other enlisted men under the charge of Captain George Otis of the 2nd Wisconsin. Otis was a man who apparently liked to stretch out on a long train ride, and, upon entering the car and finding it crowded, he said in a loud voice to a doctor traveling with the group, "What conclusion has been arrived at about that man; was it smallpox?" Otis nodded toward Sullivan. "It was not decided yet," the physician answered in just as loud a voice. Sullivan admitted later, while there "was no black eye, cuts or bruises visible on my face . . . it was covered all over with innumerable little scabs where the fellow had clawed me with his nails. . . ." Soon the passengers, one after another, "gathered up their gripsacks and other impediments" and departed, leaving the car to the soldiers. It was a dodge worked at Chicago, again at Dunkirk, and at Elmira, where the detachment changed cars. At Washington, D.C., Sullivan caught the steamer to Belle Plain, Virginia, where the Army of the Potomac was camped. He reported to Colonel Edward S. Bragg, and that was how he returned to his regiment that February, 1863.[8]

Rufus R. Dawes said later of Sullivan that "for genuine sallies of humor at unexpected times, I never saw his equal,"[9] so the Juneau County boys were glad to see the slight, bright-eyed young Irishman, with his quick mind and faster mouth, filling him in on the latest camp talk, and there was much to tell. Johnny Ticknor was now company commander. A worker in a sawmill at Germantown near Mauston when Fort Sumter was fired on, he had been one of the first to volunteer at Mauston when the unit was raised. Somewhere he had picked up the nick-

8. Sullivan, *Telegraph*, May 13, 1888.
9. Dawes, *Service*, p. 47.

name "Jerkey," for reasons not recorded, and he was much admired. The day his commission as lieutenant had come, while the regiment was at Arlington Heights, near Washington, his soldiers had carried him up and down the company street, singing, laughing and shouting in joy. And the regiment was still talking about his hot bravery in the grim fighting at South Mountain, where Sullivan had been wounded. Ticknor was six feet tall and "straight as an arrow," and the boys wondered how the rebels had missed him with their bullets.[10]

Corporal Reuben Huntley, a Dawes cousin,[11] had died at South Mountain along with Chamberlain. Ticknor had told the boys he had seen Huntley fight and fall, and with tears in his eyes, said, "I never saw better work than old Huntley did." Eph Cornish and Corporal Wilcox had survived their South Mountain wounds, but both were ailing, and word was that they would soon be discharged. Billy Harrison of Lindina and Charlie Abbott of Summit had been killed at Antietam as well and were buried in the same grave upon the field where they fell. They were remembered as "farmer boys of correct habits and upright character and good education" and mourned by friends and comrades.[12]

Jimmy Scoville's reputation had spread. He was a soldier now famed throughout the whole brigade for neglecting his brasses, never blackening his shoes, and having as "little pride of soldier appearance and soldierly bearing as any man ever born." Sullivan also said a quick hello to his uncle, Private Tommy Flynn, as well as quiet Corporal Abe Fletcher, who would always carry an extra knapsack or two for the smaller fellows; to dark-eyed Sergeant Albert Tarbox; sandy-haired Aaron L. Yates, a company favorite, and Hugh Talty of Lisbon, the smallest man in Company K, whom all the boys called "Tall T."[13]

10. U.S. Census, 1860; Dawes, Star, January 8, 1885; Milwaukee Sunday Telegraph, August 24, 1884.
11. Merton G. Eberlein, Mauston, Wisconsin, unpublished essay on the Huntley family. Reuben Huntley was a cousin of Rufus R. Dawes and grandfather of network television news commentator Chet Huntley. Reuben Huntley's wife, Sarah, lived the rest of her life in Necedah, Wisconsin, dying April 20, 1898. She was buried in the Necedah Cemetery. Members of the Dawes and Huntley families moved to Fort Winnebago at Portage, Wisconsin, May 10, 1855. Rufus Dawes' father, Henry, came to Mauston from Marietta, Ohio, shortly thereafter. Eberlein's essay was based on papers and information provided by the Dawes family.
12. Dawes, Star, January 8, 1885.
13. Dawes, Service, p. 47.

The diminutive Talty always had uniform trouble because he "was under the smallest size contemplated in the regulations, and he could never be fitted," Dawes recalled. The young captain spent much time pulling and fussing with the small Irishman's blue coat and pantaloons, and during one march, a passing soldier called out, "Who's your tailor, 'Tall T?' " Lightning fast, Talty responded: "The captain, be gob."[14] The story on Yates was that he had been the last man to volunteer for Company K, and Dawes had found him working in a field. Yates set aside his hoe, saying to the young officer that he would be along in a minute after telling his mother he was off to be a soldier.[15]

Three days after Sullivan's return, there was a rather bitter-sweet event for his brigade, the drumming from service of a handful of soldiers, including a young Irishman from the 2nd Wisconsin. Patrick Dunn of Verona in Dane County, who had enlisted at age 18 in Madison in 1861, had served well at First Bull Run and during the bloody campaigns of 1862. In fact, he was a great favorite in the 2nd Wisconsin, and there was even an old soldier story that Dunn liked to tell on himself. It allegedly occurred at the battle of Antietam, when the brigade was drawn up just before the start of the day's fighting. Dunn said Army Commander George B. McClellan himself rode up to ask the regimental commander, "Is private Dunn present?" Dunn told the boys that he called out, "Here I am general," and snapped a smart salute, palm out in the fashion of the day. McClellan nodded and, turning to his staff, said, "Let the battle begin." True or not, the yarn always got a laugh.

But, sometime that winter of 1862-63, Dunn lost all faith in soldiering and "became utterly worthless," said one 6th Wisconsin man. Finally, he was put before a court-martial and ordered to have his head shaved and be drummed out of the regiment. It was all curious, this good and brave soldier turned sour; frustrated to mutiny by inept generals; angered by arrogant officers who, just months before, had been his fellow neighbors, and totally convinced one less soldier for A. Lincoln would not make a difference in the war effort. There was a streak of pure Wisconsin bullhead-

14. *Ibid.*
15. Carroll Tracy, *Mauston Star*, 1957, Juneau County Centennial Edition. A native of Kildare Township, Juneau County, Tracy wrote a series of articles on Civil War subjects for the special edition. The story was based on local tradition.

35

edness in all this: it did not make sense to risk life and limb without at least a chance of victory. No hope, no soldier.

The brigade formed a hollow square for the elaborate ceremony that Washington's Birthday. Finally, as the drum corps played the "Rogue's March," along came "poor Pat—his head looking like a mammoth white turnip," walking slowly "and the boys who followed as a guard, with bayonets fixed, and held in unpleasant proximity of Pat's rear, were nearly convulsed with laughter." But it was ex-Private Dunn, once outside the square and a free man, who got in the last word. Turning to his former comrades, a hot glint in his eye, he yelled, "It's all right boys. Ye can squek the fife and bate the drum, and fight and fight, but I'd rather be a live ass than a dead lion."[16]

About that same time, Sullivan went down to the ordnance sergeant to draw a musket and belts. There were a good many of the "old guns"[17] on hand and a few of the new ones, the favored Model 1861 Springfield rifle-muskets, which had been issued to the regiment in January, 1862.[18] The new rifle-muskets were much lighter and a "better gun" than the old "Belgian muskets," the soldiers all agreed at the time, one remembering the Springfields "gave great satisfaction."[19]

When Sullivan went to the ordnance sergeant that February, 1863, he was after a new Springfield, but he came away with one of the "old muskets," either one of the "Belgians" or more likely a Springfield that had seen hard service during the 1862 campaigns. That put a hot flash in his blue eyes, and the fiesty Irishman stormed over to the regimental commander, Colonel Edward S. Bragg, to see about it. Looking the "little colonel" square in the eye, he demanded to "know if the regiment could not afford to

16. [Loyd G. Harris], "Stories Told in Camp," *Milwaukee Sunday Telegraph*, March 11, 1883. Harris wrote using the pseudonym "Grayson," his middle name; [Jerome A. Watrous], *Milwaukee Sunday Telegraph*, August 24, 1879. The article was not by-lined, but was obviously written by Editor Watrous.
17. Sullivan, *Star*, February 13, 1883.
18. The 6th Wisconsin Infantry was issued Model 1861, dated 1861, Springfield rifle-muskets. Ordnance Office, U.S. War Department, September 28, 1863, letter to Col. E. S. Bragg, 6th Wis. Vols. ". . . Co. Returns for your Regt. may commence from Jany. 1862, the date they received the Springfield Rifles." Edward S. Bragg Papers, State Historical Society of Wisconsin.
19. Dawes, *Service*, p. 35. See also, Claud E. Fuller, *Springfield Muzzle-Loading Shoulder Arms*, (New York, 1930); Robert M. Reilly, *United States Military Small Arms 1816-1865*, (Eagle Press, 1970). For the best non-technical discussion of Civil War arms, usage and tactics, see Jack Coggins, *Arms and Equipment of the Civil War*, (Garden City, New York, 1962).

give me a good musket." The two returned to the ordnance tent. "Sergeant, this is the man that fought the whole Rebel army at Bull Run. Let him choose a gun for himself," said Bragg, in what Sullivan admitted later was "his usual nasal jesting manner."

There was a story behind Bragg's remark, and it involved Sullivan's part in the battle of Second Bull Run. The second platoon of Company K had been ordered forward as skirmishers to see "if there were any Rebels" in a woods, Sullivan said, and had not gone far when it received a volley from the Johnnies. The bullets killed Levi Gardner of Fountain "dead in his tracks" and upended [Edward W.] Hod Trumbull of Mauston. It seemed Trumbull had his rubber blanket folded up very narrow, about three or four inches wide, and was wearing it around his waist and under his waist belt:

> He was running forward when a bullet hit him on the waist belt and rubber blanket and he turned the completest somersault I ever saw, and some of us laughed heartier at it than at the antics of a circus clown.

The bullet was just about spent, however, and Trumbull jumped up, gasping for air, only the wind knocked out of him, and the Juneau County boys gave him a friendly yell, then moved forward until they found a Confederate line of battle along a railroad embankment. Having found the Johnnies, and a good many of them, young Lieutenant Johnny Ticknor ordered his boys to retreat but, somehow, in the din, Sullivan didn't get the order. He was down behind a small tree, and began to "peg away at the Rebs until I exhausted the 20 rounds that was in the top compartment of my cartridge box," he said, "and when I stopped to refill it I saw I was alone and I dug out of there in a hurry."

The young Irishman found his company in a woods off to the left:

> I was very angry at Ticknor, thinking that he had carelessly left me there alone and not yet having arrived at the dignity of using . . . "a good mouth filling oath," but still clung to the "cuss" words of my boyhood, I asked him with an indignant "dog gone" him why he left me there to fight the whole rebel army alone. Lt. Colonel

Bragg ordered to me lay down, and all the satisfaction I got from Ticknor was, "Lay down Mickey, you damfool, before you get killed."

And that was how "Mickey" Sullivan became the man who fought the whole rebel (and Wisconsin men, then and thereafter, always spelled rebel in the lower case) army at Second Bull Run, and why Bragg made a sly remark in giving him the pick of the Springfields available.[20]

Sullivan finally selected "one with a curly stock" later mounting it "with some silver ornaments" and fixing a screw in the stock that pressed against the sear in the lock, so the trigger pull "worked almost as easy as a squirrel gun." He was pretty proud of it, he remembered, and later, at a general inspection, Division commander James Wadsworth asked the reason for the screw. "So I can hit a canteen at one hundred yards," Sullivan replied promptly, relating also that Wadsworth "asked me no more questions."[21]

In addition to the news of his Juneau County comrades in Company K, Sullivan found the ranks of his 6th Wisconsin Infantry much thinned by the hard fighting. The other regiments in the brigade—the 2nd Wisconsin, 7th Wisconsin, 19th Indiana—were also diminished, but the unit had been reinforced by a new volunteer organization from the West, the 24th Michigan, and the Wisconsin boys told of a growing reputation as a hard-fighting outfit.

As the only Western brigade assigned to the Eastern Theater, the unit had always been singled out by the other soldiers. One of the Baraboo boys in Company A, Phil Cheek, tried to explain it: "We were the only Western soldiers in the entire army [of the Potomac], and we would have died rather than have dishonored the West. We felt that the eyes of the East were upon us, and that we were the test of the West."[22] To further distinguish the unit, the brigade had been issued distinctive headgear, the Regular's dress or Model 1858 "Hardee" hat, a showy, black felt affair,

20. James P. Sullivan, "The Iron Brigade at Bull Run," *Milwaukee Sunday Telegraph*, March 16, 1884.
21. Sullivan, *Telegraph*, December 20, 1884.
22. Orson B. Curtis, *History of the Twenty-Fourth Michigan of the Iron Brigade*, (Detroit, 1891), p. 455. The quotation is from a speech by Phil Cheek of Company A, 6th Wisconsin, to a group of Michigan veterans. Cheek was active in the Grand Army of the Republic.

trimmed in brass and sporting a black plume. The hat had become a symbol for the Western brigade. After its first major fight near Gainesville, Virginia, on the Brawner farm fields, the rebels had asked Wisconsin wounded on the field about "the black hatted brigade," and said they knew the Union soldiers were Western men.[23] Sullivan himself recalled it was "a common remark with the rebel prisoners that their officers used to say: 'It's no use to fight that Big Hat Brigade, we will only get cut to pieces.'" A private from Appleton, Jerome Watrous, always said the Johnnies had "a pet name" for the Western men that was a bit stronger—"the Black Hat Devils of the Army of the Potomac."[24]

Now in the camps, Sullivan was told, the men in other Union regiments were talking not of a "Black Hat Brigade," but an "Iron Brigade." It was a mighty war name that echoed down through the decades and made the Wisconsin, Indiana and Michigan regiments famous, and if the brilliantly arrayed Washington belles and dignitaries came down to the camps to see and admire them, so be it; because it was a name earned with blood in the darkness at South Mountain and "The Cornfield" at Antietam, and they were puffed up and proud of it. But there was a reverse to having a mighty name. More was expected of soldiers belonging to an "Iron Brigade." They had to march further, shoot straighter and stand firmly in a battle line when other men just as brave gave it up. The price was paid on the first day at Gettysburg, when, with the rest of the Union army in retreat, outnumbered,

---

23. Thomas Scott Allen, Letter, September 4, 1862, *Civil War Times Illustrated*, November, 1962, pp. 32-33. This letter was under the heading "Upton's Hill, Va." Allen was a major in the 2nd Wisconsin Volunteer Infantry.

24. James P. Sullivan, "Co. K, 6th Wis. Vols." (poem), *Mauston Star*, c. 1883; Jerome A. Watrous, "A Real Reunion," *Milwaukee Telegraph*, October 30, 1897. Sullivan's creation was based on a popular post-Civil War poem, "Company K," which was re-printed in the *Mauston Star*. A clipping from the *Star* with the original poem (which deals with a "cap in the closet," not a Hardee hat) was preserved in the Van Wie Family scrapbook. Rufus R. Dawes used the original version to open Chapter One of his war memoir. Dawes, *Service*, p. 5.

Watrous wrote: "When Ewell's corps struck the advance of Reynolds' First corps a little out of Gettysburg, the 1st day of July, 1863, the Confederates soon discovered that they had something besides raw militiamen to deal with. Seeing the black hats of the Iron brigade, for it was that brigade which began the infantry fighting in the battle of Gettysburg, they set up the cry, so that it was plainly heard in the Union lines, 'Hell, these are not raw militia; they are those "Black Hat Devils" of the Army of the Potomac,' and they were."

bullets coming from three sides, the black-hatted Westerners made the brave stand that nearly destroyed them.

Much later, General George B. McClellan claimed credit for the proud fighting identification. He said the name "Iron Brigade" was first given to the Western men during an exchange he had with I Corps Commander Joseph Hooker and others as they watched the unit in action at South Mountain in September, 1862. Often told at the old soldier meetings after the war, it was a nice story that was "romanced" as the reputation of the Western Brigade expanded. Actually, there were several variations of the same story, each part truth, part old-soldier yarn, but clearly linking the name "Iron Brigade" to McClellan and South Mountain.

In one account, long after the war, Joseph H. Marston, who came into the 6th Wisconsin as First Lieutenant of the Appleton contingent of Company E, even went so far as to say the origin of the name started in his regiment with a remark by Colonel Edward S. Bragg during the fighting at South Mountain. "I remember hearing [Bragg] give an order to [his] adjutant, as I lay on the ground wounded, which I think had something to do in giving the brigade its proud name." The order Bragg gave that late September afternoon, Marston said, was: "Adjutant, go and find General Gibbon. Tell him the 6th Wisconsin is on the top of the mountain, that we are out of ammunition, but we will hold our position as long as we have an inch of iron left." And that was the report, Marston said, that "from the front went up to General McClellan, commanding the army."[25] In his careful history of the

25. "General Bragg," *Milwaukee Telegraph*, February 25, 1899. Marston's comment came as a contingent of Iron Brigade veterans visited Bragg at the general's home in Fond du Lac on the occasion of his 72nd birthday.

The most stylized version of the story of how the Iron Brigade received its name was detailed in a letter from John B. Callis, 7th Wisconsin, printed in *Indiana at Antietam*, Indiana Antietam Monument Commission, (Indianapolis, 1911), p. 111. In it, Callis quoted McClellan as remembering the exchange in this fashion:

McClellan: "What men are those fighting on the pike?"
Hooker: "General Gibbon's brigade of Western men."
McClellan: "They must be made of iron."
Hooker: "By the Eternal, they are iron! If you had seen them at Bull Run as I did, you would know them to be iron."
McClellan: "Why, General Hooker, they fight equal to the best troops in the world."

McClellan also said that after the battle Hooker had hailed him, calling out: "General McClellan, what do you think now of my Iron Brigade?"

There is evidence in two letters from Wisconsin men linking the name to McClellan. In one dated September 21, 1862, Captain Aleck Gordon, Jr., of

6th Wisconsin, Dawes never identified the origin of the name. Whatever the truth, the sobriquet was carried quickly back to Wisconsin, and in his December 31, 1862, report, Adjutant General Augustus Gaylord was already linking the 2nd, 6th and 7th Wisconsin of Gibbon's Brigade, noting "Wisconsin may well be proud of their record, which has procured for them the name of the 'Iron Brigade of the West.'"[26]

The greenhorn patriots who left Wisconsin in 1861 had marched a long way, and J. P. "Mickey" Sullivan would be the first to admit the roads they had followed were not always straight and the camps not always dry.

---

the 7th Wisconsin wrote, "Gen. McClellan has given us the name of the Iron Brigade." *Wisconsin Newspaper Volumes,* Vol. IV, pp. 21-22; Curtis, *Twenty-Fourth Michigan,* p. 463. The Curtis account indicated the name was acquired at South Mountain. Eight days later, Hugh C. Perkins, also of the 7th, wrote a Wisconsin friend that "Gen. McClellan calls us the Iron Brigade." Hugh C. Perkins, Letter, September 26, 1862. In "Letters of a Civil War Soldier," edited by Marilyn Gardner. Prepared for syndication for April 9, 1983, *Christian Science Monitor.* The letter was to Herbert Frisbie, Pine River, Wisconsin, under the heading "Camp on the battlefield of Antietam." Gardner is a great-granddaughter of Frisbie.

A 2nd Wisconsin man, William H. Harries, said his recollection was that "the name originated with a war correspondent of a New York paper," who, while writing of the Western Brigade's conduct at the battle of Antietam, "called it the Iron Brigade, and the name has clung to it ever since." William H. Harries, "The Iron Brigade in the First Day's Battle of Gettysburg," Military Order of the Loyal Legion Paper read October 8, 1895, reprinted in The *Second Wisconsin Infantry,* ed. by Alan D. Gaff, (Dayton, Ohio, 1984), p. 272.

Lewis A. Kent, who started as a private in the 6th's Company G and later commanded the regiment, wrote a quarter century afterward that the brigade was named at South Mountain. He said the unit had fought its way to a stone wall, where it "stood and fired until every cartridge was exhausted and then, lying down, held its position with the bayonet. This little part of the battle was keenly watched by General McClellan, who made the remark, 'If Jackson's men are stone, those men are iron;' and that's how and where our brigade received its name, 'Iron Brigade.'" Lewis A. Kent, "Capt. Kent's Memory," *Milwaukee Sunday Telegraph,* September 25, 1887.

Another 6th Wisconsin soldier, Jerome A. Watrous, who came in as a private and served as regimental Adjutant, also said the name was earned at South Mountain. Hooker "fairly danced with delight as he saw those blue lines of Western boys steadily moving up the long, high mountain facing showers of lead and storms of iron, and, in speaking with McClellan about it said: 'Those Western boys of yours are men of iron.' McClellan's comment upon their iron endurance and Joe Hooker's enthusiastic remark about their being men of iron constituted the foundation of the name, 'Iron Brigade.'" Watrous said in 1896. "The war correspondent of a Cincinnati paper was near McClellan when Hooker spoke of them as men of iron, and in describing the battle, the correspondent spoke of Gibbon's brigade as the 'Iron brigade of the West.' There are conflicting stories, but this is the true story of the origin of the name. . . ." "Heros of Undying Fame," *Milwaukee Telegraph,*

September 12, 1898. Watrous was interviewed by the *Chicago Chronicle* before the 1898 Iron Brigade Association Reunion at Baraboo, Wisconsin. The dispatch was reprinted in the *Telegraph*.

The commander of the Western men at the time, John Gibbon, in his written recollections of the war, said he did not know "how or where the name of the 'Iron Brigade' was first given. . . . but soon after the battle of Antietam the name was started and ever after was applied to the brigade." John Gibbon, *Personal Recollections of the Civil War*, (New York, 1928), p. 93. Gibbon's book was reprinted in 1978 by the Morningside Bookshop of Dayton, Ohio.

There is also some evidence the name "Iron Brigade" may have been earlier applied to Hatch's Brigade, which included the 2nd United States Sharpshooters, the 22nd, 24th, 30th and 84th New York [14th Brooklyn]. William F. Fox, *Regimental Losses in the American Civil War*, (Albany, New York, 1889), p. 117; and [C. V. Tevis and D. R. Marquis], *The History of the Fighting Fourteenth*, (New York, 1911).

26. *Annual Reports of the Adjutant General, State of Wisconsin, 1860-1864*, (Madison, 1912), pp. 108-109.

CHAPTER TWO

Bright eyes have looked calmly their broad rims beneath,
On the work of the reaper, grim harvester death,
And never once faltered or turned the wrong way,
When with cheers into battle rushed Company "K."
—By "Mickey"

Wisconsin's 6th

The young men who would become the "Boys of '61" went off to war with light hearts and great expectations when Governor Alexander W. Randall called for volunteers to fill Wisconsin's 6th Regiment. A Republican, the governor fought against the rebellion and for the Union with an Old Testament zeal. In a special message before a joint session of the legislature at Madison shortly after the firing on Fort Sumter, he expressed impatience with the new Lincoln administration for not moving quickly enough. "This war began where Charleston [South Carolina] is, and it should end where Charleston *was*," Randall said. "These gathering armies are the instruments of His vengeance, to execute his judgments; they are His flails wherewith on God's great Southern threshing floor, He will pound rebellion for its sins."[1]

If Randall's words were hard, he was only echoing what was being said in many towns and villages in his new state. Since the cannonade against Fort Sumter on April 12th, war fever was loose in Wisconsin. Energetic and ambitious young men canvassed their counties, anxious to find the 100 men needed to fill the rolls of a company and be off on the crusade for the Union, or a great adventure, no one exactly sure which. War rallies were held in Milwaukee, Baraboo, Fond du Lac and dozens of smaller communities. The parades, the patriotic meetings and the hot oratory

---

1. Alexander W. Randall, May 15, 1861, *Messages and Proclamations of Wis. War Governors*, (Madison, 1912), p. 63.

43

would all take on a golden glow afterward, but war fever was a raw emotion those days, and young men who did not make immediate plans to go felt unsettled, as though somehow, in some rite of passage to manhood, they had been found wanting.

"I laugh now, when I review the impressions I then had of a soldier[']s life," one Wisconsin volunteer wrote in a letter home about one year after he had left Boscobel with his company. "How enthusiastic the boys were! How idle they thought the ceremony of taking the oath! They would be soldiers for fifty years, if necessary, and then leave their muskets as a legacy for their children, enjoining them never to lay them down until the stars and stripes should wave in triumph from the St. Lawrence to the Rio Grande, and from the Atlantic to the Pacific."[2]

In the rolling country of western Wisconsin, the "Anderson Guards" marched off to war to cheers and band music that June, 1861. Named in honor of Fort Sumter hero Robert Anderson, the company left Hillsboro in Bad Ax County "full officered and partly recruited," recalled Earl M. Rogers, who enlisted in the ranks and would command his company at Gettysburg. The Guards halted the first night at Ontario, adding 29 more to the rolls and electing two more corporals. Then the new company whooped into nearby Viroqua, where another 25 volunteers stepped forward and two more sergeants were selected. They headed for Bad Ax City (renamed Genoa in 1863), where Governor Randall had ordered a Mississippi River ferryboat to pick up the company and carry it to Prairie du Chien, where it was to be taken by train to Madison.

Along the road to the river, said Rogers decades after, "youths left the field without going home for a 'change;' men hurried to the house to say good-bye, and then joined their fortunes with the company." All the while, he said, a "band of four pieces" tooted "Yankee Doodle" and "Hail, Columbia" over and over again, making, "with the small flag in the lead wagon," one of the "most inspiring, enthusiastic, liberty loving processions that had ever been witnessed in the county. Parents tried to keep the youths back, but the enthusiasm in young America was too great, and they went forward with determination that paternal demon-

2. Edward Kellogg, "Letters from a Soldier," *Milwaukee Sunday Telegraph*, September 28, 1879. Kellogg was in the 2nd Wisconsin and not related to John A. Kellogg of Company K, 6th Wisconsin.

stration and threats could not prevent." Thus, "armed with a flag and music," the company attracted volunteers, and, in the fashion of the day, elected its officers, sergeants and corporals.[3]

Two of the young soldiers in the Guards were Frank A. Wallar, a farmer, and his brother, Samuel.[4] They had stood for the Union when a portion of the company was raised at DeSoto from surrounding areas. Born in east central Ohio, the Wallars had come to Wisconsin with their parents, David and Marian, in the early 1840s, when the family sought opportunity and land in the new state.[5] A robust 5-feet-8½ inches, Frank Wallar, with light complexion, sandy hair and blue eyes, was remembered first by his comrades as the only soldier in the regiment never to "miss a roll call or a meal." But later, after a score of battles and a great deed at Gettysburg, he would become the man "who never missed a battle or a meal," and as "brave a soldier as ever fought in the ranks." Wallar was mustered into the Federal service June 16th—one month shy of his 21st birthday. He would be a corporal in the fight two years later at Gettysburg.[6] His brother, Sam, would save his life in the same battle.

Soon to become Company I of the new regiment, the "Guards" boasted lads more familiar with a pitchfork than a musket, Rogers wrote later, but they would become soldiers who would do their duty and be remembered kindly by their comrades. One was John M. Goodwin of Plymouth, who "was always ready for duty and no grumbling." He served four years and would have carried a musket "longer if necessary to whip the rebels." And there were Chester Wyman, the Hillsboro boy who was the first of the Guards to be wounded; James Wallace of DeSoto, "among the first to break down with disease" and be discharged; and Isaiah Williams of Franklin, who was "shot through the right lung at Antietam, [but who] would not die." Here as well were Gottfried Schroeber, a "German patriot, an earnest soldier, and a good man," who would be wounded at Gettysburg; T. W. McClure, "too old

---

3. Earl M. Rogers, "A Sixth Wisconsin Company," *Milwaukee Sunday Telegraph*, February 1, 1880.
4. Wallar's name is spelled "Waller" and "Wallar" in various Wisconsin records. Both Frank and Samuel "Waller" are listed in *Roster of Wisconsin Volunteers*, p. 529 and 532. However, the Descriptive Book for the 6th Wisconsin lists "Frank Waller" and "Samuel Wallar." Wallar is the spelling used on a tombstone erected by his family.
5. U.S. Census, 1850 and 1860.
6. *Roster of Wisconsin Volunteers*, p. 529.

for duty" and soon sent home; and George W. Thurber, "one of the boy soldiers, but nevertheless zealous for his flag," who would serve his three years before seeing Wisconsin again.[7]

One of the men who heard the band music and came forward would become a regimental legend. The lad walked in from a field as the Guards neared the Mississippi River. He had been plowing corn as the company passed and sought out the captain, asking to sign the roll. The officer questioned the boy about his age. "Twenty years," the boy answered with a grin. The officer asked his name. "Peter Markle, of Coon Slough," came the reply. The boy had "bright eyes, good head and fair physical development," and the captain gave him a long steady look, then entered on the roll: "Pete Markle, Coon, age 17."

It was the beginning of the unusual military career of "Markle the Straggler," and it was spoken of around the campfires with awe, admiration and shaking of heads. Markle's company commander recalled:

> Pete was careless of his clothes and of his personal appearance. His pants were baggy and slouchy; his coat too large and ill fitting; usually a sleeve partly torn out and seams rent, a button missing in one place and a button hole torn out in another. In his tailoring he would sew the seams overlapped, with white thread, and his buttons carefully sewed on upside down. His shoes were seldom blacked even for a review. The adjutant never selected "Pete" for an orderly, nor did he aspire to be of the neatness usually attained by the one complimented with the privilege of [being] the "colonel's orderly."

What Markle did possess was an independent spirit, unerring sense of direction and uncanny ability to sniff out food, his comrades discovered. He did his duty, and the boys remembered later they always felt safe when he was on a sentry post. But while on a march, Markle would "quietly and mysteriously, unbidden and unknown; even in disobedience of orders," slip from the ranks and "straggle" among the farm houses. He would always return with something "on his bayonet," and he was quick to share it with his messmates. One 6th Wisconsin man said Markle "had the instinct

7. Rogers, *Telegraph*, February 1, 1880.

of a hunter, a scent keen as a hound and could trail the regiment as a dog trails his master." Markle would disappear from the ranks of his marching regiment as it moved toward Gettysburg two years hence, but he would show up, just as mysteriously and unbidden, to take his place in ranks when the shooting started.[8]

On the other side of the state, at Fond du Lac, Edward S. Bragg, a young attorney of much promise if not physical size, was having difficulty raising his company, and in nearby Appleton, one "Professor Platche," a German teacher at Lawrence University, was well below his goal in raising another volunteer unit. Then Platche "changed his mind" about being a soldier and, after much talk by representatives of both fledgling outfits, it was agreed and shaken upon that the Appleton organization would join the Fond du Lac men, the latter to have the captain in Bragg, and the former to have a lieutenant and a share of the non-commissioned officers. The combined unit would become "Bragg's Rifles," the only one of the 10 companies in the 6th Regiment named after the man who organized it. That said something about Bragg.[9]

A native of Oswego County, New York, Bragg was descended from pre-Revolutionary War Vermont settlers. In his infancy, there was a portent of his sometime stormy adulthood when the three-month-old Edward was handed through a window to save him from a fire that destroyed his father's mill and dwellings. At 20, young Bragg was reading law, and in 1850, he rode the wave of migration west, settling in Fond du Lac.

Bragg's public career began in 1853 when he was elected county district attorney. A Stephen Douglas Democrat, he was a delegate to the Charleston Convention in 1860. But at the start of the war, he sided with the "War" Democrats, and in 1861, put aside his law books for a drill manual.[10] Bragg may have been for the Union and anxious to be off as a soldier, but that war spring he was still short of men, so he made a long swing to the small community of Weyauwega, in the sparsely populated central portion of Wisconsin. There, he probably concluded, the recruiting officers had been less active. The small Wolf River town was

8. Earl M. Rogers, "Markle, Straggler," *Milwaukee Sunday Telegraph*, October 8, 1887.
9. [Jerome A. Watrous], "Bragg's Rifles," *Milwaukee Sunday Telegraph*, January 4, 1880. Watrous was a Company E soldier, having enlisted out of Appleton.
10. *Fond du Lac Reporter*, June 20-21, 1912.

on the very edge of Wisconsin civilization, set in gently rolling countryside marked by white stands of birch trees that brightened the wooded areas. The residents were a hard lot given to independent thought.

"Excitement and expectation were raised to the highest pitch," one of the Weyauwega townsfolk, a boy of 14 at the time, reported much later. "The thrilling notes of the fife and drum, sounds which were destined to be frequently heard a little later, gave the meeting a martial character, quite unusual and the apparently out of place in the cozy, conservative village," he recalled.

Captain Bragg mounted the stand and in "his shrill squeaking voice" delivered a "stirring speech," telling how the country was in danger, the Nation's life imperiled by a "gigantic rebellion," and that it was "the duty of every man to fly to her relief." He himself, the young officer said, had dropped his law business and left court at Oshkosh, while trying a case, and "did not expect to return until the war was over."

His company was almost filled, Bragg told the gawking villagers, but "there was room for a few more," and he promised all who stepped forward "good treatment and a share in the glory which would attach to the patriotic volunteers who went forth to fight for their country." The speech, said the village chronicler, was "one of the best that the fiery little Bragg ever made," but the crowd regarded it all in silence and with cynical glances.

Finally, Bragg put forward the question: Come forward to sign the rolls. There was silence. "Each of his listeners seemed to look at his neighbor as if the whole matter of enlisting was a huge joke," remembered the villager. Bragg again called for volunteers. More silence. Then there was a shuffling in the back as Eugene F. Hardy, age 16, but "a tall loose-jointed young fellow who would easily pass for eighteen or twenty," stood up and went to the front to sign his name "amid the mingled laughter, cheers and ridicule of the crowd." But it mattered not to Hardy, said the villager. His father was an original opponent of slavery, and the boy, "with an intellect developed far beyond his years, was bred a strict anti-slavery Whig. . . ."[11] So Bragg returned to Fond du Lac with but one addition to his rolls, and that a boy of 16 who could pass for 18 in a pinch, probably wondering if he would ever

11. "War Meeting at Weyauwega," *Milwaukee Sunday Telegraph*, April 9, 1881.

Wisconsin 1861

Prescott

Fountain City

Appleton

Fox River

Lake Winnebago

Mauston

Viroqua

Wonewoc

Fond du Lac

Baraboo

Milwaukee (Camp Scott)

Prairie du Chien

Wisconsin River

Madison (Camp Randall)

Lancaster

Beloit

Mary Slough

get into the war. One thing certain: war fever had not yet reached the village limits of Weyauwega.

Finally, the rolls were filled and the company ordered to assemble. At Appleton, tall, newly elected Second Lieutenant Joseph H. Marston formed his volunteers before marching to the shanty that served as a depot for the Chicago & North Western Railroad at that point. The ladies turned out in good number for the farewell, and several of them presented to each young man a testament and a little article in which were stored a thimble, a supply of pins and needles, thread and a pair of scissors—what one Appleton recruit said was called the "Popular Housewife." He remembered that "pretty nearly the whole of Appleton followed the band to the station, where the final good-byes were said, and when the train started, cheered, waved handkerchiefs, and either smiled through tears or felt like doing so."[12] At Fond du Lac, the other men of the company boarded the train, and there was one touching incident: The volunteers, "boys from the pinery, the store, farm, factory and the printing office," saw the young Captain Bragg lift his "little black-eyed, black-haired girl of six or seven" and "tenderly kiss her and say good-bye. . . ."[13] Four of the young volunteers would have a grim meeting on the battlefield of Gettysburg. Joseph Marston of Appleton would command the company. One of the men in ranks, Michael Mangan of Fond du Lac, would be a sergeant and be wounded. Marston and Francis Deleglise of Appleton, shot himself, would try to assist the bleeding Mangan, and finally, Harry Dunn, the strongest man in the company, would carry Mangan to safety. Dunn was always remembered for his huge size, and the new officers wondered where they would find a uniform large enough to fit him.[14]

The volunteers were to become Company E of the new regiment, and they would be remembered as a mixed lot by one of their comrades, Jerome A. Watrous of Appleton, a young printer by trade and a man who then and ever after saw the war and his fellows in heroic light.[15] In addition to young Hardy with his

12. Jerome A. Watrous, "An Appleton Contribution," unpublished manuscript. Jerome A. Watrous Papers, State Historical Society of Wisconsin.
13. [Jerome A. Watrous], *Milwaukee Telegraph*, October 26, 1895.
14. Dawes, *Service*, p. 228.
15. Jerome A. Watrous was born September 6, 1840, on a farm in Broom County, New York. His great-grandfather, Benjamin Watrous, was a soldier in the American Revolution. His family moved to Wisconsin when he was quite

anti-slavery sentiments, Watrous wrote decades later, there were such men in ranks as Jake Deiner of Ellington, a youth with the "shortest legs and the longest body of any man in the regiment," who would never return to Wisconsin; steady Amos Lefler of Eden, who would receive one wound at South Mountain and another at Gettysburg; Frank King of Fond du Lac, who would die at Gettysburg two years hence; and the remarkable Edwin C. Jones, "by all odds the most awkward soldier on drill or parade, but perfectly fearless in a fight." When it came time to list his hometown, Jones had signed "Cosmopolite," and it would show up that way 50 years later when Wisconsin printed a formal list of volunteers.[16]

One other member of Bragg's Rifles, an officer named Edwin A. Brown, would leave only a few dozen letters before being shot to death in the cornfield at Antietam in 1862. In one of the earliest, from Camp Randall just days after he arrived there, he touched on the mixed emotions as the Badger men readied for the war front. Brown was concerned, he wrote his wife, that "because I did not show my feelings before the crowd at the time of parting, that I did not feel very bad at going from you. But Ruth it was pride that kept me up. I did not want people to think that soldiers were baby's [sic]."[17]

His story had a cruel ending. In the confusion after Antietam, there was a mixup, and the message that reached the Fond du Lac home of Cornelia Bragg was that her husband had fallen. There were several agonizing hours and talk of funeral preparations, when another telegram arrived from the front: it was Brown, not Bragg, killed. Mrs. Brown, the "Dear Ruth," of the letters from the young lieutenant, was in the room when the message arrived. She had hurried over to console Mrs. Bragg, and, with a knock on the door, one life had been restored and another taken away.[18]

young, and he was working as a printer at Appleton when he enlisted April 16, 1861, immediately after the attack on Fort Sumter. William H. Washburn, *Jerome A. Watrous: The Civil War Years.* Unpublished manuscript, Grand Army of the Republic Museum, Madison, Wisconsin. Mr. Washburn is a grandson of Watrous.

16. Watrous, manuscript; *Roster of Wisconsin Volunteers,* p. 14.
17. Edward Brown, Letter, to his wife. The letter was not dated, but was headed "Camp Randall," the staging area for Wisconsin volunteers at Madison. Private collection.
18. [Watrous], *Telegraph,* January 4, 1880.

In Milwaukee, meanwhile, two ambitious city factions, the Germans and the Irish, readied companies for the new regiment. The Irish Montgomery Guards, which would become Company D, was commanded by one Captain John O'Rourke.[19] The German "Citizens' Corps," soon to be Company F, was organized by substantial Captain William H. Lindwurm, a man of property who had had some modest success in the political wars between the controlling New Yorkers and New Englanders and the upstart Germans and Irish.

Lindwurm was tall, pale-eyed, gray-bearded and weighed more than 300 pounds.[20] A relatively early arrival in Milwaukee, from the Prussian Dukedom of Braunschweig, the 26-year-old had reached the city in December of 1846, where he found one of every three citizens to be German. The Germans had brought much of their Old World art, music and literature with them to Milwaukee, including Gemutlichkeit—a certain Teutonic hospitality and sense of place. Lindwurm quickly made his mark. One early city historian used a German phrase to describe him: "Einen grossen Jager vor dem Herrn," a mighty hunter before the Lord. The huge Prussian was all that and more.[21]

By 1860, Lindwurm, at 41, lived with his wife, Fredericka, a three-year-old son, William, and two-month-old daughter, Rosa. He had accumulated properties valued at $5,000 and personal effects of $1,000. In the household lived a 25-year-old domestic, Anna Koetner, and another recent immigrant, Werner Von Bachelle, who had arrived in Milwaukee less than a decade previously with Lindwurm as his citizen sponsor.[22]

At the outbreak of the war, Lindwurm mobilized quickly, establishing a recruiting office at Vogelgesang's Republican House Hotel. He was assisted by Frederick Schumacher, a former city surveyor and engineer, and Von Bachelle, touted as having been in the service of Emperor Louis Napoleon and having served in the French army in Algiers. The "Citizens Corps," *The Milwaukee Sentinel* reported April 24, was being made up of "men inured

19. *Wisconsin Necrology-1882*, Report and Collections of the State Historical Society of Madison, Vol. X, (Madison, 1888), p. 483; Bayrd Still, *Milwaukee: The History of a City*, (Madison, 1948), pp. 148-149.
20. Philip Cheek and Mair Pointon, *History of the Sauk County Riflemen, Known as Company "A," Sixth Wisconsin Veteran Volunteer Infantry, 1861-1865*, (Baraboo, Wisconsin, 1909), p. 19.
21. Rudolph Koss, *Milwaukee*, (Milwaukee, 1871), p. 221.
22. U.S. Census, 1860.

to exertion, and under the command of able officers; [it] will be a very efficient corps and will do credit to the city." Before May 10th, 60 names were entered on the rolls—all German—and by the 28th, sufficient men enlisted to conduct an election of officers. As expected, Lindwurm was named captain; Schumacher became first lieutenant and Von Bachelle second lieutenant.[23]

About this time, Lindwurm went to the Stein Studio at West State Street for a picture. He wore his newly tailored officer's frock and light-colored kepi; his cold, pale eyes looked confidently into the camera—here was a man with Germanic assurance in life's station. The portrait showed him, indeed, "einen grossen Jager vor dem Herrn."

The Irish Montgomery Guards had been organized in 1857 as a Wisconsin militia company and was part drill outfit, part attempt to gain social equality with the rival native-born "Americans" who had formed the dashing "Milwaukee Light Guard," a well-drilled, well-known militia company composed mostly of prominent young men from the city's prosperous families. The Guards made their first public appearance July 4, 1858, after receiving arms and equipment from the state.[24] With the outbreak of hos-

23. *Milwaukee Sentinel*, May 10, 1861.
24. *Ibid.*, April 28, 1861; *Reports of the Adjutant General, 1860-1864*, (Madison, 1912), p. 9. The report credited the Montgomery Guards with 48 members in 1860. The more well-known Irish company in Milwaukee was the "Union Guards," but it was disbanded by order of the governor in March, 1860, and required to return its arms to the Capitol. "The order to return the arms was obeyed after considerable delay," the Adjutant General noted in his report for 1860. "The cause for disbanding the company was repeated utterance of remarks by the commander tending to create a spirit of ill-feeling and in-subordination towards the authorities of the state. Subsequent to the dis-banding of the company, it adopted an independent organization and procured arms elsewhere. In order to obtain the means of keeping up this organization, the excursion upon the ill-fated steamer *Lady Elgin* was resorted to, resulting in the most melancholy and distressing loss of life; the 'Union Guards' not only being swept from existence, but a considerable number of members of companies attached to the 1st Regiment, besides many other persons who had joined the excursion." *Adjutant General Reports*, p. 4.
   The key figure in the Union Guards was Captain Garrett Barry, a Democrat, U.S. Military Academy graduate and treasurer of Milwaukee County. He had formed the company of 70 men, and it was the pride of Milwaukee's Irish south side. He got into trouble with state officials for saying he would obey a call to arms by the Federal government, but not obey an "illegal order" from Wisconsin officials. After surrendering the company's state arms, he managed to buy 80 muskets for $2 each. To pay for the purchase, Barry and his friends scheduled an excursion to Chicago on the steamer *Lady Elgin*, a triple-decked sidewheeler, one of the favorites on the lakes. On September 6, 1860, the *Lady Elgin* left Milwaukee with about 400 excursionists on board,

tilities in 1861, the Irish unit, like other state companies, quickly tendered its services for the war effort. It was initially slated to join the ranks of the three-month 1st Wisconsin Infantry, but upon inspection April 28, 1861, its ranks were found insufficiently filled. The city's Catholic Irish, for the most part, were suspicious of the war and unsure where it all was leading, and the neighborhoods were still shaken by the Lake Michigan *Lady Elgin* excursion boat tragedy that had destroyed the city's most prominent Irish company, the "Union Guards," in September, 1860. The Montgomery Guard's place in the first regiment was declared vacant.[25] It was all rather embarrassing for the organizers and sponsors of the Irish unit, because the rival Light Guard, the first unit accepted, was designated Company A of Wisconsin's 1st Regiment. Three days later, to make matters worse, the governor ordered an upstate company, the "Fond du Lac Badger Boys," to the unfilled place of the Guards. When the Light Guard departed June 11th from Camp Scott on Spring Street (now West Wisconsin Avenue) in Milwaukee, it was escorted by the Montgomery Guards, Milwaukee Zouaves and Milwaukee Turners. The event was rather bittersweet for the Irish volunteers, but there was some solace: the same day, orders arrived from Madison for the Guards to take "immediate possession of Camp Scott" for drills and quarters; the unit and the Citizen's Corps, under Captain Lindwurm, were being assigned to the 6th Regiment.[26] "The companies are each composed of able bodied, active, intelligent men . . . ," a reporter for *The Milwaukee Sentinel* wrote June 12. "Their ranks are full, and each of them will present themselves at camp with a maximum of 101 men, ready and anxious to serve their country when required. With such officers as Capt. O'Rourke and Capt. Lindwurm, and their subordinates, we shall expect a good report from them, under even the most unfavorable circumstances. Let the other regiments of the State look well to their positions, and post themselves in drill, otherwise the 6th if filled

---

including members of the German Black Jaeger and Green Jaeger militia companies in addition to Barry and the Union Guards. That night, the *Lady Elgin* was rammed amidships off Winnetka, Illinois, by the *Augusta*, a schooner loaded with lumber. Eventually, 227 bodies were recovered, and the death toll may have been more than 300. Richard Current, *History of Wisconsin*, Vol. II, (Madison, Wis., 1976), pp. 277-281; Still, *Milwaukee*, p. 153.

25. *Milwaukee Sentinel*, April 28, 1861.
26. *Ibid.*, June 11, 1861.

up with companies equal to them, will carry off the laurels, and prove true the old adage, that 'the last shall be first.' "[27]

At least one unidentified member of the Irish company took a dimmer view of the prospects. Two days later, as the company marched to Camp Scott, across the bridge spanning the Milwaukee River, "one of the privates coolly and deliberately announced that 'he'd be d----d if he'd go further,' and took a stand at once dignified and belligerent," reported *The Sentinel* June 14. "In vain the officers expostulated; in vain a guard was detailed to bring him; there he stood, until the matter was compromised, and he was marched to the armory."

One member of the Irish company, Corporal Tom Kerr, was more sure of himself. At age 17, Kerr had run away from home to enlist in the 2nd Pennsylvania Infantry and serve in the war with Mexico. In the fighting outside Mexico City, a shell fragment had carried away two of his fingers. The 5-foot-8½-inch Kerr had settled in Milwaukee before 1850, and was active in local politics as well as a volunteer Irish fire company. A carpenter, he, his wife, Elizabeth, and daughter, Mary, lived in the Irish Third Ward, a "somewhat disreputable" area that boasted not one church, but whose fringes contained the largest collection of saloons in the city. At the call for volunteers, Kerr, a family man with obligations and a wife in her sixth month of pregnancy, was among the first to sign the rolls. It was the action of a man trying to make something of himself, or perhaps, a man fleeing a less than promising life. Kerr would win his captain's bars two years later at Gettysburg.

More sure of his motives for signing the roll was one of the Irish privates in the Montgomery Guard, John H. Cook of Hartford in Washington County: "I enlisted (not for my country being nothing but a boy did not know what that meant; did not know what my duty to country was), but for the sake of seeing the sunny south that I had heard so much about and to be considered brave."[28]

Shortly after taking control of Camp Scott, soldiering for the Irish volunteers took a hard turn. They were called out to confront a mob of 300 Germans who had taken to the streets to protest a

27. *Ibid.*, June 12, 1861.
28. John H. Cook, "Cook's Time in the Army," unpublished manuscript, August 9, 1865, p. 1. John H. Cook Papers, State Historical Society of Wisconsin.

move by city bankers devaluating local script backed by bonds issued by Southern states. Accompanied by a brass band (and only in the Milwaukee, the "Deutsche-Athens" of America, would a mob attract a band), the Germans stoned and cursed Mayor James S. Brown and other civic leaders and looted several commercial buildings. The arrival of the Montgomery Guards produced another storm of stones and epithets. One of the casualties was new volunteer Johnny Cook, who was bruised by a brick. The Irishmen were driven away without serious injury except to soldierly pride. (Perhaps the most bruised ego was that of First Lieutenant John Nichols, who Cook said "gave up his sword to the mob.") Finally, five other companies of soldiers were called, including the Milwaukee Zouaves, and peace was restored. It was all unsettling for the young Irish volunteers. A soldier should be fighting the enemy on a battlefield, not trying to face down fellow citizens on the streets of his own hometown, even if they were the damned "Dutchmen" and their damned brass band. There was one consolation, Cook remembered: "Our Co. received three hundred dollars for their service for help quieting the mob."[29]

Two weeks later, the two Milwaukee companies departed for Madison, and no record was left whether the recalcitrant Irish private was in ranks or not. A *Sentinel* reporter described the Irish and German companies with a finely polished civic pride: "They are both composed of fine-looking, muscular men who, we are satisfied, will do no discredit to the Badger State, either in point of appearance, in their drilling, or in bravery on the field of battle. The Montgomery Guards are decidedly of the fighting order, and are brim full of zeal to get a chance at 'them d----d rebels from the South.' Their captain combines all the qualities of a good commanding officer: intelligence, sobriety, and a thorough knowledge of military tactics. As a drill-master and swordsman, he has few superiors.

"The Citizen's Corps, like the other German companies that have gone from our city, is composed of intelligent and hardy specimens of the Teutonic race, many of whom have served in more than one battle-field in the old world."[30]

29. *Ibid.*
30. *Sentinel*, June 25, 28 and 29, 1861. For a full discussion of the ethnic factor in the Milwaukee rioting, see William L. Burton, *Melting Pot Soldiers: The Union's Ethnic Regiments*, (Ames, Iowa, 1988), pp. 199-200. Burton said the event acquired "a certain ethnic coloration," but its origin and develop-

56

The departure of the Milwaukee companies was marred, however. A large number of friends, relatives and well-wishers accompanied the two companies to the depot, but the streets were less crowded than expected. Most of the curious citizens and warbackers stayed to their homes because of rumors of more possible rioting. There were some vocal agitators, but the armed mob never materialized. In the end, the Montgomery Guards and the Citizen's Corps tramped off to war through troubled Milwaukee streets amid little fanfare, fewer cheers and with the hint of violence in the air.

Despite the bright prediction of his hometown newspaper, Captain O'Rourke would resign his commission and return to Milwaukee within six months. For some unknown reason, however, much would be made in the state records of his brief military career, where he was listed as climbing "to command of the regiment" and "serving with honor to the end of the war." In fact, upon his return to Wisconsin, he moved to Linden in Iowa County, where he became a successful candidate for the Wisconsin Legislature; later he removed to Plattsmouth, Nebraska, where he worked as a banker and served as mayor. Perhaps a man trying to establish himself far from his home might make more of his military record than he actually accomplished.

In the annals of the regiment, Captain Lindwurm was accorded one other mention, and that occurred shortly after the 6th Wisconsin had been shipped to the warfront and was in camp near Washington. For two days, there had been no bread rations, and, in protest, from the ranks of Lindwurm's German company, the recruits took up the cry, "Brodt! Brodt!" Unaware of what the words meant, soldiers in other companies repeated the chant, and it went from company to company, all in all creating quite a racket that eventually reached the ears of Regimental Commander Lysander Cutler, a transplanted New Englander who had little patience for immigrant officers. He summoned Lindwurm to headquarters, and two Sauk County Riflemen, seeing the German officer "in his full regimentals," tagged along "at a safe distance, hoping to see some fun."

ment had little if anything to do with the ethnic composition of the mob. He said it was a protest "against certain city banks by depositors living in German neighborhoods, who were stirred up by fiery speakers assailing the 'monied interests' and the aristocracy."

The Captain saluted the Colonel and asked, "You want me?" Cutler returned the salute, folded his arms and turned a "very severe" look on the huge German. "I am very much surprised and chagrined that your company, Sir, should make such a show of themselves and the regiment," sputtered the six-foot Cutler. "It impairs the regiment's standing with the other troops, is unsoldierly, and shows a lack of attention on the part of the officers in permitting such a breach of good discipline to occur."

A dozen years Cutler's junior, Lindwurm drew himself to full height, and the two Sauk County boys saw he was "getting madder and madder." Finally, Cutler paused, and Lindwurm, that "mighty hunter before the Lord," had his say. "See here, Colonel Cutler, dem boys what is by my company in, are de best boys in Milwaukee," Lindwurm began. "Their father and mother come to say to me, 'Captain Lindwurm, we let our boys with you because we know you will be like a father to them,' and now my boys are all hungry; they have no bread for two days."

Lindwurm was just getting started, his fine German temper beginning to fray. "I want to tell you something, Colonel Cutler. Were I Colonel of this regiment I would have some one else besides that fool brother-in-law of yours as quartermaster [Isaac Mason of Milwaukee]. . . . I am no lager beer Dutchman, I am a German gentleman what drink my Rhinish wine, when you, sir, was a stinking fish inspector in Milwaukee. Mine boys want brodt!"[31]

While the recorders of the story noted that bread rations were thereafter received regularly while the regiment was in camp, their postwar memories embellished the story somewhat. Cutler was not accorded the position as inspector of fisheries until after the war.[32]

In any event, by December, Lindwurm had resigned his captaincy and returned to Milwaukee, his military career over. But he would always be called "Herr Hauptmann" with a doff of the hat from his neighbors; a man of standing in his community until he died in bed, surrounded by his family, in 1879.[33] What he accomplished as a soldier was the raising of a company; the sponsorship of Schumacher and Von Bachelle, two of the finest officers

31. Cheek and Pointon, *Sauk County*, p. 19.
32. *Milwaukee Sentinel*, April 11, 1866.
33. *Ibid.*, September 12, 1879.

in the regiment, and he had gotten his boys their bread.

Two hundred miles west of Milwaukee, the "Prairie du Chien Volunteers" was raised in the communities in the rolling and pleasant bluff country along the Mississippi River, one of the oldest settled areas in Wisconsin. Originally a French fur post, the community in those days had a raw edge, the street corners clustered with hard-eyed rivermen or burly miners from the nearby galena deposits. The small community was also a transfer point to the West, and there was always much coming and going.

The leader of the recruiting effort was 28-year-old Alexander S. Hooe, whose father of the same name was regarded as a hero in the Mexican War. The elder Hooe (some records spell the name Hove), a Virginian by birth, had come west to Fort Crawford at Prairie du Chien in the 1830s.[34] Phil Plummer was among the first to answer the younger Hooe's call in 1861 for a three-month company. Brother Tom followed shortly. Among others was Loyd G. Harris, a 19-year-old express agent who showed acumen and prowess in the hurly-burly Prairie du Chien community. He would, more than 20 years later, writing as "Grayson," create a series of gentle and humorous yarns about the 6th Regiment that would delight his old comrades. Harris, the local newspaper noted, was "the first to shoulder a musket and enter the ranks as high private. He is loved and respected by all. He left a good situation, and with feelings of real patriotism, he entered the army." Harris' "good situation" included a net worth of $350—a tidy sum for a 19-year-old.

Born in Buffalo, New York, August 24, 1840, Harris was eight when his family migrated to Wisconsin, settling first in Sheboygan and relocating later to Milwaukee. As a lad of 16, he marched with a volunteer fire company in the funeral of Solomon Juneau, the French fur trader-turned-town founder, who put Milwaukee on the map. Others in the funeral party included Rufus King, then editor of *The Milwaukee Sentinel*, and an Irishman by the name of Thomas Kerr. King would later command the brigade Harris served in during the Civil War, and Kerr would fight alongside Harris at a place called Gettysburg.

As one of the first to enlist in the Prairie du Chien company, Harris was presented to a Wisconsin industrialist, Norman Wiard,

34. *History of Crawford and Richland Counties, Wisconsin,* (Springfield, Illinois, 1884), pp. 497-499, 515.

who gave the young volunteer a gold watch, saying "that he did so because I was prompt . . . to enlist." Harris would meet Wiard in Washington in 1864, and the industrialist, who had perfected a steel-barreled artillery piece, took the officer to a meeting with President Lincoln. The watch was displayed, and Lincoln took the timepiece, "looked at it carefully and said, 'That is a superior piece of work, and it was done in America.' " Said Harris later: "You may be sure that I do not think any less of this watch because the great and grand man, Abraham Lincoln, once held it in his honest hand."

The Plummer brothers had arrived in Wisconsin from England with their father, John, who established himself as a land speculator. Philip and Thomas, a year apart in age, were handsome, slim and just under six-feet tall. Likely, both still bore traces of an English accent, now somewhat flattened by a half-dozen years on the American frontier. Despite striking dark looks, neither had yet married.[35]

It was an emotional time in the Mississippi River town that April of 1861. On a Friday evening, after but an hour's notice, Union Hall filled with a boisterous crowd, all talking war. Several speakers, including Hooe, addressed the audience, and a subscription of more than $300 was raised to aid in recruitment work. Within weeks, the roll nearly filled often with family pairs. In addition to the Plummers, there were others such as the Whaley boys, Edward and William. The former would rise to officer ranks and the latter would become a famous Iron Brigade musician who lived his postwar life impecuniously. From nearby Beetown came Albert and Harley Sprague. Lynxville sent Walter and William Pease. The Bottun brothers, Edwin and Henry, and the Hewitts, Ezra and Albert, arrived from Prairie du Chien. Also enlisting was father and son, John W. and John H. Fonda, the elder quickly becoming a sergeant.

At the muster in May, Hooe, as expected, was elected captain; Phil and Tom Plummer became first and second lieutenants; Harris was named first sergeant and Ed Whaley one of the corporals. Little Aleck Johnston became the company fifer.[36] One of the privates was Cornelius W. Okey of Cassville, whose later claims about a Confederate flag at Gettysburg would raise sharp words

35. U.S. Census, 1860.
36. *Crawford and Richland Counties*, p. 499.

in 1884 from a usually quiet and reserved Frank Wallar.

In assessing the prospects of the proud new company, the editor of the *Prairie du Chien Courier* wrote the volunteers had been "drilled for two weeks; and on the whole, are a fine appearing company of men. They are alive with the right feeling, desirous of perfecting themselves in military tactics." Captain Hooe, the editor noted, is a "patriotic and efficient officer [who] has a thorough knowledge of the duties of a soldier acquired at West Point. He is the most capable man in this part of the country to lead a company."[37]

The Prairie du Chien outfit would become Company C in the 6th Regiment, a light-hearted, frisky bunch known in the camps as the "Jayhawkers," perhaps for their remarkable ability to forage plump Secessionist chickens. Harris would later write about all that. But another member of that company, George Fairfield, who came in from Seneca, would never even hint at such activity in his neatly penned diaries full of weather observations and miles marched each day. He left a stiff picture showing him in frock coat and sergeant stripes, hands folded in his lap, a stern look on his face. Fairfield was not the type to romanticize camp life and doings, but he would write in post-war years of what he saw at Gettysburg, and, with some bitterness over what he felt were slights to his regiment. He would try to set the record straight.

Further north on the Mississippi River, the most experienced soldier answering the call for volunteers was John F. Hauser. Born Johann Friedrich Hauser on October 9, 1826, in Wadenswil, Canton Zurich in Switzerland, he had attended the exclusive military school at Thun. In the European wars, Hauser served on the staff of General Guiseppi Garibaldi and claimed one of his European friends was Charles Louis Napoleon Bonaparte, the third son of Louis Bonaparte.[38] Leaving behind a troubled marriage, Hauser immigrated to America in the early 1850s, initially locating on a farm in Davenport, Iowa, then moving two years later to Minnesota Territory, where he operated a general store. A short time thereafter, he moved across the Mississippi River to Fountain City, Wisconsin, where the number of German immigrants increased almost daily.

37. Jerome A. Watrous, *Milwaukee Telegraph*, September 1, 1894; *Prairie du Chien Courier*, May 2, 1861.
38. Dawes, *Service*, p. 13.

At the start of the secession crisis, in late December, 1860, Hauser had written Governor Alexander Randall to volunteer his services and Old World military experience. "In times of danger & trouble of the native or adopted country," he wrote, "the Patriots will join to the common banner." When the call for volunteers was made in 1861, the dashing 5-foot-10 Hauser led efforts to raise the "Buffalo County Rifles." By the end of April, some 60 men were enrolled, nearly 70 percent of them German-Americans. Hauser was chosen captain of the new unit, which traveled to Madison to become Company H of the new Regiment.[39]

All in all, Hauser had just the experience needed to turn the volunteers into soldiers. Rufus Dawes described him as a "commanding figure" and "rigid as a disciplinarian and exact as an instructor." Dawes told one story about Hauser, who, though he had a "voice like a trumpet," could express himself only with difficulty in English. At one drill session, Dawes recorded, Hauser became so exasperated that he halted his company and told them: "Vell, now you looks shust like one dam herd of goose."[40] Naturally, the men of Company H became "Hauser's Geese." The Swiss officer would be second in command of the regiment at Gettysburg.[41]

In addition to Hauser, three other Company H men would play key roles at Gettysburg. One was Lewis Eggleston of Shiocton, who came into the regiment as a drummer and would die a hero. Another was his friend, David Anderson of Minneapolis, a "rough looking man with a shaggy head of hair" who went down the Mississippi River to enlist in the Wisconsin regiment. The boys all called him "Rocky Mountain" Anderson, and he would avenge his pard's death.[42] The last was Edward P. Brooks of Madison. He enlisted June 11th and nine days later was promoted to regimental quartermaster-sergeant, a post he held until July 16, 1862, when he became second lieutenant of Company D. He was appointed adjutant of the 6th Wisconsin on April 1, 1863.

39. John Hauser, Letter, to Gov. Alexander Randall, December 26, 1860, Alexander Randall Papers, State Historical Society of Wisconsin; L. Kessinger, *History of Buffalo County, Wisconsin*, (Alma, Wisconsin, 1888), pp. 497-499; U.S. Census, 1860; Iron Brigade Association handwritten testimonial letter, September 13-14, 1883, State Historical Society of Wisconsin.
40. Dawes, *Service*, p. 13.
41. *Roster of Wisconsin Volunteers*, pp. 525-528.
42. *Ibid.*, p. 494; Rufus R. Dawes, "Align on the Colors," *Milwaukee Sunday Telegraph*, April 27, 1890.

"Mickey" Sullivan of Company K left an affectionate word picture of the young Brooks:

> [The boys] of high grade in the rear rank were pleased when he won (by hard and faithful service) his first straps and appeared on guard mount in all the glory of a brilliant new uniform, which was . . . 'anyhow two sizes too big mit him' and how we used to note with unbounded admiration his soldierly stride, his tremendous Grecian bend and his wonderful salute 'En high Tierce,' as he announced 'Sir, the parade is formed,' or presented the new guard to the officer of the day at guard mount. How we watched with inexpressible anxiety (and some with unspeakable envy,) the growth of his tow-colored and effeminate mustache, and how greatly we rejoiced when with the help of . . . hair dye it became visible to the naked eye when he faced the regiment at the proper distance as given in 'Hardee's Tactics.'[43]

Another of the western Wisconsin companies, raised by Captain Daniel J. Dill, called itself the "Prescott Guards" and drilled on the prairie overlooking the Mississippi River town of that name. The new officers were all very serious those first weeks of May, 1861, carefully keeping a "Roll of Prescott Guards" marked with pins to show the absentees from drills. First Sergeant Michael H. Fitch would become sergeant major of the new 6th Wisconsin when it reached Madison.[44] The company adopted as an "undress uniform" a "grey cap, red shirt and black pants," Fitch recalled 28 years later, remembering fondly "the drilling, the marching and the enthusiasm of those days," and how Captain Dill was a "natural soldier, tall, straight as an arrow and very commanding." All the men respected him, Fitch said, "not only for his soldierly qualities but for his kindness, even temper and most excellent judgment." The company's first and second lieutenants—John F. Marsh and Henry Serrill—were Mexican War

43. James P. Sullivan, "Why the Staff Lost a Chicken Supper," *Milwaukee Sunday Telegraph*, March 2, 1884.
44. Fitch resigned to become adjutant of the 21st Wisconsin in July, 1862. He joined Colonel Benjamin J. Sweet, who had been lieutenant colonel of the 6th as well as Frederick Schumacher, who had been first lieutenant of Company F of the 6th. *Adjutant General Reports*, p. 136-137; *Roster of Wisconsin Volunteers*, pp. 434, 502, 516.

veterans and "knew something about the drill," he wrote. The unit would be designated Company B and become "so mobile and well drilled" that Edward S. Bragg, who would later command the regiment, complimented the Guards at a reunion in Milwaukee nearly two decades later as "the best company of soldiers he ever saw." Fitch also remembered: "There were no stupid brains among the men." The company would leave Wisconsin with 92 members.[45] Captain Dill's worth was noted a year later when he was commissioned colonel of the 30th Wisconsin Infantry.

The fourth sergeant of the Prescott Guards was Rollin P. Converse, who would become one of the best-loved officers in the regiment. He was working as a clerk in Prescott in 1861. Born in Pierpont, Lawrence County, New York, the 5-foot-7 Converse, with his brown hair, blue eyes and fair complexion, rose quickly in the ranks and would be cited for "conspicuous bravery and good conduct" at Gettysburg.[46] He would die in the Battle of the Wilderness in 1864, before his 24th birthday. "No officer was ever more loved by his men, and none was ever more deserving of love, while he won the confidence and respect of his brother officers by his undaunted courage, and the coolness and judgment he always displayed in dangerous situations," wrote the editor of the *Prescott Journal* in a lengthy obituary May 28, 1864.

Another of the Prescott boys to play a role at Gettysburg was Isaiah F. Kelly. He was one of the company's first corporals, and though wounded, he would take up the 6th Wisconsin's shot-ripped flag and later write a remarkable letter about it. One of the other corporals in the Company B was James Kelly. The two were not related. James Kelly would receive his death wound at Gettysburg, and Rufus Dawes—in a lull in the fighting—would take special care to make sure James Kelly was remembered for having done his duty.[47]

About this time, in Rock County at Beloit, on the Wisconsin-

45. Michael H. Fitch, "Old Company B," *Milwaukee Sunday Telegraph*, March 24, 1889.
46. U.S. Census, 1860; Dawes, Gettysburg Report, July 17, 1862, U.S. War Department, *The War of the Rebellion: A Compilation of the Official Records of the Union and Confederate Armies*, (Washington, 1889-1901), Vol. 27, Pt. 1, p. 227. This is the Gettysburg Report of Lieutenant Colonel Rufus R. Dawes of the 6th Wisconsin. It cited Converse and Lieutenant Charles Hyatt for "conspicuous bravery and good conduct" in saving the gun of the 2nd Maine Battery, which had been captured.
47. Rufus R. Dawes, Journal, July 1, 1863, Rufus R. Dawes Papers, State Historical Society of Wisconsin.

Illinois line, Captain Marshall A. Northrup faced a special problem. A native of New York State, Northrup was trying to make a name for himself in his adopted city. In 1859, while corresponding secretary of the new City Republican Club, he had invited a rising Illinois politician by the name of Abraham Lincoln to make an appearance in Beloit as he returned from a speaking engagement at the Wisconsin State Fair in Milwaukee. Lincoln had accepted, and the local folks all agreed Northrup was what in those days was known as "a comer." His problem was whether Henry C. Matrau, who had enlisted in the "Beloit Star Rifles," would pass muster. A native of Bainbridge, in southwest Michigan, the underage Matrau had tried to sign up at Chicago, but was rejected. After telling the recruiting officer he "didn't know his business" and being threatened with arrest, the youngster traveled north to Beloit, where he heard recruits were needed, and was accepted. The rolls list his age as 16 and his height at 5-feet-6¾ inches, but a comrade said later that Matrau was actually 14 and probably a good deal shorter. At first, young Matrau was told he should be a fifer or drummer, but "he wanted to carry a gun like other men," and the crisis occurred at Camp Randall when the Beloit Star Rifles was mustered as Company G by a U.S. recruiting officer:

> More than a hundred men who had become interested in the little chap stood around to see if he would pass muster. He had picked out a pair of large shoes into which he stuffed insoles that would raise him up a half an inch or more, higher heels and thicker soles had been added to the shoes. The high crowned cap and the enlarged shoes lifted the little fellow up. . . . I can see him as he looked when he started to walk past the mustering officer. I can also see Captain McIntyre of the Regular Army, who mustered our regiment. The minute the boy started down the line, his eyes were fixed upon him, and he watched him until he reached the left of the company. I can see the captain's smile of approval as the little fellow took his place. He had won the day. He was mustered into Uncle Sam's service for three years or during the war.[48]

48. Jerome A. Watrous, "The Littlest Captain in the Iron Brigade," unpublished manuscript, Watrous Papers, SHSW. A graduate of the "State and National

Shortly afterward occurred the incident that won for Matrau the title "Baby of Company G." The regiment was participating in the Fourth of July parade in Madison. As the company marched by, a young lady called attention to Matrau, saying, "Look at that little fellow. He's only a baby." But the young private did his duty. "No soldier in the regiment carried a larger knapsack, kept up better in a long march or loaded and fired more rapidly than the baby of Company G, or behaved better under fire or in camp," said Matrau's comrade.[49]

In Sauk County that spring of 1861, the war was touching the Jones family in Excelsior Township. Horatio Jones and his wife, Nancy, had moved to Wisconsin from Virginia via Indiana sometime before 1850. By 1861, there were six sons—two already out on their own. In the call for volunteers, Bodley Jones and two brothers, Reuben and George, signed the roll of the "Sauk County Riflemen" on May 10th. George was only 15. Another brother, Thompson, who everyone called "Thompe," enlisted on the 28th.[50]

Despite his Virginia birth, father Jones was "intensely loyal," recorded Phil Cheek and Mair Pointon, who would write a history of the company. They remembered the elder Jones saying "if the war lasted long, he had two more younger sons, and, when the boys were all gone, if necessary, he would go himself."[51] It was all somewhat prophetic. Two sons would be killed, another would die of disease and the fourth would be wounded.

Bodley Jones, 20, made the strongest impression. He was 5-feet-7, with grey eyes and brown hair; a "little fellow," but "intelligent, perceptive, active, with an ingenuous and happy nature that made him companionable; happy in doing his duty; proud of his regiment, his state, and, above all, the colors under which he fought. . . ."[52] At Gettysburg, Bodley Jones almost captured a flag, but another man would get the glory and Jones would get an unmarked soldier's grave.

But that was all yet to happen that May, 1861, as the Jones brothers and other Sauk County boys rallied for the Union. At

---

Law School" of New York State, Northrup moved to Beloit at age 19, where he practiced law and held several municipal offices. *Beloit Journal*, October 20, 1864.
49. *Ibid.*
50. U.S. Census, 1850 and 1860; *Roster of Wisconsin Volunteers*, p. 498.
51. Cheek and Pointon, *Sauk County*, p. 11.
52. *Ibid.*, p. 75.

one of the earliest meetings, A. N. Kellogg, proprietor of the *Baraboo Republic,* "claimed the privilege" for his newspaper of furnishing one volunteer, Joseph Weirich, and arming him with "a Sharp's Rifle." Cheek and Pointon also told how, two days later, the new soldiers took off for nearby Reedsburg in "four four-horse wagons" with "martial music furnished by Rowley's band." Ten more recruits were added to the rolls, and all agreed it was a "good time." Finally, the company was off to Madison, the four Jones brothers, Cheek and Pointon in the ranks, and with Andrew G. Malloy as captain, the latter wearing the "handsome sword" given him by the admiring townsfolk.[53] The Riflemen would become Company A in Wisconsin's 6th Regiment.

At about the same time, in late April, 1861, the "largest and most enthusiastic meeting ever held in Juneau County" assembled at Mauston, and it was resolved to "henceforth recognize but two parties—the Union and Disunion party; that the Union party shall have our assistance, the Dis-Union party our most determined opposition." The *Mauston Star* also reported May 1st that when volunteers were called for a company to put down the rebellion, "FORTY-SEVEN brave fellows at once stepped forward and pledged their services—if need be their lives—in defense of the Government and laws of the United States."

The meeting was chaired by Henry Dawes, father of Rufus, and one can run a finger down that first list of volunteers and find not only the younger Dawes, but Jimmy Scoville, Aaron Yates, William Remington and John Kellogg. The meeting adjourned with "loud cheers for 'The Union, one and indivisible!,'" the *Star* said, adding the gathering showed "our people are a unit for the Union." Rufus Dawes had been elected captain, and Kellogg, the county's prosecuting attorney, the first lieutenant. Both would play key roles in the fight at Gettysburg two years later. Bill Remington came in as a private, and everybody liked the "raw-boned, good hearted and awkward" six-footer with his fair hair, blue eyes and "devil me care" attitude, one comrade remembered. The former mill hand and mail carrier soon would have his shoulder straps, command his own company at Gettysburg and, despite a nagging cold, almost capture a flag.[54]

53. *Ibid.,* p. 8.
54. Jerome A. Watrous, Letter, *Mauston Star,* January 8, 1885; *Roster of Wisconsin Volunteers,* p. 533.

The new company was to be "The Lemonweir Minute Men," a name selected from the "peaceful and gently flowing river, in the beautiful valley of which most of our men resided," Dawes remembered. One of the recruits said the name would remind the boys of home, and "this argument carried the day."[55]

In the following weeks, there was a scramble to fill the company, and Dawes wrote his brother he was "working like a beaver" to get his "Minute Men" into active service.[56] Recruiting lagged when it appeared the company would not be called, then Governor Randall sent word it would be needed, and more volunteers came forward.

On July 3rd, Mauston Star editor John Turner reported in his columns that company strength had reached 90, and those were "the best men of our county; many of them leaving property and business interests that must suffer in consequence of their absence. The patriotism of such men cannot be doubted."

One of the first of the Juneau County young men to catch war fever was James P. "Mickey" Sullivan, who had been "following a plow" as a hired man at Wonewoc. He wrote two decades later that on May 8th, he and two White Creek boys, Rescun "Reck" W. Davis and Jim Barney, went to the adjoining farm of Bill Steward, where a corporal of the new company, John St. Clair, was "acting in the dual capacity of 'hired man' and 'beau' for 'Sal,' 'old Bill's' buxom daughter." Sullivan signed the enlistment roll, then returned home, remembering how, as the family gathered around "the big lamp" in the kitchen each night after chores, one or the other would read the latest "war news" in the Mauston Star.[57]

Finally, the volunteers were called to Mauston; the Wonewoc boys getting in first, followed by a party from New Lisbon and then the "Yellow River crowd," Sullivan related later. The new soldiers found they had much to learn. With the exception of 38-year-old Corporal John Holden, a Mexican War veteran, few had even a nodding acquaintance with a drill field. Mauston Star editor Turner made much of Holden's patriotism, writing that "even though an old man," he had walked 16 miles from Wonewoc to Mauston to join the company; and "he was greeted with three

55. Dawes, Service, pp. 6-8.
56. Ibid., p. 8.
57. Sullivan, Telegraph, May 9, 1885.

cheers and a tiger." But it would be a short war for Holden: he was discharged within six months for disability.[58]

Even Holden's military experience was suspect those days, said Sullivan, because he "had been an ordnance sergeant so long that he had forgotten all drill and tactics except the 'salute'. . . ." Not a "man of the company had seen a company drill," the Irishman wrote 25 years later, "and 'right flank,' 'left flank,' 'front,' 'wheel' . . . were conundrums which the ablest of us were unable to master and the way we went 'endways,' 'sideways,' in one row and two rows" puzzled the young officers. Sullivan recalled:

> Our maneuvering was done in the public square at Mauston to the great edification of school children, fathers, mothers, sisters, friends and the girls we had not yet left behind us, and if they judged by the loudness of the tones of command and our ability to charge the school house or church, they must have felt the rebellion would soon be a thing of the past.

Young John Ticknor showed promise. He later would become a fine volunteer officer, but "then seemed to look on the thing as a huge joke." Ticknor was drilling Sullivan's squad and "one time when he had us going endways in good shape, there became imminent danger of a collision between the 'squab' and one of the outhouses," Sullivan remembered. Ticknor was up to the occasion. At the last possible second, Ticknor shouted, "Break ranks, boys, and fall in on the other side of the back-house," and the boys did just that, probably with hardly a break in step. It was a fine performance under pressure; young Ticknor was on his way up the military ladder.

Those days of drill at Mauston were not always pleasant for young Sullivan, however. Several members of the new company objected to his enlistment because of age and small size, he recalled; some muttered in loud voices the young Irishman "would disgrace the company by not being able to pitch rebels over [his] shoulder with a bayonet, or keep up on a march," and others questioning, "What good would Mickey be in a charge 'bagnets?' " Sullivan remembered how "old Ira Butterfield and several others would look complacently down from their six feet four altitude

58. *Mauston Star*, May 14, 1861; *Roster of Wisconsin Volunteers*, p. 534.

and good naturedly advise me to go home to mother and wait till I was feathered out. . . ."

It seemed for a time, the young Irishman said, that Captain Rufus R. Dawes might reject him, then Second Lieutenant John Crane, "whose ancestor, like my own, was some of the 'rale ould kind,'" came to his rescue. There was some question whether Sullivan was old enough to enlist, so Crane marched the would-be soldier before a justice of the peace. The justice appointed himself Sullivan's guardian, "granted consent to enlist, and swore me into the state service in one time and three motions, and so I became a full fledged member of the company," and that was why his enlistment was dated June 21st, 1861, instead of May 8th, the day he actually signed the roll.

The company's start for the war front was fitful and frustrating. It seemed there was some mix-up between young Captain Dawes and the Adjutant General's office over transport to Madison. Three times, Sullivan recalled, "we bid farewell to every one in Mauston, and twice we were escorted to the depot but each time no cars were provided, nor had the railroad any instruction to furnish transportation." There were some fears voiced by the young soldiers that perhaps "the state would have no use" for the company, but finally, just before midnight July 6th, railroad "Agent Fish notified us that cars were attached to the coming train, and with no time for good-byes nor any escort, we hustled to the depot and took the train which carried many of the boys away never to see Mauston again."[59]

All told, 25 who had signed the original rolls would not go, finding one excuse or another, and editor Turner, in his July 10th edition, jeered the stay-at-homes as the "Gosling Guards." It should be noted, however, at least 15 of those who stayed behind in the first call did later serve in other regiments, several with bravery and distinction.

The company—94 men in all—changed cars at Minnesota Junction and again at Milton, and on Sunday, July 7th, 1861, arrived at the east gate of Camp Randall at Madison, where it would soon become Company K.[60] The Juneau County boys—"Mickey" Sullivan, George Chamberlain, Johnny Ticknor, Hugh Talty,

59. Sullivan, *Telegraph*, May 9, 1886.
60. James P. Sullivan, "Old Company K," *Milwaukee Sunday Telegraph*, May 16, 1886. This is Part Two of Sullivan's account of his company.

Aaron Yates, Tom Flynn and dozens more—a collection of volunteers Sullivan remembered as "hardy lumbermen, rugged farmer boys and sturdy mechanics,"[61] under the command of young Ohioan Rufus Dawes, were off to save the Union. Unanswered in the records or recollections they left was whether young John St. Clair ever got a chance to say a final proper good-bye to Bill Steward's buxom daughter, Sal.

61. *Ibid.*

COL. LYSANDER CUTLER
The Men Called Him "Gray Wolf"

72

CHAPTER THREE

When with noble appearance, and line straight and true,
    And lithe springing step, they passed in review,
Their soldierly bearing forced the Generals to say,
    They march better than regulars, grand Company K."
                                        —By "Mickey"

Greenhorn Patriots

Wisconsin was alive with war news that early July of 1861 as the Lemonweir Minute Men traveled to Madison to join the 6th Regiment. The columns of the newspapers were filled with the latest sensations: Fort Sumter surrendered. A call for Union volunteers. The South and North mobilizing. Four regiments had already been forwarded to Washington by the young state. The 5th was still at Camp Randall, along with nine companies of the 6th. The Juneau County organization was to complete the 6th Regiment, and the boys piled off the railcars at Madison not far from the former fairgrounds-turned-drill field and mustering place, many loaded down with gripsacks and bundles carefully packed by the homefolk; one fellow carried just "one shirt tied up in a red handkerchief." It was exciting and threatening at the same time: the backwoods pinery and farmer boys big-eyed and skittish, and young Captain Rufus R. Dawes all business and very much in charge. During the rail journey he had received a telegram from the regiment's commander, Lysander Cutler, asking the hour of arrival; Dawes responded, taking no special note of the request. Dawes got his men in two ranks and headed them for the front entrance, the new soldiers stumbling along, "kicking each other's heels." Dawes remembered there was not much show or dash about the young volunteers: "A few wore broadcloth and silk hats, wore the red shirts of raftsmen, several . . . in country homespun, one [in] a calico coat, and another looking through a hole in the drooping brim of a straw hat." Several of the Minute Men were also wearing what Dawes said were "those ugly white caps with long capes, called 'Havelocks.'"

At the front of Camp Randall, Dawes encountered his first test as a soldier, when a young officer in a "bright uniform" and mounted on a "spirited charger" cantered up and snapped a salute that was well practiced and precise. He identified himself as Lieutenant Frank A. Haskell, the new regiment's adjutant. He told Dawes that Colonel Cutler requested the new company be formed "in column by platoon" and marched to headquarters. Behind the dazzling Haskell and his "spirited charger" was a sight that chilled the Juneau County boys: arrayed along the drill field stood the 5th and 6th Wisconsin Regiments, row after row of men, neatly aligned—nearly 2,000 soldiers—to receive the new arrivals with "becoming state and ceremony." It was almost too much for the new volunteers, suddenly awed and awkward under the steady gaze of more people than many of them had ever seen in one place in their whole lives. The company was to be marched to headquarters under escort of the Milwaukee Zouaves, Haskell said in that superior way he had, gesturing to the soldiers in colorful uniforms formed to one side of the gate. This was the same Milwaukee militia outfit that had, just weeks before, along with the Montgomery Guard, escorted the famed Milwaukee Light Guard from that city. It had a reputation as the best-drilled company in the state, and it was now designated Company B of the 5th Wisconsin. It was all overwhelming, and Dawes admitted later he was all confusion, acutely aware of the backwoods appearance of his men, but manfully trying to put a good face on it. "Good Afternoon, Sir," he answered Haskell. "I should be glad to comply with the wishes of the Colonel, but it is simply impossible." Then, still unprepared and trying to make sense of it, the Minute Men found themselves in their first tramp across a drill field, the eyes of two regiments of real soldiers upon them. The brightly uniformed Milwaukee Zouaves marched on both sides, yelling and "engaged in one of their peculiar drills" that Dawes remembered increased "the distraction of my men," who "marched worse than before." Somehow, after much pulling and pushing by Dawes and the other officers, the soldiers got into a line in front of headquarters and the assembled regimental commanders. It was a humble beginning for the company that Private J. P. Sullivan later romanced in verse as "marching better than regulars."[1]

The welcome by the regiment and the officers was at the same time well done and ill received, Sullivan wrote later, remembering how he stood in ranks for his first look at the men who would order him into battle. Juneau County was now somehow far away to the young soldiers who had drilled to loud commands between the church and the Mauston school, and the road ahead suddenly unknown and threatening. Dawes recalled that Colonel Cutler congratulated the company for their arrival, adding a few other remarks and informing the Minute Men they would be Company K; but the young officer also remembered—"in recognition of our grand entree"—the camp had already christened the new arrivals Company "Q."[2] Sullivan wrote later of the company being received by Cutler "with a few words of welcome," and by Lieutenant Colonel Julius P. Atwood, "who welcomed us in quite a speech." But it was Major Benjamin Sweet "who embraced the opportunity to spread himself (as [Tom] Flynn ironically termed it, all over the American Eagle." Sullivan recalled:

> [Sweet] had been state senator, and being restricted by the rules of the senate from talking them into insanity, he had loaded himself for our arrival and at once proceeded to fire off his "dictionary words" at us. I don't remember any of his eloquence but one sentence, and that "stuck in my crop" until he left the regiment, which was, "you call yourselves 'Lemonweir Minute Men,' but we had begun to think you were 'Lemonweir Hour Men,'" which implied that it was our fault for not reaching camp sooner; an implication which was wholly undeserving and unnecessary, for we had been (to again quote Flynn) "Pepperin for fear we'd miss a chance to be kilt" I never liked the man afterwards, and frequently thought that, after he left us that if company K [volunteers] were hour men getting into camp they were also hour men in staying in the war, and that one of the hour men who was only a lieutenant when Sweet was major, attained a position of honor which in my estimation was equal to any in the army, the command of the Iron Brigade.

1. Dawes, *Service*, pp. 11-12.
2. *Ibid.*, p. 12.

The "lieutenant" was John A. Kellogg, the round-faced Juneau County prosecuting attorney, who had, though 30 and with a wife and family, joined Dawes in raising the company. The Company K boys were always rather proud of Kellogg, who served the regiment with honor for four years: dodging a hail of bullets that ripped his hat and uniform at Gettysburg; a wound and capture at the Wilderness in 1864; an escape from a Confederate prison; and finally, promotion to command what remained of the Iron Brigade in the closing days of the war.[3]

In any event, the welcome was finally completed, and the new company dispatched to the wooden barracks built on the east side of the compound and north of the main gate. The 5th Wisconsin was billeted in tents just north of headquarters, which was "on the hill," and the mess building for the two regiments was on the north side of the camp.[4] That night, the new company was formed behind the other men of the 6th Regiment for evening dress parade, and Adjutant Haskell came to Dawes' relief, assisting him in directing his company. The young captain said later he had "an appreciative memory" of Haskell's "kindness on that occasion," but admitted "the fun he enjoyed in watching us, amply repaid his service."[5] In a letter two days after arriving at Camp Randall, Dawes wrote his sister, telling her his men were "now under the severest kind of drill" and had been moved from the barracks with their old straw, "in which there was no scarcity of fleas," to tents. "My men are no more than half supplied with blankets, and, as we have cold drizzling weather, they have suffered. It is a new life to us all, but I hope we can get broken in without much sickness."[6]

New Private Sullivan wrote later it was all a rude awakening for those who fancied a soldier's life was one of ease, and he described "a day's duties in camp as it was in Camp Randall in July, 1861, and when I describe one it covers all." At daylight, there was reveille and roll call, followed immediately by one hour's company drill. Then there were 15 minutes for preparation before being marched to breakfast. There was a "Sick Call" and "Fatigue

3. Sullivan, *Telegraph*, May 16, 1886; *Roster of Wisconsin Volunteers*, p. 494; J. A. Kellogg, *Capture and Escape*, (Madison, Wisconsin, 1908); Dawes, *Service*, p. 6.
4. Sullivan, *Telegraph*, May 16, 1886.
5. Dawes, *Service*, p. 12.
6. *Ibid.*, p. 14.

Call" and finally a "Guard Mount;" then two and one-half hours of company and squad drill before dinner:

> At one o'clock, fall in and have three hours "battalion drill" supper; dress parade. Tattoo and roll call at 9 o'clock, taps fifteen minutes later. Then the poor green-horn patriot, tired as an ox after a day's hard logging, was at liberty to lay down on the soft side of a board and dream, if he slept at all, of glory and the grave.

The young Irishman also remembered a "man called Dutcher had the contract for 'grubbing' us," and the Juneau County farmer boys, who were used to a good table, "grumbled immensely over the hash which Jim Barney called 'cononderfun'; but I think that afterwards many of us would be glad to have a dish of Dutcher's hash." Sullivan also wrote how each outfit ate at a long pine table that accommodated officers and men. At meal times, each company formed and marched in, a rank on each side of the table. Dawes would command, "Lemonweir Minute Men. Inward face. Uncover. Seats." Then the young officer, who, Sullivan related, "always did things decently and in order," offered grace. All "the little fellows on the left"—Tommy Flynn, Erastus Smith, Billy Campbell, S. Frank Gordon, Tommy Ellsworth and Sullivan—whom Smith called "the ragtag and bobtail of Company K"—would "cross our hands, assume a Sunday-go-to-meeting expression of countenance" before beginning "grace" of their own invention. There were two versions:

> Now I sit me in my seat,
> And pray for something fit to eat,
> If this damn stuff my stomach brake,
> I pray that God my soul will take.
>
> Or:
>
> Oh, thou who blessed the loaves and fishes,
> Look down upon these old tin dishes;
> By thy great power those dishes smash,
> Bless each of us and damn this hash.

They were "gay, brave, fun-loving boys," Sullivan wrote, and many of them would later face "death just as cool and unconcerned as they then ridiculed Dawes' attempts at ready-made piety."[7]

It was all new for the young volunteers, the drills, drum calls and company mess; young Dawes and the other officers learning along with the men; and always, magnificent Haskell off to the side somewhere, watching with an amused glint in his eye before moving in to straighten out a muddle as the company learned the movements. Finally, after about a week in camp, the Minute Men were marched to "headquarters on the hill" to be "rigidly examined" by the medical officers. Being "chiefly hardy lumbermen, rugged farmer boys and sturdy mechanics, none failed to pass," Sullivan recalled, "and on July 16th, we were directed to prepare for muster into the service of the U.S. Flynn, as usual, commented by saying, 'we'll be mustard now and salted and peppered afterwards,' and after events showed that he was no false prophet." The actual ceremony wasn't quite what the soldiers expected, wrote Sullivan:

> Muster into the service of the U.S. in our case consisted of forming in company line, opening order to the rear, when several officers pass along in front of each rank, the company closes order and the first or orderly sergeant calls each man's name who steps out and passes the mustering officer, saluting him in passing.

But it wasn't until the issue of uniforms, the young Irishman said, that the Minute Men began to feel they were soldiers:

> The uniform was a short gray jacket reaching to the hips, faced with black at the ends of the collar, on the upper side of the cuffs, on the shoulders and straps on the sides to hold up the waist belt, gray pants with a black welt in the outside seam, a fatigue suit of pepper and salt gray cotton cloth, (i.e., a sack coat and trowsers with red welt in outside seam,) two heavy dark blue woolen shirts, two pairs drawers, two pairs socks, a pair of cowhide shoes, a linen and glaze cloth cap cover, cap, etc., every article received from the state was of excellent quality, except the dress caps, and that was something wonderfully and fearfully made.

7. Sullivan, *Telegraph*, May 16, 1886.

The dress cap created the most amusement. "What a carpenter would call the carcass was made of hair cloth," Sullivan wrote, "the frame and studding of wire and whalebone, and the siding of gray cloth; the inside finish of black alpaca, and the cornice base board, and outside trimmings of patent leather, a front vizor or porch square with front elevation and projecting on a level; a rear vizor or piazza extending downwards at one-third pitch, and the whole heavily and strongly put together according to a specification." He remembered the caps "afforded the boys an unlimited opportunity to exercise their powers of sarcasm, and they were universally named after a useful chamber utensil and many were the theories advanced and overthrown in regard to the use of the hind vizor or tail piece." It was little Hugh Talty who finally solved what the boys remembered as "the vexed question." After much headshaking and conversation as the Juneau County boys stood in a bunch, hands in pockets, discussing the matter in that solemn Western fashion, Talty asserted in an undisputable manner "that whin we were fi'tin', the inemy couldn't tell whin we ware advancin' or retratin'," which, as Sullivan recalled, "was accepted as the only correct and reasonable hypothesis."

In the little free time the soldiers had, the Wisconsin issue uniforms of militia gray, especially the headgear, provided a good deal of entertainment. "The caps furnished the boys an excellent substitute for footballs and considerable exercise in 'hop, step and a jump,' the jump generally ending on top of somebody's cap," Sullivan remembered. But the "remarkable caps sprang up refreshed after every disaster, the hair cloth acting as an indestructible spring to restore them to the original shape after the pressure was withdrawn. . . ." But it was not until the caps "were remodeled by taking out the hair cloth and cutting off the rear vizor that the boys took to them kindly or generally," he added. The rough shoes also furnished "much harmless mirth and jokes," and there were many off-hand remarks about "gunboats," "flatboats," "schooners," "ferry boats" and "mud scows," Sullivan said, "but those were mild terms applied to the brogans worn by the taller fellows such as Ira Butterfield of Lemonweir, Joe Chase of Lisbon and Arland Winsor of Summit and others of the No. 13s," while the 5-foot-6½-inch Sullivan—as Tommy Flynn observed in his clever way—"could go through all the facings without moving the toes of his shoes from the front." Sullivan said, however, that later, when the regiment drew the federal blue uniforms, "we realized very forcibly the difference in quality in favor of our state uniform."[8]

About the same time, seven of the boys in Company E, Bragg's Rifles, went to Madison to get their pictures taken so the home-folk could have a likeness. The young volunteers wore their newly issued, gray Wisconsin kepis and dark-blue fatigue blouses. The flat-topped caps were shaped to individual style, some cocked rakishly to one side or the other, one tipped back, another forward, and one stiff and tall. Four of the seven, George W. White, John J. Dillon, Charles D. Elliott and James F. Parkhurst, were seated, and standing behind them were Worthie H. Patton, William A. Dillon and Lyman L. White, hands casually on the shoulders of the young volunteers in front of them. "They were all Appleton boys," said a comrade, "belonged to the same company lived in the same tent; sat at the same table. Not one of them was bewhiskered; they never had been the possessors of such an adornment, or encumbrance, which ever you please. They were indeed boys—beardless boys."[9] The young men facing the camera had yet to be touched by the war, although they wore real uniforms and were real soldiers. It was a good time to be young in Wisconsin and off on the great mission to preserve the Union. The seven were confident they would do their duty, and the smooth faces showed innocence as well as resolve. In the end, the seven would be in the "hottest of the great battles of the Army of the Potomac," and they would never again be the bright-eyed boys captured by the camera. William Dillon would be a sergeant at Gettysburg and would be wounded. His brother, John, was discharged for disability after the bloody summer campaigns of 1862. Charles Elliott would break down physically and transfer to the Veteran Reserve Corps, that unit for soldiers no longer able to sustain the rigors of front-line duty. Jimmy Parkhurst would be severely wounded at Antietam. Worthie H. Patton would be wounded at the Battle of the Wilderness in 1864 and go home. The White boys, who were not related, would serve their three years. But it was George W. White, the "handsome faced . . . boy" sitting on the right in the picture, who prob-

8. *Ibid.*
9. [Jerome A. Watrous], "That Group of Seven," *Milwaukee Telegraph*, March 30, 1895.

ably had the most harrowing experience of the seven.

It all started in January, 1862, when an order went out to the regiments asking for volunteers for the Signal Corps. White was summoned to regimental headquarters, a lad remembered as a "short, well-built, blue-eyed, black-haired boy of 20, whose clear complexion—whose pink cheeks any girl might be glad to possess." Colonel Lysander Cutler looked him over. "Think you would like to leave the company and enter the signal service, where you will have a horse to ride?" asked the colonel. "If the mud is always going to be as deep as it is now I think I would," said Private White. "I guess you will do," said Cutler, and so White packed his traps while the Company E boys wished him well, for he was a great camp favorite. "If Little Mack wants any more men to ride government horses, tell him I am at his service," said Frank King of Fond du Lac, with a grin, and it was all sad later, for King would die a horrible death at Gettysburg, and perhaps it was all chance White was selected and he was not. Finally, the departing private walked down the company street with downcast eyes and carrying his plump knapsack. He stopped at the tent of Major Edward Bragg, his first captain. "Do your duty as well as you have done it in the company, White, and you will have no trouble," said the little major, "but if you do get into difficulty send word to me." At the battle of Fredericksburg, less than a year later, White was assigned to the highest church steeple in the city, where he stood all day watching for and answering signals. The steeple was between the rebel artillery as well as his own:

> Hundreds of solid shot and shell roared past me, each one seeming to call for a winding up of my career. Think of it! I was over 200 feet from the ground, charged with a sacred duty that demanded ceaseless attention and any second a shot or shell might hurl me to the street. The church was struck in a dozen places, each time giving me a jar that I can never forget. A shell hit the top of the steeple and exploded, a piece of iron half as large as your hand dropping within an inch of one of my feet. A solid shot went through my perch three or four feet below my platform. How did I feel? Can't tell. Thought the hour to go had come, but at that moment a message from

81

[General Ambrose] Burnside's headquarters at the Phillips House was signaled and I repeated it. Never did a poor fellow pray for night as I did.

And that was how George White, who posed so proudly for a picture at Camp Randall, did his duty in a church steeple under artillery fire at Fredericksburg, all because it seemed having a government horse to ride was easier than tramping in the Virginia mud.[10]

But that was all ahead for the seven Appleton boys, and if some of the young Wisconsin volunteers passed the time getting their pictures taken, other companies had been in Camp Randall a longer time, and the young soldiers had discovered more sophisticated pastimes, especially an 18-year-old private in Irish Company D by the name of John H. Cook. He had enlisted in the Milwaukee unit from nearby Hartford and (despite standing a half-inch under 5-foot-4) was making a reputation for himself as the "Tough One." He remembered hanging around with such fellows as Frank Bell, who enlisted from Waukesha County, Josiah Fowler of Mazomanie, and Hamilcar McIntosh of Milwaukee, among others, and when "there was any deviltry going on, you found one or more of the crowd." Cook got into his first scrape when he, McIntosh and Bell "wanted to go to Madison through the back end of the barrack" and were caught by young Lieutenant Patrick H. McCauley of Milwaukee, who gave Cook and the others four days in the guard house. But the "Tough One" was not upset by what he called the "racket" because "our dear old Col. Cutler said he would not give a cent for a soldier that had not been in the guard-house. So I thought I would be something extra of a soldier." His second stint came just a few days later when an Irish corporal, "a little, dried up fellow, who had been in the English army and was strict," ordered Cook to walk a guard post. Cook (who admitted the corporal thought he was a "prime rascal") wasn't in the mood for any such duty, and he remembered the exchange this way: " 'Go to h-ll,' says I. 'Take that Private Cook to the guard-house!' He went." It didn't take Cook long to "put up a job" on the two-striper "that he did not forget." Cook and McIntosh went into Madison and wrote the cor-

10. *Ibid.* The 200-foot steeple White remembered was likely somewhat lower, but, as old soldiers would be the first to admit, it made a better story.

poral a note saying that his wife had just arrived from Milwaukee and was waiting for him in Madison. "We were watching out for him," Cook recalled later, "and when he went with a pass at the front gate, we skipped out our regular way through the place where the board was off in back of our barracks. We followed him, caught up with him, and before he got where his supposed wife was, he was too full [of alcoholic beverage] for utterance. We then went to the provost guard, told them there was a fellow that had deserted the camp and was drunk; he was arrested, kept overnight, came back next day without seeing his wife." And the "Tough One" added. "He always thought I had a hand in it; but I got even."[11]

The next Company D man to fall victim to Cook's bizarre sense of duty was kindly, old First Sergeant Benjamin Campbell of Watertown, who, for some unexplained reason, placed "considerable confidence" in the young private. "At one time I came near being promoted (not for my bravery) but because the 1st Sergt. thought that I was such a divil that to promote me would make a man of me."[12] Campbell sent Cook "to draw clothing at the chapel," Cook wrote later in the dry, humorous account of his days at Camp Randall. "I went up with fifteen men to draw clothes, but they were so busy that we had to wait. We filed around to the south of the chapel where they sold beer, got full, and did not know whether we were drawing clothing or drinking beer. I think we were. We were (that's me) put under arrest for disobedience of orders."

Campbell was also the victim of another prank. It was, among other things, the sergeant's duty to fire the reveille gun each morning at 5 a.m. "We woke him up at 3 o'clock, and the gun went off just the same," Cook recollected. "The old fellow's keg was always full so he could not tell whether it was 3 or 5 o'clock in the morning. He thought it was a mean trick; so do I, but I had to do something and I took that way of doing it."[13] The sergeant was more than slightly upset, Cook remembered: "Col.

11. J. H. Cook, "A Tough One," *Milwaukee Sunday Telegraph*, March 4, 1883.
12. Cook, *Army*, p. 1. Cook's 12-page war memoir is a curious document. There are two copies. The first was written May 30, 1865, in Washington, D.C. and the second, a copy, August 9, 1865 at Hartford, Wisconsin. Both are identical. For a soldier who served in three separate outfits and took part in a score of battles, the "memoir" is unusual in that it is almost a complete litany by Cook citing grievances against the officers of the various regiments.
13. Cook, *Telegraph*, March 4, 1883.

Cutler came near reducing him to the ranks and he talked awful hard to Mc and me and threatened to put us in the Guard House. We knew he wouldn't for he had promised it many a time before that."[14]

There was one other incident at Madison, and Cook recounted it with his black sense of irony. "We marched through the city of Madison on the 4th of July and paid ten cents a drink for a cup of water; it was not generally so, but some took advantage of it and charged that amount. Well, that is all past," he wrote 22 years later. "Now we look at things different. Boys then; men now."[15]

Phil Cheek and Mair Pointon in Company A, the Sauk County Riflemen, remembered the July 4th parade through Madison as a "hot dusty march," and when the regiment returned to Camp Randall about 2 p.m., the dinner of "bread, potatoes, codfish gravy and coffee" was cold. "We naturally were just a little mad," they wrote later, "and threw the whole outfit of dinner and tin plates into the cook shanties and made a break for up town for something to eat, but they had double guarded the exits; we did not make it." It all turned out in the end, however, for when the "good people" of Madison learned the facts, "they were as indignant as the two regiments." On July 18th, the townsfolk brought in a "splendid repast" for the 5th and 6th that was recalled as "the only square meal we had while in camp there."[16]

While the soldiers of lesser rank drilled, ducked through the loose barrack's board for Madison, paid 10 cents for a cup of water, kicked about the grey caps provided by the state and tricked an old sergeant into firing the wake-up gun two hours early, young Captain Dawes and the other officers of the regiment were getting to know one another, studying their drill manuals and learning about the strange and wondrous ways of Army Regulations. In addition to Colonel Cutler and Adjutant Haskell, Dawes remembered, he was impressed especially by Captain Edward Bragg of Company E, who "appeared to be much gratified that a Captain had come in, who knew less than he did about military matters." Other officers of ability, he found, included Captain Adam Malloy of Company A; Captain A. S. Hooe of Company C; the courtly German lieutenants of Company F, Frederick Schumacher and

14. Cook, *Army*, p. 2.
15. *Ibid.*
16. Cheek and Pointon, *Sauk County*, pp. 15-16.

Werner von Bachelle, whom he regarded as "two of the most highly qualified officers with whom I met in all my service"; Captain John Hauser of Company H, and Lieutenant John F. Marsh of Company B.[17] The brother officers were probably similarly impressed with young Dawes as well, with his prominent New England origins: one great-grandfather, William Dawes, Jr., was Paul Revere's companion at the start of the War for Independence, and another, Dr. Manasseh Cutler, a Massachusetts churchman of wide reputation.

With such a heritage, it was all somehow fitting Rufus was born on the Fourth of July, 1838, the second son and fifth child of Henry Dawes and his wife, Sarah Cutler. The infant was given the single name "Rufus" in honor of a remote cousin, Boston poet Rufus Dawes, but as the years passed, family members (noting the significant date of his birth) nicknamed him Rufus "Republic" Dawes. That was quickly shortened to "R.R." or "Railroad" Dawes, and in time the young man came to regard the middle initial as part of his legal signature.[18]

One of his sons later said young Rufus "had few pleasures as a child,"[19] probably due in part to the "legal separation" obtained by his parents in 1839. Rufus' father, Henry, operated a warehouse and general store at Malta, but was gone much of the time, dealing extensively in grains and real estate. Henry Dawes came to Wisconsin where, on May 18, 1855, he recorded extensive land purchases near Mauston, in what would become Juneau County. In a letter to his brother from Madison about that time, Henry Dawes noted his new purchases were near the "route to La Crosse" and were "mostly prairie with Timber enough and lots of Springs." He added: "Land warrants were selling at La Crosse for $95 for eighty acres."[20] On that same trip, Henry made arrangements to enter his two sons, Ephraim and Rufus, in the

17. Dawes, *Service*, pp. 14-15.
18. A family biographer said "one other rendition of the middle initial has come to pass, but by what process of reasoning is unknown." In the Library of Congress catalogue, Dawes' *Service With The Sixth Wisconsin Volunteers* was originally credited to "Rufus Robinson Dawes," but the family, sometime after 1900, successfully petitioned to have it changed to "Rufus R. Dawes." Rev. William E. Roe, "Brigadier General Rufus R. Dawes," *Dawes-Gates Ancestral Lines*, A Memorial Volume Containing the American Ancestry of Rufus R. Dawes, Vol. I, compiled by Mary Walton Ferris, privately printed, 1943, p. 3.
19. Charles G. Dawes, "By One of His Sons," *Ancestral Lines*, p. 8.
20. *Ibid.*, p. 56.

university at Madison and then went to see his brother, Edward Dawes, who was living at Ripon, Wisconsin, where Henry Dawes' father was visiting. The senior Dawes died there September 21, 1855. Henry Dawes also wrote a quick letter to son Rufus, noting it was doubtful he would be home for an additional month. He added a fatherly caution: "I wish you to be careful of fire and see that ashes are not thrown out near wood. Be a good boy. Don't go out nights."[21]

Rufus and Ephraim entered the university at Madison in the fall of 1856. In November, their father sent Rufus $6 to "use only for necessaries for both of you." Henry Dawes added: "Try to do with as little as you can until I sell some Wisconsin land which I shall probably be able to do next summer. . . . You should be careful to tallow your shoes."[22]

In the summer of 1857, Ephraim and Rufus returned to the family home, now at Marietta, Ohio, to spend some time with their mother, Sarah Cutler Dawes. The two returned to Wisconsin the next summer to help "clear" the Dawes farm located at Seven Mile Creek, several miles south of Mauston. Both again entrained for Marietta to attend college that fall.

In 1859, the *Mauston Star* reported Henry Dawes was starting a general merchandise business in Mauston with his son, Rufus. Most of that summer was also spent clearing land, and Rufus reported in a letter to his sister in Ohio:

> This is a tremendous job of "log rolling" or to use the dialect of the country "bush whacking." Father is prosecuting his improvements rapidly. . . . devoting his whole time, energy and business talents to the sole object of making a productive and profitable estate, to which he looks forward for a home and sustenance.[23]

But the store proved to be a short-lived venture, and the merchandise left was transferred to the large frame home Henry had erected on his farm.[24] Rufus Dawes graduated from Marietta College the spring of 1860, and again journeyed to Mauston. The

21. *Ibid.*, pp. 56-58.
22. *Ibid.*, p. 57.
23. *Ibid.*
24. The house Henry Dawes built stands several miles south of Mauston, on Juneau County Trunk K at the top of Keegan hill at Seven Mile Creek.

1860 census, recorded that June, showed Rufus and Henry Dawes as "farmers" with the land valued at $25,000 and personal property $5,000. In the fall of 1860, Henry Dawes was a candidate for Juneau County Commissioner, as well as a candidate for coroner, on the Republican ticket. He was successful in both endeavors, and, perhaps, it was during this time young Rufus Dawes, who campaigned for his father on horseback, visiting most of the voters in the county, gained the recognition that helped him in recruiting members for the Lemonweir Minute Men the next year. That he was popular was evident, as he had no opposition in being elected captain of the new company.[25]

At Camp Randall, Dawes was regarded by all as a promising young officer who, as Mickey Sullivan said, always "did things decently and in order," and a man Loyd Harris, a promising prospect himself, remembered as "never known to have any vices or use an oath."[26] One of the Company I men, Earl M. Rogers, described the Ohioan as "one of the coolest, and conspicuously daring brave men the Army of the Potomac ever enrolled, and no one can question his valor. . . ." Dawes went out of his way to "give credit where it belonged, and only when personally known to him [and that] was characteristic of the soldier Dawes," Rogers pronounced.[27]

In all things, Dawes was intelligent, orderly and effiicient, and if Sullivan thought Dawes took himself a bit too seriously, no one

25. Merton Eberlein, Mauston, Wisconsin, unpublished essay on Rufus R. Dawes. Rufus Dawes returned to Ohio after being mustered from the Army in 1864. The last documented visits of Rufus Dawes to Mauston were in 1867, when his father died unexpectedly, and in 1869, when he closed the extensive estate, valued at between $50,000 to $60,000. The auction was the largest ever held at that time in Juneau County. Dawes did attend the Iron Brigade Association Reunion at Lancaster, Wisconsin, in 1884. His four sons, including Charles Dawes, who was Vice President under Calvin Coolidge, returned to Mauston in 1926, when a pageant commemorating the Civil War was held. They took part in a ceremony placing a wreath on the grave of their grandfather, Henry Dawes, in Evergreen Cemetery in the rolling countryside near the Dawes' Wisconsin homestead. Rufus Dawes' mother, Sarah, never visited Mauston or Juneau County, and it was always the belief of Juneau County folks it was because she regarded Wisconsin as Indian County. They were apparently unaware of the legal separation. In the death notice for Henry Dawes, the *Mauston Star* noted: "He was always a prominent and active man in the community in which he lived. He took a warm interest in politics and always for the right."
26. [Loyd G. Harris], "Army Music," *Milwaukee Sunday Telegraph*, November 12, 1882.
27. Earl M. Rogers, "A Settled Question," *Milwaukee Sunday Telegraph*, July 29, 1883.

doubted the young Ohioan's ability. One of the men in the ranks, Isaiah F. Kelly, who would carry the 6th Wisconsin's shot-ripped National flag at Gettysburg, recalled Dawes as the "coolest man under fire" he ever saw. After publication of Dawes' military memoir in 1890, Kelly wrote his old commander a long, emotional letter about the old regiment and Gettysburg, and he probably said best how the soldiers felt about Dawes:

> How you ever got through without being killed is more than I can understand, as you were always in front in every fight. And it is my opinion that a braver officer than you was not in the grand old Army. Always looking after the interests of your men and officers. Never asking them to go where you did not lead. Perfectly cool under fire. A brave leader of as noble a band of patriots as ever wore the blue and fought under the stars and stripes.[28]

A careful reading of Dawes' war-time letters and his history of the 6th Wisconsin is revealing. If Dawes was intelligent and capable, he also had a well-developed ability to laugh at himself and others. He was ambitious, as a man of his promise and ability should be, and concerned enough about the feelings of others that he would carefully edit the letters and portions of his journal he re-printed in his war memoir. In an 1863 letter just after Gettysburg, for example, Dawes wrote:

> I was detached from the brigade early on the first day, and operated as an independent command. I saved my men all I could, and fought them to suit myself, and as a result I captured a regiment and suffered terribly to be sure, but less than any other regiment in the brigade. I don't know as I shall get my just credit before the country, but I have it with my men and my generals.

In his history 30 years later, Dawes edited the passage to read:

> We were detached from the brigade early on the first day and we operated as an independent command. I

28. I. F. Kelly, Letter, to Rufus R. Dawes, August 2, 1892, Dawes Papers, SHSW.

saved my men all I could and we suffered terribly to be sure, but less than any other regiment in the brigade. We captured a regiment. I don't know as we will get our just credit before the country, but we have it with our Generals.[29]

If the phrasing changed from "I shall get my just credit" to "We will get our just credit," it was the editing of a man aware of how his words might affect others. He was just as careful to avoid anything of a boastful stance, even though he had done much in the War of Rebellion and achieved lesser fame than many who had done less.

In the end, Dawes' intelligence would prove his undoing. He resigned his commission in 1864, simply unable emotionally to accept any longer the senseless killing, especially the deaths of his friends and comrades, while he himself was spared. To understand that about him was to understand much about Rufus Dawes. He expected himself to be good and brave in an insane war, where goodness and courage brought death, and finally, what he called "the carnival of blood" wore him down, almost as if he could not quite forgive himself for escaping the rebel bullets. And always, it seemed, he sensed that looking over his shoulder were his brave Revolutionary War ancestor, William Dawes, Jr., and the respected Dr. Manasseh Cutler, somehow measuring his conduct against an impossible standard.

His soldiers always respected him, and if he was not the officer of the bright uniform and profane remark about whom the men wrote home and remembered, he was trusted, as well as brave. Later, the 6th Wisconsin men came to love him and recognize just how much the character and deeds of the 6th Wisconsin could be traced to the quiet, steady Rufus R. Dawes, the boy from Ohio forever linked with Wisconsin and the Iron Brigade.

One of his men, Jerome A. Watrous, who went to war as a private and afterwards became a well-known journalist, felt Dawes never got the credit he deserved for shaping the famous regiment in which both served and he wrote Dawes to tell him just that two days after Christmas in 1894:

29. Rufus R. Dawes, Letter, to Mary Gates, July 4, 1863; Dawes, *Service*, pp. 159-160.

I thought, during the war, particularly from Gettysburg to Petersburg, while men were praising [Lysander]
Cutler, [Edward] Bragg, [Frank] Haskell and [John]
Gibbon, for making soldiers of the 6th Wisconsin, that
there was another man who had done more to bring the
regiment to its high degree of proficiency than any of
these, and, that belief has strengthened through all the
years since the war. You, as a soldier, through and
through, as a patriot; as a Christian gentleman, as a man
who never set anything but good example to the soldiers,
did more than Cutler, Bragg, Haskell and Gibbon to
make the 6th Wisconsin what it was, the noblest band
of patriots that ever marched and fought. The older we
get, the more we think of the good man we knew when
we were young; at least that is my experience.[30]

But that was all ahead those days at Camp Randall, when the
war was new and all the men young, brave and strong, and the
Rebellion sure to be put down in weeks, or a few months at best.
Dawes naturally gravitated toward other officers of his regiment,
especially Edwin A. Brown of Fond du Lac, and learned a lesson
about "Army Regulations" when he took his pay voucher to Paymaster Simeon Mills. Mills carefully studied the document, paus-
ing to look at the Ohioan. "I see, Captain, that you have omitted
to put in your servant," Mills said. Dawes, puzzled, replied, "I
have no servant." Paymaster Mills responded, "I think you certainly have as the Regulations require it." And Dawes, noting
"that he knew more about the subject than I did," made no
further objection. "My treacherous memory forbids my recording
here," Dawes wrote later, "whether my servant was described as
having green eyes and red hair or red eyes and green hair; but I
think the old pay roll will disclose a very remarkable descriptive
list of this imaginary person. . . . Few Captains had servants, but
all had one hundred and twenty-eight dollars per month" provided for a Captain and one servant.[31]

As the 5th and 6th Regiments drilled at Camp Randall, the war
news from the Eastern front became more ominous: two large

30. Jerome A. Watrous, Letter, to Rufus R. Dawes, December 27, 1894, Dawes
   Papers, SHSW.
31. Dawes, Service, p. 14.

armies were moving toward each other in Virginia, the issue of Union all in doubt, North and South making fierce statements. Then in late July, the telegraph clacked a series of forbidding dispatches: bloody battle in Virginia at Manassas Junction July 21. The National army routed. Washington in danger. President Lincoln calling in the regiments. "[At] last, when the truth [of the defeat] was reluctantly made known," recalled Private Sullivan of Company K, "we realized for the first time we were to have a chance, and telegrams were at once received directing the 5th and 6th to be sent to Washington."[32]

Suddenly, it was all a rush with much to be done. Dawes reported to his relatives the 6th Regiment had mustered 1,045 men for three years of Federal service.[33] But while the air of Camp Randall was filled with the youthful confidence of untested soldiers, one of the Shawano County boys in Company E, Julius Murray, was more realistic in his assessment. "All is excitement in regard to the late war news, and the disaster of our Troops [at First Bull Run]," he wrote in a letter to his brother. "In my opinion this war will not be brought to a close as soon as a great many imagine. I think we will have some hard and bloody fighting and a great many companies will lose some of their numbers from the Muster Roll before they return."[34]

The 5th Wisconsin left for Washington July 24th. Four days later, the 6th Regiment entrained for the war front via the Pittsburgh & Fort Wayne & Chicago Railroad. The first stop was at Milwaukee, where the townsfolk, proud of German Company F and Irish Company D as well as the regiment's colonel, fellow Milwaukeean Lysander Cutler, gave the regiment a first-rate farewell. Two Company A boys remembered the "elegant dinner" at the Water Street warehouse, during which, the Sauk County Riflemen were presented with "the largest cake we ever saw and with it a handsome bouquet and this inscription: 'Flowers may fade, but the honors of the brave, never.' "[35]

Private Sullivan fondly recalled the citizens of "the city of beer

32. Sullivan, *Telegraph*, May 23, 1886.
33. Dawes, *Service*, p. 15.
34. Julius A. Murray, Letter, to his brother, July 25, 1861. Julius A. Murray Papers, State Historical Society of Wisconsin.
35. Cheek and Pointon, *Sauk County*, p. 16; *Milwaukee Sentinel*, July 29, 1861, [Flower], *Milwaukee*, p. 709.

and pale bricks" and the elaborate preparations to welcome the regiment:

> [But] what impressed us most favorably was the kindness of the many beautiful ladies who seemed to think they could not do enough for us. That trip through Milwaukee sustained many a poor fellow afterward on a tiresome march, in the privation of the soldier life, or in the fury of battle by reminding him that at home in the center of wealth, talent and beauty of his state, he had many strong and warm friends, and nerving him with the thought that come what would, they should have no cause to be ashamed of him.[36]

Loaded with food and good wishes, the soldiers climbed back aboard the train to continue the trip to the war front. There was a delay before departure, and an Appleton private remembered how some of the volunteers got off the cars "to exchange a few last words with sorrowing and weeping friends, gathered to bid them good-bye." There was one incident that glowed for two decades after:

> On one of the cars, stretched about half way out of the window, was one young fellow who did not seem to take the same view many of his comrades did of their situation, and was disposed to treat it with considerable levity. Looking up the platform, he espied a young lady, perhaps sixteen or seventeen years of age, approaching. He waited until she was nearly opposite him, when, with a smile, he said: "Say, Miss, won't you kiss me for my mother." To his surprise and the amusement of those who heard the question, with tears in her eyes, she reached up and, clasping both arms around his neck, kissed him "for his mother," and he drew back into the car and was seen no more, while she continued on her way with the consciousness, apparently, of having done her duty.[37]

Maybe this soldiering was not such a bad business after all, the

36. Sullivan, *Telegraph*, May 23, 1886.
37. [Jerome A. Watrous], "Some Good Stories," *Milwaukee Sunday Telegraph*, April 8, 1883.

greenhorn patriots undoubtedly concluded. It was this show of patriotism that sustained the boys the next two days, as they traveled to Harrisburg, Pennsylvania. There, however, soldier life took a hard turn. "Mickey" Sullivan told the story best, his lighthearted words of two decades' vantage not disguising his black Irish anger:

We . . . were dumped like a train load of stock, outside the city and found quarters for the night in a pasture field, and next morning for the first time we partook of the bounty of our great and good government. The policys [sic] of the great and good at the time I speak of seemed to be that anything was good enough for persons willing to risk their lives to preserve that same "great and good," and in fact, it seemed all through the war as if the remark of Governor [Alexander] Randall, "that when a man enlisted the authorities seemed to think he forfeited all rights that they were bound to respect," governed all those connected with the war department. [Confederate President] Jeff Davis if in citimen's clothes, could travel the length and breadth of Washington or any city in the North; while a Union soldier who had maybe spilled his blood to prevent Jeff Davis from taking one of the aforesaid cities would be arrested at every corner or public place, if he appeared there without a pass. But to return to the bounty of our "great and good" government. Next morning after reaching Harrisburg we drew rations, but although we were a little short of those necessaries previously, we did not eat of those drawn, immediately, for the reason that most of us had been in the habit of using such things as coffee, pork, flour, etc., after having undergone a cooking process. But the brainy part of the "great and good" running things in the commissary department at Harrisburg considered cooking entirely superfluous . . . and consequently issued us damaged hard tack of the consistency and nutritiousness of sole leather, green coffee, rusty bacon, sugar, vinegar (if you had anything to get it in), and the everlasting bean. Inasmuch as there was not a coffee mill, coffee pot, skillet or kettle in company K, one may imagine how sumptuously we fared on the above menu. . . .

93

The Western volunteers were not to be denied, however. "Those who had money ran the guard, an easy proceeding, as all the weapon he had was 'halt,' and being obliged to remain on his beat, his halt was not very effective at long range," Sullivan wrote, "and in a very short time Company K was without a quorum, and bakers, pie-dealers, hotel-keepers and others in Harrisburg experienced a boom in their particular lines of trade."[38]

In a letter from "Camp Cutler, Harrisburg, Pennsylvania, August 1st," Dawes related the journey from Madison to Harrisburg was "a triumphal march," with the trip "full of exciting and pleasing incidents," especially involving a personal encounter at "Cresson, on the Allegheny Mountains," where the family of Fort Sumter hero Robert Anderson appeared. "You may be sure the Badger boys made the mountains ring with cheers for the daughters of the hero of Fort Sumpter [sic]," the young officer wrote. "His oldest daughter is a very handsome young lady. The enclosed sprig please keep for me till the wars are over, as it was presented to me by Miss Anderson in acknowledgment of our compliment to her father." And there was one other item: "The rebels are said to be advancing on Harper's Ferry. We therefore expect a fight in a few days. I wish my men were better drilled."[39] In reality, young Dawes was more than a year away from the moment his company would fire its first volley in battle.

If rations were short for the boys in ranks, that was not the case for officers, or, at least, Dawes made no mention of it. As to why the handsome Miss Anderson passed by old Colonel Cutler to present a sprig to the youngest captain in the line—overlooking even the Anderson Guards of Company I (named to honor her father)— was not explained in a satisfactory manner. Dawes said simply it was "wholly due to the superior lung power of Company K."[40]

There was one other incident at Harrisburg, at least for Company A: Paul Will of Baraboo skipped camp, never to return, and the Sauk County boys always claimed he was the only real deserter the company had during four years of service.[41] The regiment went, not to Harpers Ferry, but Baltimore, where it arrived at dusk. Baltimore was a troubled city. Several weeks before, a

38. Sullivan, *Telegraph*, May 23, 1886.
39. Dawes, *Service*, p. 16.
40. *Ibid.*
41. Cheek and Pointon, *Sauk County*, p. 17; *Roster of Wisconsin Volunteers*, p. 500.

Secessionist mob had attacked the 6th Massachusetts Infantry as it marched from one railroad depot to another. Shots were fired, and four soldiers and 12 civilians killed. That was much on the mind of the apprehensive Wisconsin boys as they prepared to march through the streets under escort of 200 armed police. They were still without weapons, and the Badgers armed themselves with brickbats and stones. The dark streets were jammed with a hostile crowd, and for the first time, the Western soldiers saw the ugly face of civil war. "Bull Run, you blue bellies!" one faceless person shouted from the dark sidewalk. "It was Yankees Run," yelled another, and the young soldiers rolled the clubs in their hands as they marched, eyes moving, ready for anything. "The sentiments expressed were spitefully hostile," Dawes wrote home the next day. "There is a slumbering Volcano in Baltimore ready to break out at any success of the Rebellion." He reported that "rebel Plug Uglies" attacked Captain Bragg's Company E boys just in front of Company K, but "it was promptly suppressed by the police." And he added a footnote: "We have come into a different atmosphere."[42] The next morning the city appeared more peaceful. Dawes wrote home that the regiment's camp was in Patterson Park, in "a beautiful grove overlooking the city, the bay, Fort McHenry and a broad extent of finely cultivated farms." The day passed pleasantly enough, and muskets were issued to Companies A and B—The Sauk County Riflemen and Prescott Guards—so they could post guards. About midnight, however, Dawes reported, "the Plug Uglies of Baltimore" opened fire "on our Guards, who promptly replied, and the bullets whistled occasionally through the camp." It was all confusion in the dark, but finally, several companies were turned out and the "quiet soon restored." In the excitement, Captain Dawes sent Lieutenant John Kellogg to Colonel Cutler for instructions. Kellogg wandered around for a time, finding Cutler in the back part of the camp where most of the shots were fired. "What instructions he received we never learned," Dawes wrote 30 years later, "as he fell into a dreadful hole in his reckless rush to bring them to us, and his condition of body and mind was such that he did nothing but swear a blue streak about his own mishap."

All in all, the young captain related, "the tragedy ended with a roaring farce," and he had one brief comment for the whole

42. Dawes, *Service*, p. 17.

affair: "Lieut. Kellogg was of quick blood and it was not always safe to congratulate him as the only man wounded in the Battle of Patterson Park."[43] The attack had one other result: authorities provided the "heavy, clumsy Belgian muskets" for the other eight companies, a shoulder arm that Phil Cheek and Mair Pointon remembered as a gun "peculiar in that you could most always tell when they were fired by finding yourself on the ground, kicked over by the recoil."[44]

On August 7th, the regiment again marched through Baltimore to catch a train to Washington. This time, the Wisconsin boys carried their new Belgian muskets loaded and "at half cock," and there were no catcalls from the sidewalks, Dawes recalled, only "respectful silence."[45]

43. *Ibid.*, pp. 17-18.
44. Cheek and Pointon, *Sauk County*, p. 17.
45. Dawes, *Service*, p. 19.

CHAPTER FOUR

'Twas at South Mountain, in that terrible pass,
  Where soldiers were falling, as a mower cuts grass;
Blood crossing the road caused McClellan to say,
  "They are men made of iron, brave Company K."
                                            —By "Mickey"

Washington Camps

The 6th Wisconsin Infantry—riding in "filthy cattle cars"—
arrived in Washington at 4 a.m. on August 8, 1861. The new soldiers made hard beds on the stone pavement in front of the Post
Office Building. After sunrise, the Wisconsin men used the fire
hydrants to wash up, then were marched to Kalorama Heights
and camped on Meridian Hill, a few rods from Columbia College,
then being used as a hospital for the wounded from the First
Battle of Bull Run. The bivouac became "Camp Kalorama," and
the soldiers recalled its "magnificent view of the Capitol and the
city."[1]

It began a period of camp life for the Wisconsin soldiers that
would last almost a year. The regiment was assigned to the Division of General Irvin McDowell, which was manning the Washington defenses, and it was here the companies drilled and drilled
some more, battled sickness and boredom, all the time feeling the
war was passing them by; and it was here the 6th was brigaded
with the 2nd and 7th Wisconsin and 19th Indiana regiments, and
where the farmer boys, mechanics and lumbermen began the
process of becoming real soldiers.

Camp life, it turned out, was all rather dull for a volunteer
expecting drums, brass buttons and glory. "We have been engaged
in clearing and cutting our roads for several days along the Potomac, that is four hundred of our Regiment," Julius Murray of

1. Dawes, *Service* p. 17.

Company E wrote his brother. "The ground is exactly similar to the road we cut out to the Oconto, only the hills are some what steeper and the timber is as much thicker than the thickest we cut through, as you can imagine I have thought of that road and you a hundred times a day as we were at work." He added: "I would not advise any one to enlist. It is irksome to be so closely confined and to have to implicitly obey all orders."[2]

One never-ending duty was drill call. In those days of mass formations and muzzle-loading rifle-muskets, there was a great emphasis on drill, and a company that "moved easily"—to use a description of the day—that is, in precise formation, was prized and admired. The volunteer infantry regiment at full strength, as prescribed in the U.S. regulations, was composed of ten companies, each of 97 men and three officers. In a tactical situation, the underlying principle of all drill was to bring the soldiers quickly and in good order to the field of battle, where they were arranged, with as little confusion and delay as possible, in a position where they would be able to fire their muskets to the best advantage. Given the relatively slow rate of fire of the Civil War rifle-musket —two to three shots per minute—the regiment usually fought its companies abreast, forming a long, double line of men. A regiment that was broken or disorganized was unable to deliver fire effectively, and, as a result, the Wisconsin officers drilled their volunteers over and over again. There was much pride in being able to fire a crisp volley, that is, the whole company, two companies or regiment delivering massed fire at the same instant. That was why, 25 years later, Michael Fitch of Company B, the Prescott Guards, recalled with pleasure the remark from his former regimental commander that his company was "so mobile and well drilled;" and "Mickey" Sullivan of Company K, writing of the first time the 6th Wisconsin was under fire, mentioned with satisfaction the initial exchange was "one of the volleys by regiment, for which it [the 6th Wisconsin] was noted."[3] But the translation from a drill manual to maintaining a crisp line when a regiment was in battle formation was a difficult one, almost impossible when the line moved over broken ground under fire. In that year in the Washington defenses, the Wisconsin boys drilled morning and afternoon, stood guard mount and dress parade and evening pa-

2. Julius A. Murray, Letter, to his brother, John, September 24, 1861.
3. Sullivan, *Telegraph*, November 4, 1883.

rade until, finally, the regiment began to move as one, each of the ten companies a part of the whole, and each of the men part of the company. They were much admired and even envied by the other regiments.

The 6th Wisconsin just may have been the best-drilled regiment in the Iron Brigade, and perhaps the whole of McDowell's Division, at least the Calico boys always thought so, and if that was true, it was due to Franklin Aretas Haskell, who forced them to learn to move so easily and smartly they could do so later under the most murderous fire. That famous back-rank high private and true Irishman himself, J. P. Sullivan, told a story about this, and it involved Second Bull Run. As the 6th Wisconsin passed through a small orchard, the line was disrupted when the color bearer was hit or the flag tangled in a tree. Haskell, then serving as an aide on the brigade staff, saw the downed flag and came up quickly. The colors were critical in the noise and smoke of Civil War combat, because the bright banners were marched in the very center of the regiment's line, the companies on each side aligning to the center. It was all momentarily a jumble, scattered bullets coming in and the flag down, then up again, the line broken and hesitant. Haskell took it all in instantly. "By heavens, these colors must never go down before the enemy," he shouted, and then, as he had done so many times on the drill fields near Washington, that "prince of good soldiers," as Sullivan called him, pumped his sword up and down and called the cadence, the voice familiar and somehow comforting amid the noise, smoke and death, "Left. Left. Left, right, left," and the regiment steadied and "marched as well as it ever did on review."[4]

Haskell may have been the best volunteer soldier produced by Wisconsin during the Civil War, and it was only an unlikely set of circumstances that kept him on the staffs of Lysander Cutler and, later, John Gibbon, and from command of his own regiment until late in the war. Ironically, Haskell would be better remembered a century later than were his old comrades. He became famous as "Haskell of Gettysburg" for his propitious action in rallying the Union line that threw back Pickett's Charge on the third day of fighting, and for a lengthy account of the battle he sent his brother a few days afterwards. The account would be published, and reprinted, and what he saw, did and wrote would

4. Sullivan, *Telegraph*, March 16, 1884.

be so important that no subsequent historian writing of Gettysburg could ignore Haskell's words. The ironic part of all this was not the fame he gained at Gettysburg, for he did a great deed and wrote well about a momentous battle, but that his major role in shaping a tough Western regiment, and later the Iron Brigade, was overlooked. Haskell had accomplished much in little time. Yet he would die a soldier's death as colonel of the 36th Wisconsin at Cold Harbor, Virginia, in 1864, and the brilliant promise was never realized.[5]

The Wisconsin boys feared and respected the stiff-backed, demanding officer, but there was little affection, at least during his lifetime. In fact, if it was easy to like and respect stern, fatherly old Lysander Cutler and the restless, energetic Edward S. Bragg, it was just as easy to despise Haskell, with his cold, arrogant manner and New England prejudices. The frisky Wisconsin farm and school boys, woodsmen, clerks, railroad hands, printers, teachers and preachers, one veteran remembered, "did not like him. He was rigid. He . . . [made] regulars of them . . . They were volunteers; they didn't want to be converted into regulars. They kicked and thrashed, but the harder they kicked and thrashed the more thorough was Haskell's discipline."

General John Gibbon, a regular army professional, called Haskell an "ideal soldier." So did other notable Union generals of the war. One 6th Wisconsin veteran wrote in postwar retrospect.:

> Frank Haskell is one of the soldiers for whom I shall always mourn. He was brave. He inspired courage in those who followed him. He was quick to see, not a little spot in the line, but every spot all along the line of the regiment, brigade, division or corps. . . .[6]

Haskell was already a man of note in Wisconsin when he accepted appointment as adjutant of the 6th Wisconsin Infantry when it assembled in 1861 at Camp Randall. A native of Vermont and the grandson of a new Hampshire captain of the Revolution, Haskell was 33. He had followed his brother to Wisconsin in

5. For a full biographical study of Frank Haskell, including copies of his war letters, see Frank L. Byrne and Andrew T. Weaver, eds., *Haskell of Gettysburg*, State Historical Society of Wisconsin, (Madison, 1970).
6. [Jerome A. Watrous], "About the Boy Patriots," *Milwaukee Sunday Telegraph*, November 27, 1897.

1848, then, in 1850, traveled East to attend Dartmouth College, where he graduated in 1854. Haskell returned to Wisconsin that year and entered the practice of law in the Madison firm of Julius P. Atwood, who would become lieutenant colonel in the new 6th Regiment. Haskell had been active in a Wisconsin militia company, the Governor's Guards, and, after Fort Sumter was fired on, assisted in the organization of the Anderson Guards, which would become Company I of the new regiment. Standing one inch short of six feet, Haskell had a long face marked by sharp, intelligent, hazel eyes under rather heavy brows. At Dartmouth, one of his professors had made a cruel assessment of his student, writing Haskell was intelligent and able, but "ambitious as Lucifer."[7] His school picture showed curly hair worn long over his ears and neck, but by wartime, Haskell was balding, the hair trimmed close to his head and the face marked by long sideburns and a carefully trimmed mustache. He wore a uniform well, with studied dash, and his movements were neat and contained, almost as if he had been a soldier all his life.

Old Cutler took the younger man, saw his promise and came to rely on him perhaps more than he realized. With Haskell supplying the technical knowledge and the sad-eyed "old colonel" the heavy-handed discipline, the 1,000 volunteers of the 6th Wisconsin quickly became soldiers, and when they finally stood up to rebel bullets, as Mickey Sullivan wrote much later, their "lithe springing step . . . and soldierly bearing" forced the generals to say, "they march better than regulars." Credit for that must go to Frank Haskell, although that recognition came much later. Said one Wisconsin veteran: "Yes, he was a martinet—a soldier from the foundation up—and had to be known before he could be liked."[8]

In the drill camps, there was a testy rivalry among the regiments at first, with the 2nd Wisconsin men, those veterans of First Bull Run, making much of the fact they had stood up to rebel bullets. The 2nd and 7th Wisconsin soldiers called 6th Wisconsin men "the Calico boys," or the "Baby 6th." No record has been left how the 6th became the "Calicos," except perhaps many of the companies had rural origins, but the second name

7. Byrne and Weaver, *Haskell*, p. 1.
8. [Watrous], *Telegraph*, November 27, 1897.

resulted from the habit of the soldiers to refer to the regiment as Brigade Commander Rufus "King's pet babies." A good story was told about that time how the wife of a Wisconsin congressman, who in 1861 was visiting Arlington Heights and, seated in a carriage when the 6th Wisconsin passed, asked the name of the regiment. "The Baby 6th, M'am," a nearby lieutenant answered. The lady indignantly replied, "Sir! I am from Wisconsin, and allow me to inform you, that we send no infants to war from there." Almost every soldier in camp called the 7th Wisconsin boys "the Huckleberries." Edward Bragg always said it was because "they liked to talk about pies and things to eat." The "lean, lank" men of the 19th Indiana were simply known as "old Posey County" or "Swamp Hogs No. 19," and one Wisconsin soldier remarked, "Every man of them did not care a goll darn how he was dressed, but was all hell for a fight." The volunteers in all three regiments made loud remarks about the "Ragged Assed 2nd." (Long afterwards, in writing of their soldier days, the veterans softened the term to "Ragged Backed 2nd.")[9] "They [the regiments] had not lived on the best of terms [that first year]," one veteran remembered. "They were separate and distinct communities."[10] But after the brigade's first battle, in August, 1862, "where they had been tested as few soldiers ever are tested," the four regiments were "brought together as family." Mickey Sullivan of Company K put it in stronger terms: "If any one wanted to get into . . . difficulty, all that was necessary for him to do was go into the 19th [Indiana camp] and say a word against the 'Wisconsin boys,' and the same held good in any of our regiments about them."[11]

Young Loyd Harris of the Jayhawkers of Company C wrote dozens of delightful stories of those months in camp, and one of them involved those worldly and envied veterans of "the Ragged 2nd." It seemed that after the battle of First Bull Run, the state issue grey militia uniforms of both officers and men were "sadly depleted" to the point there was, Harris related, nothing quite like "a view of their rear ranks when they attempted a dress parade." President Abraham Lincoln, a Western man himself, had heard

9. [Jerome A. Watrous], "Heroes of Undying Fame," *Milwaukee Sunday Telegraph*, September 26, 1896; Ethel Alice Hurn, *Wisconsin Women in the War Between the States*, (Madison, 1911), p. 105; "General Bragg," *Milwaukee Sunday Telegraph*, February 25, 1899; Curtis, *Twenty-fourth*, p. 466.
10. [Watrous], *Telegraph*, September 26, 1896.
11. Sullivan, *Telegraph*, March 16, 1884.

of the famed Wisconsin regiment, and, "one bright day," he and Mrs. Lincoln drove up "in an elegant carriage" to take a look at the Badger outfit just as the 2nd had formed for dress parade. There were a few anxious moments, Harris remembered, but it all went off pretty well. Then, "to the horror and consternation of the entire regiment, especially the lively boys in the rear ranks, who were more like Highlanders minus kilts than model infantry soldiers," the driver of the carriage decided to swing around past the rear of the formed lines. "The excitement was great, and just as the colonel, as a forlorn hope, was about to command 'About face,' " Harris recalled, "a gallant officer stopped the driver and informed him that the road was impassable in that direction." The carriage turned away and carried the President and Mrs. Lincoln back to Washington. As it disappeared, "the modest youths, almost to a man, gave one great sigh of relief," Harris said, and the colonel joyfully exclaimed just one word—"Saved!"[12]

About this time, the commander of Company A wrote home describing his Sauk County boys as "the most intelligent and moral set of men in the regiment. We have no cases of drunkenness or quarrels, every man does his duty promptly and faithfully." A private recalled his messmates were sure the war would be over in just a few short weeks, and the cry of the day was "Hurrah for Baraboo."[13] That was all comforting to the homefolk, but Irish Company D's "Tough One," John H. Cook, who took to camp life with a flourish, described a less-assuring picture. The first night, camped near Washington, he and several others ran the guard to go into the city. "When I returned to camp, I got what I deserved, and so did the rest; but we had a bully time. Three days on short rations and clothing. Of course you other fellows don't know anything about such things," he wrote 20 years later with a smirk. Cook admitted he found the soldier business all rather confining, and quickly discovered two stumps, about two feet apart, which the camp guards neglected. "A certain few of us knew it, and when we wanted to get out we would file through between the stumps," he recalled, telling also of the passes he and the boys carefully signed "Brig. Gen. King" and "Col. L. Cutler" for Brigade Commander Rufus King and Regimental Commander Lysander Cutler. And, he admitted, "while in that camp

12. [Harris], *Telegraph*, March 11, 1883.
13. Cheek and Pointon, *Sauk County*, p. 18.

I was only put in the guard-house four times for going to Washington without a proper pass. We of course had passes, but they were up for each especial occasion. You know how it is yourself," with a wink to his old comrades.

Another time, Cook and his pard, Hamilcar McIntosh (who, by the way, would become an officer of the regiment and a good one) were looking for some fun and, believing the company had too many non-commissioned officers, decided to reduce them all to ranks. "It was mighty fine work to do," he said later. "We got away with all the stripes there were in the company except Sergt. Gilmore's [Andrew U. Gilmore of Milwaukee]; he was always sober." The stripes were carefully placed in an envelope and sent to the captain. "He found in the morning that he had one non-commissioned officer left out of thirteen," the "Tough One" wrote later, adding: "Of course it got out. Cook and Mc. were in [the guard house] for three days."

There were also incidents involving young Lieutenant Patrick McCauley and Captain John Marsh, named to command Company D after the resignation of John O'Rourke. McCauley thought "the small fellows on the left of the company were pretty tough," Cook recalled, but did not always line up as quickly as they should. "Get up there on the left, you jumping Jesus Christers!" the young officer admonished the boys one time. Cook admitted the boys "got up," but they also got even. One night, the young lieutenant's tent went down. "He never knew who did it. We did. I tell you, there was some tall swearing. But to no use, the deed was done. Although he was a good officer, as we see it now, we thought him a terror then." Captain Marsh also made it "warm for the boys and we made it warm for him," Cook remembered. "One cold sleety night in '61 . . . the crowd put up a job on him; his tent went down. Nobody knew who did it, at least he did not. Another time he had eight of us in the guard house at one time, which we did not object to, for it was easier than knapsack drill. Col. Cutler told the captain he had better go to the guard house and take charge of his company." It was an unusually wry remark from the sober and dignified Cutler, and, perhaps, that was why Cook also wrote he "revered" the old colonel.

The litany of Cook's pranks ranged from getting fined $10 for calling "a sergeant a bad name," destroying Edward Brooks' new officer uniform, running the guard posts to spree in Washington and building a frame inside his knapsack to trick his officers into thinking he was carrying 30 pounds. But there was one episode he regarded as topping them all—blowing up the log shanty housing the non-commissioned officers. It seemed, he remembered, there was a stump in the middle of the shanty, and one night he and Private Charley Sprague of Kenosha, upset after a few hours of disciplinary knapsack drill, bored into the stump, filled it with powder, plugged it and laid a train of powder outside. "We then set it and it did go off," Cook wrote slyly two decades later. "Nary a shake [shingle] was left on the roof, nor nary a stump inside, but lots of dirt, all over everything belonging to the high-toned members of the 'white gloved six.'"[14] Sprague developed into a steady soldier, and was one of the men who fell at Gettysburg.

So the 6th Wisconsin Volunteers drilled, stood guard and wondered about the war; they were still fresh and frisky, and the stories told of those days reflected their "Western" independence. Private Albert Young of Fond du Lac recalled he first arrived at the Washington camps "with a heavy knapsack on my back, with two days' rations in my knapsack, 40 rounds of ammunition in my cartridge box, a full canteen, and a Belgian musket" on his shoulder. Not far away from the regiment's first camp, he said, was a unit commanded by a German of some reputation named Louis Blenker, and "all of its sutlers kept lager beer, and many who did not belong to the German division filled up on lager beer and sang funny songs on their way back to the brigade camp."[15] Loyd Harris wrote, of Arlington Heights outside Washington, of how the Prairie du Chien boys constructed winter huts, using logs and tents. Each had mud chimneys, and there was much discussion about the design. "One squad, in building, contended that in order to draw successfully the chimney must be smaller at the top than the bottom," Harris recalled, but Henry Petitt and the Lynxville boys "swore and argued the reverse; a widening at the top." Finally, both chimneys were completed and the two squads laid a fire, and, after a short time, both were "smoked out into the street, where they stood in rain and cold, unhappy to the last degree." Although Petitt's chimney was the proper one, it had

14. John H. Cook, "The Tough One Again," *Milwaukee Sunday Telegraph*, March 11, 1883.
15. [Albert V. Young], "A Pilgrimage," *Milwaukee Sunday Telegraph*, March 9, 1890; [Harris], *Telegraph*, March 11, 1883.

105

failed also, because "the boys in the other squad fearing a failure on their part, and success on his, had secretly stuffed an old pair of pants in his. It caused considerable swearing, but was voted the best joke that week."[16]

About this time, Bragg, the Fond du Lac attorney-turned-soldier, was establishing himself as a favorite with the boys in ranks. One Company E soldier described the officer as "small and wiry; eyes and hair black as coal; voice penetrating . . . ,"[17] and Mickey Sullivan said the little colonel had a "cool, indifferent way" in a battle, watching the fighting with "one eye shut and the other not open,"[18] while Harris recalled how Bragg, on hearing the Germans in Company F complaining they had no rations, went to the commissary non-commissioned officer. "Sergeant, have the men any rations?" asked Bragg. "Well, colonel, they are supposed to have four day rations, but really have none." "Oh blank your supposition," Bragg snorted. "Soldiers cannot live on supposition; issue five day rations at once."[19] However, the "Tough One," Cook of Company D, had a less flattering memory of Bragg at South Mountain. He recalled the boys were upset when Bragg formed the regiment in solid column for a charge with "all of those great big boulders to buck against. Of course, we forget all about those things—of course!"[20] Lieutenant Edwin A. Brown also left a disturbing letter on Bragg, warning his wife:

I wrote to tell J.H.G. that I would be Captain as soon as he would. It was the same as to say that Bragg would get something higher. Well, Mrs. B wrote to her husband about it and he wrote her to find out where it come from. She inquired and finally called on you, then wrote her husband that it was I that had let the cat out of the bag. He was provoked with me about it as if he had failed to get a higher place, it would have made talk.[21]

Many wrote postwar stories about one another and the pranks played on other regiments. In writing of those days, sometimes

16. [Harris], *Telegraph*, March 11, 1883.
17. Jerome A. Watrous, "The Old Captain," pamphlet, undated. Watrous had his story on Bragg printed and distributed as a "Holiday Greeting."
18. Sullivan, *Telegraph*, March 16, 1884.
19. [Harris], *Telegraph*, March 11, 1883.
20. Cook, *Telegraph*, March 11, 1883.
21. Edwin A. Brown, Letter, to his wife, September 21, 1861.

the hard memories of the veterans were couched in light-hearted phrases, but the humor was black and grim. Cook, for example, asked if any of the boys in the Iron Brigade remembered the time when one of the "Jersey Brigade" went to the front and was fired on for a Johnny by his comrades. "They picked him up, that part that was left, which was not much." Cook also told of the time at Arlington Heights, when he and some of the boys unofficially relieved all the guards of the 7th Wisconsin, then went to quarters. "It was a very good one," he said, "but very mean."[22] Harris recounted a yarn about the "Huckleberries" and their first colonel, who, during a drill on firing by front and rear ranks, confused the orders, telling his men, "Rear rank, about face!" Ready, aim. . . ." This "sudden innovation brought the long line of file closers and officers to their knees, while the gallant lieutenant colonel and major were seen charging toward some friendly trees," Harris recalled. The adjutant shouted, "Colonel, that is not correct; you will shoot the file closers." "I don't care a tam," responded unbending Colonel Joseph Vandor of Milwaukee, a Hungarian new to America. "If your colonel ish te mark, fire away," and "a thousand muskets emptied their blank cartridges at the noble colonel." Harris said the officer was, a few days later, "promoted to a foreign consulship, a polite way Mr. Lincoln had of banishing general officers who were not wanted in the field."[23]

Even white-haired Cutler of the 6th was not spared from the pranks of the enlisted men. It happened when a widow lady who lived near the camp complained her chickens and hogs had disappeared. She went to Cutler and "revealed the astounding news that she was Union to the back bone, or to use an army phrase, 'words to that affect,'" noted Harris. Cutler, who was then serving as Brigade commander, believed her and accused his old unit, that military organization Harris piously styled "the most moral and law abiding regiment of the brigade, the 6th, with the mighty offense, and thus he made a great mistake, for they claimed to be innocent, and in their leader, Colonel [Edward S.] Bragg, they had the best lawyer in the whole army." There was little Cutler could do, but "in a most persistent way the gallant old veteran sought to fasten the guilt where he really believed it belonged, but all in vain."

22. *Ibid.*
23. [Harris], *Telegraph*, March 11, 1883.

It seemed that the woman claimed the men seen carrying away the pigs wore the numeral "6" on their black hats, but to this the 6th Wisconsin had a ready reply: It was, after all, they noted, "a common thing for the 19th Indiana regiment, whenever they in a hungry mood raided a henroost, to remove the figure 1 from their hats and inverting the 9, and were able to pass as the old 6th and make themselves the terror of the country." But Harris said this time, because of certain signs, the Calicos in the 6th blamed the men of the 7th Wisconsin as the "guilty ones." But the old officer would not believe it, and perhaps the next day, noticed the 6th Wisconsin men "seemed to have ample suppers" despite a shortage of rations. Cutler called in Private Jones of Company E to get to the bottom of the matter. Edwin C. Jones, who had listed himself a "Cosmopolite" on the company rolls and "the only private who repeatedly refused an officer's commission, preferring to carry a musket," was, Harris explained, "a remarkable character with a compound of cunning and patriotism." This was how the young officer remembered the interview:

Cutler—(cautiously) Jones, what do you know about this pork affair?

Jones —(boldly) I know considerable.

Cutler—(greatly encouraged to find at least he had found a clue.) Do you know who killed the hogs?

Jones —(confidentially) I saw a man carry half a dead pig from near the woman's house.

Cutler—(greatly encouraged) Aha! You did! And you are sure it was the woman's pork?

Jones —(positively) I can swear to it.

Cutler—(very excited) Now Jones, who was the man? One of the 6th, wasn't it?

Jones —No General, it was not, and I really hate to tell you who it was.

Cutler—(sternly) Jones, you must tell. I command it.

Jones —(sadly and looking the very picture of humility) Well, General, the man I saw carrying that pork was your servant, Pete, and I further saw him cook it for your supper.

That, said Harris, not only concluded the interview but the search for the pig thieves, and he added. "I will state that Jones,

108

and only 'our Jones,' would have ever dared to lead Cutler into such a trap." But in writing the story about an "Item of Pork" some two decades later, Harris admitted:

> I for one knew that the dare-devils . . . [of the 6th Wisconsin] killed the hogs, cooked and ate them almost under the general's nose, and what was left was smuggled into Col. Bragg's headquarters wagon . . . and while the gallant Cutler was interviewing Jones, the 6th was still feasting on that pork.

There was a rationalizing postscript:

> [The 6th Wisconsin men] never believed that [the widow was] a Union woman . . . , or they would have willingly collected enough to have paid her loss. I have not betrayed the part that Col. Bragg sustained while all I have described transpired, but will reveal this much. His efforts alone saved us from paying for that pork and above all, from being disgraced in the eyes of all soldiers, who at that time did not believe that stealing pigs or chickens in Virginia was a sin, but to be convicted of it was a stain that nothing could wipe out.[24]

It was a curious period for American soldiers, when stealing a pig was winked at by shoulder straps but getting caught was "a stain nothing could wipe out."

So the 6th Wisconsin soldiers continued to drill together, mess together and train together. Now and then, they captured a rebel pig together, and, wrote Loyd Harris, the Prairie du Chien volunteer who carried a violin with him when he went off to war, they sang together. It was a time when the soldiers made their own entertainment to lighten the drill days. The regiment boasted some fine singers, among them Johnny Ticknor of Juneau County's famed Company K, Orrin Chapman of Company C and Edwin A. Brown of Company E. Of all the men in Wisconsin's 6th, it was Harris who remembered best the camp songs and the music. "No army in this or any other civilized country is complete without

24. [Loyd G. Harris], "A Celebrated Case," *Milwaukee Sunday Telegraph*, August 5, 1883.

music," he concluded two decades later, when he was in charge of a Military Order of the Loyal Legion singing school in St. Louis. "The brass bands, drums, fifes, the song and chorus on the march or by the camp-fire, are a necessity to infuse a national spirit[,] keep the men cheerful and assist in making the army a successful one."[25]

On the march, Harris related, after the regimental band stopped playing, his own outfit, the "Jayhawkers" of Company C, would sing:

O never mind the weather, but get over double trouble.
For we are bound for the happy land of Canaan.

That concluded, the Juneau County boys of Company K, "despite the religious warnings" and scowls from proper Rufus R. Dawes, Harris recalled, "in stentorian tones, as in one voice," would sing several verses of "Joe Bowers," even the scandalous sequel where "Sally had a baby and the baby had red hair." The middle-aged veteran recalled the regiment "was always cheered" by that verse. The Appleton-Fond du Lac boys in Company E, Bragg's Rifles, had another variation of the same song that started, "My name is Jake Kaiser," and then the Irish in Company I, the Bad Ax County boys from southwestern Wisconsin, would contribute:

Here's a health to Martin Hannegan's aunt.
And I'll tell ye the reason why.
She eats because she is hungry.
And drinks because she is dry.

But Harris said it was the Germans in Company F that he most enjoyed. "How often . . . did I steal quietly to their camp-fire and, perhaps concealed by the shadow of a friendly tree, listen . . . as in the bright fire-light, their voices in pure harmony rang out on the quiet scene."

In reflective times, the Germans sang:

Blue is the flower called the forget me not,
Ah, lay it on thy heart, and think of me.

25. [Harris], *Telegraph*, November 12, 1882.

Or in merry times:

> The Pope he leads a happy life.
> He knows no care or married life.

The favorite song of the day, at least for the Eastern regiments, Harris noted, was "John Brown's body lies a moldering in his grave," while the Wisconsin soldiers enjoyed "Tramp, tramp, the boys are marching," and "Rally around the flag." The volunteer officers especially enjoyed a tune they had picked up from graduates of the U.S. Military Academy, "Benny Havens, O."[26] Tall Johnny Ticknor was the regiment's great soloist, and 6th Wisconsin men insisted he had a role in creating the great war song of the Rebellion. Rufus Dawes said it occurred after a review of Irvin McDowell's Division. A lady visitor, Julia Ward Howe, rode with the soldiers as they marched back toward their camp. As the 6th Wisconsin marched, the "evening dews and damps" gathered, Dawes wrote:

> . . . [O]ur leading singer, Sergeant John Ticknor, as he was wont to do on such occasions, led out with his strong, clear and beautiful tenor voice, "Hang Jeff Davis on a sour apple tree." The whole regiment joined the grand chorus, "Glory, glory hallelujah, as we go marching on." We often sang this, the John Brown song. To our visitor appeared the "Glory of the coming of the Lard," and in our "burnished rows of steel" and in the "hundred circling camps" on Arlington [Heights] which were before her. Julia Ward Howe, our visitor, has said that the singing of the John Brown song by the soldiers on the march, and the scenes of that day and evening inspired her to the composition of the Battle Hymn of the Republic. We at least helped to swell the chorus.[27]

If the 6th Wisconsin boys marched to their own voices, drilled in the sprawling camps around Washington, and learned to be soldiers, they were also much concerned with their station in the new brigade and overly conscious about their self-perceived short-

26. *Ibid.*
27. Dawes, *Service*, p. 29.

comings. There was one thing, however, in which they excelled over the other regiments, especially the much-scorned, know-it-all 2nd Wisconsin, and that was in the dashing figure of Drum Major William Whaley. Even less-than-effusive Rufus Dawes was awed, telling homefolk that Whaley was regarded "with pride and affection as the finest adornment of the regiment," a drum major of "stately" military bearing who "snuffs the air and spurns the ground like a war horse." Whaley "can hold his head higher, and whirl his baton faster than any other drum major in the Army of the Potomac." Alas, while Drum Major Whaley was a great favorite, during the war and after, there was one story his comrades repeated about him. It occurred during a great review staged by General George B. McClellan in November, 1861.

Sixty-thousand infantry, 9,000 cavalry and 130 pieces of artillery passed in review before "Little Mac" that day—taking five hours to do so—but what was remembered by 6th Wisconsin men was how Whaley was singled out by the dashing little general. McClellan was "so overcome by the lofty pomposity of drum major William Whaley," Dawes wrote later, "that he took off his hat when Whaley passed." The acknowledgment came to a sour end. So overcome by this recognition, which took place while he was indulging in a "top loftical gyration of his baton," Whaley's concentration broke, and, to the horror of the Badger men, the twirling baton slipped through his hand, and, Dawes glumly recorded, "from the topmost height of glory he was plunged into the deepest gulf of despair."[28]

The greenhorn patriots of Wisconsin's 6th were boastful of Drum Major Whaley and proud of his dazzling abilities, but fate dealt him and the regiment a puzzling hand. If the regiment had the Army of the Potomac's best drum major, it also had the Army of the Potomac's worst regimental band, an organization so lacking in musical ability its reputation brought groans from the Wisconsin veterans for half a century. "[E]ach and every regiment believed and were ready to take an oath that their band was the best in the army," Harris, the chronicler of songs and music, wrote later. "Our men were just as ready to wager anything from a box of cigars to a month's pay, rations included, that our band was without exception the worst of all."[29]

28. *Ibid.*, p. 30.
29. [Harris], *Telegraph*, November 12, 1882.

That there was a serious problem became apparent August 23, 1861, when Brigade Commander Rufus King ordered a review of his regiments. Writing the next day to his brother, Dawes admitted it had not gone well and the regiment "never before appeared so meanly." It was, the young captain wrote, "enough to try the patience of a martyr, the performance of that contemptible brass band of ours. They played such slow time music that we passed the review officer at about forty-seven paces a minute [about half the normal cadence]. We had to hold one leg in the air and balance on the other while we waited for the music." An old friend from Dawes' college days at Madison, Theodore D. Kanouse, was a member of the musical organization, "pumping up and down on a big toot horn"; however, he wanted to get out of the musical organization because "if any man in the regiment is caught in a rascally trick, the whole regiment yells, 'Put him in the brass band.'" Kanouse told Dawes "he had undertaken to crush the Rebellion with a trombone and, willing to admit his own failure, he hoped the Government would not rely wholly upon its brass bands to accomplish that result." Dawes added: "It is enough to make one sad to see the stately Whaley leading that execrable brass band on dress parade, eternally playing the Village Quickstep. . . ."[30]

If, in those first months of soldiering, Dawes found the regimental band "contemptible" and "execrable," Private "Mickey" Sullivan of the Juneau County Boys in Company K stated flatly the band's "discordant tootings" should have "brought a deserved shower of defunct eggs, but at that time we were willing to endure anything to whip secession."[31] But it was young Loyd Harris, with his fine ear for good music, who detailed how that "unfortunate brass band" brought low 6th Wisconsin men:

If ever a regiment went to the front with light hearts, well officered and eager for the fray, it was ours. . . . Our pride was immense, and we had an enlarged opinion of our appearance—and how we longed for the time when we could show the other regiments of the brigade that we could fight. [There was much regimental honor involved in all this and the 6th Wisconsin boys] . . . hesi-

30. Dawes, *Service*, p. 30.
31. Sullivan, *Telegraph*, May 16, 1886.

tated about being too neighborly with a certain regiment [the 2nd Wisconsin] which had been so actively engaged in the 1st Bull Run battle that had changed their appearance wonderfully, and their uniforms, if gray, ragged coats and tattered pants could be called such, hardly concealed their Apollo like forms; also with another regiment [7th Wisconsin] which the ragged set had named "Huckleberries." Yes, it was with great reluctance that we got up even a calling acquaintance with those other regiments, yet some of us had friends, cousins and even brothers in their ranks. But pride must have a fall; and our's [sic] tumbled, simply on the merits of our brass band.

What did it matter if old Colonel Cutler drilled the regiment "until we thought we could never survive?" Harris questioned. What if Adjutant Frank Haskell made the regimental guard mounting "a model for the whole army?" And no matter how bright the regiment's arms, buttons and brasses, "there was that unfortunate brass band."[32] The 6th Wisconsin musicians played just one tune, "The Village Quickstep," and the bandsmen tooted it over and over again, at guard mounting, dress parade and on the march, Harris said, and even 20 years later, the recollection of it "makes a cold chill creep over me." He recalled later how he and "Brave [Lieutenant Frederick] Schumacher [of Company F] would walk a mile any pleasant evening to hear the Indiana band play one air; and we were just as willing to walk five miles away when our band wrestled with the one old tune."[33]

The ineptitude of the band eventually so grated the soldiers that there was trouble. The unrest started in the German company from Milwaukee, Harris said, shortly after the regiment marched from Kalorama to the Chain Bridge. One of the Company F boys, who had "a very accurate musical ear," broke "his leg in a vain effort to keep time to that same old tune," Harris said. A few days later, the Germans, very upset over the whole matter, and, in their forthright Teutonic manner, organized a

32. [Loyd G. Harris], "Music in the Army," *Milwaukee Sunday Telegraph*, November 26, 1882.
33. [Loyd G. Harris], "Our Brass Band," *Milwaukee Sunday Telegraph*, August 16, 1885.

protest, "prompting a couple of hundred men to visit the headquarters of the band" wherein they began "drumming on their tin
plates" and whistling "the old tune until the band nearly went
wild." Colonel Cutler finally had to order in the guard to disperse
the serenaders.

The situation did not improve, Harris wrote later:

> I remember how mortified we were once on a division
> review, where we were anxious to excel another regiment
> of our brigade. We had to march to the music of an Indi-
> ana band, a good one by the way, but just as we wheeled
> into column of division and started to pass the general
> with his staff, also a brilliant array of Washington belles
> and citizens, who were expecting a great deal of us, the
> band struck up an operatic selection, no doubt very ele-
> gant for a grand concert, but a flat failure for marching.
> Our men lost step and those in the front ranks muttered
> subdued curses on the rear ranks who were stepping on
> their heels and trying to climb over their knapsacks; the
> line looked like a rail fence, and our mild and gentle . . .
> [Rufus R. Dawes], who was never known to have any
> vices or use an oath, lost his temper and was heard
> shouting "blank that blank band." The [Hoosier musi-
> cians] must have heard him, for suddenly the tune
> changed, the step was taken—and in perfect time the
> crack regiment of the division, passed in review; yet how
> much easier it was for the old 2d, with their band play-
> ing the one only tune their colonel allowed them to play,
> no matter how grand the review—"Rory O'Moore." No
> opera for them.[34]

After a few weeks, there was a glimmer of hope. "Old Wad"
[Bandleader Abner H. Wadsworth of Fond du Lac] was sent
home and a new band master, "a brother of the great Patrick S.
Gilmore,[35] of Gilmore's band," was named to head the 6th Wisconsin musical organization. "How our spirits revived," Harris
recalled. "What cared we for that famous Indiana band, or that
'Rory O'Moore' crowd of the 2d. We even had hopes to humiliate

34. [Harris], *Telegraph*, November 12, 1882.
35. Gilmore was the most famous bandmaster of his time.

the 5th [Wisconsin], although outsiders swore that they had the best band in the Army of the Potomac. And I now think the outsiders were correct."

Finally, the much-heralded Gilmore arrived, and "for a while the woods back of the camp was made hideous with practicing." Groups of soldiers came in from the company streets to stand at the edge of the trees and listen to the music, and there was much headshaking by the Badger soldiers. Gilmore played what Private Henry Petitt, one of the Lynxville boys in Company C, described as "an exceedingly active clarinet," Harris recalled, and the band leader "could draw more shrill tones, both full and shaky, quavers and semi-quavers, than his salary required, never failing to elicit a loud response from the four intelligent mules commanded by Private Bill Winney of company C, whenever they heard it."

An anxious week passed, and finally Bandleader Gilmore announced the band was ready to play the new selection for the regiment. The result was even more dismal than before, and, that week, Harris recorded, tongue firmly in cheek, "a private died in Company C, and small-pox broke out in the regiment." Finally, the band was dissolved, and, for a while the 6th Wisconsin "fell back on our old drum Major Whaley, who with his gay young fifers and drummers did challenge every thing in sight. They played with the drum corps of C. C. Augers' brigade on a wager and won." Ultimately, Harris said, the brigade formed its own band, "a good band," and it "cheered us to victory, soothed us in defeat and made life half way endurable." Harris had one other conclusion:

> It was a serious mistake when the higher powers allowed that band to go back "from whence they came." They should have been sent to the front to frighten the rebels with that one old tune—then followed by a charge of the entire brigade.[36]

There was a postscript to the whole story of the 6th Wisconsin band and its one tune, "The Village Quickstep," and it was played

36. *Ibid.* All regimental bands were ordered mustered from service in 1862, in favor of brigade bands. The Iron Brigade band basically was formed from musicians taken from the band of the 2nd Wisconsin Infantry.

out in 1899 on the street outside the Fond du Lac home of Edward S. Bragg on the occasion of his 72nd birthday. A contingent of Iron Brigade veterans had gathered to honor the old brigade commander, and they formed on the sidewalk before a brief formal ceremony to present him an engraved "Loving Cup." With them was the drum corps of the Edwin A. Brown Post of the Grand Army of the Republic, named for the young Captain of Company E, who sang "Benny Havens, O" so well and who wrote touching letters to his wife before being killed at Antietam. And the song the fifers piped that day to draw Bragg from his home was the old regimental standby—"The Village Quickstep." It was probably the last time that song was played for a detail of 6th Wisconsin men.[37]

Left to his own devices, Harris, that "dull winter" of 1861-62, organized his own "orchestra of ten performers and a quartet of singers. We had violins, flute, guitar and three brass instruments," he recalled. It was about that same time Colonel Lysander Cutler "received a supply of groceries from Washington among them a box of wine." Harris recalled:

[A] secret consultation of the younger officers was held, and without a selfish or mercenary motive, it was decided that although our colonel did not know one tune from another, he was justly entitled to a serenade from the orchestra. Several officers were not performers and as they were anxious of joining, I hit upon a happy idea by which they could enjoy the old gentleman's hospitality. That night the orchestra and the officers invited stood in line before his tent and in a lively manner the orchestra performed the old "Souderbach Waltz." As expected, when the tune ceased, the colonel threw open the entrance of his tent and invited us in. In a marvelous manner the band swelled in number to twenty-five. The colonel's inexperienced eye failed to detect that while one performer carried a violin, his neighbor held only the violin box, and the same with the guitar and flute,

37. "General Bragg," *Telegraph*, February 25, 1899. The account noted Bragg was presented with a "loving cup" engraved with the words: "Presented to Gen. Edward S. Bragg, Commander of the Iron Brigade, Feb. 20th, 99, by his Comrades on his 72nd Birthday." An attached plaque displayed the Iron Brigade emblem and the words: "War for the Union, 1861-1865."

but at last, when passing a glass of wine to Captain Edwin Brown, who blushingly held one half of the brass bass tuba, the old gentleman smiled grimly, and exclaimed, "I declare, captain, I always knew you had many accomplishments, but I was not aware that you could play on that big brass horn," and without awaiting a reply, passed on. Though promoted to general afterwards, he never learned the conspiracy the young officers of the 6th worked so successfully against that box of wine.[38]

It was one of the few times old Cutler was fooled. A stern New Englander, he was six feet tall, with deep-set gray eyes overhung with heavy eyebrows. Prematurely gray, his hair and beard turned white during the war. Cutler was 53 when Fort Sumter was fired on and was active with state officials in forming the early Wisconsin regiments, even to the point of being commissioned to travel to New York to purchase many components of the state's grey militia uniforms. He was named colonel of the 6th Wisconsin and the raw 20-year-old backwoods boys were impressed, awed and frightened by the grim officer they always called "the old colonel." Cutler had worked in the rough Lake Superior mining country prior to the war where the Indians called him "Gray Devil." Young Captain Rufus Dawes said Cutler was a "very strict disciplinarian [who would] tolerate no nonsense . . . ," but was "as rugged as a wolf, and the regiment has great confidence in him, both as a man and an officer."[39] In those early days of the war, much was made of Cutler's experience leading a regiment of militiamen in the brief but unbloody 1839 border dispute between the United States and Canada known as the "Aroostock War."

Born in Royalston, Worcester County, Massachusetts February 16, 1808, Cutler was a farmer, surveyor and schoolmaster before he emigrated to Dexter, Maine, where he entered a partnership with a wealthy townsman and built what became the largest woolen mill east of Massachusetts. In its heyday, the mill employed 2,000 workers. Cutler also became a member of the town board of selectmen and served on the boards of Tufts College

38. [Harris], Telegraph, November 26, 1882.
39. Dawes, Service, pp. 18, 25.

118

and the Maine Central Railroad. He was elected to the Maine State Senate as a Whig, serving from 1839 to 1840.

The financial Panic of 1856 destroyed his mill business, and Cutler followed the path of many Yankees before him, emigrating to Wisconsin where, with his knowledge of surveying, he was employed by a mining consortium seeking clear claim to portions of the Penokee Range on the southern shore of Lake Superior. He traveled north into the wilderness from Milwaukee that summer of 1857, amid rumors of Indian trouble. One surveyor had already been found dead, possibly slain. Unperturbed, Cutler spent two winters in the trackless wilderness, organizing a town that was 30 miles from the nearest supply post. The community relied on half-breed packers to transport supplies and there was one incident (or at least that was the story that circulated among the greenhorn patriots at Camp Randall) where Cutler roused two reluctant packers from a saloon at gunpoint and forced them to deliver supplies to his snowbound village.[40]

In 1859, he returned to Milwaukee, where he engaged in the grain and commission business with modest success. The outbreak of Civil War roused the old militia officer, and one historian wrote the 53-year-old "showed the war-like enthusiasm of a young man of thirty" and that only the remonstrations of friends prevented him from enlisting in the 90-day first regiment as a private.[41] In the end, he was assigned to command Wisconsin's 6th Regiment, stamping it with much of his own character, a man first feared, then respected, and finally, loved by his soldiers, even if his sly young officers could trick him out of his wine.

All in all, Cutler was a rigid, unbending officer, sure of the rightness of his prejudices. One of his soldiers, who came in as a private from Appleton, could remember only one occasion the "old colonel" allowed himself "to indulge in . . . a smile that was unreserved, a broad, full-grown, generous smile,"[42] but Cutler was a man who did his duty as he saw it.

There was a dark side to all this, and it showed that fall of 1861, outside Washington, when Cutler, or perhaps those other New Englanders, Bragg and Haskell, came to the conclusion that some of his young officers had bad habits or lacked military prom-

40. [Flower], *History of Milwaukee*, pp. 789-791.
41. *Ibid.*
42. [Watrous], *Telegraph*, March 26, 1898.

ise. Even Dawes, with his New England origins, was troubled. Julius Atwood triggered the events when he resigned as lieutenant colonel; Benjamin Sweet was promoted to fill the vacancy, and Bragg of Company E became regimental major. Dawes, at the time, said Cutler would have preferred Haskell in the third spot, and there was some political tugging before Bragg was named. Then, "under the thin disguise of failure to pass examination before a certain commission of officers . . . several very promising officers were arbitrarily driven out of the regiment," Dawes wrote almost 30 years afterwards. As a result, Irish Company D was stripped of Captain John O'Rourke, First Lieutenant John Nichols and Second Lieutenant Patrick H. McCauley. In the Beloit Star Rifles, Company G, the "examinations" claimed Captain M. A. Northrup, First Lieutenant George C. Montague and Second Lieutenant William H. Allen. Other forced resignations included First Lieutenant Daniel K. Noyes of Company A; Second Lieutenant Amos S. Johnson of Company I and young Second Lieutenant John Crane of Company K, the Irish officer who had come to "Mickey" Sullivan's aid in those troublesome days at Mauston.[43]

Dawes was disquieted by the development. He had written his brother on September 29 that Crane was "making a fine young officer" and was "one of the best instructors in the manual of arms in the regiment."[44] But that counted not at all among those "Americans," Cutler, Haskell and Bragg, who held strong opinions about the immigrant classes. In Wisconsin, the Germans were organized and numerous, while the Irish were scattered, fewer, and, as a result, more vulnerable to prejudice. More than a quarter-century later, Dawes blamed Crane's "too close a sympathy" with the Irish officers of the Montgomery Guard, Company D, for bringing the "attack upon him."[45]

The purge claimed six lieutenants and four captains. "There was much bitter feeling in the regiment over these matters," Dawes wrote. "Some, however, of the displaced officers had

43. *Adjutant General Reports*, p. 49.
44. Dawes, *Service*, p. 26.
45. Dawes, *Service*, p. 27. In reporting on Wisconsin's first regiments, the state Adjutant General broke his listing into Americans, Irish, Germans (including former residents of Switzerland and Holland), Norwegians and Swedes, and lumped together the English, Canadians, Welsh and Scotch. *Adjutant General's Reports*, p. 83.

proved incompetent, and others might be termed incorrigible, so far as the discipline of the regiment was concerned."[46]

In an October 22nd letter to his wife, Edwin A. Brown wrote of the incident and blamed ambition, an emotion as strong as prejudice, for the purging:

> We have been having quite a time among the company officers of the Regiment since Bragg was promoted Major. He exercises great influence over the Colonel, and seems inclined to remember his enemies. They [Cutler and Bragg] have caused several Capts and Lieutenants to be reported for a vigorous examination while myself and others have been allowed to go scot free altho we probably knew no more than those who were examined. Some who passed the ordeal, that they desired to get rid of, have been annoyed in other ways. So much so that 4 captains and 6 lieutenants sent in their unconditional resignations today. The consequence is quite a bad state of feeling in some of the companies which I fear will impair our efficiency when called upon to fight. *Most of those officers* [who resigned] *opposed Bragg's promotion* [to major]. This much of my letter must not be made public at all, as my head would come off if it were known that I had "let the cat out of the bag."[47]

The day Brown wrote his letter, Captain Northrup of Company G, the Beloit Star Rifles, called his non-commissioned officers to his tent and announced his intention of resigning. Lieutenants Montague and Allen said they were quitting as well. It was neatly done, with no grumbling or hint they were being forced out. "The boys feel 'down in the mouth' about it [the resignations] —most of them," Levi Raymond, one of the Beloit boys, wrote in his diary that night. "Several other commissioned officers also will resign—a general 'tune' in camp." The diarist added a sober footnote to his entry of October 23: "I hate to see the Capt. & Lt. Montague go back: it can't be helped."[48]

So Northrup, who had brought Lincoln to Beloit, went home

46. Dawes, *Service*, p. 26.
47. Edwin A. Brown, Letter, to his wife, October 22, 1861.
48. Levi G. Raymond, Diary, October 23, 1861.

without hearing a shot fired in anger. He cast about here and there for a time, trying to set his life back in order, but it just wasn't enough, being home while other men were winning glory. On April 20, 1863, he wrote Governor Edward Salomon seeking another post. "I have several times made application for a commission in the service again—I have a letter from Col. L. Cutler to the Sec. of War as to my competency to fill any place in a Regiment," he wrote in a letter of a man near the end of his rope. "Which with other testimonials I would like to present to you, and ask a situation in the army if there be any place which you could give. I could enter upon the duties of such position upon a very short notice. I would like an answer as soon as you could conveniently determine."[49] But it was not to be; troubled by failing health, Northrup died October 6, 1864, almost three years from the day he had resigned.

Looking back over more than a century, the episode forcing the resignations of 10 officers remains unclear. At first glance, it would appear the Irish were singled out. Yankee Whig Cutler, along with Bragg and Haskell, all "Americans," may have been unreasonable and vindictive in their feelings toward the Papist Irish. The departing officers seemed to fall into four classes: They were incorrigible, incompetent, opposed Bragg for major, or they were Irish. The curious, unexplained detail in the whole story is Cutler's letter of recommendation for Northrup to the Secretary of War. Perhaps Cutler felt Northrup was adequate to be an officer in another regiment, but certainly *not* in his regiment.[50]

The final resignation was that of Captain William Lindwurm, who had earlier squared off against Cutler over bread rations for his Company F boys. It was submitted a month after the others. Dawes and Edwin Brown, in letters at the time, included the stocky German among the officers forced to give up their commissions. Perhaps he tried to fight his "resignation," being a German of standing and political ability, but more likely the 300-pound Prussian probably realized he was physically unfit for field

49. M. A. Northrup, Letter, to Governor Edward Salomon, April 20, 1863.
50. *Beloit Journal*, October 20, 1864. Northrup's obituary also raises the possibility he suffered from some physical or mental disability that forced him to resign his commission. The weekly noted he worked his last months "laboring under embarrassment known only to his most intimate friends." Northrup was buried "in occurrence with the ritual and usage of the Masonic Fraternity; to which order he belonged," the newspaper reported.

service, especially since Rhinish wine would be in short supply.

Even Wisconsin state officials took notice of the changes, and comment was made in the Adjutant General's Report for 1861. "For some reason not known to this department, there has been more change, in the 6th Regiment among the commissioned officers by resignations and otherwise than all the other regiments combined." The Adjutant General continued, however: "It is due to this Regiment to say, that no better body of men have left the State. They have had no opportunity as yet show their fighting qualities, but they possess the ring of the true metal, and whenever an opportunity offers to bring out their qualities, there will be another gem added to the wreath of Wisconsin glory."[51]

Some of the appointments to fill the vacancies were curious: Lieutenant Philip W. Plummer of Company C was promoted Captain of Company G; named his lieutenants were First Sergeant William Reader of Company E and First Sergeant James L. Converse of Company G. Loyd Harris of Prairie du Chien was advanced from first sergeant to second lieutenant of Company C. Lieutenant John Kellogg of K became captain of Company I, and Clayton E. Rogers of I was promoted from ranks to be second lieutenant. David Quaw became first lieutenant and Sergeant John Ticknor second lieutenant of Dawes' Company K, while Lieutenant John Marsh of Company B was named captain of Company D; Michael Fitch, the sergeant major, initially of Company B, became first lieutenant of the Milwaukee Irish.[52]

The changes brought muttering, especially in Irish Company D. "This appointment of strangers to command of the company, and disregard of their natural and reasonable preference as to nationality, made bad feelings among the men of that company," Dawes wrote long afterwards:

Marsh and Fitch were excellent officers and discreet men, and less difficulty resulted than was anticipated. This changing around of officers, indiscriminately from company to company was a new departure, and it gave our regiment a violent wrench. Colonel Cutler had in all matters of command discipline, the courage of his con-

51. *Adjutant General's Reports*, p. 48.
52. *Ibid.*, p. 49.

victions, and his justification must be found in the fact that good results ultimately followed.[53]

Private Johnny Cook, the "Tough One," left a less reassuring picture of the change in commanders for Company D: "Capt. O'Rourke resigned and a Brute from Co. B (Capt. Marsh) came in his place. . . . I could not get along with Capt. Marsh and consequently I was put in the Guard House *Several Times.*" Lieutenant Samuel Birdsall, Cook remembered, told the boys flatly "he did not know anything about military [matters] and he be damned if he wanted to know [about them]."[54]

In the end, however, the purging of some officers and promotion of others, as expected, produced mixed results. It showed the ethnic classes, especially the Irish, had a way to go before complete acceptance and that the leadership of at least this Wisconsin regiment (despite its large immigrant contingent) was still firmly in the hands of Americans. Left unanswered was whether some of the officers forced to resign, such as young John Crane of Company K, would have developed into good line commanders in the 6th Wisconsin. Even Dawes, decades later, remarked that the promotions missed men such as Milwaukeean Thomas Kerr of Company D, a Mexican War veteran and soldier of ability. Ultimately, he would become lieutenant colonel of the regiment.[55]

The purging had a positive side as well. It brought men of promise and ability to positions of responsibility and blurred forever the strong and sometimes parochial ethnic characteristics of individual companies. That opened promotion opportunities for such men of ability as John Hauser and, within a year or so, Tom Kerr. The Irish, Germans and "Americans" also found they could work together, a significant lesson they carried back to Wisconsin and the old soldier associations which became so politically active after the war. Thus, the 6th Wisconsin became more Regiment than assembly of companies, and it was a distinction that had much to do with creating a stout fighting organization, and, as Dawes noted, "good results ultimately followed."

Except for the turmoil caused by the resignations, the early winter days passed slowly with never-ending guard mountings,

53. Dawes, *Service*, p. 27.
54. Cook, *Army*, p. 4.
55. Dawes, *Service*, p. 27.

drill, dress parades and inspections. It was a time of boredom and homesickness, and the approaching holiday season added to the gloomy feelings of the young soldiers, most facing their first Christmas away from home. In addition to the usual ailments, measles swept the camp, leaving many companies, for a time, at half-strength. Then there was the strange, unexplained death of Second Sergeant Benjamin E. Smith of Company E. Young Edwin Brown, the Fond du Lac attorney now commanding Bragg's Rifles, was troubled about it. He remembered Smith as a "middle aged man with a short, thick set figure" who enlisted with hope of quick advancement. "I feel quite grieved at his loss as it was so peculiar a case," Brown wrote his wife, trying to explain it all to her as well as himself. It seemed Smith, he said, "did not get as high a position as he would have liked, and became sick and tired of the army." An application for a discharge was denied, "whereupon he began to grow sick. Most everyone supposed he was shamming illness until I saw that he lost flesh and appetite. I then began to intercede for him. The surgeon could not see that anything was the matter with him, except that he was discouraged and homesick. Yet he partly promised to get him discharged." With that news, Smith began to perk up, Brown said, and was soon walking outdoors and eating "with a relish." But the next word the young officer received was that Smith had been sent off to a hospital in Washington, where two weeks later he died. "It appears that the Surgeon thought he was getting so smart as not to need a discharge and then poor 'Ben' gave right up again," Brown wrote, adding: "A singular case isn't it? To think that a man . . . should die more from homesickness and despondency than disease. Altho no fault attaches to me on account of his not getting a discharge, yet I am afraid I did not have charity enough for his feelings. It seemed so much like shamming illness for a purpose." He added a disturbing sentence: "I am afraid I shall be as hard hearted as 'Nero' if I stay in the Army 3 years."

For Brown, Smith's strange death added a bleakness to the Christmas season that was hard to dispel:

> Next Wednesday is Christmas. I don't know what I shall do, unless it be to drill. "No peace for the wicked" you know. I should like to sit with my little family around the paternal hearthstone with a good blazing fire in front,

friends by my side and the usual delicacies on the table. . . . Take good care of the "babies." Tell them good things of their pa. Repeat tho many assurances of my regard to relatives and friends, and be sure not to forget your soldier husband.

The letter was signed, "Affectionally Yours, E.A. Brown."[56]

Bragg's letters home in this same period reflected a curious mixture of homesickness and ambition. He cited a recent disagreement with Cutler:

He likes all the credit of doing things in such quarters as they were creditable, but when there is any ill feelings growing out of what has been done, he insinuates that somebody else did it. In this way, he has created temporarily considerable ill feeling, on the part of some officers toward me, but I shall be able to live it all down, and him with it unless he is more mindful of what is right, than he has been. He fancied he had a boy to deal with, but like many men before him, he found out he had caught a Tartar.

The relationship would worsen in coming months.

On a Brigade review, Bragg reported he felt the "men never looked better, with their knapsacks neatly placed and their new blue overcoats nicely rolled up and strapped on the top." He added a conclusion as well: "My being a Col. is a wonderful remote point—if I should succeed in the next year, it will be wonderful and rapid luck." In the same letter:

Tell Kit and Will that from what I have seen of Santa Clause [sic] in Washington, I think he has heard they are naughty and do not mind, for when I told him what they would like for presents, this year, He said, that he had heard so many bad things about them, that he did not believe he should come and see them. At all events, it would do them no good to hang up their stockings, unless they learned to be better children and mind their Mama, without being whipped.[57]

56. Edwin A. Brown, Letter, to his wife, December 20, 1861.
57. Edward S. Bragg, letter, to his wife, December 7, 1861. At the time, Bragg had three children, William Kohl Bragg, Kate Colman Bragg and Margaret Bragg, called "Will, Kit and Daisy."

As the greenhorn patriots waited out the winter of 1861-62 there was one matter to resolve. The volunteer regiment was composed of friends, relatives, neighbors and former schoolmates, and that produced a casual relationship between enlisted man and officer. An example of the problem was the March 20, 1862, diary entry of Private Levi B. Raymond of Company G—the Beloit Star Rifles—noting he had been pitched onto a stump and hurt while "scuffling and fooling" with an officer of his unit. If the regiment was to be a disciplined military organization, such free and easy "scuffling and fooling" between private and officer would have to end.[58]

On May 7, 1862, an event occurred that would have far reaching affects on not only that curious relationship between enlisted man and officer in the 6th Wisconsin, but the other regiments as well: John Gibbon was named permanent commander of the Western Brigade. Born in Pennsylvania in 1827, Gibbon grew up in North Carolina. A graduate of West Point, he served in the Mexican War and against the Indians.[59] Despite his Southern background, he sided with the Union when the war started. The slightly built Gibbon, with his deep-set eyes and short hair, had been in command of Battery B of the 4th U.S. Artillery, and as the battery had long been associated with the brigade, was not an unfamiliar figure to the Wisconsin black hats. In fact, when he had needed some men to fill out his gun crews in Battery B, Gibbon had obtained gunners from the infantry regiments and was impressed favorably with the Westerner volunteers.[60] In outlook, Gibbon was a stiff professional soldier, but he quickly learned how to adapt the rigid discipline of the Regulars to the requirements of an army of civilians. The Badger boys did not like him much at first, but soon he would become "Johnny the War Horse" and the officer whom the "Tough One" of Company D, Johnny Cook, described as "the boss soldier." After the war, Gibbon was a great favorite at the old soldier gatherings, and he served as president of the Iron Brigade Association until his death.

But that May of 1862, he had a great job in front of him, and he admitted he was puzzled just how to go about turning the frisky volunteers into real soldiers. One who caught his eye was

58. Raymond, Diary, March 20, 1862.
59. *Dictionary of American Biography*, (New York, 1946), Vol. VII., pp. 236-237.
60. Gibbon, *Recollections*, pp. 27-28.

polished Frank Haskell, whom he accepted on his staff when the acting brigade commander, Lysander Cutler, returned to the 6th Wisconsin. It was a joining of two officers of like mind, and Haskell quickly won not only Gibbon's respect, but his affection. Haskell, in turn, acquired from his new commander much of the viewpoint of the professional soldier. One soldier in the regiment recalled:

> . . . [T]he time was mostly spent in camp duties and drilling—company, battalion and brigade drill—under Gen. John Gibbon, and I do not believe any body of men could attain higher efficiency in drill and discipline than we had attained. Mornings at 5 o'clock Gen. Gibbon and . . . Adjt. Haskell would ride in and around the camp, taste coffee in the company cook kitchen, and look after all sanitary matters pertaining to the general well fare. . . .[61]

In the back ranks, there was muttering that Dane County neighbor Frank Haskell had perhaps become more Regular than volunteer, at the time, a hard assessment.

In his six months commanding the Western brigade, Gibbon proved to have just the right knack in shaping the four volunteer regiments of his command into a cohesive fighting brigade. He found the boys and men to be intelligent, willing, and more responsive to reward than punishment. ". . . I was already impressed with the conviction that all they needed was some discipline and drill to make them first class soldiers and my anticipations were more than realized," Gibbon later wrote. He also found the 2nd and 6th Wisconsin "had decidedly the advantage" over the 19th Indiana and 7th Wisconsin, and "each strove to become the 'crack' regiment of the brigade."[62]

If he was pleased with the men he was to command, Gibbon also walked into a personality squabble between Colonel Lysander Cutler and the regiment's lieutenant colonel, Benjamin Sweet. At the same time, another of his colonels, Solomon Meredith of the 19th Indiana, a politician "backed by strong political influ-

61. J. O. Johnson, "Army Reminiscences," *Milwaukee Sunday Telegraph*, November 30, 1884.
62. Gibbon, *Recollections*, pp. 27-28.

ence," was also grumbling openly over Gibbon's appointment. Meredith thought that the command of the volunteer brigade should have gone to a Western man, leaving unsaid, of course, that the Westerner he had in mind might just be one S. Meredith of Indiana. Fortunately, according to Gibbon, "his action in the matter might have produced more harm than it did but for the fact that not being anything of a soldier and too old to be made one, his influence in the command was not very great and he did not gain the support of the best military element in it."

As a result, Gibbon found himself walking a narrow line in trying to settle the dispute. He first called upon old Cutler, whom he remembered as a "natural soldier though somewhat inclined to be arbitrary and dictatorial." Next, he met with Sweet, and finally, little Major Edward S. Bragg. Sweet declared an order published by Cutler had contained a falsehood; he accused the officer of being "arbitrary and tyrannical," and flatly told Gibbon there could be no peace. Bragg, however, gave a "calm straightforward dispassionate" account of the dispute and won Gibbon's confidence and respect. Gibbon settled the matter by sending a letter to Cutler, upholding the old Colonel, but asking the charges he had leveled against Sweet be dropped for the good of the regiment. He also said the letter was to be read in the presence of the commissioned officers. It worked. Cutler was satisfied, and Sweet soon resigned to accept the commission as colonel of the new 21st Wisconsin Infantry.[63]

All in all, it was nicely done, and Gibbon then turned to the more important task of training his new brigade. He instituted regular drills and noticed an immediate improvement. The Westerners were known to knock down a rail fence now and then for firewood or to construct a shelter; Gibbon instituted a rule that when a fence was torn down, the regiment camped nearest to it was required to rebuild it. Soldierly bearing and appearance at inspection and drill were encouraged with a policy of giving the well-turned-out soldier a 24-hour pass to allow him to go blackberrying. (Two soldiers who surely never enjoyed such privilege were Privates Pete Markle of Coon Slough of Company I and J. Scoville, late of Juneau County, Wisconsin, now a file closer in Company K.) A circular was also sent down to the regi-

63. *Ibid.*, pp. 27-30.

ments directing commanders to "see that their men bathe regularly at least once a week. . . ."[64]

One problem persisted, however, Gibbon remembered, and that was teaching the sentinels to walk their posts in the prescribed manner:

> Men who had been working hard all their lives for a purpose could see no use in pacing up and down doing nothing. Hence logs of wood, a convenient rock or campstool, were frequently resorted to as resting places, and often I would ride by a sentinel without any attention being paid to me whatever, the men on post being entirely too much occupied enjoying his ease, perhaps even smoking a cigar, to notice my approach.

One of the problem soldiers was Company D's "Tough One," Johnny Cook, who was making life difficult for recently appointed Captain John Marsh. Cook recalled how, on one occasion, he was on duty when Marsh came up to the guard post and "wanted to know why I did not walk my beat." Cook had a quick answer: "I told him, Marsh, that he did not know much." There was another clash a short time later:

> One day I was standing on picket . . . and [Marsh] . . . , wishing to make a fuss with me, commenced with—"Cook do you know your duty?" Told him I did. "Why don't you present Arms to me when I came up?" Told him it was not required on picket. He told me he would learn me my duty and used abusive language to me. I called him a tyrant and a brute, not fit to command a squad of Government Mules (which was the truth). At this time I was standing on [a] RR crossing with my musket loaded. Striking the butt end on the crossing it went off into the air. I told him I wished it had went through his black heart. (And I meant it). He ordered me under arrest and sent me to the camp.[65]

General Gibbon had about the same success with the Irish private. He passed Cook's sentry post one day and did not get the required salute. "He walked through the line and stopped,"

64. First Brigade Order Book, Circular, May 13, 1862.
65. Cook, *Army*, pp. 3-4.

130

Cook wrote later, in that dry manner of his. "Wanted to know if I knew him. Told him I did. Wanted to know why I did not salute him. Told him I could not see any shoulder straps. He looked at his shoulders and saw he had his old Army blouse on. Wanted to know where I belonged. Told him to the 'divils of the 6th.'" Gibbon nodded and moved on, probably thinking this turning volunteers into real soldiers might take a day or two longer than he first anticipated.[66]

Gibbon finally found a solution. One day, "perhaps being in a less amiable frame of mind than usual," he admitted, he ordered a lax sentry relieved from his post, stripped of his equipment, and placed for several hours on the head of a barrel in front of the guard-tent. "He soon attracted many observers and when it was known for what he was placed there, he was most unmercifully ridiculed by his comrades," Gibbon wrote later. "I never had any more trouble after that about my sentinels, either saluting me or walking their posts, and that is the only instance in which I ever resorted to arbitrary punishment in that command."[67]

One other thing had to be done. The regiments of his new brigade mainly wore Federal-issue uniforms, but a few remnants of the state-issued clothing persisted. In October, 1861, when the Wisconsin-issue grey uniforms became tattered and unserviceable, the 2nd Wisconsin had been issued the dark-blue, nine-button regulation frock coats, dark-blue trousers and the black felt Model 1858 hat of the U.S. Regulars. The 6th and 7th had been issued the frock coats and sky-blue trousers the month before, but retained some of their state-issue clothing, including the famous caps Private Sullivan and others so enjoyed. On May 5, 1862, Acting Brigade Commander Lysander Cutler of the 6th Wisconsin ordered black hats for the 7th Wisconsin. When Gibbon assumed command May 7th, he determined to make the Model 1858 dress hat a consistent item of his brigade. Accordingly, the 6th Wisconsin Infantry was issued the new headgear about May 17, and presumably, the 19th Indiana at about the same time.[68] It was, as later events proved, a significant step in transformation of volunteers into an "Iron Brigade."

66. Cook, *Telegraph*, March 11, 1883.
67. Gibbon, *Recollections*, p. 37.
68. Howard Michael Madaus, see Appendix III for a full discussion of the development of the Iron Brigade uniform.

The entire Western Brigade was also issued white linen leggings and white cotton gloves. In the 6th Wisconsin, the new hats and other items were "received with the greatest merriment." There was some grumbling because the new outfits depleted the clothing allowance. The displeasure of the men in ranks was displayed one morning when Gibbon came out to find his "pet horse" equipped with leggings.[69] But Rufus R. Dawes remembered the boys "all felt proud of the fine appearance" of the regiment, and his journal for that time recorded: "General Gibbon attended our dress parade to-day and the regiment was in 'fine feather.'"[70] It may all have been a bit fancy for the farmer boys and piney workers, but the Calicos and the men in the other regiments were all rather pleased with how they looked in their tall, new black hats and trim uniforms. One Badger wrote the homefolk: "We have a full blue suit, a fine black hat nicely trimmed with bugle and plate and ostrich feathers; and you can only distinguish our boys from the regulars, by their [our] good looks."[71] Soldiers in other outfits were less appreciative, however. A week after the issue, Dawes noted in his journal some soldiers in Shield's Division had made rude remarks about a "bandbox brigade," but the Badger boys had retorted they "would rather wear leggings than be lousy," and Dawes added with a proper sniff: "Shield's division are the dirtiest ragamuffins we have yet seen in the service."[72]

In the end, Gibbon was proud of his Western brigade, and they were proud of him. What he gave the volunteers was a professional's discipline. In writing his recollections of the war, he explained:

> The mere efficiency in drill was not by any means the most important point gained . . . The *habit* of obedience and subjection to the will of another, so difficult to instill into the minds of free and independent men became marked characteristics of the command. A great deal of the prejudice against me as a regular officer was removed when the men came to compare their own soldierly appearance and way of doing duty with other

69. Dawes, *Service*, p. 44; Cheek and Pointon, *Sauk County*, p. 27.
70. Dawes, *Service*, p. 45.
71. *Mineral Point Tribune*, October 22, 1861. The quotation was from a soldier in the 2nd Wisconsin Infantry.
72. *Ibid.*

commands, and although there were still malcontents who chafed under the restraints of a wholesome discipline and would have chafed under any, these were gradually reduced in number and influence.[73]

And that was why a free and independent volunteer such as "Tough One" Johnny Cook finally accepted Gibbon as "the boss general," and why he greeted him so warmly 20 years later at an Iron Brigade Association meeting.

For a time that Spring, it seemed the 6th Wisconsin might be getting into the war. There was much excitement when General George McClellan took the Army of the Potomac to the Peninsula, but McDowell's Division was left behind. The brigade was marched here and there, but finally settled down near Fredericksburg, Virginia, where it was halted. McDowell's Division had been considered as a reserve for McClellan's force outside Richmond, but there was enough concern by alarmed politicians to keep it close enough to protect Washington as well. The brigade engaged in various duties, including the construction of a 500-foot-pole trestle bridge on the Aquia Creek Railroad over Potomac Creek. Photographers carrying bulky cameras visited the area, taking both individual and group images for posterity. But nothing of serious note occurred, and the Badger soldiers told one another, with much wagging of heads, that the war was going to be over before they "saw the elephant." In late May, there were some alarms and marching, as elements of McDowell's command tried to intercept the soldiers of Stonewall Jackson, but it came to nothing, and the most noteworthy excitement erupted with a regimental row involving the ambitions of Frank A. Haskell.

It started with Benjamin F. Sweet's resignation, finally, to take command of the 21st Wisconsin. Bragg was expected to move up to Sweet's spot, creating a field-grade opportunity for Haskell, or so Haskell hoped. He had the considerable backing of Gibbon, Cutler and Division Commander Rufus King. But it was a curious time in American military history. The "officers of the line" petitioned the governor by letter, asking they be consulted about the filling of any vacancy involving field officers. In the style of the day, they noted: "With becoming deference for your position and

73. Gibbon, *Recollections*, p. 37.

undoubted confidence in your discrimination and ability to select competent men for any position in our regiment, we still trust that your Excellence, in appointing men to whose hands our lives and honor are to be entrusted, will not ignore our ideas of the fitness of the men to command us."[74]

Cutler, the former New England selectman, tried to resolve the matter in town hall fashion, and, as a result, he lost control of the situation. The "old Colonel" first had the four captains of equal seniority draw lots to determine precedence. He then attemped to induce a caucus of all his officers to choose Haskell, his favorite, in preference to the winner of the draw, young Rufus R. Dawes. The caucus, however, by a vote of 14 to 13, recommended Dawes to be major. Haskell, supported by Cutler, refused to accept the close result, and the dispute was sent off to Wisconsin Governor Edward Salomon, who had succeeded Louis Harvey. (Harvey had drowned on April 19, while on a relief expedition to Wisconsin troops in Tennessee.) A German-American from Milwaukee, Salomon was a Democrat drafted on a war ticket put together by Republicans in an appeal for German votes and war support. Beset on all sides by Haskell's friends, the new governor resented the pressure from the inner circle of Madison politicians. When William F. Vilas, the young Madison attorney to whom Dawes had entrusted his application, called on Salomon to discuss the vacancy, the governor at first refused to hear him, saying, "The friends of Mr. Haskell have already harassed me beyond my patience." But, learning Vilas was on the other side, he listened to Dawes' advocate. Sweet, who had quarreled bitterly with Cutler, also joined the political infighting. He visited the governor to oppose Cutler's protégé. Thus, during the independent-minded governorship of Edward Salomon, Republican Haskell, with his Madison connections, had little chance of promotion. The major's commission went to Rufus R. Dawes.[75]

In a letter home, Bragg recounted the events, noting that no sooner had the lieutenant colonelcy opened up than "Cutler and

74. May 13, 1862, letter to Gov. Edward Salomon, Regimental Papers, 6th Wisconsin Infantry, State Historical Society of Wisconsin. Among the signers were Philip Plummer, John Hauser, R. Converse, Thomas Plummer, John Marsh, John Kellogg, Clayton Rogers, Edwin A. Brown, Earl M. Rogers, Joseph Marston, R. R. Dawes, John Ticknor, and Jerome B. Johnson.
75. Byrne and Weaver, *Haskell*, pp. 20-21. The editors mistakenly list Bragg as opposing Dawes for Major.

his toadies set themselves at work, to procure a recommendation of one of their own kind [Haskell], for the vacancy." For two days there was much heated talk amongst the young officers, and finally Cutler called in the captains, advised them to have a meeting and recommend somebody, and he would approve their choice. The 27 officers met, with 19 voting for Bragg for lieutenant colonel and 14 for Rufus R. Dawes as major. "This surprised them so much," Bragg wrote, "that they have refused to recognize their own caucus. Old Cutler says, he was opposed to a caucus, and he cannot approve it."[76] In a letter to "Dear Ruth," young Edwin Brown of Fond du Lac put it plainer:

> They tried hard to elect the Adjutant—Frank A. Haskell—to the office of Lieut. Col. over Bragg—jumping him as we call it. My influence saved Bragg. Then they tried said Adjutant for Major, and we elected my friend, Capt. R. R. Dawes by one majority. Glory enough for one day! Altho Haskell was a good officer, yet he was of lower rank and—*I hated him.*

No reason for Brown's feelings against Haskell was given.[77]

In his Journal that tense week, Dawes followed the ups and downs of the debate:

> June 16, 1862: Now comes a tug of war. Colonel Cutler wants Haskell appointed Major.

> June 17: Colonel Cutler has asked an expression of the officers for Major. A caucus called for to-night. . . . Was appointed officer of the brigade guard, and did not attend the caucus. Final vote: Haskell, thirteen, Dawes, fourteen.

> June 18: A very exciting day in the regiment. No report made of the caucus. It did not come out right. Captain Brown battles for me like a hero. Haskell told me he should get the appointment if he could. I told him, I should do the same, as it was my right in order of rank, and we shook hands over it. . . . Major Bragg works hard

76. Edward S. Bragg, Letter, to his wife, June 22, 1862.
77. Edwin A. Brown, Letter, to his wife, June 22, 1862.

for me. He says, "this attempt to dragoon the officers into over-riding the rights of captains, will not win."

June 29: Colonel Cutler, General Gibbon, General King, and, I suppose, all Madison, Wisconsin, recommended Haskell. Lieutenant Colonel Sweet, Major Bragg, seven captains, fourteen lieutenants and three regimental staff officers recommended my appointment.

Dawes was finally appointed major, and Haskell stayed on the brigade staff. "It was an unfortunate step," Dawes wrote 30 years later, "as it put entirely out of the line of promotion one of the finest officers Wisconsin sent to the war." In a July 1 letter home, Dawes noted his own promotion "comes very fortunately just before active operations against the enemy, which I doubt not will soon take place, since Gen. Pope has been sent to command our army."[78]

The "Gen. Pope" of Dawes letter was John Pope, who had been brought East after some success in the West. McClellan's attempt to capture Richmond had ended in failure. Pope was brought in to take command of a new army created from several divisions and given instructions to do something about one T. J. Stonewall Jackson, who was roaming around in his old Shenandoah Valley haunts, scaring the dickens out of official Washington. McDowell's Army Corps was assigned to Pope's new "Army of Virginia."

It was the end of blackberrying for the 6th and other regiments in the brigade. On August 28, 1862, while marching along a roadway near the old Bull Run battlefield, the brigade was attacked by Jackson's soldiers. It was a stand-up fight in an open field. Outnumbered, the Westerners refused to yield to the Confederate veterans and began to earn the reputation that would make them famous. They fought at Second Bull Run the next two days, then at South Mountain and Antietam, Fredericksburg and Chancellorsville. "Mickey" Sullivan was out of the war and back in it. Young Captain Edwin A. Brown was killed at Antietam, along with the dashing Werner Von Bachelle, late of Germany and, more recently, Milwaukee. Johnny "Tough One" Cook left the regiment to serve in Battery B of the Fourth U.S. Artillery, where he found opportunity for mischief more far ranging. John Gibbon

78. Dawes, *Service*, pp. 49-50.

was promoted to a Division command in the II Corps, taking Frank Haskell with him. Lysander Cutler was promoted to command of his own brigade of New York and Pennsylvania soldiers and would play a major role at Gettysburg. Sol Meredith's long ambition was also realized when he was named to succeed Gibbon as commander of the Iron Brigade. Finally, the Wisconsin boys who had left home two years before were on a road to a place called Gettysburg, in Pennsylvania. Although at the time they did not know it, the fate of the Union was resting on their strong legs and Western courage.

MAJ. RUFUS R. DAWES
A Hard-won Promotion

138

CHAPTER FIVE

When our lines they were broken, and backward did lag;
And old "Daddy Wadsworth," rushed up to Bragg,
Saying the Rebs were triumphant, you must save the day,
They charged like a whirlwind, old Company K.

—By "Mickey"

Marsh Creek

The campaign that ended in the Civil War's most notable battle
began with what 6th Wisconsin men felt was the Army of the
Potomac's most humiliating defeat. The soldiers always were at
a loss to explain how the army had been whipped at Chancellorsville, Virginia, in early May of 1863.[1] But by the end of that
month, the Army of the Potomac found itself again in its camps
on the strong Rappahannock River line, waiting on Robert E. Lee
to decide what was going to happen next. There was general
agreement that Lee would head north again to feed and supply
his soldiers, as well as attempt to lure the Federal army into a
decisive battle that might win the war. There was also a feeling
in the camps that a showdown was near. The big question was
where and when, and top Union officers rode back and forth,
much occupied with bringing the troops to readiness.

One thing accomplished in those days of waiting was a reorganization of the I Army Corps. The muster-out of the two-year
New York regiments and a brigade of nine-month New Jersey
volunteers who had temporarily replaced some of them, cut the
list of regiments drastically, reducing some divisions from four to

---

1. Edward S. Bragg, Letter, to his wife, May 22, 1863. Bragg wrote: ". . .[I]n
my opinion, [the defeat at Chancellorsville was caused by] lack of comprehensive power [on General Joseph Hooker's part] to grasp so large a subject."
He added: "Never an army, had such confidence as we, when we gave battle,
in no single instance were we outfought, but we gained nothing, and in a
great degree lost our confidence in the head of affairs."

two brigades. The Iron Brigade, now commanded by Brigadier General Sol Meredith, the former colonel of the 19th Indiana, was designated the 1st Brigade in the 1st Division headed by steady James Wadsworth. The brigade of New Yorkers and Pennsylvanians led by Lysander Cutler, the first colonel of the 6th Wisconsin, became the 2nd Brigade of the small division. There was much harmless but loud boasting by the black hats over his change, because it made the Iron Brigade the 1st Brigade of the 1st Division of the I Army Corps. But it was the Sauk County boys in Company A who put on the most airs, telling anyone who would listen (and most would not) that they were in the 1st Company of the 1st Regiment, of the 1st Brigade, of the 1st Division of the I Corps of the whole damned Army of the Potomac.[2]

In early June, the Confederate brigades began shifting westward. That triggered a series of false starts, orders and counter orders, until, finally, the blue soldiers marched north. The men were uneasy about the outcome of the coming campaign, and unsure of "Fighting Joe" Hooker, he of the bluff manner and whiskey-flushed face, who, for all his dash and personal bravery, they believed, as army commander had somehow cheated them out of even a chance for victory at Chancellorsville. But there was a feeling in the ranks, one Wisconsin soldier recorded, that the next battle must be a Union victory: "To speak it plainly the Army of the Potomac was mad clear through; every man's pride was touched."[3]

It was one thing for General Hooker to decide to move the army, but quite another to get it on the road. The brightly uniformed, energetic young men on the general's staff galloped to the headquarters of the various Army Corps, and the marching orders went down to the divisions and brigades, telling the field commanders to take this road or that, and organizing a timetable, everyone in a great rush. The infantry columns moved out first, followed by the miles and miles of wagon trains carrying food and ammunition. It required a mighty effort to get the tens of thousands of men and thousands of horses and mules in the right

2. For details of the I Corps reorganization, Alan T. Nolan, *The Iron Brigade*, (New York, 1961), pp. 223-224; Cheek and Pointon, *Sauk County*, p. 68.
3. George H. Otis, *Second Wisconsin Infantry*, ed. by Alan D. Gaff, (Dayton, Ohio, 1984), p. 83. This account originally was serialized in 11 parts in 1880 issues of the *Milwaukee Sunday Telegraph*.

place at the right time on the network of roads west of Washington, but, finally, the massive, twisting blue columns flowed north over the dusty roads, the officers and soldiers out of sorts over the frustrating hurry-wait. The whole army was a dull tangle of men, artillery, animals and wagons marked by the sounds of shuffling feet, rolling wheels, creaking harness leather, the animals, and, as usual, much cursing and shouting. It was the beginning of the Gettysburg campaign.

The march, for the 1st Division of the I Army Corps, began with an unsettling incident—the shooting of Private John Woods of the 19th Indiana. It was something that stuck in the minds of the veterans for half a century. Woods had somehow obtained a Confederate uniform and tried to pass himself off as a deserter from the 19th Tennessee. It was a thin ruse to get himself out of the war, but Woods was recognized by a regimental clerk, tried and sentenced to be executed. The call had come two days earlier for each regimental commander of the Iron Brigade to detail "two lieutenants and twenty wholly reliable men" to report to Division Provost Marshal Clayton E. Rogers for execution duty. It was all unpleasant, and Rogers, a 6th Wisconsin officer before being appointed an aide to General Wadsworth, told a friend that he "feels very badly [sic] that he is obliged to perform this duty."[4] The night of June 11th, marching orders arrived, and the columns took to the road at 2 o'clock the next morning. The prisoner, handcuffed, shackles on his feet, sitting on a rough wood coffin, was brought along in an ambulance at the rear of the division. About midday, after traveling 20 miles,[5] the column halted to allow the soldiers to eat, then the regiments were deployed "in sort of a hollow square with one side open."[6] A grave was dug, and the

4. Rufus R. Dawes, Letter, to Mary Gates, June 10, 1863; Dawes, *Service*, pp. 149-151. This and other letters also appear in Dawes, *Service*, but in some cases were slightly edited for publication. The original text is used in the event of variations.
5. [Howard J. Huntington], *Milwaukee Sunday Telegraph*, March 1, 1885. The article was signed "H." See also Dawes, *Service*, p. 150; Curtis, *Twenty-fourth*, p. 144; E. R. Reed, "Shooting a Deserter," *Milwaukee Sunday Telegraph*, April 12, 1885; Clayton E. Rogers, "Woods the Deserter," *Milwaukee Sunday Telegraph*, May 24, 1885; Cheek and Pointon, *Sauk County*, pp. 68-69; George Fairfield Diary. Cheek and Pointon quote from a letter from Howard J. Huntington of the 6th Wisconsin, which appeared in the *Baraboo News-Republic*. It was "written soon after" the event and published in the *News-Republic*. The "H" of the *Telegraph* account was likely Huntington.
6. [Huntington], *Telegraph*, March 1, 1885.

coffin pulled from the ambulance and placed in front of the hole. The hapless prisoner was brought and seated on the coffin, under the eyes of the 3,000 soldiers. From the men named by the five regiments, a dozen were selected, and they formed a line. General James Wadsworth addressed them briefly and then the 12 filed before a line of guards and the two files faced each other. One by one, rifle-muskets were taken from the guard and handed to the anxious detail. Rogers inspected each weapon to ensure the lock was functioning. The executioners then marched single-file in front of the coffin, some 10 paces distant. It was one thing to kill in battle, but another to stand and look into the eyes of a helpless victim, and a 6th Wisconsin soldier remembered the execution detail "manifested more uneasiness than the criminal."[7]

A chaplain, who had earlier spoken to Woods, was summoned again. "Some moments [were] spent in solemn conversation and prayer, both kneeling, and . . . the very air [grew] still with the hush of death's angel and each heartbeat of the thousands standing around them seem . . . measured by minutes, they [rose] to their feet," recalled one of the witnesses.[8] Finally, the clergyman pressed the young soldier's hand and turned away.

Eleven of the muskets carried by the detail were loaded; the 12th contained only a blank, but that was not reassuring. The veterans would know by the kick of the weapons if their musket fired the heavy bullet. Rogers moved forward with a blindfold, remembering Woods later as "a simple-minded soldier without any force or decision of character." The young Hoosier asked that his eyes not be covered, but Rogers denied the final request, tore open the condemned man's shirt and stepped back. He gave the command "Attention!" and lifted his hat. Musket locks clicked to full cock. The hat swept down and there was a ragged volley and puff of smoke. The detail had aimed low, and only four of the bullets struck Woods, toppling him back over the coffin. He was not dead. A member of the detail, quiet, reliable Sam Wallar of Roger's own Company I of the 6th Wisconsin, grimly re-loaded under the eyes of the hushed division, stepped forward and carefully put the killing ball into Wood's head. Somehow the lone shot seemed louder than the volley. It was all over. The medical

7. Cheek and Pointon, *Sauk County*, p. 69. The quotation is credited to Huntington.
8. Curtis, *Twenty-fourth*, p. 144.

director came forward and pronounced Woods dead. The body was manhandled into the coffin and buried. A band struck up a quickstep and the columns faced right and moved out on the road. ". . . I can [still] see that poor trembling, moaning fellow drop back on the coffin. It seemed hard, but it was just," one 6th Wisconsin soldier said 25 years later.[9]

The next few days were marked by marches over dusty roads, the sun hot, the columns closed. The Confederate Army of Northern Virginia moved northward, and the Army of the Potomac followed at a grinding pace. In the 6th Wisconsin, the regimental flag was cased, and there was very little talking amid the clank of accoutrements. The heat was brutal and water in short supply.

9. Clayton E. Rogers, *Milwaukee Sunday Telegraph*, May 24, 1885. Details of the shooting of Woods were taken from Rogers, except as noted. In his account, Rogers said he consulted his war diaries in writing the story. He indicated Woods, in a butternut uniform, was taken to Gen. John Reynolds' I Corps Headquarters for interrogation; here the deserter insisted he was a member of the 19th Tennessee. But further questioning revealed he could not name the Confederate unit's officers or describe the state's geography. Suspicions hightened, and he was later identified by a 19th Indiana clerk.

"H" claimed Woods went over to the Rebel side, intending, later, to desert. He had acquired a butternut uniform when he came into the Iron Brigade lines, where he was identified by a member of his regiment.

Reed, a 2nd Wisconsin man, claimed Woods was marching Rebel prisoners to the rear when he clandestinely laid down his musket and fell into their ranks. He traded his uniform for one of butternut to effect the ruse. He said it was Woods' third attempt at desertion, and that the Hoosier was trying to take advantage of legislation permitting Rebel deserters who swore an oath to be released North and "remain unmolested so far as demanding of any military service."

Some accounts also claim Rogers used a handkerchief to signal the execution volley, but Huntington clearly states Rogers used a hat. He also wrote one of the muskets contained a blank.

There were also discrepancies in the recollections about Woods' final words. "H" wrote Woods was asked if he had anything to say before death. He "stood up and made a manly and pathetic speech. He told the troops he was very sorry he had deserted from the army, and that his death he hoped would be an example and warning to others. He trusted that in time it would be found that he had really died for his country, as his present death would, he believed, put a stop to desertion and in that way help in the great Union cause. The sentiments uttered were noble and good." Reed remembered no final speech. Woods was "like a lamb, dumb before the slaughter—he opened not his mouth," and was not given an opportunity to do so. Rogers recalled no final speech, but he did write that, in a conversation with the accused an hour before the execution, Woods said he had been persuaded by Indiana friends—"presumedly the Knights of the Golden Circle," who would protect him—to desert and return home. Rogers, too, may have been somewhat gulled; at least he was guilty of embellishment about the vaunted Knights, exaggerated in the Civil War mind to extensive Fifth Column proportions.

The quotation is from Jerome A. Watrous, "Three of a Kind—Reminiscences," *Milwaukee Sunday Telegraph*, August 6, 1882.

Lieutenant Colonel Rufus R. Dawes was in command. Colonel Edward S. Bragg was in Washington, recovering from a kick from his surly horse that left him lame. He would miss the entire campaign.[10] In his letters, Dawes wrote the "heat was like a furnace. . . . Many a poor fellow marched his last day yesterday. Several men fell dead on the road." If the soldiers collapsed from sunstroke, dozens more dropped out of the marching columns simply unable to go on, physically. Officers carried the muskets and knapsacks of their used-up men and cursed the shirkers, but still the regiments grew thinner and thinner from straggling. The shuffling feet stirred up immense dust clouds that caked the throats and nostrils of the weary soldiers. The 6th Wisconsin men passed through such places as Centreville, Leesburg and Broad Run in Virginia. In a letter home, Dawes reported:

> We broke camp at daylight Friday morning, (the twelfth [of June].) We marched that day about twenty miles under a scorching sun and through suffocating clouds of dust. You can hardly imagine what our poor loaded soldiers suffer on such marches. We camped Friday night at Deep Run. We marched at daylight Saturday and camped for the night near Bealton station. We marched Sunday morning and all day Sunday and all night, and until the middle of the afternoon to-day, when we reached this point, tired, sore, sleepy, hungry, dusty and dirty as pigs. I have had no wink of sleep for two nights. Our army is in a great hurry for something.[11]

10. Rufus R. Dawes, Letter, to Mary Gates, May 31, 1863; Dawes, *Service*, pp. 145-146; Rufus R. Dawes, Letter, to Mary Gates, June 7, 1863; Dawes, *Service*, p. 149.

11. The contemporary accounts of the march to Gettysburg give much sharper detail about the heat and fatigue when compared with accounts written after the war. See Dawes, Letters, to Mary Gates, June 15, 1863, June 18, 1863, June 21, 1863 and June 27, 1863; Dawes, *Service*, pp. 151-157; Charles Walker Diary; George Fairfield Diary. Walker served in Company B of the Seventh Wisconsin. "Our march yesterday was terribly severe. The sun was like a furnace, and the dust thick and suffocating. Many a poor fellow marched his last day yesterday. Several men fell dead on the road," Dawes wrote June 18. On the 27th, Dawes questioned: "What do you think of trudging along all day in a soaking rain, getting as wet as a drowned rat, taking supper on hard tack and salt pork, and then wrapping up in a wet woolen blanket and lying down for a sleep . . . ? Well—that is soldiering, and it is a great deal more comfortable soldiering, than to march through suffocating clouds of dust under a hot sun."

The hot weather, he reported, made the soldiers "morose, silent and sullen" amid the clouds of dirt.[12]

At the Leesburg halt, newspapers reached the marching column with headlines reporting: "Rebels in Pennsylvania." But the morale of the soldiers, at least in the Iron Brigade, was strong. One Wisconsin black hat wrote in his diary for June 17th the news about the rebels was "exciting, but I think we shall be enough for the Johnnys when we get at them. The Iron Brigade has always acquitted themselves like men and they can do so again after we get a little rest."[13]

That same day, with the division bivouacked at Guilford Station, Virginia, Jerome Watrous and Earl Rogers (Rogers known by all as "Bona," for a fancied resemblance to Napoleon Bonaparte), "thinking a 'square meal' in a Virginia mansion would relieve the monotony of hard tack and fat pork," rode out in the country a couple of miles and were "hospitably entertained." Rebel partisans had dogged the marching Union columns the past few days, but the lure of a "square meal" outweighed caution and the two gave it no thought. Just before dusk, after tea, they made their good-byes and began the ride back to the army. About one-half mile into a heavy woods, the Wisconsin men came upon six or eight men in gray uniforms. "Quick as a flash, they were in their saddles and rushing in our direction," Watrous recalled. "Not caring to make the acquaintance of so many of Mosby's men all at once, we wheeled in our saddles, gave them two or three shots from our navy revolvers, and put spurs to our horses. The last half mile of that ride in the woods has no legal or moral right to be compared with the first half mile." (Watrous always enjoyed telling the story, and he related it 24 years later at an old soldier dinner in Milwaukee. The guest of honor was a former rebel of some reputation, one John Singleton Mosby, to whom Watrous bowed and smiled as he added: "As one soldier of the Grand old Army of the Potomac, I take this occasion to thank our guest for his efficiency as a file-closer of the Union Army.")[14]

Rogers and Watrous made much of their narrow escape, but at Broad Run in Virginia, where the brigade halted June 20, there

12. *Ibid.*, June 15, 1863; Dawes, *Service*, p. 151-152.
13. Walker, Diary.
14. Jerome A. Watrous, "Mosby and His Men," *War Papers*, Vol. 2, (Milwaukee, 1896), pp. 303-307.

was a more important matter—a mail call. Dawes received 12 letters, and one hopes most were from Miss Mary Beman Gates of Marietta, Ohio. They had met a year earlier at her home culminating in a heated discussion over the military abilities of one George B. McClellan. Happily, Dawes would write later, those differences, and indeed all others, were resolved. "She was twenty years of age, and of her charming qualities of mind and person it is not for my partial pen to write."[15] At the start of the march to Gettysburg, he had written her: "The regiment will go out strong in health and cheerful in spirit, and determined always to sustain its glorious history. It has been my ardent ambition to lead it through one campaign, and now the indications are that my opportunity has come. If I do anything glorious I shall expect you to be proud of me."[16] (They would marry within six months, and she would save his letters, and he hers, and nearly 30 years later the letters would become a most important component of Dawes' history of his regiment).[17]

The column marched through a region not previously devastated by either army, and foraging was good, so plentiful, in fact, that not only were privates and non-commissioned officers involved, but line officers as well. "Shoulder straps were becoming so numerous among the raiders," one Brigade soldier recalled, that a circular was sent down from First Corps headquarters June 20, establishing a camp guard to surround Wadsworth's and the other divisions. It was an order designed more to keep hungry Union soldiers from the nearby loyal farms (and especially loyal chicken coops) than to keep the rebel soldiers at bay. The circular reached the Iron Brigade June 21st, and the next day, Commander

15. Dawes, *Service*, p. 154.
16. *Ibid.*, p. 151.
17. Of New England ancestry, Mary Gates attended public schools in Marietta until her 18th year, when she was sent to the Female Seminary at Ipswich, Massachusetts. Her father also arranged for her to visit New York, Philadelphia and Washington, opportunities rarely accorded young Ohio women in the 1860s. She married Rufus Dawes January 18, 1864. "It became the part of the young wife at home to follow with mental anguish the varying fortunes of her husband through the fearful fighting of the succeeding summer [of 1864]," her daughter, Mary Frances (Dawes) Beach, wrote of her mother. "In after years she could seldom bring herself to speak of these months when she waited and watched for news from the front." Rufus Dawes died in 1899, and Mary lived 22 years longer. Mary Frances (Dawes) Beach, "Mary Beman (Gates) Dawes," *Dawes-Gates Ancestral Lines*, A Memorial Volume Containing the American Ancestry of Mary Beman (Gates) Dawes, Vol. II, Compiled by Mary Walton Ferris, privately printed, 1931.

Solomon Meredith issued an order forming a "Brigade Guard" to be "mounted at the same hour each day when circumstances will permit until further orders." The detail was to be made up of 30 privates from the 2nd Wisconsin, 15 from the 6th Wisconsin, 20 each from the 7th Wisconsin and 19th Indiana, and 29 privates from the 24th Michigan. Each regiment was to supply one sergeant and one corporal, with the exception of the 24th Michigan, which was to supply two corporals in addition to the lone sergeant.

Meredith's order contained a curious paragraph. From the details would be selected "each day one Sergeant, three corporals and fourteen privates for special guard duty at HeadQrs." The men were to be picked "with special reference to cleanliness and soldierly bearing," and they were to be brought to the guard formation about 9 a.m., "band playing."[18]

No reason was given for the makeup of the "special" headquarters detail. Given the hard marching as the Iron Brigade and the

18. General Order No. 24, Order Book, 1st Brigade, 1st Division, 1st Army Corps.
Headquarters, 1st Brig. 1st Div. 1st A.C.
Near Guilford Station, Va.
June 22, 1863
    General Order
No. 24.
    A Brigade Guard will be mounted at 9 a.m. tomorrow, June 23d, under the direction of Capt. Wood A.A.G. Such Brigade Guard will be mounted at the same hour each day when circumstances will permit until further orders.
    The following is the detail for June 23d.
    The 2d Wis. One Captain for Officer of the day. The 7th Wis. one First Lieut. and the 24th Mich. one 2d Lieut. as officers of the guard.
    2nd Wis. Vol. One Sergt., One Corpl. and 30 Privates.
    6th Wis. Vol. One Sergt., One Corpl. and 15 Privates.
    7th Wis. Vol. One Sergt., One Corpl. and 20 Privates.
    19th Ind. Vol. One Sergt., One Corpl. and 20 Privates.
    24th Mich. Vol. One Sergt., Two Corpl. and 29 Privates.
    From the above details there will be selected each day one Sergeant, three Corporals and fourteen Privates for special guard duty at HeadQrs.
    The detail will be chosen with special reference to cleanliness and soldierly bearing.
    The Adjutant of the 6th Wis. Vol. will act as Adjutant of the day for the 23d Inst. He will be assisted by the Sergt. Maj. from the same regiment.
    The Drummer of the Brigade Band will sound the Guard call when the several details are turned out upon their respective Regimental Parade Ground and be thoroughly inspected after which they will be conducted by the senior officer to the guard formation, band playing.
    By Command of
Brig. Gen. Meredith
J. D. Wood
A.A.G.

147

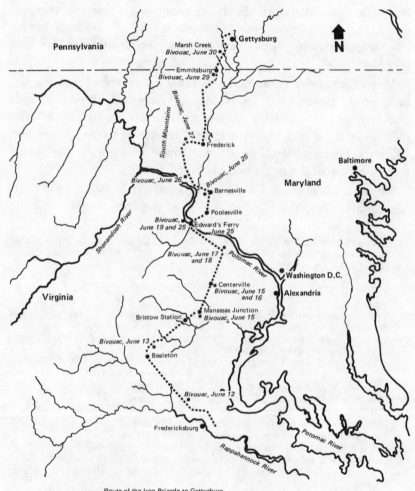

Pennsylvania

Gettysburg

Marsh Creek
Bivouac, June 30

N

Emmitsburg
Bivouac, June 29

Bivouac, June 27

South Mountains

Frederick

Bivouac, June 26

Bivouac, June 25

Barnesville

Maryland

Baltimore

Poolesville

Shenandoah River

Bivouac,
June 19 and 25

Edward's Ferry
June 25

Potomac River

Bivouac, June 17
and 18

Washington D.C.

Centerville
Bivouac, June 15
and 16

Alexandria

Virginia

Bristow Station

Manassas Junction
Bivouac, June 15

Bivouac, June 13

Bealeton

Bivouac, June 12

Fredericksburg

Potomac River

Rappahannock River

▪▪▪▪ Route of the Iron Brigade to Gettysburg
▪ Bivouac sites, 1863

Mary Slough

rest of the Army of the Potomac pushed to keep up with the northward moving rebels, it would seem unlikely a commander would require his brigade's guards to turn out each morning with the "band playing." Somehow, the ceremonial turnout and "special" headquarters detail smacked of Roman spear bearers to satisfy the enormous ego of Indiana politician Meredith.

But despite his political posturing and his earlier squabbling with General John Gibbon, the boys in the ranks always liked the imposing officer they called "Long Sol." Meredith, who had come from humble North Carolina beginnings to make a name for himself in Indiana, had come a long way up from far down (as they put it at the time), and the boys understood the blunt, loud Western style of the former backwoods stump speaker. They also admired his bravery. "Mickey" Sullivan always said Meredith took double the risk in battle because he was twice as big as most men, and he recalled how, on one occasion, "Long Sol" had called on the boys for "three backwoods cheers, and three more and a tiger!"[19] Ironically, Meredith's Brigade Guard would play a key role in the upcoming clash of infantry at Gettysburg, certainly a more important one than anyone could have envisioned.

One of the details "guarding" the Iron Brigade contained soldiers from Company K of the 6th Wisconsin. They came in one late afternoon "in the highest kind of glee, shouting, whooping and hellowing as though they were all 'filled with new wine.'" The story made the campfire rounds that evening. As "old soldiers," the Badger men had marched their beats as strictly ordered:

If a private soldier came along the guard turned and walked the other way and didn't see [him]. A private soldier on horse back was every where passed as a mounted orderly. But when a commissioned officer came along the boys were only too glad—yea, suffering for an opportunity to do their full duty; no manner of reasoning, coaxing, persuading, stamping, swearing, or threatening could prevail.

The recorder of the incident told of one exchange (which prob-

19. James P. Sullivan, "Charge of the Iron Brigade at Fitzhugh's Crossing," *Milwaukee Sunday Telegraph*, September 30, 1883.

ably improved in the two decades he had to think it over). It came as one 6th Wisconsin private halted a mounted field officer, galloping forward "with the air of one 'born to rule.'"

What the hell you doing here?
Doing guard duty, sir. You can't pass this way.
Who put you on guard here?
Gen. Meredith.
What are your instructions?
To pass nothing but generals and mounted orderlies.
Well you get out of the way and let me pass.
Can't do it, sir. I've got positive orders.
Well, I don't care for your orders; I'm going past.
No you ain't; this gun's loaded, and I will shoot you if you attempt it.
But I've got important dispatches for General Doubleday.
All right; you go back and give them to a mounted orderly and he'll take 'em out.
Well, this beats thunder.
I expect it does, but I can't help it.

The fuming officer turned away and rode back. A short time later, similar reports coming in from other quarters, the guard was relieved as unnecessary.[20]

The story of the sly private broke the boredom, at least for a time, but the hard marching along what one soldier remembered as "a long and weary road"[21] soon again consumed all attention and energy. One of tthe near-victims was a "fat cheeked, sleepy boy" from the Jayhawkers in Company C. Dawes remembered the young private had been brought in by a divisional guard detail for sleeping on his picket post. The penalty for such offense, in the presence of the enemy, was death. "The poor fellow . . . [who] slept because of a big supper on rebel chicken, was sadly frightened," Dawes wrote home. "That demon, official duty, required that I should prefer charges and send him to a general court martial for trial. But with a sharp lecture and warning, I released him from arrest and sent him to his company." The

20. Harries, MOLLUS, October 8, 1895, Second Wisconsin, p. 272.
21. John A. Kress, "At Gettysburg," Missouri Republican, December 4, 1886. Kress was an aide to General James Wadsworth.

officer also recalled how, in that incident at least, dodging his duty "gave me pleasure."[22]

The column clumped across the pontoon bridge over the Potomac River at Edward's Ferry into Maryland, and Loyd Harris, the young commander of the Prairie du Chien Guards of Company C, remembered several incidents during the seemingly endless days of marching, one about a soldier who lost his eggs and another involving a pretty girl.

Harris, who after the war had a nice way of turning a good yarn into a better one, said the first encounter started in the 2nd Wisconsin, as a staff officer of I Corps Commander John Reynolds rode along the marching column. The boys in the 2nd took up a shout, "Hen's eggs! Hen's eggs! Hen's eggs!" keeping it up until the young aide hunkered down in his saddle, spurred his horse and hurried away. Somewhat astonished and puzzled by the outcry, 2nd Wisconsin Commander Lucius Fairchild rode along his marching regiment, warning that he would punish the next man who raised the cry "Hen's eggs."

The whole uproar caused much wonder in the ranks of the 6th, and that night some of the boys wandered over to the 2nd Wisconsin camp to get the story. It seemed, Harris recalled, one of the 2nd Wisconsin men, "desiring to do justice to his stomach, that had in his opinion been somewhat neglected, invested his hard earned money in two dozen fresh eggs." Carefully nesting them in his black hat, he was on his way to rejoin his regiment, thinking "some they would fry and the rest 'bile' for the next day," when he was halted abruptly by the mounted staff officer and his orderly. "Give me those eggs," demanded the officer. "But captain, I bought them and want them for my use," answered the hapless private. The officer snorted, "Bought them? I don't believe any such story." Other words were exchanged, and finally the private surrendered his prize. The Wisconsin men always believed, somehow, the eggs found their way to the captain's table. It was shabby treatment, the Badger men agreed with solemn faces and shaking of heads, and they decided on a plan.

The next day, the marked captain again passed along the line, and the high privates in not only the 2nd, but the 6th Regiment as well, set up "such cock-crowing and cackling" never

22. Rufus R. Dawes, Letter, to Mary Gates, June 24, 1863; Dawes, *Service*, pp. 155-156. The sleepy private was William P. Armstrong of Prairie du Chien.

"heard before in the whole army." Fairchild, with more heat this time, passed a new order: no more "hen's eggs" or "crowing and cackling as well." Now, the blood of the Badger soldiers was up, and they were not to be denied the voicing of their displeasure with the young officer. On the third day, the whole brigade had heard the story and "hen's fever" had spread through the ranks. Again the captain appeared, and this time, a "thousand throats" began to chant, over and over, "Hen's fruit! Hen's fruit! Hen's fruit!" until the red-faced officer scurried off to escape the taunts. Harris wrote later he always thought that the young officer found it "so hot among 'those western men,' that he resigned his position on the staff and resumed his place with his company with another corps." And he added his own footnote: "From every old soldier methinks I hear the response, 'Served him right.' "[23]

The other incident triggered several minutes of delightful confusion as the column neared the Pennsylvania line. Harris remembered a "beautiful girl, scarcely twenty" (he always had an admiring eye for the ladies) came to the gate of her home, waving a large American flag at the marching men. At the head of the 6th Wisconsin, Dawes and the other officers doffed hats and bowed, but the men in the ranks were smitten to silence. Harris said "every last man seemed ready to give his life if necessary for that patriot, yet did not seem to know just what to do." The young officer took matters in hand, ordering his men to bring their rifle-muskets to "Right shoulder, shift!" It was a bright moment in his memory 20 years later:

> They caught the idea; every head was up; the fours perfectly aligned—then as we were just opposite the maiden, I commanded, "Carry arms!" Down came the very bright shining muskets. The next company did the same and all the companies of the Iron Brigade as they passed gave her a salute as if she were general of the army.

Harris had one additional comment:

23. [Loyd G. Harris], "Hen's Fruit, A War Story," *Milwaukee Sunday Telegraph*, June 6, 1880. As usual, Harris wrote using his middle name, "Grayson." The aide was probably William H. Wilcox, a member of Reynolds' staff during the Gettysburg campaign. Edward J. Nichols, *Toward Gettysburg*, (University Park, Pennsylvania, 1958), p. 213.

It remains an unwritten history whether she full realized the compliment; yet as a rich blush glowed over her face she no doubt felt that in some way the veterans were saying by their action, "thank you pretty miss for your loyal efforts."

A short distance further on, the regiment came upon something Company C Private Billy Florence called "immensely practical." A "very nice matron, sort of 'fair, fat and forty,' instead of waving the old flag" had brought her table to the roadside and on it placed a "large jar of apple butter, surrounded by a breastwork of bread." Those "Maryland and Pennsylvania loaves . . . seemed to me more the size and shape of a gunny sack filled with corn and my mouth waters now when I think how good they were," Loyd Harris said later in describing the scene. The woman, her sleeves rolled up, stood behind the table loaded with large slices of bread well spread with apple butter. She smiled and offered the lunch to the men of the 6th:

> To my amazement, the first company passed by without taking any. I noticed an air of embarrassment with the good lady, and felt like throwing something at those stupid boys. They had been away from "America" and in the southern confederacy for so long a period where they either paid for or borrowed everything, that they were afraid the lady might want a half of a dollar a slice.

After the first company marched silently by, German Company F, whose boys were "always hungry" for good "brodt," neared the table. Harris walked over. "Pitch in boys," he said quietly, and the shy Germans did with smiles and nods. The lads in his Company C required no invitation and "in a very respectful manner some carried away the slices already prepared, many saying a hearty 'Thank you, ma'am.'" The young officer moved on, remembering the "matron's arms were flying like the rods of a locomotive, spreading the apple butter," and he smiled and decided it "will make some think of the good old mothers at home."[24]

24. [Loyd G. Harris], "Fredrick City [sic] to Gettysburg," *Milwaukee Sunday Telegraph*, January 25, 1885; Doc [Cullen B.] Aubery, *Recollections of a Newsboy in the Army of the Potomac, 1861-1865*, (Milwaukee, 1900), pp. 111-112.

But an aide to Division Commander James Wadsworth, John A. Kress of the 94th New York Infantry, remembered a less friendly welcome in Maryland and Pennsylvania:

> We had looked forward with great expectations to the pleasant campaigning to be experienced in the North, to be welcomed as deliverers of the country from a hated foe, to live on the fat of the land, milk, chickens, honey, eggs, butter and potatoes in profusion, without much money, and not at very high price. Bitter was the disappointment and sour the buttermilk doled out at 25 cents a glass, and other things in proportion.[25]

The roads were very rough, Kress recalled, and the need to replace the worn-out shoes of the soldiers became critical; so much so, in fact, General Wadsworth ordered the "seizure of every pair of suitable boots and shoes" that could be obtained along the road. "They were frequently taken from the feet of citizens and transferred immediately to the pedal extermities of bare-foot soldiers," said Kress, remembering one incident:

> The general and his staff officers rode up to a fine stone flour mill, the proprietor of which sat on the steps looking at the troops marching past. The miller was a middle-aged man of well-to-do appearances, fairly well dressed in flour-dusted gray clothing. Gen. Wadsworth bade him "good morning," and, as he did so, noticed that the miller wore an excellent pair of shoes. The general halted, and not having time to make examinations, asked him if he had any boots or shoes. The miller said he had none.
>
> "You have a fine pair of shoes on your feet, sir, I will take them, if you please, for one of my bare-footed soldiers."
>
> "No, sir; you shall not take the shoes off my feet; I am a free American citizen, the owner of this mill and of much of the property hereabouts; I will not submit to such an outrage."

25. Kress, *Republican*, December 4, 1886.

"I must have the shoes and cannot waste time parley-
ing with you."

Turning to an aide, the general directed him to have
two or three of the orderlies dismount and remove the
man's shoes. The miller concluded that discretion was
the better part of valor and gave up his shoes.[26]

The regiments of Wadsworth's Division camped Saturday, June
27, just north of Middletown, Maryland, the soldiers much used-up.
Sergeant George Fairfield wrote in his pocket diary that his Company C, and others from additional companies, were on picket duty
near "an old man's house who owns but 1 acre of land. He
seemed to live well. His right arm was badly palsied." Fairfield
noted the distance covered that day—10 miles. On Sunday, the
column moved toward Frederick, Maryland, arriving after dark:
another 10 miles covered. Rain made the roads so muddy and
slippery that the men had to march in the fields alongside them.
Fairfield did not find the incident with the private who lost his
eggs, or the pretty girl and her flag, or the matron with her apple
butter of significance; there was no mention of them in his diary.[27]

That Sabbath morning, before the columns moved through
Frederick, the two officers of Company C, Loyd Harris and Orrin
D. Chapman, enjoyed a pleasant hour. The company was on picket
duty with "no enemies within miles of us," Harris said, when
young Chapman "scraped an acquaintance" with a farmer and his
family. The farmer had a "very good parlor organ" and it was
carried outside to the porch. Some hymn books were found. And,
with the Crawford County boys of Company C clustered around
the porch listening, the farmer's daughters singing the soprano,
the old man a deep bass, and Harris and Chapman joining in "on
the still quiet air of that bright sunny morning," the group sang:

> The morning light is breaking—
> The darkness disappears.
> The sons of earth awaken
> To penitential tears;
> Each breeze that sweeps the ocean,
> Brings tidings from afar,

26. *Ibid.*
27. Walker Diary; Fairfield Diary.

Of Nations in commotion,
Prepare for Zion's War.

That Sunday night, after an easy march of only 10 miles, Harris, Chapman, and John Ticknor of Company K gathered to sing with Gilbert Woodward of the 2nd Wisconsin and Amos Rood of the 7th. A comrade remembered the officers ("all young, brave and handsome") had earlier formed a musical society to entertain the boys. One of the first members, Captain Edwin A. Brown of Company E of the 6th, had been killed at Antietam. At previous programs, he had always been the one to call out with a cheery smile, "Now let's sing 'Benny,'" for "Benny Havens, O" was a great camp favorite, but now, the veteran recalled, there was always "an unwonted tremor in the voices" as the officers sang that song. The Frederick medley was the "sweetest, and strange as it may seem, saddest music ever heard." Perhaps it was the off-hand remark by Chapman as the officers broke up, the young man wondering aloud if they would ever sing together again. They never did. After Gettysburg, the regimental officers refused to sing "Benny," and Harris admitted he was one of them. That night, as he and Chapman pulled on their blankets, Harris remembered Chapman remarking, "That singing [this morning] was like my old home. It is the best treat I've had for many months."[28]

The next day, Monday, the 29th of June, the column marched in a "mist like rain," passing through several towns and finally, Emmitsburg, Maryland, before camping in a field at sunset. The march was 26 miles. It rained again the next morning. The 6th Wisconsin was in the advance and was the first regiment to cross into Pennsylvania.[29] Wadsworth's small division of two brigades was in front of the rest of the Army of the Potomac. The Confederate army was even farther north and west, but the Union soldiers were unaware of it. The division moved only about four miles before camping at noon near Marsh Creek, south of the Adams County borough of Gettysburg in Pennsylvania.[30]

The Marsh Creek bivouac was a damp but pleasant one. The

28. [Harris], *Telegraph*, November 12, 1882; [Harris], *Telegraph*, November 26, 1882; [Jerome A. Watrous], *Milwaukee Sunday Telegraph*, August 24, 1884. The incidents of hymn-singing and refusal to sing "Benny Havens, O" after Gettysburg were told by Harris. The story of the officers was signed by "Camp Fire," a pseudonym for editor Jerome A. Watrous.
29. Dawes, Letter, to Mary Gates, June 30, 1863; Dawes, *Service*, p. 158.
30. Fairfield Diary.

6th Wisconsin and other regiments in the Brigade were mustered for pay. The completed rolls of the regiment showed a total of 359 enlisted men, but 22 were absent on other duties and 16 were sick. The regiment's combat strength was 321, plus 21 officers. It was also time to settle up with Uncle Sam for extra clothing and equipment drawn in May and June. In Company A, Private Bodley Jones owed $9.25, while Company B Corporal James Kelly paid $10, and Private Charles Keeler, $15. Sergeant George Fairfield of Company C, who kept an orderly diary, was also meticulous about equipment and uniforms, especially if he had to pay for them. He owed only $1.30.[31]

Dawes also formed the ranks of the 6th Wisconsin to read to the soldiers an address from newly named Army of the Potomac Commander George Gordon Meade, appointed two days earlier to replace Hooker. There was little enthusiasm. Meade was not well known, and Dawes noted in a latter home that night he was somewhat surprised by the move.[32] The soldier campfire talk was the command should have gone to Major General John Reynolds of the First Corps, and some discussed the possibility that former commander George McClellan might be just off-stage, ready to ride back to the army, waving that little cap of his with a twirl to let his boys know things were going to be all right in the end.[33] A century later, it is difficult to understand this affection for "Little Mac," in light of his failures outside Richmond and at Antietam the previous year, but it was there—a faith that he would lead them to victory and not sacrifice them without cause.

But that created only a minor stir. The regimental officers turned to nagging paperwork, and the soldiers tried to dry out, hanging damp clothing across their small tents, cleaning equipment and resting sore feet. Company I Commander William Remington nursed a cold he picked up marching in the rain the past week. He wrapped cloths around his neck and head to ease the discomfort.[34]

31. Muster Roll for two months ending June 30, 1863, 6th Wisconsin Volunteer Infantry. The amounts owed are from the Muster Rolls for Companies A, B and C, covering the same period. The Regimental Muster Roll shows the following enlisted men present for duty: Field Staff 5; Co. A 15, Co. B 32, Co. C 36, Co. D 28, Co. E 26, Co. F 46, Co. G 31, Co. H 34, Co. I 34, Co. K 34.
32. Dawes, Letter, to Mary Gates, June 30, 1863; Dawes, *Service*, pp. 157-158.
33. Augustus Buell, *The Cannoneer*, (Washington, D.C., 1897), p. 61.
34. U.S. Pension Office, William Remington File.

Cutler's 2nd Brigade camped in a cultivated field south of Marsh Creek, while the 6th Wisconsin and the other Iron Brigade regiments erected their tents on the north bank. Water spilling over a nearby mill dam attracted some of the boys, and they ambled over to wash clothing and frolic. Others surveyed nearby farms for food, and Private Sullivan of Company K made arrangements with a Pennsylvania farmer for a canteen of milk, or at least that was his official story.[35] He had a good working knowledge of cows, and certainly there were several about, far from the watchful eyes of their owners.

In the afternoon, as the soldiers drew rations, some cavalry clattered up the Emmitsburg road—General John Buford's men. Some infantry wandered over to watch the horse soldiers and exchanged pointed banter. The cavalrymen had some news: Johnnies just ahead, and in great numbers.[36] But the infantrymen shrugged off the report and returned to their chores. Horse soldiers were a shiftless lot, the black hats agreed, and known to frighten easily. That night, some of the Wisconsin soldiers sniffed the air and caught whiffs of roasting chicken from the camps of the New York and Pennsylvania regiments in the 2nd Brigade.[37] There was no record the Badger men were as successful in their forays to neighboring farms.

At his tent, Harris displayed a harmonica he purchased from a music store while passing through Frederick. It was a "simple affair," he admitted, "yet if well played makes enjoyable music." Chapman was his audience that night. It was all very sad later, for one of the songs he played was "Home, Sweet Home," and Chapman, the Westfield, New York, boy who enlisted as a private at Prairie du Chien, and who had been promoted to Second Lieutenant just five months earlier, listened quietly to the haunting

35. James P. Sullivan, "The Old Iron Brigade at Gettysburg," *Milwaukee Sunday Telegraph*, December 20, 1884. Three versions of Sullivan's account of Gettysburg have been found: James P. Sullivan, "The Old Iron Brigade at Gettysburg," *Mauston Star*, March 22, 1883 and March 29, 1883; J. P. Sullivan, "The Charge of the Iron Brigade at Gettysburg," *Vernon County Censor*, August 1, 1883 and August 8, 1883; "Mickey, of Company K," [James P. Sullivan], "The Charge at Gettysburg," *Milwaukee Sunday Telegraph*, December 20, 1884 and December 28, 1884. The first two are almost identical, but *Telegraph* editor Jerome A. Watrous edited some of Sullivan's more critical comments from the version printed in his Milwaukee newspaper.
36. Buell, *Cannoneer*, p. 61.
37. Tevis and Marquis, pp. 80-81.

melody, "little dreaming that before the noon of the coming day he would be killed in the great battle of the war."[38]

The Wisconsin men bivouacked on Marsh Creek had marched a good many miles since being called together at Camp Randall at Madison in 1861. The soldiers were much changed after two years of war, and the written record left by 6th Wisconsin men about those months revealed more than they intended. The Badgers didn't quite understand all of it, at the time or with 20 years' hindsight. The bright hopes of 1861 were tarnished by 1863. The good and brave soldiers died too easily because they were good and brave. J. P. Sullivan could write of the death of his friend, George Chamberlain, and his wound at South Mountain in an almost lighthearted fashion, but there was no expression of mourning for Chamberlain, almost as if, nearly a quarter of a century later, something was better left unsaid. The soldiers camped at Marsh Creek were in close, tight little squads, drawing on each other for support. While they marched and died, enduring unspeakable hardship, the homefolk "growled" about high prices and short money. The army casually tossed out the used-up soldier, and the "patriotic" speculators fleeced him of 10 percent of his pay. Bragg and Sullivan wrote the soldiers fought well, but were denied victory by incompetent generals. Officers used their rank to steal a private's eggs and to get through sentry posts to forage. Sam Wallar could shoot a deserter in the same offhand fashion a farmer kills a hog.

The march that began June 12th and ended June 30th on Marsh Creek was perhaps the most grueling of the war for the Wisconsin men, but, decades later, the memory of those three weeks was selective: forgotten were the dust, heat, thirst, muddy roads, poor food and worse water, sore feet, heavy straggling and false starts and stops; remembered were the pretty girl waving a flag, the singing around campfires and the matron passing out apple butter to passing soldiers.

Only one of three soldiers was still in ranks from the regiment of 1861, the others dead from battle or illness, scores more sent home sick and disabled; some gone who knows where. The survivors were emotionally dependent on the men of their campfire and then on the small companies and slightly less on their regi-

38. [Harris], *Telegraph*, January 25, 1885.

ment and brigade. They felt isolated from the homefolk, misused by their generals and the country's leaders, cheated by sutlers, snubbed by the Eastern soldiers because of their Western origin; trusting only their comrades in battle and immediate officers who had proved to be skillful and brave. They were a hard lot, good soldiers, proud of their fighting reputation. And the next day, the Badger men would fight the battle they always regarded as the turning point of the Civil War. In many ways, Gettysburg would be the last great battle for the "Boys of '61," those bright volunteers who flocked to the flag. The army itself was changing. In the camps, the veteran soldiers were unsettled by the appearance of recruits who enlisted to collect bounties, and disgusted more by the trickle of drafted men reaching the front. After Gettysburg, the Army of the Potomac, the Iron Brigade and the 6th Wisconsin would be different, partly due to a change in the way the war was fought, and partly to the men being brought in to fill the battle-diminshed regiments. But late in the war and afterwards, at the great old soldier reunions and campfires, even those bounty and drafted men would be accepted, simply because they were there and shared the hardship while the stay-at-homes had not.

But the Wisconsin men camped near Gettysburg would do their duty. There was something of the "Western" frontier mentality in all this, a quiet determination to see the job through with the same resolve it took to clear a field of stones, build a rail fence or wait out a Wisconsin winter. Part of it was typified in the words of John Ticknor on the death of Reuben Huntley at South Mountain: Huntley was "doing good work" that late afternoon. Some of it was in the off-hand remark by Sullivan, as he reenlisted for nine months, that chances were good that he would be killed before the term was up, but he was going anyway. The time of brave bayonet charges in the sunlight and stand-up battle lines was passing, the fighting grim and brutal now, but the soldiers, despite realizing the war was not what they expected, did not want to give up entirely on those bright expectations of 1861. But there was to be one more shining moment for the Wisconsin "Boys of '61" sleeping at Marsh Creek, and it was coming up fast at an unfinished railroad near the Chambersburg Pike west of Gettysburg.

The 6th Wisconsin men were awakened before daybreak the Wednesday morning of July 1st for a "hearty breakfast of coffee and hardtack" before packing their "traps."[39] The brigade ordnance wagons rumbled through camp. An order from Army headquarters the day before directed Corps commanders to provide the men with "60 rounds of ammunition in the boxes and upon the person."[40] The Wisconsin Black Hats shoved two packets of 10 cartridges each in the tin containers of their cartridge boxes, broke open two more and put the individual paper cartridges in readiness at the top of the tins. The paper twists containing percussion caps were also broken open and the caps added to the small leather boxes looped to their waist belts. The remaining two packets of cartridges were stuffed into haversacks, knapsacks and pockets, or tossed into the grass at the first opportunity; the veterans were much stripped down for hard marching and not carrying extra weight.[41]

Dawes had started a letter the night before to Mary Gates. "I don't think I ever before saw at this time of year such continued, misty, drizzling storms as we have been marching through since we crossed the Potomac," he related. "I am kept full of business on such hurried marches, scarcely from morning to night getting a moment I can call my own." At the top he had written, "June 30th, Bivouac in Pennsylvania on Marsh Creek near Gettysburg." This morning, he added a few quick lines: "July 1st A.M. Orders have just come 'pack up, be ready to march immediately.' I will finish this letter the first chance I get.[42]

As the 6th Wisconsin soldiers began forming their companies, some observed Cutler's Brigade already marching onto the roadway. The soldiers also watched General Reynolds and his staff lead off the day's march, followed by Division Commander Wadsworth and his aides. The men in the ranks respected the quiet Reynolds, a Regular Army officer. One Wisconsin soldier recalled how, on the long or short march, the general would send an aide to the regiments with word whether there was time to make coffee. "If we did not receive that order no man started a fire, and

39. Sullivan, *Telegraph*, December 20, 1884.
40. *O.R.*, Series One, Vol. 27, Part Three, pp. 416-417.
41. A study of the reports concerning the ammunition issued to the I Corps at Gettysburg determined the 8,700 soldiers expended about 68 rounds per man. See Dean S. Thomas, *Ready . . . Aid . . . Fire . . ., Small Arms Ammunition in the Battle of Gettysburg*, (Biglerville, Pennsylvania, 1981), p. 13.
42. Rufus R. Dawes, Letter, to Mary Gates, June 30, 1863, July 1, 1863; Dawes, *Service*, pp. 157-158.

during the whole march there was never a fire lighted in vain."[43] Then, Cutler's regiments swung past, followed by Hall's 2nd Maine Battery. The 2nd Brigade's 7th Indiana was left behind to guard the division wagon train.[44]

Meredith was slow ordering his men to "Fall In" and Cutler's Brigade got well ahead—almost a mile—before General Wadsworth sent a galloper with orders to "close up" on Cutler. The Iron Brigade filed onto the roadway. The 2nd Wisconsin led the way, followed by the 7th Wisconsin. A short distance ahead, the soldiers of the 19th Indiana, which had been on sentry duty, filed onto the roadway behind the 7th. The 24th Michigan closed up behind the Indianans. The 6th Wisconsin marched last, followed by the Brigade Guard of 100 men and two officers.[45]

An artilleryman in Battery B, 4th U.S., watched the two brigades: "The little creek made a depression in the road, with a gentle ascent on each side, so that from our point of view the column as it came down one slope and up the other, had the effect of huge blue billows of men topped with a spray of shining steel, and the whole spectacle was calculated to give nerve to a man who had none before." There were some Wisconsin men in the battery, and some friendly joshing developed as the infantry column rolled past. "Tell the Johnnies we will be right along," an artilleryman yelled. One of the infantrymen had a quick answer: "All right. Better stay here till we send for you."[46]

The regiment, Dawes remembered, was in "high spirits" that pleasant morning, the boys full of fun.[47] Before long, the Mil-

43. R. K. Beecham, *Gettysburg*, (Chicago, 1911), p. 120. Beecham was in the 2nd Wisconsin.
44. *O.R.*, Series One, Vol. 27, Part One, Report of General James S. Wadsworth, commanding 1st Division, pp. 265-267; Report of Colonel Henry A. Morrow, 24th Michigan, pp. 267-278; Report of Major John Mansfield, 2nd Wisconsin, pp. 273-275; Report of Lieutenant Colonel Rufus R. Dawes, 6th Wisconsin, pp. 275-278; Report of Colonel William Robinson, 7th Wisconsin, pp. 278-281; Report of Major General Abner Doubleday, commanding 3rd Division, I Army Corps, pp. 243-257. A hand-written copy of Dawes' Gettysburg report, dated July 17, 1863, shows slight editing. The text of that report is used if it differs from the printed version.
45. 45. Earl M. Rogers, "The Second, or Fifty-Sixth—Which?" *Milwaukee Sunday Telegraph*, June 22, 1884. Rogers quotes his brother, Clayton, an aide to General Wadsworth, as saying the gap was "one mile" due to Meredith's "delay in giving orders . . ."; *O.R.*, Series One, Vol. 27, Part One, Doubleday's Report, p. 245.
46. Buell, *Cannoneer*, pp. 63-64.
47. Dawes, *Telegraph*, p. 164.

waukee Germans in Company F started a "soul stirring song" in their native tongue, "such as only the Germans can sing." The regiment took up the step and gave the Milwaukeeans three rousing cheers. Then the bully Juneau County boys in Company K, with "about as much melody as a government mule," Sullivan later admitted, picked up a tune of their own. It began:

On the distant prairie, where the heifer wild,
Stole into the cabbage, in the moonlight mild.
Everyone that knew her said she was a thief,
And should be killed and quartered and issued out for
beef.

There were a number of verses, and the whole marching column roared the chorus, "On the distant prairie, Hoop de dooden doo," scattering livestock in nearby pastures and getting curious stares from the local folk who had ventured out to see the marching army. The song went on and on without seeming end, Sullivan remembered, chorus after booming chorus, until the whole line broke down in laughter and catcalls. Private Thomas Flynn of Company K rendered "Paddy's Wedding," and finally the boys settled down. Sullivan said later he found it "odd for men to march toward their death singing, shouting and laughing as if it were parade or holiday."[48] Some cavalry and artillery hurried up the Emmitsburg Road, causing the marching column of the 6th Wisconsin to open right and left. As they passed, Flynn, always one with a sharp Gaelic remark, gave them "a parting benediction" that turned out to be a prediction: "May the devil fly away with the roofs of your jackets; yez going now to get us into a scrape and thin walk off and let us fight it out like you always do."[49] None of the Wisconsin soldiers left a record of undue haste or concern those first miles from the Marsh Creek bivouac to Gettysburg. Loyd Harris remembered the column "plodded along."[50] Meticulous diarist George Fairfield of Company C termed it a march of "unusual quietude."[51]

Ahead, Cutler's men halted near an orchard, to rest and allow

48. Sullivan, *Telegraph*, December 20, 1884.
49. *Ibid.*
50. [Harris], *Telegraph*, February 15, 1885.
51. Fairfield Diary.

the Iron Brigade to close the gap. Lieutenant Colonel Dawes recalled it "was a beautiful morning."[52] and he decided to "make a show on the streets of Gettysburg." He passed instructions to Adjutant Edward Brooks and the company commanders. The sheath was pulled off the National flag, the ranks closed and the drum corps moved to the front of the regiment. Drum Major R. N. Smith directed his fifers and drummers to strike up the fierce rallying song of the clans, "The Campbells are Coming." Dawes remembered he had selected the song "through a fancy that the people would infer that 'the rebels are running,' or would run very soon after so fine a body of soldiers as the 6th Wisconsin then was, confronted them."[53]

No one would ever again see the 6th Wisconsin of that morning of July 1, 1863, as it tramped toward Gettysburg. The drum corps, all feverish thumping and shrill piping (famed Drum Major Whaley gone home, but his dash still part of the tradition of the fifers and drummers) passed first, followed by the "Star Rifles" of Company G from Beloit. The talky men from the Mississippi River country, the Jayhawkers of Company C, were the second company, with quiet Lieutenant Orrin Chapman in command and, in ranks, Cornelius Okey and Sergeant George Fairfield; Okey ready to seize a moment of glory if it came his way, and Fairfield already thinking about his nightly diary entry. The Jayhawkers were followed by the bully Juneau County boys of Company K: bright-eyed James P. "Mickey" Sullivan, Tommy Flynn, unsoldierly Jimmy Scoville, Corporal Abe Fletcher and Sergeant Albert Tarbox. Sullivan had his canteen of fresh milk and Johnny Ticknor his captain's bars; both just minutes from a grim meeting alongside a rail fence not far from an unfinished railroad cut. Companies E—"Bragg's Rifles"—and B were combined into the regiment's color company. Isaiah Kelly marched with the Com-

52. Dawes, Letter, to John B. Bachelder, March 18, 1868.
53. Dawes, Service, p. 164; Rufus R. Dawes, "Align on the Colors," Milwaukee Sunday Telegraph, April 27, 1890. The Telegraph account was actually written five to seven years previously by Dawes, but editor Jerome A. Watrous held the copy, apparently because he wanted to reproduce sketches of the maneuver Dawes had sent with the article. It is probably the earliest account Dawes wrote for publication, and contains many details he eliminated in writing about Gettysburg for his book. With its sometimes awkward sentence structure and additional detail, it is the best account of the battle by Dawes. He was much more circumspect in his other published descriptions of Gettysburg.

pany B boys, looking pale and thin. He had been suffering from a nagging intestinal complaint the boys called the "Virginia Quickstep." He had dropped out of ranks several times on the march north, but had finally caught up with his unit south of Gettysburg. He and his comrade, James Kelly, would do their duty. Among the Appleton and Fond du Lac boys under Captain John Marston in Company F, Frank King was nervous, and he recognized there was more to the feeling than the usual fear felt by any soldier. It would be his last fight.

In the very center of the line, the color guard of eight noncommissioned officers carried just one flag, the bullet-shredded national banner, the silk still bright in the morning sun, though much marked by the battles of the past months. The colorbearer was Sergeant Thomas Polleys of Company H, late of Trempealeau, Wisconsin, and the banner he carried was the same flag sent to the regiment by Governor Alexander Randall those first weeks after the 6th Wisconsin had reached Washington. The blue regimental state flag had been used up and sent back to Madison with a careful letter from Colonel Edward S. Bragg that made a proud claim:

> History will tell how Wisconsin honor has been vindicated by her soldiers, and what lessons in Northern courage they have given Southern chivalry. If the past gives an earnest of the future, the "Iron Brigade" will not be forgotten when Wisconsin makes up her jewels.

Before midday, all eight men in the color party would be dead or down.[54]

Behind the color party came Company F, the Germans of Milwaukee, who sang so well in the still night air "of a hundred

54. Dawes, *Service*, p. 131. Regimental General Order 23 named Polleys as colorbearer. Regimental General Order No. 11, March 25, 1863, Paragraph 2, named the following corporals to the color guard: William Day, Patch Creek, of Company C; Francis A. Deleglise, Appleton, of Company E; Milo G. Sage, Delafield, Company F; C. L. Jones, Mauston, Company I; Charles Mead of Company B; Arland F. Windsor, Summit, Company K, and Clarence E. Bullard, Menomonie, Company B. For the best study of Iron Brigade flags, see Howard Michael Madaus, "The Flags of the Iron Brigade, 1861-65," *Wisconsin Magazine of History*, Vol. 69, Number 1/Autumn, 1985, State Historical Society of Wisconsin, Madison. The National flag carried by the 6th Wisconsin has since been restored and is displayed at the Grand Army of the Republic Museum in the State Capitol at Madison.

circling camps." They were the largest single company in the line, was 46; Private John Raeder of Milwaukee was one of the few soldiers still wearing white leggings. They were followed by the Buffalo County crowd of Company H, still known throughout the regiment as "Hauser's Geese." The Sauk County Boys of Company A were combined with the famed "Devils of Company D," the Irish Montgomery Guards from Milwaukee. The Sauk County boys, those fellows who boasted so long and so loud, were down to just 15 enlisted men. In the middle of his squad was Bodley Jones of Excelsior Township, marching into his last fight. The final company was I, the famous Anderson Guards, late of Bad Ax County; in ranks brothers Frank and Sam Wallar, two of the toughest men in the Army of the Potomac, and one straggler of some reputation, Pete Markle of Coon Slough, who, somehow, had appeared from nowhere the day before in time to collect his two months' pay.[55] Captain Bill Remington of Mauston was just behind the regiment with a squad of Company I boys hurrying up the slow and footsore. Suffering from his cold, he was out of sorts and looking foolish because of the cloths he had wrapped around his head and neck to ease the discomfort; he was an unlikely looking officer for serious work. Just behind them came the Brigade Guard, 100 soldiers from the five regiments of the Iron Brigade, under the command of Lieutenant Loyd Harris of Prairie du Chien. He had his new harmonica tucked in a pocket, and would play a brave rendition of "Tramp, Tramp, Tramp, the Boys Are Marching" a few hours later, as an Army surgeon cut a rebel buckshot from a muscle in his neck.

The Wisconsin men, marching in step to the music in a 140-yard-long closed column, four abreast, the Brigade Guard tight behind them,[56] began to hear a disturbing thumping noise over the rolling countryside to their left. There was some confusion at first. "For some reason the sound was very dull, and did not attract our attention as indicating any serious engagement," Dawes said

55. 6th Wisconsin Regimental Order Book, General Order 12, March 26, 1863. This order changed the alignment of the companies and combined companies A and D as well as B and E. In line of battle, the companies would be arranged, from left to right, as follows: I, A-D, H, F, B-E, K, C and G.
56. For a detailed description of Civil War drill and formations, see: Col. W. J. Hardee, *Rifle and Light Infantry Tactics*, 2 Volumes, (Philadelphia, 1861); Capt. Henry Coppee, *Field Manual of Evolutions of the Line*, (Philadelphia, 1862); and *Field Manual*, Ordnance Bureau, (Richmond, Va., 1862).

later.[57] Harris, one of two officers in command of the Brigade Guard, leaned over to Lieutenant Levi Showalter of the 2nd Wisconsin. "The Pennsylvanians have made a mistake and are celebrating the 4th three days ahead of time," he said, somewhat puzzled. Then there was a "boom, boom, boom,"[58] and this time it was recognized by the veterans of Second Bull Run, South Mountain and Antietam—artillery being fired in haste. The word passed through the ranks that General Buford's cavalry had "found the Johnnies over at York or Harrisburg," Sullivan recalled.[59]

Then the brigade adjutant, James D. Wood of the 2nd Wisconsin, galloped along the brigade shouting over and over from regiment to regiment, "Boys, Little Mac is in command of the Army of the Potomac!"[60] It was an incident that puzzled the Wisconsin men the next 50 years. Even though they had been read Meade's address the day before, even though, in hindsight, it was all so improbable, the 6th Wisconsin men yelled for joy. "Our fellows cheered like mad," Sullivan said in describing the scene, "glad to be rid of . . . vainglorious fools. . . ."[61]

Why Wood spread the spurious story of McClellan's return, and where it came from, was never determined. If, taking the worst case, it was a calculated ploy by some officer to boost the fighting spirit of the soldiers, it worked. George H. Otis, marching with the 2nd Wisconsin, much later labeled it all "a rumor," but recalled the soldiers immediately had "a lighter and more elastic step. Our hearts were full of gratitude."[62] Dawes, always careful about what he wrote, contemporaneously and a quarter-century later, never mentioned the incident. Two other 6th Wisconsin soldiers, Philip Cheek and Mair Pointon of Company A, later re-

57. Dawes, *Telegraph*, April 27, 1890.
58. [Harris], *Telegraph*, February 15, 1885.
59. Sullivan, *Telegraph*, December 8, 1884.
60. *Ibid.*
61. Sullivan, *Star*, February 13, 1883. The full quotation reads: ". . . And our fellows cheered like mad, glad to be rid of such vainglorious fools as hindquarters in the saddle and old-stick-in-the-mud, to say nothing about drunken Joe, who had Lee where he would have to fight him on his own ground or seek safety in inglorious flight. Our fellows thought Hooker did the inglorious part to perfection on that occasion. . . ." He referred to Union Generals John Pope, Ambrose Burnside and Joseph Hooker. In his *Milwaukee Sunday Telegraph* account, the passage was edited to read, "And our fellows cheered like mad." The *Telegraph* account otherwise varied only in detail.
62. Otis, *Second Wisconsin*, p. 83.

corded that "thousands of soldiers believed that General McClellan had been restored to command," but they said the source of the report was never discovered.[63] Otis said the announcement was "sufficient to create the greatest enthusiasm," and tried to explain McClellan "was the idol" of the army's rank and file, "the one in whom our confidence remained unshaken."[64] Fairfield, the chronicler of weather and miles marched, did not mention it.[65]

Before the McClellan cheers died away, the sound of cannon intensified, mixed now with the popping of small arms fire. From their position in the back of the brigade, the 6th Wisconsin men saw the outskirts of Gettysburg just ahead and "our fellows straightened up to pass through it in good style," said Sullivan, remembering the Brigade Band was playing "Red, White and Blue" when "all at once, hell broke loose . . . in front."[66]

Cutler's Brigade had turned left off the Emmitsburg Road, marching crosslots through the fields and yards along the southwest edge of Gettysburg, followed by Hall's 2nd Maine Battery. The Iron Brigade was now only about one-quarter mile behind the 2nd Brigade.[67] The 2nd Wisconsin also turned off the roadway, followed closely by the 7th Wisconsin, 19th Indiana and 24th Michigan, and finally, the 6th Wisconsin and the Brigade Guard. The Brigade Band swung off to one side of the road and played "Yankee Doodle" in double-quick time.[68] The men passed through hastily created gaps in the rail fences around fields, and near gardens and yards. Ahead, the 2nd Wisconsin surged forward after being ordered to the double-quick, a pace of 140 steps a minute. Then the 7th Wisconsin started to run, followed by the 19th Indiana and, finally, the 24th Michigan. The brigade's column

63. Cheek and Pointon, *Sauk County*, p. 70.
64. Otis, *Second Wisconsin*, pp. 83-84.
65. Fairfield Diary.
66. Sullivan, *Telegraph*, December 20, 1884.
67. The quarter-mile distance between the Iron Brigade and Cutler's Brigade is an estimate. Clayton E. Rogers of Wadsworth's staff put the Iron Brigade "about one mile behind" at the start of the morning. For a detailed description of Cutler's Brigade in the opening of the battle of Gettysburg, see James L. McLean, *Cutler's Brigade at Gettysburg*, (Baltimore, 1987). McLean estimated Cutler halted "about 10 minutes" to allow the Western Brigade to close up. However, he quoted Major Grover of the 76th New York telling his soldiers they could go into a cherry orchard. See pp. 55-56. It is unlikely the halt was only 10 minutes, given the time it would take to reform. In 10 minutes, a marching column could cover 700 to 1,100 yards. *Ordnance Manual*, p. 134.
68. Sullivan, *Telegraph*, December 20, 1884.

snaked forward, gaps opening between the regiments, accoutrements bouncing, black hats bobbing and rifle-musket barrels twisting every which way. Over his shoulder, Dawes shouted, "Forward, Double Quick!" and the regiment lurched forward with a clatter of canteens and tin cups barely heard above the growing sound of battle just ahead.[69]

The soldiers skirted knapsacks and other items discarded by Cutler's men, who were running in formation ahead of them. The Black Hats passed frame homes and farm fields, splashing through a shallow run at one point. It was harder going now, the Wisconsin men breathing in labor, the heat of the day coming up, but there was no stopping. The field officers of the 2nd and 7th Wisconsin dismounted, sending horses and noncombatants to the rear. Now and again, an artillery shell cleared the ridge to the front, crashing through the tree tops.[70] Just ahead, the advance regiments of the Iron Brigade, still in column, double-quicked through some scattered trees and began to move to the crest of a low ridge adjacent to a large, stone school building. The Wisconsin men would later learn it was a Lutheran seminary. One by one, the regiments disappeared over the crest. Captain Bill Remington and a squad from his Company I were well behind now, gathering up the winded and footsore stragglers and hurrying them forward.[71]

More gunfire rattled just over the ridge, and the smell of burnt powder grew more pronounced. When the head of the 6th Wisconsin reached the crest, an aide from General Meredith, Lieutenant Gilbert M. Woodward, rode up on the run. "Colonel, form your line and prepare for action," Woodward shouted to Dawes. The command was difficult to hear over the growing noise. Dawes reined his horse around and stood in the stirrups to give the orders. Ahead, the ground dipped, then gently rose to another low ridge 500 yards away. In the line of trees on the second ridge, Dawes saw soldiers moving, but he was unable at first to determine the color of their uniforms. Here and there, smoke puffed as a musket fired. In the swale between the ridges, the 2nd Wis-

69. Rufus R. Dawes, Letter, to John Kranth, April 20, 1885. John M. Kranth was secretary of the Gettysburg Association.
70. R. K. Beecham, "Adventures of an Iron Brigade Man," a series of articles published in the *National Tribune*, (Washington, D.C., 1902), n.p.
71. William N. Remington, "Wm. N. Remmington's [sic] Story," *Milwaukee Sunday Telegraph*, April 22, 1883.

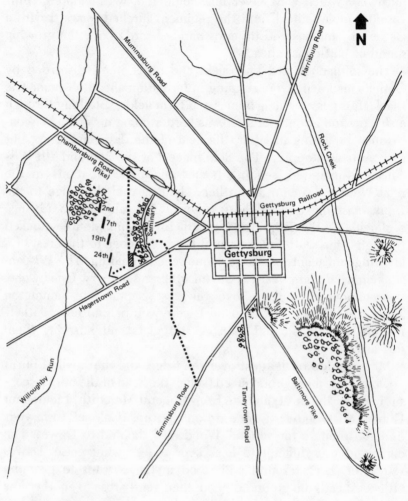

- **•••••** Route of the 6th Wisconsin
- **▨▨▨▨** 6th Wisconsin
- **▬▬▬** Iron Brigade regiments
- **••••** Intended direction of the 6th Wisconsin

Mary Slough

consin was in line of battle: two ranks sweeping toward the trees on the opposite ridge, a faded blue ribbon moving slowly across the green of the field, rifle-muskets and black Hardee hats distinctive in the bright sun. The other Iron Brigade regiments were close behind, also in battle line, moving en echelon, flags tilted forward, the men carrying their rifle-muskets at the shoulder. The line of four small regiments appeared painfully thin. Here and there, scattered squads of Buford's cavalry moved to the rear as the infantry came up, some of the cavalrymen joining the line as it moved toward the trees, the morning sun at their backs. To the north, the leading regiments of the 2nd Brigade crossed another roadway. There was scattered small arms fire across the whole front now, heavier to the north. "I saw also, a line of rebel skirmishers, running back from my own front," Dawes remembered.[72]

Giving the commands as quickly as he could, the dapper, bearded lieutenant colonel ordered the regiment to form "By Companies into Line!" Then, "Forward into Line! By Companies, Left half wheel, double quick, March!" The companies slowly began the evolutions that would array them in a line of battle. Dawes waited until they wheeled out of company column, then shouted, "Forward, guide right. March!" and then "Load at will, Load!" The men stumbled and bumped one another as they fumbled with the paper cartridges, trying not to spill powder as they poured it in the muzzles. The ramrods clanked as they were pulled and the lead driven home. The soldiers struggled to keep their alignment as they thumbed percussion caps on the firing cones. The rifle-muskets were returned to the right shoulder. Twenty-five years later, in a letter responding to an inquiry from a stranger, Dawes would draw a precise diagram of the maneuver to show "this intricate evolution performed by that unequalled body of skilled veterans."[73]

Ahead of him that July morning, the Wisconsin men from Prairie du Chien and Wonewoc, Milwaukee, Baraboo and Mauston, and dozens of towns in a new state hundreds of miles from the battlefield; who had drilled at Camp Randall at Madison, Wisconsin, and in the camps around Washington; and who stood fire in the sunset in the Brawner farm fields, along the National

72. Dawes, Letter, to Kranth, April 29, 1885.
73. *Ibid.*

Road at South Mountain, and in the bloody stubble of the bullet-shredded cornfield at Antietam, ran down the gradual slope into the battle of Gettysburg.

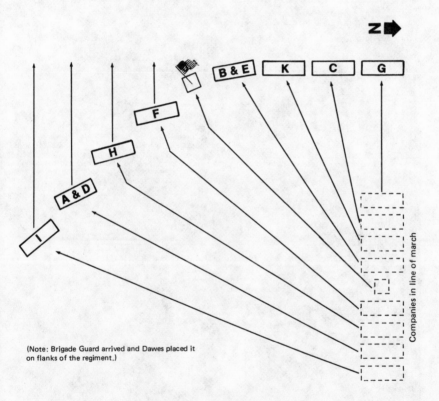

Z ➡

B & E   K   C   G

F

H

A & D

I

Companies in line of march

(Note: Brigade Guard arrived and Dawes placed it
on flanks of the regiment.)

"By companies into line. Forward into line!"

Mary Slough

173

CHARLES KEELER
Shot Through Both Legs During the Charge

CHAPTER SIX

And where are the comrades, so kind and so brave,
Who proudly left Mauston, the Union to Save,
The death-roll, so lengthy, does mournfully say,
How foremost in battle went brave Company "K."
—By "Mickey"

Go Like Hell

The opening clash of infantry at Gettysburg on July 1, 1863—
6th Wisconsin men always said—was a stand-up-and-knock-down
fight, and it was a statement that was delivered, at the time and
thereafter, with a sharp, satisfied nod. The collision of the two
Confederate brigades and two Union brigades occurred on the
farm fields west of the town, along a ridge called McPherson's for
the family owning the land and small woods on it. As the 6th
Wisconsin and the Iron Brigade double-quicked over Seminary
Ridge and ran down into the swale, over the second rise, 500
yards ahead, still out of sight, two strong Confederate brigades,
in lines of battle, moved with the steady, swaying step of veteran
infantry toward Gettysburg. Two others were in close support.
John Buford's overmatched horse soldiers, with the assistance of
a Federal rifled battery, slowed the Confederate advance, but the
rebels had not been in a great hurry, marching astride the Chambersburg Pike with the carelessness of veteran infantry dealing
only with pesky cavalry and perhaps some Pennsylvania militia.
Confederate Commander Henry Heth always said he marched to
Gettysburg to look for shoes for his foot-sore soldiers, but what
he found was the Army of the Potomac.

Off to the right of the 6th Wisconsin, the woods on McPherson's
Ridge ended near a cluster of farm buildings along the Chambersburg Pike. The roadway itself was flanked on each side by a
"stake and rider" fence. Cutler's 2nd Brigade was almost out of

175

sight to the north. The other Iron Brigade regiments, in line of battle, were moving en echelon toward the woods.[1] On the other side of the trees, Confederate General James J. Archer directed his brigade of four regiments and a battalion of Alabama and Tennessee troops across a shallow run toward McPherson's Woods.[2]

The 6th Wisconsin men could see Union cavalry squads in the trees, but they were pulling out with the hurried, jerky motions of soldiers convinced they had done their duty. Here and there, rebel skirmishers poked out of the shade in places where the Federal horse soldiers had vacated. Scattered shooting sputtered along the whole front, mixed with the faint, distant commands of the Iron Brigade line officers directing their companies. Farther north, the gunfire was a steady roar. Hall's 2nd Maine Battery of Cutler's Brigade was in position near the Chambersburg Pike, the crash of the rifled guns adding to the noise and tatters of smoke along McPherson's Ridge. Before the 6th Wisconsin reached its place on the flank of the Iron Brigade, a rider from General Sol Meredith, perhaps on direction from Division Commander James Wadsworth or Acting I Corps Commander Abner Doubleday, brought orders for Dawes to halt his regiment. The running Wisconsin black hats pulled up in a jumble, the soldiers dressing on the flag as they had done so many times on so many drill fields. They were down in the swale between the two ridges, well southwest of the Lutheran seminary, the regiment's left near the Fairfield Road. Ahead, a crash of musketry rolled along the ridge from the north as the 2nd and then 7th Wisconsin, the brigade's leading regiments, plunged toward the woods line.[3] From the Brigade

1. Edwin B. Coddington, *The Gettysburg Campaign*, (New York, 1968), pp. 266-277. Coddington's careful study put Archer's strength at 1,132 in his fight against four regiments of the Iron Brigade mounting 1,048.
2. Douglas Southall Freeman, *Lee's Lieutenants*, Vol. 3, (New York, 1944) pp. 78-81. Freeman wrote: "As fate would have it, Archer encountered the Iron Brigade, a command of Michigan, Wisconsin and Indiana soldiers who deserved their name. . . . At any time they were formidable."
3. One of the lingering questions about the morning of July 1, 1863, at Gettysburg is who first halted the 6th Wisconsin, holding the regiment in reserve, until it was needed to assist Cutler's Brigade. The answer is two-fold. Dawes clearly stated in his July 17, 1863, report on Gettysburg his regiment was halted twice. At the first halt, Dawes reported, "by direction of General Meredith," the Brigade Guard was assigned to the 6th Wisconsin. He was then ordered forward again to align on the left flank of the Iron Brigade, only to be halted a second time, by a staff officer from General Abner Doubleday. From the evidence, it would seem it was General Meredith, perhaps acting at the direction of Division Commander James Wadsworth or General Abner

Guard, Lieutenant Loyd Harris ran up for instructions. Dawes told the young officer to divide the reserve into two 50-man companies and place one on each flank of the regiment. Harris ran back and did so, assigning the right company to Second Lieutenant Levi Showalter of the 2nd Wisconsin. In that minute before he moved his detachment up—the soldiers still trying to catch their breath after the hard half-mile run in knapsacks and equipment—Harris, who admitted he was "feeling keenly my situation," commanding "old veterans in the service who no doubt felt a novel sensation in fighting under a strange officer, and away from their companies, and regiments," acted on an impulse. He stepped before his panting soldiers and told them: "I know how much you

---

Doubleday, who first held the 6th Wisconsin in reserve, then ordered it forward again to join the attack of the Iron Brigade on McPherson's Woods. Doubleday clearly deserves credit for the key decision halting the 6th Wisconsin the second time as a reserve for the division, then ordering it to the assistance of Cutler's Brigade.

Earl M. Rogers, writing in the *Milwaukee Sunday Telegraph,* June 22, 1884, indicated Wadsworth directed Meredith to hold the 6th Wisconsin in reserve. Rogers cited a letter "written a few months ago" by Rufus Dawes from which he quoted Dawes as saying that when Meredith's Brigade reached the field, the 6th Wisconsin "was taken from Meredith's column by direction of a member of Gen. Wadsworth's staff. . . ." Dawes then went on to quote at length a statement he had recently obtained from Clayton E. Rogers (Earl Rogers' brother), Wadsworth's aide at Gettysburg:

Nearing Gettysburg, Gen. Cutler filed obliquely to the left, in the direction of the Seminary, and to a point beyond where the Union cavalry was skirmishing with rebel infantry. Gen. Cutler's brigade was placed in line of battle, and then went forward to develop the rebel strength. It was found that a division of rebel troops was in front and more coming. The enemy extended past Cutler's left and beyond his right. Gen. Wadsworth directed Rogers to "hurry up Meredith" to Cutler's left. He rode back and met Gen. Meredith, directing him to move up and take a position pointed out on Gen. Cutler's left. The 6th Wisconsin was the rear regiment of the brigade. When Col. Dawes came up he was taken from Gen. Meredith's brigade. . . .

John A. Kress, an aide on Wadsworth's staff, however, in his article, "At Gettysburg," in the *Missouri Republican,* December 4, 1886, wrote:

Gen. Meredith was in the rear of his brigade, riding in company with Gen. Doubleday. At the suggestion, or order, of the latter, Meredith held back the Sixth Wisconsin from the charge, keeping it in reserve temporarily.

That would seem to indicate it was Meredith, under order from Doubleday, who halted the 6th Wisconsin the first time. However, whoever made the decision also ordered Dawes forward again to join the Iron Brigade attack. It was Doubleday's action holding the regiment in reserve that proved the significant decision.

177

would like to be with your own commands, and I am just as anxious to join company C over there on the right of the 6th, but it cannot be so; do the best you can and I will do my duty toward you."[4] He ordered them forward to the left flank of the 6th Wisconsin.

Just as that was completed, another rider arrived from Meredith with instructions to move forward again. But before Dawes could execute the order, "Mickey" Sullivan saw a "very boyish looking staff officer" ride up.[5] It was Lieutenant Benjamin T. Marten of Major General Abner Doubleday's staff. "Colonel," the young officer shouted to Dawes, "General Doubleday is now in command of the First Corps, and he directs that you halt your regiment." Marten's appearance was puzzling, as Doubleday was supposedly off to the rear somewhere with his 3rd Division of the I Corps, but Dawes quickly ordered his men down, and the Badgers flopped to the ground, all sweat, heaving chests and tangled equipment. Here and there a lagging soldier came up and elbowed back into his spot in the line. One of the Fond du Lac men on Company E, Private Albert Young, in one of those moments seared into memory, recalled the field was planted with "fast ripening wheat."[6] Nearby, in the Company E line, Frank King of Fond du Lac, shaken by a premonition, turned to Corporal Lyman White of Appleton. "Lime, this finishes my fighting," said King. The corporal tried to make light of it, but later White remembered King's words.[7] In the shade of the woods, the 2nd and 7th Wisconsin exchanged near muzzle-to-muzzle, ripping volleys with Archer's Brigade, the big lead bullets splintering trees and knocking down men in a thin swirl of chest-high powder smoke. The Calico boys burrowed deeper into the new wheat. It was shaping up to be a hard morning for Wisconsin mothers.

In a few minutes, Staff Officer Marten was back. "General Doubleday directs that you move your regiment at once to the right," the staff officer shouted, pointing to the north. Dawes ordered the regiment to its feet. "Right, Face!" he shouted over the growing

4. [Loyd G. Harris], "The Iron Brigade Guard at Gettysburg," *Milwaukee Sunday Telegraph*, March 22, 1885.
5. Sullivan, *Telegraph*, December 20, 1884.
6. [Albert V. Young], "A Pilgrimage," *Milwaukee Sunday Telegraph*, April 22, 1888.
7. [Jerome A. Watrous], "Some Premonitions," *Milwaukee Sunday Telegraph*, July 27, 1895.

noise of the battle, and the regiment shifted; facing north in a column of fours. "Double-quick, March!" Dawes yelled, remembering "the musketry fighting along the whole front of the division was very sharp" with only his regiment not engaged. James Wood of General Solomon Meredith's staff was also there, all excited, riding alongside Dawes as the Wisconsin regiment double-quicked through the open field. The situation just ahead was not good, Wood explained. Cutler's Brigade was in trouble. Finally, reining his horse off to the side, Wood yelled: "Go like hell! It looks as though they are driving Cutler."[8] Seconds later, Company I Lieutenant Earl Rogers saw his brother, Clayton, an officer on Division commander James Wadsworth's staff, riding alongside the running column conferring with Dawes.[9] Wadsworth's instructions were the same: Go to the north and form on Cutler's right.

Running in the low ground between the ridges, the 6th Wisconsin passed the Lutheran seminary. Dawes looked ahead. Across the Chambersburg Pike, he could now see Hall's rifled guns "driving to the rear" and the men of Cutler's Brigade "falling back toward town. . . ."[10] From the left "company" of the Brigade Guard at the rear of the running regiment, Loyd Harris saw the 147th New York outflanked and "in full retreat" with a Confederate line in "hot pursuit."[11] In Company C, Sergeant George Fairfield could make out Federal infantry with "knapsacks on" but "not enough to make a heavy skirmish line . . . flying before the enemy." He wrote in his diary that night it was the 147th New York.[12] Across the roadway, Fairfield saw more Federal infantry "scattering like sheep, leaving the . . . artillery . . . and outrunning the enemy."[13] Just in front of the runing 6th Wisconsin, a group of Federal officers carried a body in a blanket. Dawes learned later it was I Corps Commander John Reynolds, who had been

8. Rufus R. Dawes, Letter, to John B. Bachelder, March 18, 1868.
9. Earl M. Rogers, Letter, to Jerome A. Watrous, undated. Rogers' account was presented for possible publication in the *Milwaukee Sunday Telegraph*. Rogers' brother, Clayton, also writing of Gettysburg, could not resist taking an infantryman's swipe at horse soldiers, noting he had hurried to the field at Gettysburg "greatly excited at the prospect of seeing a cavalry fight, having been two years in the service without seeing one." Clayton E. Rogers, "Gettysburg Scenes," *Milwaukee Sunday Telegraph*, May 13, 1887.
10. Dawes, *Telegraph*, April 27, 1890.
11. [Harris], *Telegraph*, March 22, 1885.
12. Fairfield, Diary, July 1, 1863.
13. George Fairfield, Letter, to Jerome A. Watrous, undated.

shot and killed in the opening fire. Later, some said Reynolds made his stand at McPherson's Ridge (even though the bulk of his forces were not yet on the field) because he saw the deep defensive positions south of Gettysburg; others said it was simply that the general was a Pennsylvania man fighting on home soil. Whatever the truth, John Reynolds, who turned down Abraham Lincoln's offer to command the Army of the Potomac, would not have to answer for it, and he would never have to worry about his soldiers and their coffee again.[14]

The small Wisconsin regiment passed Reynolds' body and moved steadily through the smoke, noise, scattered bullets and wounded soldiers behind the Iron Brigade's battle line. In the woods on their left, the sound of heavy fighting rattled southward along the ridge as the 19th Indiana and 24th Michigan roared into the woods; to their left front, scattered squads of Union soldiers drifted to the rear; and ahead, across the roadway, the heavy Confederate line rolled past with yips and yells, chasing a broken line of Union infantrymen running for the cover of a tree line on Seminary Ridge. The rebel brigade pushing Cutler's right was composed of three strong regiments—the 2nd and 42nd Mississippi and the 55th North Carolina—under the command of Brigadier General Joseph R. Davis, the likeable, but inexperienced nephew of Confederate President Jefferson Davis.[15] The Federal soldiers on the 6th Wisconsin's left front were the left and center regiments of Cutler's broken brigade: the 14th Brooklyn, 95th New York and 147th New York. The first two units were still holding formation as they bent back before Davis' Brigade. The 147th New York, however, had moved north of the Chambersburg Pike and never received Cutler's order to retreat. After a gallant but short stand, the soldiers had to run for it, all order lost, barely escaping capture by the charging Mississippians and North Carolinians. North of the road, the 76th New York and 56th Pennsylvania of Cutler's Brigade had been hit just as they formed their lines. The rebel line extended well past the exposed right of the two Union regiments, and the New Yorkers and Pennsylvanians

14. Dawes, *Service*, p. 166. For a detailed discussion whether Abraham Lincoln offered John Reynolds command of the Army of the Potomac, see Edward J. Nichols, *Toward Gettysburg*, Appendix, pp. 220-223.
15. Coddington, *Gettysburg*, pp. 266-277. Coddington said Davis had about 2,100 men in his line against about 1,625 in Cutler's Brigade plus 344 in the Sixth Wisconsin and 100 in the Iron Brigade Guard.

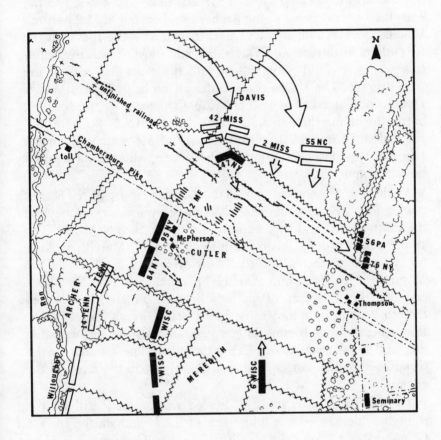

N

unfinished railroad

DAVIS

42 MISS

2 MISS   55 NC

Chambersburg Pike

toll

41 NY

2 ME

95 NY

McPherson

CUTLER

84 NY

56 PA

76 NY

ARCHER

14 TENN

7 TENN

Thompson

Run

2 WISC

Willoughby

7 WISC

MEREDITH

6 WISC

Seminary

J. Heiser

The 6th Wisconsin is ordered to assist
Cutler's Retreating 2nd Brigade.

181

had fought bravely, but the converging fire from front and flank was too much for any soldiers. Finally, they had been ordered to pull back. When the two Union units withdrew, Davis' men surged forward in pursuit, the Confederate regiments piling up until the officers lost control.

In those confused moments on the field at Gettysburg, the fighting was still undecided: John Reynolds dead and carried to the rear; the Iron Brigade driving Archer's soldiers out of McPherson's Woods; three regiments of Cutler's Brigade on the run with the two others in retreat; and Davis' Brigade slowly reaching a position where it could pour volleys into the right and rear of the Iron Brigade. The Union commander of the field, General Abner Doubleday, later called it the "critical" moment of the opening battle "involving the defeat, perhaps the utter rout of our forces." He added: "I immediately sent for one of Meredith's regiments (the 6th Wisconsin), a gallant body of men, whom I knew could be relied upon."[16]

As the 6th Wisconsin neared the Chambersburg Pike, Dawes saw "a long line of yelling rebels coming over the ridge beyond the railroad cut" and the "opportunity to attack their flank." The young officer ordered his column to "File right, March!" moving his regiment to the east until it was even with the flank of the "strong but scattered line of rebels" pursuing the 76th New York and 56th Pennsylvania of Cutler's Brigade. Finally, he ordered the 6th Wisconsin to move "by the left flank" into a line of battle. It was neatly done by the Badger veterans, despite an increasing fire, and Dawes explained: "This threw my line parallel to the turnpike and R.R. cut, and almost directly upon the flank of the enemy."[17]

The 6th Wisconsin soldiers, loaded rifle-muskets still on the right shoulder, faced left into a line of battle and started for the Chambersburg Pike. Private Albert Young of Company E said he and the men near him bowed "heads to the leaden storm and dashed forward."[18] Dawes, now riding at the front of the regiment, had just turned his mare forward toward the roadway when she was hit by a rebel ball. "She was struck in the breast, the bullet

16. *O.R.*, Series One, Vol. 27, Part One, p. 246. This is the report of General Abner Doubleday.
17. Dawes, *Telegraph*, April 27, 1890.
18. [Young], *Telegraph*, April 22, 1888.

glancing on the shoulder bone and, passing outside of that bone, lodged under the skin 14 inches from where it struck her." The horse reared, and Dawes, unaware of the cause of the plunging, spurred her savagely, until the mare fell heavily on her haunches. "Fortunately I was not caught under the animal," the young officer said. "My advancing line of battle sweeping forward on the double-quick passed by me as I scrambled from the ground, shouting at the top of my voice, 'I am all right, boys.'" Dawes was on foot the rest of the battle. The Calico boys gave him a friendly yell, the line opening left and right to pass around the officer and his downed animal, then they reached the first rail fence at the roadway. "When I got to my feet . . . I ran forward shouting: 'Fire by file, fire by file.' I could see the enemy coming over the hill now by the railroad cut in a heavy line. I looked back and saw that my gallant old mare was on her feet and was hobbling sturdily to the rear on three legs," Dawes recalled. Much later, he learned the animal was headed for the brigade's wagons. Just ahead, Dawes said, his 6th Wisconsin men fired their first shots of the battle: "The fire of our carefully aimed muskets, resting on the fence rails, striking their flank soon checked the rebels in their headlong pursuit. The rebel line swayed and bent, and suddenly stopped firing and the men ran into the railroad cut, parallel to the Cashtown [Chambersburg] Pike."[19]

19. Dawes, *Telegraph*, April 27, 1890; Dawes, *Service*, p. 167. In his book, Dawes added: "For years, she carried the bullet, which could be felt under the skin behind the left shoulder blade—but woe to the man who felt it, as her temper had been spoiled."

Abner Doubleday, in his revised report on the fighting of the morning of July 1, 1863 (in which he claimed more credit than due him even though he had accomplished much), said he had positioned the 6th Wisconsin on the flank of Davis' Brigade. In his wartime memoir published several years later, Dawes, in quoting from Doubleday's report, dropped Doubleday's claim of ordering the change of front to a footnote, and glossed over it. Dawes, *Service*, pp. 173.

The commander of the 147th New York, at war's end, on the proud occasion of returning the regiment's battleflag to city fathers at Oswego, New York, recalled how, at:

. . . [T]hat critical moment, a little band of men . . . emerged from the woods at the left. They were what remained of the Sixth Wisconsin Volunteers, a regiment which had been two years in the service, and to whom the leaden rain and iron hail of battle had become as familiar as the showers of heaven. Every man of that band was a host in himself. Steady, swiftly and furiously, they charged upon the enemy's flank. [Jerome A. Watrous], "Gettysburg," *Milwaukee Sunday Telegraph*, November 26, 1879.

It had a nice ring—"every man a host in himself"—and the tribute from a

In the left center of the line, Private Young said the fire by file by the 6th Wisconsin, a rippling crash of musketry from right to left (and a remarkable feat of regimental discipline, given the excitement of the moment), caught the rebel infantry by surprise. "The Johnnies were so intent upon following up their advantage that they did not for some time discover what was going on on their right . . . ," he remembered. "Now, we are face to face. They jump into an old railroad cut which is immediately in front of them and here about five feet deep and opened upon us."[20] Corporal Frank Wallar of Company I recalled the regiment under a "slow fire and the nearer we got the hotter the fire."[21] On the far left of the regiment, Loyd Harris said that when "the enemy discovered us coming, they gave up the pursuit of Cutler's men and wheeled to the right to meet . . . [us]. I could not help thinking, now, for once, we will have a square 'stand up and knock down fight.' No trees, nor walls to protect either, when presto! their whole line disappeared as if swallowed up by the earth. . . . They had taken advantage of a deep railroad cut, a splendid position for them, and threatened death and destruction to any regiment that attempted to dislodge them."[22] In Company K, "Mickey" Sullivan saw the Confederate line running down the slope toward his regiment and "then it seemed as if the ground had opened and swallowed them up; but we soon found that they were still on top of it—as they opened a tremendous fire on us, from an old railroad cut."[23] To Company E Private Augustus Klein, the rebels were "kowardly [sic] sons of bitches" for taking cover.[24]

At the Chambersburg Pike, bullets coming in everywhere, thudding into the ground, splintering rails and ripping furrows in the meadow, the 6th Wisconsin men scrambled over the first fence. "In the road our fellows straightened up their lines and waited for all hands to get over the fence," said Sullivan, who found his

fellow soldier of how they came running into the fight at Gettysburg was always remembered by 6th Wisconsin men and, in the end, it became woven into the myth of sturdy Western men who belonged to an Iron Brigade.
20. Dawes, *Telegraph*, April 27, 1890.
21. Frank A. Wallar, "A Settled Question," *Milwaukee Sunday Telegraph*, July 29, 1883.
22. [Harris], *Telegraph*, March 22, 1885.
23. Sullivan, *Telegraph*, December 20, 1884.
24. Augustus Klein Letter, quoted in Nolan, *Iron Brigade*, p. 239; page 359, note 21.

rifle-musket (the same Springfield he had pestered Colonel Bragg into giving him the previous March on his return to the regiment) would not fire.[25] One of the men in his company, Frank Gordon, recalled the boys pulled down sections of what Young called a "high rail fence."[26] Elsewhere along the line, the Wisconsin boys climbed over or knocked down the second fence, then stood and fired in the hail of bullets from the railroad cut 175 paces away. It was a "galling fire," Young said, "a fire that is fast decimating our ranks. Several of our poor boys are left dangling on the fence. We are in a smooth pasture field now, and but a few rods from the enemy although their heads only are exposed we open fire, still pressing on."[27] To Dawes, the Confederate fire was "murderous" and "to climb that fence in face of such a fire was a clear test of mettle and discipline."[28]

Once over the fences, the Wisconsin men frantically began to load and shoot in an effort to beat down the Confederate fire. Slowly, leaning into the storm of bullets from the railroad cut, the blue line moved away from the pike toward the largely obscured rebels. Later, Private Young would puzzle about that moment:

> It is almost universally the case—it has been our experience up to this time that either the charging party is forced to retire without having accomplished its purpose or the troops attacked break and fly the field. But the rebels do not budge and we have no thought but to do what we set out to do. It is a terrible moment. Success or failure trembles in the balance. . . . The air seems full of bullets. The zip, zip, of the little leaden messengers of death is incessantly in our ears. Our boys are dropping at a fearful rate.[29]

Loyd Harris noted proudly: "We never hesitated."[30]

The line was well into the field, "advancing and firing," when Dawes saw "about 100 men" of the 95th New York forming on his left. The 14th Brooklyn, further west, was out of sight and not

25. Sullivan, *Telegraph*, December 20, 1884.
26. Dawes, Letter, to Bachelder, March 18, 1868.
27. [Young], *Telegraph*, April 22, 1888.
28. Dawes, Letter, to Bachelder, March 18, 1868.
29. [Young], *Telegraph*, April 22, 1888.
30. [Harris], *Telegraph*, March 22, 1885.

as close as its colonel would later claim. The young Ohioan said he did not know the 14th Brooklyn was nearby, but "we would have charged the cut exactly the same if they had not been there." He hurried over and found Major Edward Pye of the 95th New York. "Let's go for them, Major!" Dawes shouted over the gunfire. Pye nodded grimly and replied, "We are with you!" The major moved off, swinging his sword, shouting to his New Yorkers: "Guide Right! Forward! Forward! Charge!"[31]

In Company C, Cornelius Okey and his comrades pushed out into the field. "The enemy's fire became so hot, and we were losing so many men with no chance for retaliation, that our boys commenced to yell, 'Charge! Charge! Charge!'" he said. The only way they could see the rebels "in front of us was by their flag, which was planted on the edge of the excavation, and by the smoke from their muskets as they gave us volley after volley." The flag would, in a few seconds, prove more a temptation than Okey could resist.[32]

Dawes ran back to the rear of the 6th Wisconsin. "Forward! Forward! Charge!" he yelled. "Align on the Colors! Align on the

31. Dawes, Letter, to Bachelder, March 18, 1868. In his war memoir, Dawes had a slightly different version, writing he told Major Pye: "We must charge." The major then replied, "Charge it is." In the Bachelder letter, Dawes said he told Pye: "Let's go for them Major."

In his own reminiscence of the fight at the Gettysburg railroad cut, A. H. Belo, who was in command of the 55th North Carolina Infantry, noted:

> After the repulse of Cutler's Brigade we continued our advance and soon saw another Federal force coming on the field, one regiment, which afterwards proved to be the Sixth Wisconsin, marching at right angles with us. They formed a line of battle and changed front to meet us, and at the same time were joined by the Ninety-fifth New York and Fourteenth Brooklyn. I was so impressed with the fact that the side charging first would hold the field that I suggested to Maj. [John] Blair, commanding the Second Mississippi on my right, that we should charge them before they had their formation completed. He agreed to this, but just at that time we received orders to form a new alignment. At the same time the Federals, taking advantage of this, were advancing, and before our new alignment could be completed, charged up to the railroad cut. . . .

Belo remarked that he and Major John Blair, commanding the 2nd Mississippi, had almost the same conversation as Dawes and Major Pye just before the charge of the 6th Wisconsin. A. H. Belo, "The Battle of Gettysburg," *Confederate Veteran*, 1900, pp. 165-167.

32. C. W. Okey, "Echoes of Gettysburg," *Milwaukee Sunday Telegraph*, April 29, 1883. A slightly revised version was also printed in Aubery, *Recollections*, pp. 156-160, under the title "An Echo from Gettysburg."

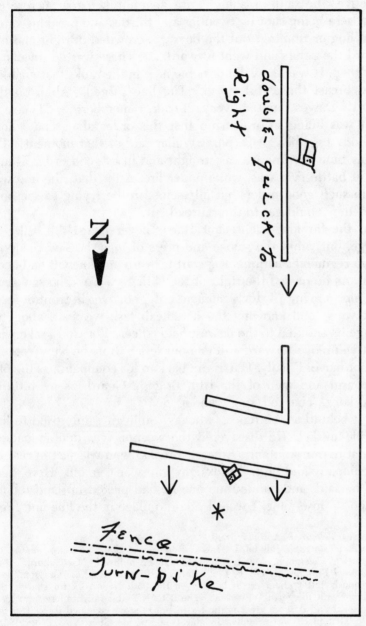

An 1885 sketch by Rufus R. Dawes showing the 6th Wisconsin
moving "By File Right" to flank Davis' Brigade.

Colors!" The firing from the railroad cut was "fearful" and "destructive," he said, crashing "with an unbroken roar before us. Men were being shot by twenties and thirties and breaking ranks by falling or running. But the boys . . . crowded in right and left toward the colors and went forward. . . . There was no royalty in rank then. It was the valor of noble men in the ranks that enabled us to breast the awful storm." The line surged. "Align on the Colors!" Dawes shouted over and over, remembering: "The regiment was being so broken up that this order alone could hold the body together."[33] Corporal Wallar said of that moment: "Up to this time our line was as straight and in as good order as any line of battle ever was, while under fire. After that, the line was not in such good order, but all seemed to be trying to see how quick they could get to the railroad cut."[34]

On the far left, Lieutenant Harris never heard the order to charge, but, amid the smoke and press of men, he saw the Wisconsin regiment's national flag start forward and knew it had been given. As he passed the right of the 95th New York, he saw they were not moving. "I, for a moment only, ran over in front of their right wing, and knowing the herculean task we were about to engage in, shouted to the nearest field officer, 'For God's sake why don't you move forward and join our left.'" But the New Yorkers did not move. Finally, Harris ran back to his command, as the 6th Wisconsin and men of the Iron Brigade Guard, as he bitterly noted later, "charged, singly and alone."[35]

Left behind at the fence, "Mickey" Sullivan vainly tried to fire his rifle-musket. He discovered the weapon was double-loaded. "I went to our adjutant, [Edward Brooks] who was just in rear of our company and said: 'Brooks, my gun won't go off.' 'Here, take this,' he said, and handed me one he had picked up, and telling him not to lose mine, I went back into place in the line and fired

33. Dawes, *Telegraph*, April 27, 1890.
34. Wallar, *Telegraph*, July 28, 1883.
35. [Harris], *Telegraph*, March 22, 1885; J. P. Sullivan, "Gettysburg," *The National Tribune*, March 26, 1885. Harris, writing as usual as "Grayson," was obviously bitter about credit later given the 95th New York for sharing the charge with the Sixth Wisconsin: "The 95th N.Y. did rally and re-form their regiment and deserve great praise for it, but they never joined the left of the 6th. That place was occupied by the 'Iron Brigade Guard' . . . They [95th N.Y.] failed to respond, and 'truth of history' compels me to state that the 6th, with the brigade guard, charged, singly and alone." Sullivan flatly stated: "The 6th Wis. received no support, morally or physically, from any New York or Pennsylvania regiment, but charged alone and unaided."

it off but when I loaded up and tried again it would not go, and then I knew my [percussion] caps were bad." It was a fine fix for a soldier who had fought the whole rebel army by himself at Second Bull Run. Sullivan ran over to Captain John Ticknor who was advancing with his company. The tall officer took it all in, and said: "Take Crawford's," pointing to wounded Corporal Charles A. Crawford of Kildare, face down on the ground, looking as though he might be dead. "We rolled him over and I took the cartridge box and buckled it on myself. As I turned around I saw Capt. Ticknor start for the rear in a spread out, staggering sort of way. After a few steps he fell," Sullivan remembered. "As I reached the line, first sergeant, Erastus Smith, my tent mate, started for the rear saying 'Jerkey' (our nick-name for Capt. Ticknor) is shot and I think he's killed and I am going to see about him." Sullivan pushed his way back into ranks and moved forward. Behind him, Sergeant Smith knelt on the ground and watched the life seep from Johnny Ticknor, the Juneau County sawmill worker who sang "John Brown's Body" in his fine tenor voice in the "evening dews and damps" of the Washington camps. The damned Johnnies, who had tried at so many places, from the Brawner farm fields at Gainesville, to the cornfield at Antietam, had finally killed him. Ticknor would return to Wisconsin in a tin coffin with the lid soldered shut.[36]

Not far away in the bloody meadow, the acting second lieutenant of Company E, Sergeant Michael Mangan of Fond du Lac, was down, blood streaming from a wound that had shattered his ankle. He tried to rise, only to fall again. Around him, other wounded Wisconsin men were loading their rifle-muskets, then pulling themselves up for another shot or two at the Johnnies. Another Company E man, Corporal Francis Deleglise, who was in the color party, came upon the wounded Mangan as he hopped to the rear after being hit. Deleglise had received a wound in the calf of his right leg and another in the knee of the same limb that splintered the bone to the hip. Dropping beside the downed soldier, Deleglise tried to bandage Mangan's ankle with his right hand, but found his muscles rigid with the shock of his own injuries. He told the sergeant he could not help him and headed for the rear. Captain Joseph Marston came up in the smoke and

36. Sullivan, *Telegraph*, December 20, 1884.

bullets and pulled Mangan to his feet. Nearby was Private Harry Dunn, the strongest man in the company,[37] and Marston ordered Dunn to get the wounded sergeant to the rear, then ran to catch up with the charging line of Wisconsin men.[38]

The 175 paces from the second rail fence to the railroad cut was a swirling hell of bullets, smoke, shouts and confusion. In Company C, the Jayhawkers from Prairie du Chien, Lieutenant Orrin Chapman, who listened to a harmonica playing "Home, Sweet Home" just the night before, was down and dying. On the left of the line, the man who played it for him, Loyd Harris, was struck in the neck by a buckshot. A rebel bullet smashed into Sergeant George Fairfield's canteen, slashing his lip, but he ran forward. Private William Armstrong of Prairie du Chien, the "fat cheeked" farm boy who fell asleep at his guard post on the march to Gettysburg, was killed, trading one death for another. In Company E, Amos Lefler of Eden was shot in the face and went down, spitting blood and teeth. Frank King of Fond du Lac took a rebel ball in the stomach and was left sprawled on the ground groaning in pain. The national flag went down, then up again. It fell a second time, and a third, and Earl Rogers of Company I saw Dawes push forward at one point to pick it up, only to be shouldered aside by another corporal from the color party in the frantic rush

37. Harry G. Dunn enlisted in Company E, June 28, 1861, and served three years, mustering out July 15, 1864, at the expiration of his term. Edward S. Bragg said Dunn was "Scotch-Irish" and his father a "man of position in Edinburgh." In a letter to Dawes after the war, Bragg wrote: "Harry, you know, deserted at Belle Plaine, because, being so large, he could not get any clothes that he could get into, but he was brought back, sentenced to some dire punishment, and pardoned for being so good a soldier. He had committed a crime in a foolish pet. Harry that morning [at Mine Run], when we were waiting orders to charge, called me to one side and said: 'Write a good report to the old Governor about me, and tell him I was a brave soldier, and please don't say anything about that Belle Plaine affair.' said I: 'Why, what's the matter Harry? I am as likely to be killed as you,—why give me the message?' 'Oh, no,' said he, 'you ain't half as big as I am. My chances are two to one against yours,' and,—the orders were countermanded and no charge was made at all." Dawes, *Service*, p. 228. In coming to Wisconsin, Dunn settled in Menekaunee (once known as East Marinette), where lumber barons were establishing mills. Irish males working the lumber camps comprised one of the larger identifiable groups in the area's population of 1860. Carl E. Krog, *Marinette: Biography of a Nineteenth Century Lumbering Town, 1850-1910*. University of Wisconsin PhD Thesis, 1971, pp., 99, 103, 104-108. Details of Dunn's postwar life are unknown.

38. *Soldiers' and Citizens' Album of Biographical Record*, Two Vols. (Madison, Wisconsin, 1909), Vol. 1, pp. 170-172, 247-248, 721-724. Mangan's promotion to second lieutenant was dated July 1, 1863. *Roster of Wisconsin Volunteers*, p. 513.

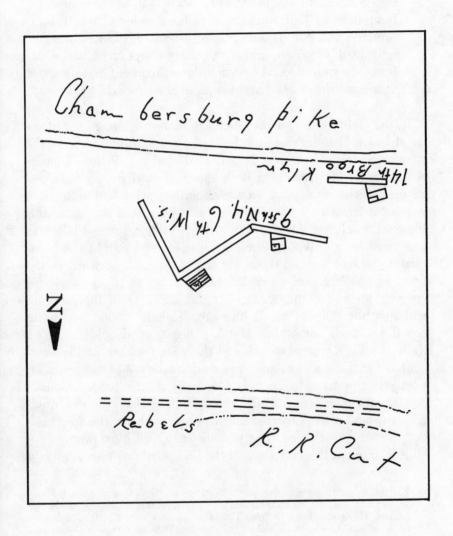

An 1885 sketch by Rufus R. Dawes showing the charge of the
6th Wisconsin on the unfinished railroad cut.

191

to charge the cut. It was a horrible moment for the Bad Ax and Dane county boys, said Rogers:

> Andy Miller of Company I falls dead, near him Gottlieb Schreiber wounded, but a few yards more and Boughton is killed, then Sweet falls wounded. Then Jim McLane and Alf. Thompson are wounded. Now Sutton falls dead, Goodwin and [color party Corporal] Charlie Jones are wounded. They reach the railroad cut and Levi Steadman drops dead and Ed. Lind is wounded.[39]

In the right center of the line, a buckshot thumped into Corporal Isaiah F. Kelly's leg, but he kept going, limping torward the smoke and bullets coming from the railroad cut. Private Charles A. Keeler was shot through both legs. Corporal Joseph Fachs, at 32 one of the older men in the regiment, who had suffered a wound at Brawner's Farm the previous year, was hit again, this time in the left leg. Another Company B soldier, James Kelly, was staggered by a bullet, but he kept his feet and sought out Lieutenant Colonel Rufus Dawes. As the two jostled forward in the press of soldiers, Kelly opened his "woolen shirt" to show his commander a "red bullet mark" on his chest. Over the shooting and shouting, Dawes heard him say, "Colonel, won't you write my folks" and "something about being a good soldier." "Yes, Kelly, I will," Dawes replied, and the young soldier nodded and started for the rear to find a place where he could get some assistance or perhaps to die.[40] In Company K, the Juneau County boys went down at a frightful rate: Abe Fletcher, the tall, quiet corporal who always carried an extra knapsack for the small fellows, was hit in the leg. The wound would kill him. Jimmy Scoville, running at the very front of the line, went down, never again

39. Earl M. Rogers, Letter, to Jerome A. Watrous, undated. Rogers obviously was writing the account for the *Milwaukee Sunday Telegraph*, but it never appeared. Miller was from DeSoto. The other soldiers were Gottfried Schoeber of Hillsboro, Lewis M. Boughton of Tomah, William Sweet of Wonewoc, James McLane of Webster, Alfred Thompson of Harmony, George W. Sutton of Viroqua, John M. Goodwin of Plymouth, Charles O. Jones of Mauston, Levi Stedman of Brookville, the tallest man in the Sixth Wisconsin, and Edward Lind of DeSoto. Sergeant Miller, according to his company commander, Earl Rogers, had "marched with the Second [U.S.] Infantry under [A. S.] Johnston to Salt Lake, in 1856; and returned in the fall of 1860."
40. Dawes, *Service*, p. 168.

having to worry about blackening his shoes or shining his brasses. Wallace Hancock was shot in the arm, and his brother, Billy, in the breast. Eugene Rose of Lemonwier was knocked off his feet by a ball that struck his right leg; Chauncey Wilcox was hit in the right arm and Lon Pratt in the leg. "Tall T"—Hugh Talty—was hit, but stayed in the fight. Little Tommy Flynn was banged up.

Captain Joseph Marston, who came into the regiment from Appleton as First Lieutenant, was in command of Company E. He was the second tallest soldier in the regiment at well over six feet, and the boys all called him "Tall Sycamore." Dawes said the young officer drew himself up to full height despite the swarm of bullets, "long arms stretched out as if to gather his men together and push them forward," and he marveled, "how the rebels happened to miss Captain Marston I cannot comprehend." In Company A, a bullet shattered Private John Raeder's left arm. The wound would kill him in less than three weeks. Private Henry Steinmetz of Milwaukee fell wounded. Sergeant Henry Schildt of Mazomanie was placing a percussion cap on his rifle-musket when a rebel ball plowed through his side and exited below his shoulder blade. Corporal Yost Zweifel of Milwaukee took a ball that would cost him his right leg. In Company D, Dugald Spear of Black Earth was hit, and Michael Hayden of Milwaukee was struck in the head. Another ball grazed Lieutenant Tom Kerr. Major John Hauser's shouts of "Forwarts, forwarts!" were heard over the gunfire. Dawes said the charging Wisconsin line was a "V-shaped crowd of men, with the colors at the point, moving hurriedly and firmly forward, while the whole field behind is streaming with men plunging in agony to the rear or sinking in death upon the ground"; his men were "leaving the ranks in crowds."[41]

About two rods from the cut, Sergeant George Fairfield noticed the rebels holding their fire "and it became evident we should get a volley, which we did when we were within one rod of the enemy's line." The leveled rebel muskets crashed, and at that very instant, Fairfield glanced down the line to his left: "The volley had been so fatal that it seemed half our men had fallen."[42] Then, said Corporal Frank Wallar, "there was a general rush and yells

41. Rufus R. Dawes, *Sketches of War History*, p. 351; Dawes, *Telegraph*, April 27, 1890.
42. Fairfield, Letter, to Watrous, undated.

enough to almost awaken the dead."[43] On the far left of the line, Loyd Harris said his Brigade Guard contingent "never faltered but held their own with the 6th. . . . The fire was the worst I ever experienced, yet not a man failed to move promptly forward and closed in to the right as the men fell before the murderous fire of the rebels in the railroad cut. . . ."[44] On the far right, Lieutenant Levi Showalter was wounded.

In that instant before the two lines crashed together, Lieutenant William Remington, whose Company I boys were on the regiment's left with the Iron Brigade Guard, saw a chance for glory. The Johnnies had been driven back from their red battle flag, which was stuck in the ground on the edge of the cut. ". . . I thought I could take their flag," Remington said, telling how he moved one or two companies to his right, then through a gap in the 6th Wisconsin line, at a run for the Confederate flag:

> I got hit just at this time on the left side of my neck. It was not of enough account to hardly draw blood. I got quite near the flag, was changing my sword to my left hand, where my revolver was, when I saw a soldier taking aim at me from the railroad cut. I threw my right shoulder forward and kept going for the flag. He hit me through the right shoulder and knocked me down. When I fell I threw my right shoulder forward and kept going for the flag. I crawled forward, got up, walked backward until I got through our regiment, spoke to Major Hauser, got d----d for going after the flag and started for the rear on my best run. Flag-taking was pretty well knocked out of me.

Looking back on that moment, Remington said he was within 15 or 20 feet of the Confederate flag when the bullet knocked him down, and no one was in front of him but the rebels, although at least three soldiers, including Jasper Donglis of the 2nd Wisconsin, who was in the Brigade Guard, rushed the colors immediately after Remington was shot. "The reason I was not hit before, I think was that our fire was too hot for them to show themselves

43. Wallar, *Telegraph*, March 22, 1885.
44. [Harris], *Telegraph*, March 22, 1885.

on top of the cut. I think I was right in thinking I could take the flag . . . ," said Remington.[45]

One of the Wisconsin men rushing the Confederate colorbearer and his red flag was Cornelius W. Okey of Company C:

> I remember seeing Lt. Wm. Remington, Drummer L. Eggleston and myself—there may have been others, but we were close together and making for the rebel flag at the top of our speed, Remington in the center, Eggleston on the right and I on the left. At this time the firing from both sides was very hot, and as we got well out between the two lines it seemed almost impossible to breathe without inhaling a bullet. Lt. Remington was wounded through the right shoulder and Eggleston and myself pressed on, expecting every moment to be shot, but it was too late to turn back. I reached the flag a little in advance of Eggleston and bending over grasped the staff low down, but he was so close to me that before I could draw it from the ground, the staff having been driven well down in the dirt, Eggleston had also got a hold of it. As I straightened up, I noticed a rebel corporal on his knees, right in front of me in the act of firing, his bayonet almost touched me; as quick as thought almost, I made a quarter face to the left, thus pressing my right side to him and bringing Eggleston, who still retained his hold on the flag, as well as myself, at my back. The rebel whom I had noticed fired. His charge, a ball and three buck-shot passed through the skirts of my frock coat in front and lodged in my left fore-arm and wrist. Almost at the same instant Eggleston fell to the ground, having been shot through both arms. . . .[46]

One of the Company H boys, John O. Johnson of Stevens Point, tried to save Eggleston even though his own rifle-musket was fouled, the ramrod jammed halfway down the barrel:

> As I arrived at the edge of the railroad cut, I saw that

45. Remington, *Telegraph*, April 29, 1883. His account was dated December 17, 1882.
46. Okey, *Telegraph*, April 29, 1883.

the rebel color sergeant had stuck the end of his flag staff into the ground and was holding on it with both hands. Louis [sic] Eggleston, one of my mess-mates, whom I loved as a brother, also had hold of the staff and was trying to wrest it from the rebel's grasp. Seeing other rebels raising their guns as if to shoot or bayonet Eggleston, I stepped in front of him and raised my musket to defend him as best I could. While thus in the act of striking, I received a wound that disabled my right arm. Poor Eggleston also went down, and I think from the same bullet that wounded me.[47]

In that same instant, the running 6th Wisconsin men reached the edge of the cut, the Badgers shouting, "Throw down your muskets! Down with your muskets!" to the hundreds of rebels looking up through a swirl of musket smoke from the railroad cut. It was a grim moment, Earl Rogers said:

Bayonets are crossed. The fight was hand to hand amidst firing and smoke. The men are black and grimy with powder and heat. They seemed all unconscious to the terrible situation; they were mad and fought with a desperation seldom witnessed.[48]

With the cries for surrender from his men, Dawes realized his regiment was upon the enemy. He pulled his way through the line. "I found myself face to face with hundreds of rebels, whom I looked down upon in the railroad cut, which was, where I stood, four feet deep," said Dawes. To the right of the regiment, Adjutant Edward Brooks threw a few dozen men across the east end of the cut and they began shooting into the massed Confederates.[49]

47. John O. Johnson, "One Rebel Flag," *Milwaukee Sunday Telegraph*, July 17, 1887.
48. Rogers, Letter, to Watrous, undated.
49. In Dawes, *Service*, p. 169, Dawes said Brooks placed "about twenty men" across the cut. In his March 18, 1868, letter to John B. Bachelder, Dawes said Brooks "with great promptness and foresight threw about fifty men square across the end of the cut toward Gettysburg. . . ." In the handwritten July 17, 1863, Gettysburg Report (probably copied by Brooks himself), Dawes said Brooks "moved a detachment of twenty men" across the cut. Cheek and Pointon, *Sauk County*, p. 74, reported "a part of the 6th . . . got across the end of the cut to enfilade it. . . ." In Dawes, *Telegraph*, April 27, 1890, Dawes does not mention the incident.

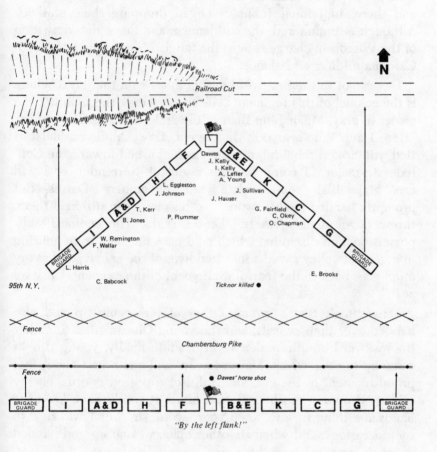

Railroad Cut

B & E
Dawes
J. Kelly
I. Kelly
A. Lefler
A. Young
F
J. Sullivan
H
L. Eggleston
J. Johnson
J. Hauser
K
A & D
T. Kerr
P. Plummer
G. Fairfield
C. Okey
C
B. Jones
O. Chapman
I
W. Remington
F. Wallar
G
BRIGADE
GUARD
L. Harris
BRIGADE
GUARD

95th N.Y.

C. Babcock
Ticknor killed ●
E. Brooks

Fence

Chambersburg Pike

Fence

● *Dawes' horse shot*

| BRIGADE GUARD | I | A & D | H | F | B & E | K | C | G | BRIGADE GUARD |

"By the left flank!"

Mary Slough

197

As the two lines confronted each other at the cut, Loyd Harris said, it was "an even question who should surrender."[50] The charge of the Wisconsin men was furious and determined, and, in the deeper portion of the cut, the Confederate infantrymen, frantically trying to reload, could not see the thinness of the Union line, just hard faces and black hats and pointed muskets. The railroad cut, which first provided protection, now was a trap. Bullets swept the massed, disorganized Confederates, and, here and there, individual Johnnies began dropping their muskets. Although outnumbered, the suddenness and fierce determination of the Wisconsin charge caught the tangled Mississippi and North Carolina soldiers off balance.

Dawes got in the first word and perhaps won the day. "Where is the colonel of this regiment?" he shouted over the shooting. An officer in gray, Major John Blair of the 2nd Mississippi, looked up. "Here I am. Who are you?" In the cut, Dawes pulled aside startled, still-armed rebel infantrymen as he pushed toward the Confederate major. "I command this regiment. Surrender, or I will fire." Major Blair "replied not a word," remembered Dawes, "but promptly handed me his sword, and his men, who still held them, threw down their muskets." Dawes said: "The coolness, self-possession, and discipline which held back our men from pouring in a general volley saved a hundred lives of the enemy, and as my mind goes back to the fearful excitement of the moment, I marvel at it."

Dawes took Blair's sword. Other officers came up and also handed over their swords, and the young Ohioan tried to gather the awkward bundle under his arm, until, finally, young Brooks came up to relieve him. Dawes always had one regret about that proud moment in the cut, an armful of captured swords, enemy soldiers dropping muskets around him: "It would have been the handsome thing to say, 'Keep your sword, sir,' but I was new to such occasions, and when six other officers came up and handed me their swords, I took them also."

Loyd Harris, who had not witnessed the surrender, said he later heard a different version, how, in the deadly instant when victory and defeat hung on a word or movement, Blair had demanded that Dawes surrender, and the young Ohioan replied: "I will see

50. [Harris], *Telegraph*, March 22, 1885.

you in hell first!" But Harris admitted he doubted the story and said Dawes himself did not remember it.[51] The regiment's color company that day was Company B, and Corporal Isaiah Kelly, blood streaming down his trouser leg, was in the crush of soldiers near Dawes and Blair, he and the other Calico boys "on the look out" to keep the Johnnies from shooting Dawes. When the Confederate major was told the Union regiment confronting him was the 6th Wisconsin, Kelly said, the rebel officer replied: "Thank God. I thought it was a New York regiment."[52]

As Dawes was getting the surrender of Major Blair, a "deadly melee" still swirled around the exposed Confederate flag of the 2nd Mississippi. Wounded and flag taking knocked out of him, Bill Remington was backing out of the fight. Private Bodley Jones, who left Sauk County with his father's blessing two years earlier, put his hand on the Confederate flag, only to be shot dead.[53] Cornelius Okey, Lewis Eggleston and John Johnson were down. When Eggleston was shot, his partner, "Rocky Mountain" Anderson, swung his rifle-musket like a club, crushing the skull of the rebel who had shot young Eggleston. Around the Confederate

51. [Harris], *Telegraph*, March 22, 1885.
52. Dawes, *Service*, p. 169; Kelly, Letter, to Dawes, August 2, 1892. The Dawes account, written almost 30 years after the fact, had the nice touch of an old soldier story: Officers on both sides gallant in victory and defeat; brave words exchanged despite the excitement and heat of the moment, and the voiced regret over how it could have been better done. Even ex-Confederate John A. Blair, in an October 31, 1890 letter to Dawes from Tupelo, Mississippi, where he was practicing law, played his role as honored foe. "It seems that you did not know of that railroad cut at Gettysburg nor did we," Blair wrote after Dawes had sent him a copy of his war memoir:

> After driving the first line of battle we met and seeing no other troops in our front (you must have been concealed by an eminence between us) we concluded we would capture Gettysburg without further difficulty or bloodshed and end the war right there. It was therefore, a great surprise to us when we came up to the railroad cut, and greater one when you swung around on our left and bagged us.

Blair added a final question, brother officer to brother officer: "What became of the sword I gave you?"
53. Dawes, *Service*, p. 169. Cheek and Pointon, *Sauk County*, p. 47. The two Company A men said Wallar told them: "Bodley Jones of A Company had made for the flag in the charge and had captured it and had it in his possession when killed. I grabbed it as Jones fell and carried it back and surrendered it to our proper officers and I got the medal of honor for the capture. But if he had not been killed, he and not I would have had the medal." The Cheek and Pointon account is the only reference linking Bodley Jones as being involved in the fight for the flag. However, it is likely Jones was one of those who rushed the colorbearer of the 2nd Mississippi.

199

flag, said Earl Rogers, "the men stood in the flash and smoke of the contending lines, shooting, thrusting and parrying thrusts."[54] In the tangle of fighting and downed soldiers, Corporal Frank Wallar quickly moved toward the flag, his brother, Sam, at his side. One of the Confederate soldiers pointed a musket at Frank, but Sam parried the barrel as the gun went off, reversed his own rifle-musket and clubbed down the Johnny with the butt.[55] Nearby, John Harland of Company I, was shot just as he reached for the Confederate flag, his body tumbling into the railroad cut at the foot of the soldier who killed him. His friend, Levi Tongue, brought his rifle-musket up, drawing down pointblank on the rebel. "Don't shoot! Don't kill me!" the Johnny cried, but Tongue grimly answered, "All hell can't save you now." Tongue fired and the heavy bullet knocked the rebel backward onto Harland's body.[56] Frank Wallar neared the red Confederate battleflag:

> I had no thought of getting the flag till at this time, and I started straight for it, as did lots of others. Soon after I got the flag, there were men from all the companies there. I did take the flag out of the color bearer's hand . . . My first thought was to go to the rear with it for fear it might be retaken, and then I thought I would stay, and I threw it down and loaded and fired twice standing on it. While standing on it there was a 14th Brooklyn man took hold of it and tried to get it, and I had threatened to shoot him before he would stop. By this time we had them cleaned out. . . .[57]

The target of the furious assault by the 6th Wisconsin men was W. B. Murphy of Company A, 2nd Mississippi. Murphy, the senior corporal of the color party for the Confederate regiment, carried the flag that morning because Color Sergeant Christopher Columbus Davis was sick.[58] Murphy said his brigade drove Cutler's Union battle line from the field and his 2nd Mississippi was

54. Rogers, *Telegraph*, July 29, 1883.
55. *Ibid*. Rogers said the story was told to him by Sam Wallar.
56. Rogers, Letter, to Watrous, undated.
57. Wallar, *Telegraph*, July 29, 1883. In later years, several other 6th Wisconsin soldiers claimed they had actually captured the flag of the 2nd Mississippi. A full discussion of the old soldier controversy is contained in Appendix II.
58. W. B. Murphy, Letter, to Rufus R. Dawes, June 20, 1892; D. J. Hill, Letter, to Rufus R. Dawes, September 12, 1893.

THE BOYS OF '61

(Front l. to r.) George W. White, John J. Dillon, Charles D. Elliott, James F. Parkhurst, (Rear) Worthie H. Patton, William A. Dillon, Lyman L. White.

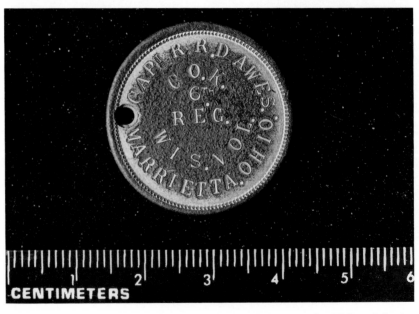

RUFUS R. DAWES DOGTAGS
Found 100 Years Later Near Fredericksburg

MARY BEMAN GATES
The "My Best Girl" of the Rufus Dawes Letters

LT. JOHN CRANE
Helped Mickey Enlist

GEORGE FAIRFIELD
Maintained a Neat Diary

Sauk County Rifleman

MAIR POINTON
Wrote the History of Company A

LT. PATRICK McCAULEY
Ran Afoul of the "Tough One"

EARL M. ROGERS
Postwar Photo
They Called Him "Bona"

LT. JOHN KELLOGG
Helped Raise Company K

MAJ. JOHN HAUSER
He Led "Hauser's Geese"

LT. COL.
EDWARD S. BRAGG
The Little Colonel

Capt Jw...
Plummer
6th Wis

THOMAS W. PLUMMER
One of Company C's English Brothers

PHILIP W. PLUMMER
One of Company C's English Brothers

CAPT. WILLIAM H. LINDWURM
Raised the German Citizens' Corps

LEVI B. RAYMOND
Upset When Company Officers Resigned

JOHN GIBBON
They Called Him "Boss Soldier"

at the cut when the soldiers first noticed the approaching 6th Wisconsin. The Wisconsin regiment, he said, halted at the roadway "for some time" to fire before they charged:

> My color guards were all killed and wounded in less than five minutes, and also my colors were shot more than one dozen times, and the flag staff was hit and splintered two or three times. Just about that time a squad of soldiers made a rush for my colors and our men did their duty. They were all killed or wounded, but they still rushed for the colors with one of the most deadly struggles that was ever witnessed during any battle in the war. They still kept rushing for my flag and there were over a dozen shot down like sheep in their mad rush for the colors. The first soldier was shot down just as he made for the flag, and he was shot by one of our soldiers. Just to my right and at the same time a lieutenant [Remington] made a desperate struggle for the flag and was shot through the right shoulder. Over a dozen men fell killed or wounded, and then a large man made a rush for me and the flag. As I tore the flag from the staff he took hold of me and the color. The firing was still going on, and was kept up for several minutes after the flag was taken from me. . . .[59]

59. W. B. Murphy, Letter to Dr. F. A. Dearborn, Nashua, N. H., June 29, 1900. Murphy had earlier been sent by Rufus R. Dawes a copy of *Service With The Sixth Wisconsin Volunteers*. In this letter, which was found in the papers of Edward S. Bragg, Murphy said he was "about fifty spaces East of the cut, and on the side toward Gettysburg, and I and my color guard were about ten spaces South of the railroad. There was no cut there at all; the ditch was not more than two feet deep where I passed over the railroad. Our regiment stopped in the railroad for protection. . . ." He also added:

> I have learned through Gen. R. R. Dawes that Sargt. Francis A. Waller of Co. I, 6th Wisconsin, who seized the flag from me received a medal of honor for the deed. I have heard that one, Anderson, of Co. I, 6th Wisconsin threw his musket aloft and split the head of the rebel that killed Eggleston of Co. I, 6th Wisconsin. If he did I did not see it. I am willing to swear that no rebel soldier was killed there that day with the butt of a gun. Though, he might have killed one of our soldiers cowardly after we prisoners were taken off the field of battle. . . . Gen. R. R. Dawes is in error when he says that the rebels began to throw down their guns and arms when his command reached the railroad in token of surrender, and also he is in error when he says that Adjutant Ed Brooks placed a detachment of men in the railroad cut to enfilade [sic] the rebels

In that instant while Corporal Murphy, 2nd Mississippi, was manhandled by a "large man" named Frank Wallar, and Lieutenant Colonel Rufus R. Dawes and Major John Blair negotiated a battlefield surrender, the shooting still rattled along the railroad cut. With Lieutenant Orrin Chapman killed, George Fairfield, bleeding from a hip wound, found himself in command of Company C. Despite being outnumbered, he said, the "old 6th stood firm and would have made great slaughter down the cut had they [the Confederates] not surrendered." He jumped into the cut, passing in the rear of a line of prisoners and found Aaron Yates, whom Rufus Dawes had called from a farmfield so long ago, in

---

if they should try to make a break to escape through the railroad cut. The cut was more than sixty yards through and about ten feet deep at the highest point, and about fifty spaces to my right. . . . I was captured about 10:30 a.m. . . . I was color bearer of the 2nd Mississippi Volunteers in the late Civil War between the states. But there is no North, nor South to-day with me, and it was a great blessing for the American people that we had the war, for now we are one and live under the best government in the world.

In 1890, Rufus Dawes had sent a copy of his war memoir to Murphy. Former rebel Murphy and Dawes exchanged friendly letters. In one dated June 20, 1892, from Mooresville, Falls County, Texas, Murphy addressed Dawes as his "Dear Friend." In his August 1, 1892 letter, Dawes had become "My comrade and friend." Both letters were the rambling accounts of an old soldier, but there were a few additional details on Gettysburg. In his June 20 letter, Murphy claimed his regiment shot and killed Union I Army Corps Commander John Reynolds:

. . . [T]he first regiment of U.S. troops was in line just north of where you captured us in the railroad cut. We attacked them with a very heavy loss and the rest of them that was not killed and wounded retreated. It did seem to me that there was about half their number killed on the field, and just at that critical moment Genl. Reynold [sic] and staff rode up in about 100 yards to our right just over the hill in some timber to our right and our Reg. 2nd Miss, gave him one volley from our rifles and I was told that Genl Reynold was killed and nearly all of his staff were killed or wounded.

Murphy also wrote:

You will remember that our Reg. killed several of your command in the cut before you and Maj. Blair could cease hostilities. There was three or four men killed or wounded before they got the colors from me. . . . My Dear Genl. I would like very much to have my old flag back again for a keep sake; there is nothing that I would appreciate more highly than to see it once more in my life as I am 50 years in July 13, 1892 and by the time you receive this letter say July 1st, 1892, twenty nine years go since you or some one of your command took the flag out of my hands. Oh, it seems as if were only yesterday since that deadly conflict in the Rail road Cut at Gettysburg.

"deadly combat" with a rebel lieutenant armed with a sword: "The demand was made that Yates withdraw his bayonet, which he did. The Lieut. was then commanded to sheathe his sword which he did with thanks and moved out his men as prisoners of war. Yates would have been killed had he persisted, as the enemy had their arms." Looking back on the moment, Fairfield concluded: "Davis' whole brigade was in the cut and could neither fight nor retreat . . . on account of the high banks. . . ."[60] When the sergeant reached the left of the 6th Wisconsin line, he found "the rest of Davis's Mississippi Brigade had broken off and were retreating out the other end of the cut, as the cut was too deep for them to see the scarcity of our numbers or make attack. The 2d Miss. lay in the water, mud and blood at the east end of the cut where the cut was coming out to a grade."[61]

In the cut just left of where Corporal Wallar captured the flag of the 2nd Mississippi, Captain John Marston of Company E ordered a rebel captain to hand over his sword to Lyman White of his company. The Appleton soldier, Marston said, "in the line of his duty, was about to bayonet the captain, but as I detected a command from this officer or his men to surrender, at this instant I sprang and caught Lyman's gun and saved the captain's life."[62]

One of the Confederates who escaped capture was 2nd Mississippi Private D. J. Hill:

> I was in [the railroad cut] and soon found to my dismay that I was in a tight place, saw no chance of escape,

60. Fairfield, Letter, to Watrous, undated; George Fairfield, "The 6th Wis. at Gettysburg," *National Tribune*, December 14, 1905.
61. Fairfield, *Tribune*, December 14, 1905.
62. Joseph Marston, *Milwaukee Sunday Telegraph*, April 24, 1881. In writing of the incident for a Milwaukee weekly newspaper nearly two decades later, Marston added:

> Now, my soldier boy Lyman is no more on earth. His mother and father are also dead. I have the sword in my possession. Now, as I call to mind the manly appearing officer, I have but one wish, and this is, if he is living, to return him his sword, as I drew my sword not in hatred. If this communication should reach the officer and he will inform me of the inscription on the scabbard as it was presented and by whom, with any other little incident that he may remember in connection with this charge, I will return him the sword and at the same time will give your paper a further account.

The dispatch was marked: "Mississippi papers please copy." No record exists whether Marston ever found the "manly appearing" rebel whose sword he had captured in the railroad cut.

was disgusted with the idea of surrendering and in fact became very much demoralized. I saw a bloody, muddy blanket lying on the ground also two wounded men lying near me. I tumbled down by them and covered myself with that blanket I then went to practicing all maneuvers and moaning that I thought would become a badly wounded and suffering man.

Some of the black hats "eyed" him, Hill said, but he was left there "as sound and well as I ever was in my life. I tell this not that I think it is a sharp or brave trick but that it is true and may go for what it is worth."[63]

In Company K, on the right side of the 6th Wisconsin line, as the fighting sputtered down, high private James P. "Mickey" Sullivan, who just may have been the unluckiest Irishman in the I Corps, suffered his third battle wound:

Some of the Johnnies threw down their guns and surrendered. Some would fire and then throw down their guns and cry, 'I surrender,' and some of them broke for the rear. I jumped into the railroad cut and a rebel officer handed me his sword and I passed through the cut with the intention of stopping the Johnnies, who were limbering to the rear. Just as I climbed up the side of the cut, a big rebel broke for the rear and I called on him to halt, to which he paid no attention, and I flung the rebel sword at him with all my might, but I never knew whether I hit him or not, for just as I turned to throw the sword, a bullet him me on the left shoulder and knocked me down as quick as if I had been hit with a sledge hammer. The first thought I had was that some rebel had hit me with the butt of his gun, for I felt numb and stunned, but I was not long in finding out what was the matter. I think that when I turned to throw the sword it saved my life, as otherwise I would have been shot square through the body. Sergeant [Albert] Tarbox came up the side of the cut and seeing me says, "they've got you down, Mickey, have they?" and then fell for-

63. D. J. Hill, Letter, to Rufus Dawes, September 12, 1893, Dawes Papers, SHSW. The letter was written from Blue Mountain, Mississippi.

ward dead, some of the damned rebs who had surrendered having shot him as he straightened up. They did a good deal of that kind of work that day. In all my experience of battles before or since, I never saw so many men killed in such a short time, as it was not more than fifteen or twenty minutes from the time we saw the rebels until we had them, officers, colors and all. Frank Wallar, of Co. I, got their flag, and I learned afterwards 27 of our men were killed or wounded trying to get it.[64]

The target of Sullivan's thrown sword was probably A. H. Belo, who was in command of the 55th North Carolina since the wounding earlier that morning of the unit's colonel:

> One officer, seeing me, threw his sword at me and said: "Kill that officer, and we will capture that command." One of my men, however, picked him off and we were able to get out of the railroad cut after a severe struggle.

At least, that was how the two soldiers remembered that furious moment. Belo, seeing the sword Sullivan was carrying, apparently assumed he was a Federal officer; Sullivan's demand to halt probably contained stronger words than the rather polite phrasing Belo remembered.[65]

In any case, the shooting slowed and almost stopped. On the east side of the cut, the 6th Wisconsin men and officers pushed the captured rebels into a line. Other Johnnies escaped out the west end of the cut, and another ragged Confederate line north of the unfinished railroad pulled back. From a woods on Seminary Ridge, John Kellogg, a 6th Wisconsin officer serving on 2nd Brigade Commander Lysander Cutler's staff, watched his old regiment clean out the Johnnies. He recalled it was "three minutes," after the 6th Wisconsin reached the unfinished railroad, long enough for Frank Wallar to capture a Confederate flag and load and fire twice, before the 95th New York and 14th Brooklyn reached the west end of the cut, pouring a volley into the fleeing, massed Confederates. The 55th North Carolina, retreating up the

64. Sullivan, *Telegraph*, December 20, 1885.
65. Belo, *CV*, pp. 165-168. The article was based on a talk by Belo before the Sterling Price Camp of Dallas, Texas, January 20, 1900.

slope north of the cut, fired back, and the fighting flared with yells and more shooting until, finally, it sputtered again to a few scattered shots.[66]

Afterward, Colonel Edward B. Fowler of the 14th Brooklyn (officially the 84th New York Infantry) inflated the role of his soldiers, even claiming in his official report that it was he who directed the 6th Wisconsin, and it was he who ordered his regiment, the 95th New York and 6th Wisconsin to charge Davis' Brigade so "all the enemy within our reach surrendered—officers, battle-flag, and men." It may have been that Fowler, senior officer on a field where a brave deed had been accomplished, claimed a bit more than he should have, but if that puffed up the 14th Brooklyn and 95th New York—and its colonel—it diminished the independent, deliberate decision of Rufus R. Dawes to attack the flank of an entire Confederate brigade with his small regiment, and forever blurred the credit due the 6th Wisconsin men. Dawes and the others spent the rest of their lives trying to set the record straight, but it was never accomplished.[67]

The letters, reports and published accounts came later, however, and on the field west of Gettysburg, near the unfinished railroad cut, the 6th Wisconsin, 95th New York, 14th Brooklyn and soldiers from the Brigade Guard tried to get their prisoners to the rear. No one was sure if there were more Confederates over the hill or what might happen next. Division Commander James Wadsworth and his staff rode up just after the surrender, accompanied by a few squads of cavalry to help with the prisoners. The old general and his officers had anxiously watched the charge and the savage fighting at the railroad cut. When the national flag carried by the Wisconsin regiment lifted in victory, Wadsworth turned to his young officers, waving his hat, and shouted: "My God, the 6th has conquered them!"[68]

Lieutenant Colonel Rufus Dawes ordered Major John Blair to have his men fall in without arms and directed Major John F. Hauser to march the body of prisoners to the provost-guard. The

66. John Kellogg, Letters, to John B. Bachelder, November 1, 1865, and March 31, 1868; Fairfield, *Tribune*, December 14, 1905; Rogers, *Telegraph*, May 13, 1887; J. P. Sullivan, "The Sixth Wis. at Gettysburg," *National Tribune*, June 21, 1885. For a full discussion of the action of the 14th Brooklyn in the charge on the railroad cut, see Appendix II.
67. See Appendix II.
68. Rogers, Letter, to Watrous, undated.

6th Wisconsin, with assistance from the 95th New York and 14th Brooklyn, had bagged seven officers and 225 enlisted men, including the battle flag, Major Blair and 87 men of the 2nd Mississippi.[69] Dawes called for volunteers to form a skirmish line, and Lieutenant William Goltermann of Company F took charge of the "10 or 15" men who stepped forward. They ran off and took possession, without opposition, of "the ridge toward the enemy" to guard against a surprise return by the Confederates. Near the Chambersburg Pike, the 2nd Maine Artillery had left a disabled gun. Captain Rollin P. Converse gathered a detail of Company I men and began to pull it to the turnpike so the artillerymen could reclaim the piece. Private Levi Tongue of Company I recalled, with some satisfaction, the Maine artillerymen "thank us a thousand times."[70]

One of the wounded men to hitch a ride on the artillery piece claimed by the Maine gunners was Sergeant Michael Mangan. Private Dunn helped him on the rifled cannon and held the wounded soldier as they moved toward Gettysburg. On Seminary Ridge, Dunn found a door to use as a stretcher, and he and others carried Mangan to the makeshift hospital being set up in Washington Hotel in the town.

Among the wounded men still in the cut, Union and Confederate, "Mickey" Sullivan was coming around:

> After a while I began to feel better, and like a true Irishman I spoke to myself to see if was dead or only speechless, and finding it was only the latter, I picked up my gun and tried to shoulder it, but I found that my left arm was powerless. I went around to the other side of the cut where our fellows had a heavy line of prisoners, and a very thin skirmish line of themselves, and took my place outside the rebs, intending to help guard them, but I felt sick and faint and the blood was running down

69. Dawes probably underestimated the prisoners his regiment captured. Shortly after the charge, his reduced 6th Wisconsin again marched through the unfinished railroad cut and "about one thousand muskets lay in the bottom of it." Dawes also noted: "The ninety-fifth New York took prisoners, as did also the fourteenth Brooklyn. All the troops in the railroad cut threw down their muskets, and the men either surrendered themselves, or ran away out of the other end of the cut. Dawes, *Service*, p. 173.
70. Levi Tongue, Letter, to wife, July 2, 1863.

inside my clothes and dropping from my pants leg and my shoe was full and running over. I had a canteen of fresh milk that an old Pennsylvania Dutchman had given me that morning, and one of the rebs took it off for me and held it while I took a big swig, which helped me a good bit.[71]

Corporal Frank Wallar, his rifle-musket still warm in his hands, volunteered to join the skirmish line. Before he ran off with the others, he asked Dawes what he should do with the flag. "Give it to me," Dawes said. The red, square flag was marked with the names "Manassas," "Gaines Farm," "Malvern Hill," and "Seven Pines." Nearby, Sergeant William Evans of Company H, who had been shot through the upper legs, was hobbling to the rear, using two muskets for crutches. "It is a rule in battle not to allow sound men to leave the ranks," Dawes said; so he took the flag from its staff and tied it around Evan's body under the coat, telling the wounded sergeant to "keep it safely against all hazards."[72] Evans joined the stream of wounded men making for Gettysburg. Adjutant Brooks also turned his bundle of captured swords over to another wounded man, keeping one, which he buckled on his belt. The swords were delivered to Surgeon A. W. Preston, but were lost when the Confederates captured the town later in the day. In later telling the story, Dawes added: "No discredit to the doctor is implied, as his hands were full of work with wounded men."[73]

Just after the surrender, Corporal Kelly of Company B, responding to shouts from the right of the line "They are getting away!" ran down the unfinished railroad bed with several others to halt more Johnnies trying to flee from the east end of the cut. There were angry shouts and some pushing and shoving, then a rebel lieutenant fired his revolver at the Wisconsin men and was shot dead by John Killmartin of Company G. The captured soldiers, Kelly said, were finally turned over to some Union cavalry, and he and the others took their place in line as the regiment reformed north of the cut.

At that instant, a lone Confederate soldier jumped up and

71. Sullivan, *Telegraph*, December 20, 1884.
72. Dawes, *Service*, p. 172.
73. *Ibid.*, p. 170.

started to run up the ridge. "Jones [Enoch Jones of Portage] and I fired at him and he fell," Kelly said, and the two Badgers chased up the slope, where they found the downed Johnny with a broken leg. Further on, Kelly said, there was a "56th Penn. boy shot through the body. . . ." From near the railroad cut, Rufus Dawes yelled up to Kelly to take a "look around," and the corporal did so, finding no more rebels:

> I returned to the regiment and had just taken my place on the right of the Co. when two shots were fired from the old fence from which I had just returned. One shot struck Corporal [Charles W.] Mead [of Company G] on the head and killed him and the other went through the rim of my hat so close to my head that it almost burned a blister. Mead was the last one of the brave color guard who went into the fight.

Company B commander Captain John Hyatt picked up the downed national flag. The officer asked Corporal Frank Hare and one or two others to take the banner, Kelly said, "but for some reason or other, they did not do it." Rufus Dawes was standing behind the company, and finally, Kelly turned and told his commander he would carry the flag. "All right, Corporal," Dawes replied. And that was how Corporal I. F. Kelly, wounded in the knee in the charge on the railroad cut, so sick with dysentery he was reduced to "a skeleton" and had barely kept up on the march from Fredericksburg to Gettysburg, was handed the "old flag" of the 6th Wisconsin and "carried it through the rest of the fight."[74]

In the thin line of Badgers guarding the Confederate prisoners to be marched away to the provost guard, "Mickey" Sullivan of Company K was in worse shape. General Wadsworth noticed the bleeding private and went up to the slight Irishman. "My man, you are too badly hurt to be here," Wadsworth said. The general called a cavalry sergeant and directed him to assist Sullivan onto his horse and take him to a hospital established in Gettysburg, and not to leave the wounded private "until he saw me in care of a doctor."[75] Finally, Sullivan was helped on the sergeant's horse and taken to Gettysburg. The fighting by his regiment that

74. Kelly, Letter, to Dawes, August 2, 1892.
75. Sullivan, *Telegraph*, December 20, 1884.

Wednesday of July 1, 1863, was not over, but the farmer-turned-soldier was out of it, at least for a time, and behind him that midday he left a badly wrecked 6th Wisconsin infantry.

In the lull in the fighting, Dawes dispatched several soldiers from his small battle line to assist 6th Wisconsin wounded on the field near the Chambersburg Pike, while others searched the railroad cut itself for downed comrades. In McPherson's Woods, south of the Chambersburg Pike, the other Iron Brigade regiments had been successful in driving Archer's soldiers from the trees, capturing the commander himself—the first general officer of the Army of Northern Virginia to fall into enemy hands since Lee had taken command—and, in fact, nearly wrecking the Confederate Brigade. North of the Chambersburg Pike, Davis' Brigade had been so sharply repulsed by the fierce charge of the 6th Wisconsin that Confederate Division Commander Henry Heth pulled it out of line because he believed the regiments too badly banged up to fight again that day.[76] In the final tally, the successful charge of the 6th Wisconsin, "singly and alone," as Loyd Harris said, saved the Union position. It was an action that would have far-reaching results. McPherson's Ridge covered the western approaches to the town, and the woods on it afforded protection for Union soldiers to fire on enemy columns moving on either the Chambersburg Pike or the Fairfield Road. Davis' Mississippians and North Carolinians had driven off Cutler's regiments and were slowly wheeling to where they could hit the right and rear of the Iron Brigade as it battled Archer's soldiers in McPherson's Woods. Although outnumbered, the 6th Wisconsin and Brigade Guard hit Davis' three regiments at the critical moment, with such fierce determination the Confederate soldiers tumbled backwards in confusion, breaking off the attack. That meant the fighting in the afternoon of July 1 took place west of Gettysburg, and, in the end, the Union line along McPherson's Ridge severely delayed Confederate units trying to seize the town before elements

76. *O.R.*, Series One, Volume 27, Part Two, p. 638. This is the report of Confederate General Henry Heth, who noted: "Davis' brigade was kept on the left of the road that it might collect its stragglers, and from its shattered condition it was not deemed advisable to bring it again into action on that day." One of the reasons Heth took the action could have been that many of the soldiers in the Confederate brigade lacked weapons. Many of Davis' men left their muskets behind in fleeing the cut. Rufus Dawes said his men counted about 1,000 muskets dropped by Confederates as they retreated from the cut. Dawes, *Service*, p. 173.

of the Army of the Potomac occupied the key high ground south of Gettysburg.

But the cost was frightful. Seven of 12 company commanders in the 6th Wisconsin were shot. The rebels killed Captain John Ticknor of Company K and Lieutenant Orrin Chapman of Company C. The wounded officers included Howard F. Pruyn, the quiet commander of Company A; impetuous Lieutenant William Remington of Company I; the German lieutenant of Company H, John Beeley; and the two officers commanding the companies of the Brigade Guard, Lieutenants Harris of Company C and Showalter of the 2nd Wisconsin.

Finally, when it appeared the Confederates would not immediately return, the regiment pulled back into the woods on Seminary Ridge, east of the railroad cut, where Dawes dismissed the Brigade Guard, returning the men to their regiments; then "a sad half hour was spent calling the dead roll and reorganizing the companies."[77] Of the 340 soldiers Dawes took into the battle, more than 160 were down, dead or missing, most of them in the few minutes the regiment dashed from the pike to the railroad cut. He never determined how many of the soldiers in the Brigade Guard had been lost.[78]

One of the wounded soldiers left on the field between the pike and the cut was Private Frank King of Fond du Lac, the Company E boy who had just missed out on being assigned to the Signal Corps the previous year. He was a regimental favorite, a soldier "who never missed a fight or neglected a duty," a "rollicking young fellow," and who was "always cheerful, full of stories and the delight of his comrades," said a friend. He was one of the camp singers, and one of the men who came into the company with him

77. Dawes, *Telegraph*, April 27, 1890.
78. Dawes, *Service*, p. 168; Rufus R. Dawes, Letter, July 19, 1863, to Aug. Gaylord, Adjutant General, State of Wisconsin. In his report to state officials, Dawes put his regimental loss at 165. The breakdown included two officers killed, six wounded, 27 enlisted men killed, 105 wounded and 25 men missing. Sergeant Mangan was listed as the acting second lieutenant of Company E. William W. Dudley, a 19th Indiana officer wounded at Gettysburg, in his "official report" on the Iron Brigade at Gettysburg, listed 22 soldiers in the Brigade Guard as wounded, including the two officers. However, a number of the wounded and killed credited to other regiments were probably injured while serving with the Brigade Guard. A reasonable estimate of the Brigade Guard's casualties would be between 30 and 35. William W. Dudley, *The Iron Brigade at Gettysburg*, (Cincinnati, Ohio, 1879), p. 15.

in 1861 remembered he "always drew an audience."[79] King had been shot through the body and knew he was dying. Several times, he had called out to the Wisconsin soldiers moving amid the wounded, "You are my friend. I beg you to end my misery, shoot me." But that was a hard thing, and those young men who could face anything could not face the wounded soldier's eyes and what he asked, so they hurried away carrying a dark memory. Finally, George M. Keyt of Rockford, Illinois, who had enlisted in Company G at Beloit, passed by, and King called out, "I have asked a dozen of the boys to help me, Keyt, but they declined." Keyt went over and took in the whole situation. The two did not belong to the same company, but were friends. "What can I do for you, Frank?" Keyt asked. "I want you to shoot me, George, and end my misery. I am shot through the body and must die. I want to die now. Please shoot me," King begged. Telling later of that grim minute, Keyt said he drew back for a second, then brought up his rifle-musket, aiming it at King's heart. One long second passed, and another, Keyt looking down his musket barrel, then, instead of firing, he broke and fled, remembering he ran "as he never ran before."[80] Three days later, a burial party would find King's body where Keyt had left him.

A short time later, during a lull in the fighting, as the Union soldiers arranged their lines for the next Confederate attack, Rufus R. Dawes took a few minutes to keep a promise he had made during the charge of his regiment on the railroad cut. He withdrew the small journal he carried in his pocket, found a pencil and began to write: "Battle Field near Gettysburg, July 1st, 1863. 2 p.m., Bloody desperate fight." He started another line, only to scratch it out and begin again: "Major Stone [sic] of the 2nd Miss. Infantry surrendered his sword and regiment to me—230 men. If I am killed today let it be known that Corporal James Kelley [sic] of Company B shot through the breast, and mortally wounded, asked to tell his folks he died a soldier. . . ." From that day, Rufus R. Dawes, in writing or telling of the charge of his 6th Wisconsin Infantry on an unfinished railroad cut at Get-

79. [Watrous], *Telegraph*, July 27, 1895.
80. Jerome A. Watrous, "Soldier Stories," *Milwaukee Telegraph*, November 24, 1894.

tysburg, always related the story of Corporal James Kelly of Company B, a boy who left his Wisconsin home to be killed on a faraway battlefield so a Union of states could be preserved.[81]

81. Rufus R. Dawes, Journal, July 1, 1863, Dawes Papers, SHSW. Dawes later added a note to his entry: "Memorandum in pencil kept by myself on the battle of Gettysburg as the fight progressed." His usual neat, tight handwriting was a nervous scrawl as he wrote the first entry.

JEROME A. WATROUS
Chronicler of the Sixth Wisconsin
214

CHAPTER SEVEN

But the heavenly Commander has said, we have heard,
    That duty, well done, shall have its reward.
When the long roll is sounded, the great muster day,
    May we all meet in Heaven—brave Company "K."
                                        —By "Mickey"

Gettysburg

Private J. P. Sullivan rode into Gettysburg on a cavalry horse
ordered up for him by a general. But the farmer-turned-soldier,
late of Wonewoc, Juneau County, Wisconsin, never made much
of it as being out of place for a soldier boy wounded doing his
duty on a battlefield. Sullivan found the streets of Gettysburg
crowded with soldiers, some wounded and others not, but as yet
no panic was evident. Despite the heavy fighting of the morning,
the townsfolk were out in force, assisting the steady stream of
Union wounded. "Ladies and gentlemen . . . had wine and re-
freshments of all kinds on tables and trays, and in their hands,"
the Irishman said, "and urged them on every wounded man, and
assisted them in every way." The cavalry sergeant pulled up in
front of the Courthouse, which had been converted into a temporary hospital:

> [T]here I found "Old Syntax," (Dr. Hall) [Dr. John C.
> Hall] and Dr. [O. F.] Bartlett and a good many more
> "quinines," citizens and military, busy cutting up and
> patching up the biggest part of the sixth regiment, and
> in due time I was put together with sticking plaster and
> bandages and was served with some good strong coffee
> that the citizens brought in, and feeling faint, I lay down
> on the floor and tried to rest myself, and after awhile,
> I felt well enough to look around and see how many of
> Company K had got punched. I found that nearly every

215

man in the company was in the same fix I was, and some
a great deal worse.

Sergeant Eugene Rose of Lemonwier had lost a leg and Corporal Abe Fletcher, from the same town, had his leg cut off at the thigh "for all the world like a sugar-cured ham," said Sullivan. Billy Van Wie of Lafayette was "grunting about a crack he had got," and Peter Everson of Mauston "had a hole in his thigh, big enough to put one fist in," while the Hancock brothers lay in one corner—Wallace shot in the arm and Billy in the breast. Sullivan also found wounded Sile Temple of Newport, and two other Lemonweir boys, Chauncey Wilcox and Lon Pratt, as well as Charley Crawford, whose cartridge box and belts Sullivan had taken on the battlefield. Even little Hugh Talty, "Tall T," was there. Talty had gotten his canteen filled with whiskey by one of the citizens, Sullivan said, and he "didn't feel his wound" and was bragging "how the ould sixth, be gob, could niver be whipt, be gob." More of the wounded Company K boys were also being treated in a nearby railroad depot, but Sullivan said, "I thought there were enough here out of the little squad of a company that went into the fight that morning."[1]

Corporal Cornelius Okey of the Jayhawkers of Company C, who tried to pull in a rebel flag and got a blast of buckshot in the left forearm and wrist for his trouble, reached Gettysburg and the make-shift Courthouse hospital about the same time. Okey had pulled out as soon as he was hit. "On my way to town, near the seminary and passing a house, I noticed the door standing open, and, thinking I might get my arm bandaged up, I went in," Okey said. "Found the house deserted, a baby's cradle was standing there and looked as though the mother had hastily taken the child out of it and left all the little bed clothing in the cradle." In the bed was a "small pillow," and Okey used it to support his shattered arm until he reached Gettysburg where he was directed to Courthouse.[2] Also reaching the town about that time were Private Harry Dunn and Sergeant Michael Mangan. Dunn carried the wounded non-commissioned officer into the Washington Hotel, where a surgeon a short time later amputated Mangan's leg.[3]

1. Sullivan, *Telegraph*, December 20, 1884.
2. Okey, *Telegraph*, April 29, 1883.
3. *Soldiers' and Citizens Album*, p. 171.

Wounded Color Corporal Francis Deleglise was also making to the rear as best as he could, having fallen in with a group of Confederate prisoners being herded to the provost guard. He was helped along by the Johnnies until two Union cavalry troopers came up and finally carried him to the cellar of a brick house in Gettysburg, where a dozen or so wounded soldiers, both Federal and Confederate, were lying side by side on the stone floor, "no longer divided by factional opinion, but united in a common suffering."[4]

On the fields west of Gettysburg, the 6th Wisconsin, now attached to Cutler's 2nd Brigade, was in line north of the railroad cut when the heavily reinforced Confederate lines again started for the town. The Union I and XI Corps were on the field, spread in a line along McPherson's Ridge and north of Gettysburg, but the Union regiments were outnumbered, and the confident, yelling Confederate brigades hit the blue line like hammer blows. Soon, north of town, the regiments of the XI Corps began to fray and give way, and the trickle of blue soldiers making for the town became a steady stream.

The 6th Wisconsin had been fighting in support of Battery B of the 4th U.S. Artillery, as it had on so many fields from Brawner's Farm to Antietam. "During this time the [Confederate] attack was progressing," Rufus R. Dawes said, "I stood among the guns of battery 'B.' Along the Seminary ridge, flat upon their bellies, lay mixed up together on one line of battle, the 'Iron Brigade' and Roy Stone's 'Bucktails.' For a mile up and down the open fields in front, the splendid lines of the veterans of the army of Northern Virginia swept down upon us." The battery opened with a roar and soon the Wisconsin men and Stone's Pennsylvanians poured in a steady fire. The rebel line faltered, then broke and retreated, Dawes said, as his men yelled, "Come on, Johnny! Come on!"[5] In a short time, the Confederates came again, more determined, and the fighting was grim and furious. Up by the six smoothbores, watching the rebel advance, Dawes had left Captain Rollin Converse in command of the 6th. Lieutenant Clayton Rogers, from General Wadsworth's staff, came looking for Dawes, and Converse stepped forward, pointing toward the guns. Corporal I. F. Kelly watched the two officers talk for a few minutes,

4. *Ibid.*, p. 723.
5. Dawes, *Service*, p. 175.

then "Rogers . . . ordered the Regt back and Converse about faced us. We had not moved far when . . . [Dawes] rushed through the ranks, jerked the old flag out of my hands and halted the Regt. Converse here explained matters, and . . . [we fired] a volley at the Johnnies, who were so close that we could hear them yelling at us to halt and surrender."[6] The orders from Wadsworth were, said Dawes, to retreat beyond the town" and "hold your men together." The young Ohioan said he was at first "astonished," as the cheers of defiance along the line of the First Corps on Seminary Ridge "had scarcely died away." But "a glance over the field to our right and rear was sufficient," he remembered. "There the troops of the eleventh corps appeared in full retreat, and long lines of Confederates, with fluttering banners and shining steel were sweeping forward in pursuit of them without let or hindrance. It was a close race which could reach Gettysburg first, ourselves, or the rebel troops. . . ." With the flag aloft, Dawes said, his "little regiment marched firmly and steadily" toward Gettysburg.[7] Company E Private Albert Young remembered the withdrawal as less orderly. The command was not simply to retreat, but to "Break and run!" he recalled:

It is not for a soldier to question an order, but to obey! We obeyed this literally, and how we did run! As we came out of the smoke of the battle what a sight burst upon our gaze! On every side our troops were madly rushing to the rear. We were flanked on the right and on the left. We were overwhelmed by numbers. My heart sank within me. I lost all hope.[8]

Clayton Rogers also found Sergeant Jerome Watrous of the 6th Wisconsin, who was assisting with the ammunition train for Wadsworth's Division, trying to get to the rear with the several wagons he had brought to the front to replenish the cartridge boxes of the soldiers of the two brigades:

The sergeant had a very warm gallop across the rail road embankment into Gettysburg on the retreat. About the time that a shell struck and killed a span of mules,

6. Kelly, Letter, to Rufus R. Dawes, August 2, 1892.
7. Dawes, *Service*, p. 175.
8. [Young], *Telegraph*, April 22, 1883.

while another shell broke a wheel of the ammunition wagon, causing it to be abandoned to the pursuers, after the ammunition was saved. Sergeant Watrous compelled the driver to hold his team in the concentrated fire of a confederate division and a Battery. It seems impossible that a single man should have escaped through such a narrow passage, yet few except dead and wounded were left by the way.

Rogers also recalled the 6th Wisconsin and Battery B "were the last to leave the field, and they brought off every gun." In the retreat, Rogers found his brother, Earl, with the Wisconsin regiment. Behind them, the Confederate line was sweeping toward Gettysburg, and Clayton Rogers told his brother, not completely in jest, "Bona, those rebs look to me not less than sixteen feet high, and the flag-staffs at least twenty."[9]

From a north window in the courthouse, Dr. John Hall could see the retreat of the XI Corps:

Away went guns and knapsacks, and they fled for dear life, forming a funnel shaped tail, extending to the town. The rebels coolly and deliberately shot them down like sheep. I did not see an officer attempt to rally or check them in their headlong retreat.[10]

Word the Union position west of Gettysburg had collapsed quickly spread, Sullivan recalled:

All of a sudden some one rushed [into the courthouse] . . . and said the 11th corps had broke and run and the rebels were driving our fellows through the town, and sure enough solid shot and shell began to crash through the courthouse and burst in the yard. The doctor ordered all who could march to leave and put up a hospital flag . . . , and after a bit no more shot struck near it. By and by a rebel officer came in and demanded our surrender. The doctors told him there were none there only medical men and the severely wounded, and the band men who were nurses. After some palaver and a drink

9. Rogers, *Telegraph*, May 13, 1887.
10. John C. Hall, Journal, July 2, 1863, Dawes, *Service*, p. 176n.

or two of hospital brandy, the rebel told our doctors to have the nurses tie a white string around their arm and the wounded to keep inside and they would not be disturbed. I was mad as the devil to think that all our hard fighting that morning had went for nothing and here was over two hundred of our brigade all smashed to pieces, to say nothing of all that were at the other hospitals.

There was angry muttering and fist-shaking by the wounded men, Sullivan said, as well as some curses directed at the "Flying Moon Corps" [The XI Corps wore a crescent corps badge], and Hugh Talty pulled himself up, wanting "to go out and fight, be gob," but another soldier told Talty "that the rebels would gobble him and take him to Libby [prison] and that took the fight out of Hugh." After a time, Sullivan said, "things quieted down and the firing ceased."[11] Along toward night, Sullivan said he "began to skirmish around for some better place to sleep than the floor of the court house where having no blankets or knapsack for a pillow, I was not very comfortable." He and Corporal Hancock discussed the matter, the corporal noting "our fellows had a good place in the railroad depot," and the two injured soldiers made their way there. Sullivan recalled:

I slept with a dead officer who had been mortally wounded in the cavalry fight; and some citizen had brought out a feather bed and some bed clothes and had fixed him on it; not being able to roll him off I lay down with him and some time in the night I went to sleep.[12]

Loyd Harris, Bill Remington and Lieutenant John Beeley were also in a make-shift Gettysburg hospital, getting patched up. Just as a surgeon was about to "probe for a buckshot in the fleshy part of my neck," Harris recalled, the "good old lady" who had been assisting as a volunteer nurse "declared her nerves" would not allow her to witness such a sight:

Here was my chance. Taking the harmonica from my pocket I said, "Madam, the surgeon will be so gentle

11. Sullivan, *Telegraph*, December 20, 1884.
12. *Ibid.*

that while he is operating I will play on this little musical affair. So, while he in no delicate manner probed around with his torturing instrument, [I] recklessly played "Tramp, Tramp the Boys are Marching," until he had finished, when the old lady, with uplifted hands, exclaimed, "no wonder you men are called the 'Iron Brigade.' "

At least, that was the way Harris remembered it all some 20 years later.[13] In any event, the buckshot was removed and he, Beeley and Remington, finding the hospital filled with wounded soldiers, decided to seek better quarters. An orderly named "Jimmy" was on the scene, having just announced to Dr. Andrew J. Ward of the 2nd Wisconsin: "Docther, Col. [Lucius] Fairchild of the Second, sinds his compliments, and wants ye in a divil of a hurry to cut off his left arrum." (Fairchild, wounded in the charge of the 2nd Wisconsin into McPherson's Woods, was a brigade favorite. He was on his way out of the war and to a long political career that would see him as one of Wisconsin's most popular governors, and a man not above using his empty sleeve and military career to political advantage.) Jimmy was directed by Harris and the others to seek "pleasant quarters," and a short time later returned, face beaming, to announce: "I have found a splindid place, wid such kind and beautiful ladies."

The contingent was soon domiciled in the nearby home of a "Mr. Hollinger, a true Union man," said Harris, who always had a way of romancing his war experiences:

> His wife was an invalid, but his daughters, two very pretty and sensible young ladies, assumed charge of the house-hold affairs, and we were soon made to feel that for the first time in two years of the hardest kind of campaigning, we were to enjoy a peaceful rest; under a roof, with comforts that too forcibly reminded us of home, sweet home.

After a hasty dinner, the wounded officers discovered Sergeant William Evans of Company H was in the same house, as was the flag of the 2nd Mississippi captured by the 6th Wisconsin. The

13. [Harris], *Telegraph*, January 25, 1885.

reunion of the wounded soldiers was joyous, if subdued, and the flag was displayed. ". . . [B]ut what cared we for that crimson rag," Harris said later of that strange moment standing in a strange home in a strange town in the middle of a battle:

> We had fought the bloodiest fight of the war to win it [the flag]. [John] Ticknor, [Orrin] Chapman and thirty brave comrades lay unburied on the field and one hundred and fifty more were maimed and crippled, all sacrificed to trail that haughty flag under ours; yet we had the esprit du corps to hold it before our new-found young lady friends, and, in a modest manner told the story of the charge.

It was one of those moments the old soldiers always treasured: brave, wounded officers holding a bloody trophy before the admiring eyes of two young ladies, telling them how a flag was captured near an unfinished railroad cut. "No Desdemona ever listened with more heartfelt sympathy than those two young ladies," Harris remembered, "and the story finished, we felt that in their eyes every man of the old Sixth was a hero."

The little circle was very pleasant, but soon a "heavy cannonading" erupted west of the town and a "shell went tearing through a grape-arbor just in front of the house." As the most able of the wounded officers, Harris went to an upper porch. "I shall never forget that sight," he said:

> The Eleventh corps had made a gallant stand, but, outflanked and charged by greater numbers, the two divisions were in full retreat, pursued by the victorious enemy. My emotions were sickening, as I vainly gazed for the First army corps, that Spartan band who had routed all before them in the morning fight. They were no where in sight—Brave men, I knew they would sell their lives dearly; almost bewildered by the maddening scenes that were happening in rapid succession but a rifle shot distant, I thought of my wounded friends, Remington and Beeley; they must not be captured.

Back in the cozy kitchen, Harris began to gather up his things. "You must get out of this on the run," he told the two wounded officers. "We have lost, and the rebels are in the next street." Beeley and Remington, "weak from loss of blood," were quickly out of the house, making for the safety of the Union lines. Sergeant Evans, too badly wounded to be moved, was left in the bedroom. The scene in the kitchen was all excitement. The "invalid mother" fainted, and the two young ladies cried as they fluttered about her. Harris was at the door, ready to bolt into the street, when he paused to take it all in. ". . . [T]he father, brave, but at fault what to do, looked the picture of despair." Harris made a quick look around. "Have you a cellar?" he asked. "Yes," the young lady he remembered only as "Miss Julia" replied. "Then we must carry your mother there," Harris explained. Helping the father with the wheelchair, the two struggled down the narrow staircase, carrying the mother to safety. Finally, the family was settled and Harris again readied to leave. "Good-bye, many thanks for your kindness," he said, "I shall always—" But one of the young ladies cut him short, "Oh, hurry away or you will be lost."

She was right. At the door, the young officer found rebels in the front street. There was a board fence and Harris ran for it, and as he cleared it "a dozen bullets rattled on it." But he was down in another yard on the run. Harris crossed through another house which had been vacated by its occupants, then scampered into a cross street crowded with fleeing Union soldiers. In the surging crowd, an army ambulance carried wounded soldiers, including Beeley and Remington. There were yells, and Harris was pulled into the vehicle by "strong arms." The stream of soldiers passed a Federal battery placed in a street. As soon as the crowd cleared the muzzles, the guns crashed, and the rebels pulled back for a time. Soon, the three Wisconsin officers were safe behind Union lines. Harris always had one regret: "Oh, misery and shame, comrades forgive us, we left behind the rebel flag [of the 2nd Mississippi], that dearly bought prize."

Left behind in the house, Sergeant Evans and the two young ladies hid the flag by cutting a hole in the bed-tick beneath the wounded sergeant, pushing in the banner and sewing up the rest. Outside, they heard rebel soldiers in the street as the Confederate army seized the town.[14]

14. [Loyd G. Harris], "Adventures of a Rebel Flag," *Milwaukee Sunday Telegraph*, January 29, 1880. For a full discussion on what happened to the captured flag, see Appendix I.

Not far away, on a place called Culp's Hill, southeast of Gettysburg, the Calico boys of the 6th Wisconsin were about to spend an uneasy night behind the makeshift breastworks they had thrown up. The regiment had to make a run for it through the crowded, bullet-swept streets of the town. Rufus Dawes had kept his men together despite the crush and tangle of retreating soldiers, ambulances, artillery and wagons. In the town, he recalled, "the cellars were . . . crowded with men, sound in body, but craven in spirit, who had gone there to surrender. I saw no men wearing badges of the first army corps in this disgraceful company."[15]

With few exceptions, the retreating Union soldiers had less order than "found in a herd of cattle," said Sergeant George Fairfield. "The enemy were pouring into town on two if not three sides, and sweeping the streets with a terrific cross fire of musketry, while the solid shot tore the buildings and ploughed through the living mass, the shell screeched through the air scattering deadly missiles as thick as hail from the town to Cemetery Hill."[16] At one point, a board fence enclosing a barnyard blocked

15. Dawes, *Service*, p. 178.
16. George Fairfield, Letter, to Jerome A. Watrous, undated. Watrous Papers, SHSW. Fairfield's diary included the following passages involving the battle of Gettysburg:

Wed. [July] 1st. Got up early, ate breakfast and moved with unusual quietude to Gettysburg. Here all of a sudden the artillery opened and we were double quicked into the fight unexpected till the very moment came. The 2nd brigade broke and as our Regt was the General reserve of the 1st brigade we moved to their support and drove the enemy back with heavy loss and recaptured some artillery. A terrific fight ensued till about 5 p.m. from 11 a.m. We were flanked and our rear nearly occupied when we fell back through town and took up a position on Wolf hill which we fortified in the evening. Lieut. O.D.C. [Orrin D. Chapman], Armstrong [William Armstrong of Prairie du Chien] and Marston [A. Richard Marston of Seneca] killed. J. Lemans [Jacob Lemans of Eastman] and 16 others wounded. 8 mi.

Thurs. 2nd. Co. C. relieved Co. F on picket. Artillery lively. The enemy charged out left at about 4 p.m. and was repulsed at every point. The enemy moved to our right and charged the whole right from Cemetery hill except a single point where our regiment was. We rallied on the battalion after dark and they were gone. We were then ordered to deploy and stop stragglers in the rear of the line. The enemy was again repulsed and we lay down to sleep and slept till morning.

Frid. 3rd. Infantry on our right opened heavy this morning. our Regt returned to its place where we joined them. All became quiet on the right. At 2 p.m. artillery opened heavy all along the line. It finally slackened as if by common consent and the infantry opened with a perfect roar and again the artillery opened with fury. Enemy repulsed.

the way. One or two boards were off the fence, making what the Wisconsin men called "a hog hole." Dawes instructed the men to follow him in single file, then ducked through the hole, while the whole street was swept with bullets. "When any man obstructed the passage way through it, I jerked him away without ceremony or apology, the object being to keep the track clear for those yet to come," Dawes said.[17] Weak and wounded, one of the soldiers who had trouble at the fence was Corporal Kelly. "It was so crowded that I could not get through at once," he remembered. "Here . . . [Dawes] and Capt. [Rollin] Converse both took hold of me and got me out, or through all right."[18] Behind the regiment, two more Wisconsin men were left wounded on the street.

Further on, an "old citizen" appeared with two welcome buckets of fresh water, and the Wisconsin men, whose canteens had been empty for hours, crowded around him. After the quick drink, Dawes, holding his small regiment together in the stream of fleeing soldiers, ordered his men to give "three cheers for the good and glorious cause for which we stood in battle." That attracted some fire from Confederates crowding into the town, and the Wisconsin men fired back. After a time they reached Cemetery Hill, where Lieutenant Clayton Rogers brought orders from General James Wadsworth that the regiment should re-join the Iron Brigade on nearby Culp's Hill.[19] It was a grim moment, Dawes recalled:

> Our men were now conscious of defeat; they were overdone with heat and almost dead with thirst. . . . The enemy was all around us, and closing in, firing and yelling. History now shows us that the whole fate of the battle turned on rallying these troops on Cemetery Hill and Culp's Hill and forming them at once in line of battle. When I got my regiment to the hill, I found everything in disorder. Panic was impending over the exhausted soldiers. It was a confused rabble of disorganized regiments of infantry and crippled batteries. To add to the confusion and peril, Brigadier General [Thomas A.]

17. Dawes, *Service*, pp. 176-178.
18. Kelly, Letter, to Dawes, August 2, 1892.
19. Dawes, *Service*, pp. 178-179.

Rowley, who was in command of . . . [the 3rd Division], had become positively insane. He was raving and storming, and giving wild and crazy orders. Cool, courageaus and efficient men, at that supreme crisis in the history of our country, brought order out of chaos. In the midst of this, Clayton Rogers rode up and boldly placed General Rowley under arrest, and called on me for bayonets to enforce the order. This was perhaps the only instance in the war where a First Lieutenant forcibly arrested a Brigadier-General on the field of battle. I saw all that transpired; and during the half hour of confusion, Rogers, who was well mounted, by his cool, clear-headed and quick-witted actions, did more than any other one man to get the troops in line of battle.[20]

Clayton Rogers himself recalled:

There was no halt till Cemetery Ridge was reached. There all was confusion. General Rowley, in great excitement, had lost his own 3d division, and was giving General Wadsworth's troops contradictory orders, calling them cowards, and whose conduct was so unbecoming a division commander and unfortunately stimulated with poor commissary [whiskey]. Not having seen General Wadsworth since the retreat commenced, the writer did not hesitate to arrest the crazy officer, on his own responsibility, and called on Col. Dawes to execute the order with the bayonets of the 6th Wisconsin.[21]

Along the way, the regimental wagon joined the 6th Wisconsin

20. Rufus R. Dawes, "A Gallant Officer," *Milwaukee Sunday Telegraph*, February 3, 1884. The editor said the quotation was in a letter from Dawes printed in the *Chippewa Herald*. Rowley was later assigned to the draft mustering station at Portland, Maine. He returned to the Army of the Potomac before the campaigns of 1864 and was court-martialed at Culpeper, Virginia, in April on charges of drunkenness on duty on the battlefield, conduct prejudicial to good order and military discipline, conduct unbecoming an officer and a gentleman and disobedience of orders. He was found guilty of all accusations except the last. Secretary of War Edwin M. Stanton, however, disapproved the sentence and reassigned the general to command the District of the Monongahela until the cessation of hostilities. Ezra J. Warner, *Generals in Blue*, (Baton Rouge, Louisiana, 1964), p. 414; Coddington, *Gettysburg Campaign*, pp. 307-308.
21. Rogers, *Telegraph*, May 13, 1887.

soldiers moving toward Cemetery Ridge. Corporal I. F. Kelly, carrying the regimental flag, made the march despite his wounded knee. Dawes said when his small regiment reached the hill, a dozen spades and shovels were pulled from the wagon and the soldiers began constructing an earthworks. "The men worked with great energy," Dawes said. "A man would dig with all his strength till out of breath, when another would seize the spade and push on the work."[22] Once the breastworks was completed, Captain John Hyatt sat Colorbearer Kelly down, sliced open his trouser leg and applied a bandage, but, the corporal remembered, "the wound bled profusely and filled my shoe with blood."[23] Sergeant George Fairfield of Company C counted "but five men of the 6th around the colors" after it arrived on Cemetery Hill, but in "an hour or two the roll was called and 65 men answered to their names."[24] Sometime later, Private Levi Tongue of Hillsboro took a count and found only 18 men left in Company I.[25]

On the fields west of Gettysburg, the famous Iron Brigade of the Army of the Potomac had been wrecked once and for all. It would never again roar into battle as it had on so many fields: Brawner's Farm, Second Bull Run, South Mountain, Antietam and, finally, Gettysburg. It was a somber moment, Dawes remembered:

Our dead lay unburied and beyond our sight or reach. Our wounded were in the hands of the enemy. Our bravest and best were numbered with them. . . . We had lost the ground on which we had fought, we had lost our commander and our comrades, but our fight had held the Cemetery Hill and forced the decision for history that the crowning battle of the war should be at Gettysburg.[26]

Another 6th Wisconsin man caught in the crush of retreating soldiers was Sergeant Jerome A. Watrous, who was trying to get

22. Dawes, Service, p. 179.
23. Kelly, Letter, to Dawes, August 2, 1892.
24. Fairfield, Letter, to Watrous, undated.
25. Tongue, Letter, to his wife, July 2, 1863.
26. Dawes, Service, p. 179.

his division ammunition wagons to safety. Finally, he reached the rallying point:

> As we reached the cemetery hill, about the first general officer we saw was [O. O.] Howard, sitting upon his horse with as much coolness as though he was watching a Fourth of July parade, and just beyond him, all excitement—not nervous—looking in a thousand ways every minute and giving directions as carefully and precisely as though he was preparing for a great parade, was Gen. [Winfield Scott] Hancock [of the II Corps] . . . He was saying to this man and to that: "Take your guns in that direction;" "Collect your men;" "Prepare for immediate action."

Thinking he'd report for orders, Watrous saluted. "Great God, what have you got here? What have you got a wagon here for? You haven't been out into action?" Hancock questioned. Watrous replied: "Yes sir, just came back with the rear guard." "Well, said Hancock, "did you lose all your ammunition?" "No, sir; distributed nearly all of it." "Lose any of your wagons?" "Well, I got back with some of them." Hancock took it all in, then said, "You did well, Sergeant. Just move your wagons down there and report to me in half an hour." (Of the chance meeting with General Hancock on the battlefield of Gettysburg, Watrous later wrote: "It makes it rather personal, but that is one of the things that a non-commissioned, or a commissioned officer would never forget when we take into account the character of a man that Hancock was.")[27]

As the sun went down that day, Lieutenant Loyd Harris of Company C was with other wounded in "a little church" behind the Union lines. Lieutenant Beeley and Bill Remington were there, as well as one or two other Iron Brigade officers, including Gilbert Woodward. Remington and Harris had stopped at a farmhouse, but were refused admittance, and, after a time, the officers made their way to a blacksmith shop, where they stopped for the night. "I never felt so lonely in all my life," Harris said.

27. Jerome A. Watrous, *War Papers*, Commandery of Wisconsin, Military Order of the Loyal Legion of the United States, Vol. I, (Milwaukee, 1891) pp. 298-300.

"For two years I had been accustomed to sleep in the company of hundreds of brave men. Then I thought of Chapman, Ticknor and the men who had been slain, the battle yet undecided. It was so dark and lonely in that old blacksmith shop; we were weak and hungry, but the fatigue of the day was so great we fell asleep like two healthy 'babes in the woods.'"

The next morning, acting on the advice of a surgeon, Harris procured two wagons and, gathering up Beeley, Woodward, and a few others, started for Littletown and Westminster. "It was dark when we reached the latter place and the wagon trains, camp followers and others had filled the town and the small hotel was crowded with guests," Harris said. "I was the most active of our party, and volunteered to find a haven or rest for them, some of whom were suffering badly for want of attention and rest." After a time, he located a "fine brick mansion" where he was greeted by an "elderly gentleman." Harris announced: "Sir, I am here with nine wounded officers and hope you can give us a room where we can spread our blankets and rest for the night." What followed, Harris said, was the following exchange:

Old Gent—"No, Sir; I haven't any room."
"Then can we occupy the barn?"
Old Gent—"No sir, my barn is filled with horses."
But I persisted: "Let the horses out in the yard."
Old Gent—"Can't do it; your soldiers would steal them."

The young officer paused. "That last unfortunate remark settled me as to the proper course to pursue," he recalled. Harris drew his revolver ("and it was a good one, presented to me by Mr. John Lawyer, Chas. Rau and John Conger, at old Prairie du Chien") and pointed it at the "old gentleman's" head. "You have refused to do a kind act," Harris said. "Now if you have a wife you can retire to your room with her, and that room shall be held sacred; the rest of this house is for hospital service, for this night, at least." Harris said he was "just marching him off in good order" when an orderly came up to announce there was a special train ready to convey the wounded officers to Baltimore. As they readied to leave, Harris recalled: "I could not leave without paying my respects to the old gentleman, simply telling him that when any wounded officers politely requested his kitchen to

229

sleep in he had better grant the request." The next morning they were in Baltimore, where the ladies . . . ("Southern by the way") cared for the Union officers kindly. Then, with the exception of Lieutenant Alphonso D. Kidd, who was hospitalized, the other eight made their way to Washington and safety.[28]

On Culp's Hill, the soldiers of the 6th Wisconsin were trying to rest behind their breastworks, but as Rufus Dawes noted: "It is a troubled and dreamy sleep at best that comes to the soldier on a battlefield." At 1 a.m., a soldier in the nearby 7th Indiana "cried out so loudly in his sleep" that he woke the men around him, and there was a great alarm. Dawes, "half bewildered" by sleep, ordered his regiment to "Fall in!" and musketry erupted left and right as the sleepy Union soldiers opened fire on shadows and trees in front of them. Finally, things quieted down again, but at 3 a.m. the sleeping soldiers were awakened to take their positions. On the firing line, 20-year-old Private Levi Tongue from Hillsboro wrote a letter to his wife, Anna. "Yesterday we were in another engagement, and a severe one it was too. We lost 17 out of our company. Andy Miller I expect is dead. I saw him hit above the right eye. Bill Sweet was shot right through the belly. First lieutenant Remington, commanding our company, was wounded," Tongue wrote:

> . . . [T]his battle will go by the name of Gettysburg, for it is right by it. We are in the rear of the city behind some piles of rails we have thrown up. This is all I have time to write. I can count myself lucky. I will write and let you know more of this when it is over, if I live.[29]

Not far away in Gettysburg that July 2, 1863, as Tongue was writing his wife, hungry rebel soldiers plundered stores and houses, "carrying away pails of sugar, molasses, groceries of all

28. [Harris], *Telegraph*, October 26, 1884.
29. Tongue, Letter, to his wife, July 2, 1863. Tongue would be one of the "lucky" ones, but his service took a harder turn a year later, when he was captured while part of a raiding party sent to burn the Danville Bridge in Pittsylvania County in southern Virginia. He was a prisoner the rest of the war, including a four-month period at the infamous Andersonville prison in Georgia. When he was finally freed March 5, 1865, Tongue, who had been 190 pounds when he enlisted, weighed a skeletal 73 pounds. He would return to Gettysburg in 1913 to take part in ceremonies marking the 50th anniversary of battle.

kinds, clothing and bales of goods, silks, calico and cloth," recalled Sullivan:

> They were good to our wounded boys and shared their stolen whiskey, tobacco and baker's bread freely, but the Rebel officers were surly, and one of them wanted a Reb soldier to take a good pair of balmoral shoes I had on, but I told him there would be an Irish row first, and the fellow said they would not fit him, that they were too small. They had not yet fairly begun to strip our wounded and Hays' brigade of Louisiana Tigers were stationed in Gettysburg, and they felt very jubilant over yesterday's battle, and their officers exalting told us that "you uns" were whipped, and they were going to take Washington, Baltimore, Philadelphia, and end the "wah." Our fellows although they felt down in the mouth, defiantly told them they would have to whip the Army of the Potomac first, and if half the Rebel Army was barely able to whip part of the first Corps they would find a different job when . . . the 2d, 3d, 5th, 6th and 12th Corps [came up] and that if [XI Corps Commander O. O.] Howard spent his time in praying during a battle and his corps their time in running, there were plenty of fighting men in the Army of the Potomac, and that McClellan was in command, and would serve Lee worse than he did at Antietam. That kind of took the brag out of them, and we did not hear any more about "you uns" being whipped.[30]

Sullivan also got a look at a rebel general when Jubal Early and his staff rode through the city, remembering the officer as a "short, pussy, grey-haired, bull-headed reb, with no great amount of intelligence in his look." But the rebel soldier who pointed him out to the Irishman said Early was "a fighting d---l," and Sullivan remembered, "We were willing to agree with him."

Not far away, Private Harry Dunn was caring for his sergeant and friend, Michael Mangan. Noticing the rebels were butchering beef, Dunn ventured out to see if he could beg some fresh

30. Sullivan, *Telegraph*, December 28, 1884.

meat, but the Johnnies were not in a friendly mood: a detail gathered in the hapless Dunn and he was on his way to a rebel prison. It would be weeks before he would be paroled and returned to his regiment.[31] In his cellar refuge in Gettysburg, Corporal Francis Deleglise of Company E witnessed a touching incident. A rebel officer ducked in the door, taking in the somber scene with a grim face. After a few seconds, he carefully stepped his way through the wounded soldiers until he "reached a place where the outlines of two figures could be discerned under a protecting quilt which had been wetted with cold water to alleviate the sufferings of the two men it covered." The officer ("a man of superb physical proportions, more than six feet in height") asked the two wounded soldiers about their regiments. The nearest man answered he belonged to the 25th Georgia. "I belong to the Federal Army," came the faint response of the other. Deleglise always remembered what happened next. "The officer drew from his pocket his canteen filled with milk punch and first gave a drink to the Union soldier and afterwards to the man who belonged to his own side," he said later, carrying with him a feeling about Gettysburg somehow stronger than the memory of the desperate fighting.[32]

Otherwise the day passed quietly enough, though there was firing every now and then south of Gettysburg. "The Rebel army all came up and the fields back of the town were full of their wagons and cattle that I suppose they had taken from the poor farmers," said Sullivan. "Their artillery was moving out to the right of the town toward the seminary, and some of our fellows who had climbed up to the observatory on top of the railroad depot said that their army was massing on our centre and right flank." Two or three times during the day, a detail of rebels made the rounds of the Union wounded, asking their names so they could parole them. "The boys would tell them the worst jawbreaking name they could think of, and we all belonged to the 199th Wisconsin, and that McClellan would parole us tomorrow," said Sullivan. "Anyhow we never heard anything about it afterwards as they did not have time next day to do anything but look out for themselves."[33]

31. *Soldiers' and Citizens Album*, p. 171.
32. *Ibid.*, p. 723.
33. Sullivan, *Telegraph*, December 28, 1884.

The Union surgeons tending the wounded in captured Gettysburg were also busy, patching up Federal and Confederate alike as best they could. One of the men they worked on was Corporal Crawford, whose rifle-musket and belts Private J. P. Sullivan had taken the day before on the battlefield. The 24-year-old Crawford, one of the Juneau County boys in Company K, had been shot through the knee joint, and the doctors amputated the leg "at the lower third of the thigh."

Late in the afternoon, Doctors Hall and Bartlett made arrangements for a mess-room in a saloon, and the soldiers got coffee, tea and hardtack. Some rebel wounded were also brought in, and soon soldiers from both sides were lying side by side. Some of the Union soldiers with lesser injuries were gathered up and marched off. Billy Hancock and Sullivan, looking for a place to sleep, went back to the feather bed Sullivan had used the night before. They rolled the dead officer off and, as he said, took "possession by divine right." His wound was bothering the young Irishman, however, "and I did not enjoy our conquest very much." He remembered: "What added to our uneasiness was the fact that the Rebs might clean out the army of the Potomac and take Washington, then 'Old Abe' and the country was gone for certain. The Reb wounded said that Lee had reinforcements from Beauregard and Bragg's armies, and that Charleston and Savannah had left the Home Guard in the works at Richmond, were going to end the war in this battle, and things looked mighty blue."[34]

Rufus Dawes and the 6th Wisconsin soldiers spent the morning of the 2nd of July on the battle line dodging an occasional bullet fired by a rebel sharpshooter. But there was little rest, Private Albert Young of Company E recalled:

> Troops were hurrying to different points of the field to take the positions assigned to them. Preparations were made at all points for a renewal of the conflict. Batteries were being placed in advantageous positions as fast as the already jaded horses could be lashed into drawing them. Ammunition wagons came to the front on a keen gallop. Cartridge boxes were replenished. All was noise,

34. Ibid.

hurry and confusion. Each soldier felt that a desperate struggle was to come and that the result no one could foretell. All felt they must nerve themselves for the ordeal.[35]

Later, the Wisconsin soldiers would learn Confederate General Robert E. Lee had ordered an attack against both Union flanks. James Longstreet's main thrust would come on the Federal left near Little Round Top. To the front of the 6th Wisconsin and other regiments, Confederate General Richard S. Ewell was preparing his lines for an assault on Culp's Hill and East Cemetery Hill. "For hours I watched the rebel troops with a field-glass, as their heavy columns of infantry marched toward our right. We could see them forming in the fields beyond Rock Creek, and knew they were preparing to attack Culp's Hill," Dawes wrote later. Heavy fighting had erupted on the Union left:

> We could plainly see that our troops were giving ground. Thousands were streaming to the rear. Our suspense and anxiety were intense. We gathered in knots all over the hill, watching the battle. . . . As the sun was low down a fine sight was seen. It was two long blue lines of battle, with twenty or thirty regimental banners, charging forward into the smoke and din of battle. To all appearances they saved the field.

But before that could be determined, the rebel yell went up in the woods to the right of the Union line on Culp's Hill and the Confederates charged the soldiers of the nearby XII Corps. In the gathering darkness, the opposing lines fired volley after volley, and, after a time, Dawes and the 6th Wisconsin were ordered to take possession of an earthworks on the right. "We received no fire until we neared the breastworks, when the enemy who had possession of them, lying on the lower side, and who were completely surprised at our sudden arrival, rose up and fired a volley at us, and immediately retreated down the hill," said Dawes. "This remarkable encounter did not last a minute. We lost two men, killed—both burned with the powder of the guns fired at them. The darkness and the suddenness of our arrival caused the

35. [Young], *Telegraph*, April 22, 1888.

enemy to fire wildly."[36] Colorbearer Kelly always remembered the scramble in the darkness. "What a time I had to get the flag through the brush," he said later. "While in the trench here I was wounded in the neck. A ball struck a rock and splattered, as the boys called it, a piece of it striking me in the neck. I bled terribly and to make it look twice as bad as it really was, the boys put a wet towel around my neck."[37] A short time later, the 14th Brooklyn also came up, and finally other soldiers from the XII Corps appeared and the 6th Wisconsin was returned to its original position.

In Gettysburg that next morning, Sullivan awoke to find the streets deserted. The sky was clear and "everything seemed as still as if there was not a soldier within a thousand miles." Later, some firing erupted along the line, but it soon quieted down. During the lull, Lee and his officers busily prepared a two-hour bombardment of the Federal lines on Cemetery Ridge and Cemetery Hill. It would be followed by a desperate mass attack on the center of the Union line by some 12,000 Confederate infantry. If successful, the assault could have meant the end of a Federal Union of states.

In Gettysburg, Union prisoners and wounded knew something was up. "Our lookout in the observatory said that all their artillery was gathering on the right of the town and their infantry was being massed in solid blocks. We knew they meant to make trouble pretty soon," Sullivan said. "After dinner . . . , the Fife Major who was in the observatory came down and said the Johnnies were moving. Just then 'bang, bang' went a couple of guns, and then such a roar of artillery as I have never heard before or since, Bull Run was not a patching; the ground shook, and the depot building fairly trembled. Our fellows answered just as loud, and it seemed as if the last day had come."

Sullivan found one of the band boys, who were acting as nurses, to help him, and, hanging onto the railing on the stairs, climbed to the cupola of the depot for a look himself:

> I saw [what] appeared like the whole Rebel Army in
> a chunk start for our lines with their infernal squealing
> yell. It seemed as if everything stood still inside of me

36. Dawes, Service, pp. 171-172.
37. Kelly, Letter, to Dawes, August 2, 1892.

for a second or two, then I began to pray. Now I never was, and am not yet noted for the frequency and fervancy of my prayers, but that time I prayed from the bottom of my heart that they would catch h--l, and they did. It seemed as if the fire from our lines doubled and doubled again, and I could see long streaks of light through the Rebel columns, but they went forward. I was afraid they would capture our guns, but all of a sudden they seemed to melt away as our infantry opened on them and we could hear the Northern cheer. We knew that the rebs were scooped, and the old Army of the Potomac was victorious. There were ten or fifteen of us in the observatory, and they were wild with joy, some cried, others shook hands, and all joined in the best cheer we could get up. I forgot all about my wound, and was very forcibly reminded of it when I went to shout as I had to sit down to keep from falling.[38]

When the cheer went up in the cupola, Union wounded in the depot also began to yell. A rebel officer came in asking what the racket was about, and he was told "Lee was cleaned," and at that, Sullivan said, "he growled out if we d----d Yankees were able to cheer we were able to go to Richmond." The officer left in a huff, Sullivan said, and "we could see that it was all up with the Johnnies; their wagons began to hustle off, and the cattle were driven after them. The streets were filled with wounded and stragglers from the front, and everything indicated that Lee had been badly beaten." The Irishman added: "Our fellows were as much pleased as if the paymaster had just come into camp, and night settled down quietly."

Sullivan spent a restless night. His wound was painful and he could "hear the roll of artillery wagons all night in the retreat." At daybreak, he and Hancock went out in the street. It was raining, and, as Sullivan had no coat, Hancock went back into the depot to get a bed quilt that Sullivan could wrap around his shoulders. Before that happened, however, a Union skirmish line came down the street "followed by a support and the battle flag of the 11th Corps. Then I knew that our fellows had Gettysburg," Sullivan said. "I told the officer about the artillery moving

38. Sullivan, *Telegraph*, December 28, 1884.

all night, and he sent an orderly off to Headquarters with the information and his command passed on through the town after the Rebs." Sergeant Michael Mangan of Company E recalled: "It would be impossible to describe my feelings when our boys rushed in . . . , took our guards prisoners and released us, as I had given up all hopes of such an event."[39]

After a time, Dr. Bartlett called the wounded Wisconsin boys together and advised all who could walk to go to Littletown, seven or eight miles distant, where the care would be better. "The city was overflowing with wounded Rebels," Sullivan said, as he and the other Wisconsin men able to walk gathered their things and formed a "limping squadron with broom sticks for crutches, and any means of assistance they could lay their hands on, [and] started out on the pike toward Cemetery Hill where we found the regiment about the size of a decent company supporting a battery in the center of the horseshoe in which our line was formed."[40] Sullivan and Hancock and the others found Juneau County Company K down to "seven or eight men." First Sergeant Erastus Smith was in charge and Corporal William Campbell the only other officer of any kind left. Sullivan and Smith, his tentmate, compared notes and found "the company had lost five killed and eighteen wounded out of the thirty-three who went into battle on the morning of the first."[41] One of the wounded soldiers who arrived from the town was Sergeant Evans of Company H, and he proudly presented Rufus R. Dawes with the captured flag of the 2nd Mississippi, which had been hidden in his bed during the Confederate occupation of Gettysburg. Another wounded soldier brought Dawes a bouquet of flowers and the compliments of one "Miss Sallie Paxton," who had watched the regiment's charge on the railroad cut the morning of July 1.[42]

After a time, Sullivan joined other wounded making for the I Corps hospital, some two miles off. He spent the night there, and the next morning again started for Littletown "as the surgeons told us the wounded were being sent to Harrisburg and Philadelphia from that point." The wounded private made about

39. *Soldiers' and Citizens' Album*, p. 171.
40. Sullivan, *Telegraph*, December 28, 1884.
41. *Ibid.*
42. Rufus R. Dawes, Letter, to Mary Gates, July 4, 1863; Dawes, *Service*, pp. 159-160.

237

two miles that day, spending the night in a barn with 25 or 30 other wounded. "The old Pennsylvania farmer furnished us with quilts, supper and breakfast," Sullivan recalled. "In the morning, he took a spring wagon and carried myself and three others to Littletown, where we were loaded on freight cars and taken to Baltimore." The next day he was transferred to Philadelphia and assigned to Ward B, Germantown hospital, with 29 others of the 6th and 7th Wisconsin and, Sullivan said, "it was a long time before I was able to go back to the regiment."[43]

At midnight on July 4, 1863, in line of battle on the field of the greatest battle of the Civil War, Rufus R. Dawes wrote to Mary Beman Gates to tell her he was safe despite the three days of "bloody struggle." His regiment had captured the flag of the 2nd Mississippi Infantry, he said, during a great charge on an unfinished railroad cut. "Their battle flag is now at General Meade's headquarters, inscribed as follows: 'Captured by the 6th Wisconsin, together with the entire regiment, kept by Sergeant Evans for two days, while a prisoner in the hands of the enemy.'" It was a proud thing for a young officer to be able to write his future wife, but Dawes also noted:

O, Mary, it is sad to look now at our shattered band of devoted men. Only four field officers in the brigade have escaped and I am one of them. I have no opportunity to say more now or to write to any one else. Tell mother I am safe. There is no chance to telegraph. God has been kind to me and I think he will yet spare me.[44]

Eighteen hours later, Dawes wrote again: "What a solemn birthday [He was 25]. My little band, now only two hundred men, have all been out burying the bloody corpses of friend and foe. No fighting to-day. Both armies need rest from the exhaustion of the desperate struggle. My boys until just now have had nothing to eat since yesterday morning." His regiment had been nearly wrecked and the Iron Brigade all but destroyed, but the Army of the Potomac finally had its victory, and perhaps, somewhere down at the end of a long road, all the deaths and sacrifice

43. Sullivan, *Telegraph*, December 28, 1884.
44. Rufus R. Dawes, Letter, to Mary Gates, July 4, 1863; Dawes, *Service*, pp. 159-160.

and suffering would bring peace. If that all happened, then there was one other thing to be said of Wisconsin's 6th Regiment, Volunteer Infantry, and Dawes added a sentence to his battlefield letter to Mary Beman Gates that summed it up, then and thereafter: "No regiment in this army ever did better service than ours."[45]

In a letter to his brother, printed in the *Milwaukee Sentinel* July 20, 1863, Private George Fink of Company F painted a brighter picture and raised an ominous note:

> I think the back bone of the rebellion is broken, or soon will be. They have played their hand long enough, and now we will try the best hand and play the trump and euchre them at last. . . . And when the war is over, copperheads look out for your bacon.[46]

Young John Kellogg, the 6th Wisconsin officer serving on the staff of 2nd Brigade Commander Lysander Cutler, touched on the same theme in a long letter to his hometown newspaper two months later. In it, he warned the homefolks to disregard those who would have peace at any price. The Wisconsin volunteers would have nothing less than complete victory, Kellogg wrote:

> It was for this purpose we left our homes, wives and

45. *Ibid.*
46. George Fink, Letter, to his brother, printed in the *Milwaukee Sentinel*, July 20, 1863. Fink served in Company F. His letter is typical of the reporting by common soldiers during the Civil War, especially as they wrote to hometown newspapers:
> With such impetuosity and hurry was it [the charge on the railroad cut] done, that we captured a whole brigade of rebel officers and all, together with their flags. Our regiment captured one with four battle marks on it. It was red, with a white cross and thirteen stars, the battle marks being on each corner.
> The rebels fought bravely, for they thought we were the militia, but when they found their mistake, they soon slackened their fire. We made a charge then and gave them the cold steel. An overwhelming force of theirs, however, soon drove us and compelled us to take a new position [on Culp's Hill], where we were reinforced and peppered them until they could stand it no longer.
> This was one of the hardest fought battles of the war. The thunder of cannons and the rattle of musketry was incessant, making the very foundation of the earth tremble and the buildings in the vicinity quake. The ground was plunged by cannon shot, and the trees were rent and scarred by the shower of shot and shell that filled the air, cutting down men on every hand. . . .

children. It was for this we have freely faced danger and death on a score of battle-fields. For this we have offered our lives, and for this thousands of our brave and best have fallen, and with their blood sealed the solemn covenant made when they with uplifted hands swore before Almighty God that they would defend the Constitution and Government against all enemies and opposers whatsoever.

He concluded:

... [W]e are confidently looking forward to the time when we can meet these men [opposing the war] face to face, and tell them they are traitors to a Government that has successfully coped with treason in arms and in their own detestable selves and has conquered both.[47]

Perhaps, just perhaps, the Wisconsin men were beginning to sense, the long, uncertain road they started on so long ago at Camp Randall at Madison just might lead to peace and, finally, Milwaukee and Mauston and Wonewoc and Fond du Lac and De Soto and Prairie du Chien and all the places they called home. And when they got there, in addition to picking up their lives, there was still a reckoning for those who stayed behind and for those who had taken up arms to threaten a Union of states.

That night on the Fourth of July, 1863, on the grim battlefield at Gettysburg, Pennsylvania, Army Commander George G. Meade ordered the bands up behind the center of the Union line. The musicians played "the national airs," said 6th Wisconsin Sergeant Jerome A. Watrous, and he always claimed the last song they played that night was "Yankee Doodle."[48]

47. John A. Kellogg, "From the Army," *Mauston Star*, September 23, 1863. The letter was written September 6, 1863.
48. Jerome A. Watrous, *Richard Epps and Other Stories*, (Milwaukee, 1906), p. 102.

CHAPTER EIGHT

This is to be a kind of bummer's meeting;
A go-as-you-please Camp-Fire.
—General John Gibbon

Lancaster: 1884

With a blast of its whistle, the Chicago & North Western train lurched into life, couplings clanking as it slowly pulled from brick station adjacent to Lake Michigan on Milwaukee's east side. The insides of the cars were already hot that August morning of 1884, and a small knot of middle-aged men, a few in old, worn, blue army blouses despite the heat, chatted in anticipation of their destination—the fourth annual reunion of the Iron Brigade Association at Lancaster in southwestern Wisconsin. It was to begin that Thursday evening, August 27th, and run through the next day. Hundreds of comrades who had marched with the "Grand Old Brigade" in the war for the Union would be there to renew friendships and enjoy the camaraderie.[1]

As the train slowly edged its way west through the expanding metropolis (J. P. "Mickey" Sullivan had, years before, called it the "city of beer and pale bricks"), tall, balding, walrus-mustached Jerome Watrous withdrew a notebook from his pocket, dipped a pencil to his tongue and began taking notes. Born in New York State, like several of his old war friends, he had migrated to Wisconsin with his parents as a youngster, had become a printer's devil and fallen in love with the newspaper business. He was running a small weekly at Appleton, Wisconsin, when, at 21, he enlisted in Edward Bragg's company of volunteers and marched away to war. He had found soldiering to his liking, too, and ultimately rose to the rank of brigade adjutant, winning commendation for his impetuosity and bravery in the war's latter campaigns.

1. [Jerome A. Watrous], "Brothers All" *Milwaukee Sunday Telegraph*, December 7, 1884.

Now the 44-year-old Watrous ran *The Milwaukee Sunday Telegraph*, a society and feature weekly that was tapping into the rising tide of the post-war veterans' movement. He wrote and solicited stories and vignettes about Wisconsin men, their units and the battles in which they fought. The newspaper business, for Watrous, was as important as soldiering, and he was pardoned by some readers for favoring the Iron Brigade and his 6th Wisconsin in his writings, polishing the two most significant facets of his life. He may have been considered a hack writer, even in that era, but with a few others, the gregarious editor assumed the mantle of torchbearer, carrying forward the flaming memory of his regiment and brigade; fueling it, in some instances, with legend, enlarging it with a pantheon of heroes, to almost mythic proportions. Nearly all 6th Wisconsin and Iron Brigade men, to his pen, were handsome and true, almost all served with gallantry and, surely, Watrous readily wrote, they all had died nobly and for a great cause. The written and oral accounts he received, solicited and edited, his own reporting at reunions and elsewhere would, with other sources, comprise one of the larger bodies of literature about one Union regiment and the brigade with which it fought through four years of Civil War.

Also aboard the hot railcar that forenoon was another fixture at the brigade gatherings, a man who would, like Watrous, contribute to the reputation of the 6th Wisconsin and the Iron Brigade. Cullen Aubery, called "Doc," had never been a soldier, but was fondly remembered as the young newsboy who hawked Washington, New York and Philadelphia papers in the camps around the nation's capital. After the war, "Doc" had migrated to Milwaukee, continuing his association with the Wisconsin veterans. A dapper, fleshy man, Aubery had gained employment as a nightwatchman at a local dry goods emporium, and, in 1880, he attended the formation of the Iron Brigade Association, securing an honorary membership. Despite his meager personal accomplishments, his stature was enhanced by the fellowship with the veterans. Aubery, like Watrous, was a collector of war stories and yarns; he would, after the century's turn, publish a pastiche of these called *Recollections of a Newsboy in the Army of the Potomac*. Basking in the reflected reputation of his old soldier friends, he contributed to the body of their literature. Aubery would die February 8, 1908; his only true accomplishment was a

242

small book. But his memory would be sanctified by the survivors of the brigade.[2]

Seated near the two writers on the gently rocking rail car, now picking up speed as it cleared Milwaukee's western environs, was a 6th Wisconsin man who had been in the fight at Gettysburg. Tom Kerr, the short-statured immigrant from northern Ireland, veteran of the Mexican and Civil Wars, was scarred with five battle wounds. In a small purse, he carried a handful of dull, misshapen rebel bullets and balls that had been meant to kill him. What had galvanized him these past few years was the burgeoning veterans' movement, a post-war phenomenon of the Gilded Age that would elect a series of legislators, governors and presidents, and successfully pressure for passage of pension acts and other legislation favorable to former Civil War soldiers. In June, 1880, when tens of thousands of old soldiers had assembled in Milwaukee for the Grand Army reunion, Tom Kerr had dusted off his old army coat and limped in the miles-long parade—a highlight of week-long festivities. To his old friend, Loyd Harris, the Irishman still had the look of "the fighting chief of the 'skull crackers' "; and though the uniform "showed the ravages of time. . . . Tom is good for many years to come."[3]

One of Kerr's wounds had been sustained that hot Wednesday morning of July 1, 1863, when the 6th Wisconsin made its impetuous rush upon the railroad cut west of Gettysburg. Kerr had risen from the ranks of Company D, the Irish Montgomery Guard, to become lieutenant in command of the Milwaukee unit that day. He had been grazed across the chest by buckshot, but it was a minor wound, he had insisted, and had remained in the line. On Culp's Hill the next day, he won his captain's straps. Kerr ultimately rose to the rank of lieutenant colonel and was second in command

2. Vermont-born Aubery had first come to the war front as a lieutenant's attendant, and later sold newspapers among regiments of the Iron Brigade, getting to know the black-hatted soldiers. He had been captured in 1862 and imprisoned at Libby, but after his exchange he had again taken up selling newspapers, this time amid regiments of the Iron Brigade. In 1882, Aubery's comely daughter, Hattie, had been enrolled as the "Daughter of the Iron Brigade," and the young woman regularly sang and recited for the appreciative veterans at reunions. She had also crafted a silk flag for the Association. Upon her marriage, some years later, the veterans presented her with a silver tea service. *Soldiers' and Citizens' Album*, Vol. II, p. 650-652; Aubery, *Recollections*, p. 149, 161-163; *Milwaukee Free Press*, February 3, 1908.
3. [Jerome A. Watrous], *Milwaukee Sunday Telegraph*, July 11, 1880.

of the remaining fragments of the Iron Brigade late in the war.[4]

In post-war years, Kerr, like most of his old comrades, never attained success or stature. But he had been stirred by the old soldier gatherings—they provided a measure of acclaim—and Tom Kerr regularly attended the Iron Brigade Association meetings. The fighting spirit burned within the scarred body: at the 1883 reunion in LaCrosse, Watrous had quoted Kerr as saying, ". . . [n]ot for ten thousand dollars would I have missed this meeting. But I would like to go into just one more fight with the old regiment." He was taciturn about his war exploits, and it had taken old comrades like Watrous, Bragg, and others to tell his story. And they would join his children at Kerr's simple gravesite after his death on June 12, 1903.[5]

The Chicago & North Western train rolled through the pleasant farm country west of Milwaukee for the next few hours. Around one o'clock that Thursday, it slowed and whistled into Madison, the state capital. Several middle-aged men, most from the old 2nd and 7th Wisconsin, waited on the station platform. They helloed greetings as they boarded the cars, shook hands and took seats. Conversations began quickly, mostly of their old soldier days; but there was talk, too, of families, business and, of course, politics, for some were prominent in their communities.

4. Dawes, *Service*, p. 168; U.S. Pension Office, Thomas Kerr file, affidavit of September 9, 1866. By July, 1864, the attrition in officer ranks left Kerr senior captain of the 6th Wisconsin; but his battle injuries, more serious than he cared to admit, had prevented him from leading the regiment in the battle of Globe Tavern in August. Turning 35 that month, the stubby Kerr had been promoted to major and then was quickly elevated to lieutenant colonel. His much-reduced brigade consisted of the 6th and 7th Wisconsin, and 91st New York. The final grueling months of the war south of Petersburg had resulted in Kerr's most serious wound: a ball fractured his spine during the confused assaults and retreats at Gravelly Run; the injury would hobble and plague him for the remainder of his days. There was some consolation when John Kellogg, who commanded the brigade, commended Kerr for "gallantry" in his official battle report. U.S. Pension Office, Thomas Kerr file, affidavit of September 25, 1866; O.R., Part One, Volume 46, p. 884.
5. *Milwaukee Sunday Telegraph*, September 30, 1883. ". . . [D]ear old colonel, lame and full of pain from numerous gunshot wounds," a reporter had once observed, "I wonder if the people of Milwaukee appreciate what he did for their city, state and nation in the great war." It is likely they did not. An historian would later make note of Kerr in the twilight of his years: "He is still living in Milwaukee, but for years has been a constant sufferer from wounds received in battle." In the first year of the new century, Kerr, weighted with wounds, would move into the National Soldiers Home on the city's west side; there he would spend his final days. *Daily Wisconsin*, October 19, 1883; Conard, *Milwaukee*, p. 114; *Milwaukee Sentinel*, June 13, 1903.

As the train worked west, across a landscape that was beginning to roll, conversations reawakened memories about times bright and dark, that marked the days since the war. And there was good-natured jibing about how much the years had changed "the boys" since the time they had left home for the great adventure of 1861. Anticipation mounted, too, for Johnny Gibbon, who had taught them to be soldiers 20 years ago, would be in Lancaster. There would be scores of others there as well, many not seen in the past two decades.

But many others would not be there. They lay buried in quiet church and soldier cemeteries in Mauston, Milwaukee or Fond du Lac, or at faraway places with names such as South Mountain, Antietam, and Gettysburg, some of them resting, only God knew where. Among them were quiet Abe Fletcher, Reuben Huntley and Albert Tarbox, all of Company K; the drummer boy from Shiocton, Lewis Eggleston, Company H, and his pard, "Rocky Mountain" Anderson of Company B; the tragic Frank King of Fond du Lac and remarkable Pete Markle of Coon Slough, both of Company E; and brave Bodley Jones of Sauk County; Jimmy Scoville of Mauston, as well as three of the regiment's fine singers—Lieutenant Orrin Chapman, and Captains Johnny Ticknor and Edwin Brown.

Pete Markle, the boy from Coon Slough in Bad Ax County, was one Earl "Bona" Rogers always remembered. At reunions, he talked of the lad's coolness in battle and of his prowess with a musket: when a "ball from his rifle was sent to a human mark . . . woe to the man on whom he took aim," Rogers would tell anyone who would listen. Markle had been there at Gettysburg (and likely marked a Johnnie or two), and he had followed the majority of his 6th Wisconsin comrades in 1864 reenlisting for three more years. His renown as a straggler had spread throughout the brigade, his wanderings overlooked by officers who knew he would take his place in the ranks when lead started flying. But for all his courage and resourcefulness in wandering and foraging, Markle, ironically, had been sensitive to the harsh army woolen trousers; he chafed badly, and sores developed on his legs. In the tangle and horror of the Wilderness in May, 1864, Pete Markle fought well and, as expected, had not answered the evening roll. Initially unconcerned, Rogers had later been gripped by foreboding when Markle failed to appear. The lieutenant began

245

a nightmarish search for the missing youth among the tents and buildings used as field hospitals. Amid the screams, groans and reek of putrefaction, Rogers moved along row after row of stretchers and pallets, calling, over and over again: "Pete Markle of Coon Slough?" No answer. Finally, there was a weak response, barely a whisper: "Aye, aye, sir." Rogers found the farm boy on a cot. Chafing had opened a sore on Markle's leg; gangrene had developed, and the surgeons had amputated. "I shook the fevered hands and saw death stamped on his pallid features," Rogers said later of that grim final visit. Young Markle died soon thereafter, his demise attributed to wounds sustained at Laurel Hill. Decades after the untimely death, Rogers eulogized:

> And could I have the privilege of standing by his grave, I would, with uncovered head, say, "Long live the memory of Pete Markle, of Coon Slough, a boy hero, an unpolished, straggling diamond, whom [sic] we hope is in that happy land where troubles cease."[6]

A hero was placed in the regiment's pantheon.

Earl Rogers looked forward to these reunions. Only a week before, he had written to Watrous: "Gray hairs, wounded bodies and rheumatics do not lessen the enthusiasm for the Reunion. . . ." Though erect, "firmly knit," and crowned with a full head of dark hair, Rogers was still troubled by a gory thigh wound he sustained late in the war. It never completely mended, and his gait favored the leg. Earl, like his older brother, Clayton, had spent much of his military career on staff duty. General James Wadsworth had selected the Rogers boys from the 6th Wisconsin's Company I, perhaps attracted as much by their Pennsylvania upbringing as their apparent organizational abilities. Earl had been with Wadsworth in the Wilderness May 6, 1864, when the old division commander was killed. Camp talk at the time had it that "Bona" vaulted from his horse under rebel fire to retrieve a watch from the dead general, but Rogers always denied it. Rogers had sustained his awful wound at Petersburg in June, 1864. He was near death for weeks, and his family traveled from Wisconsin to provide comfort. "Earl, do you know me?" his mother had softly asked at his sickbed. "Yes, mother," came a

6. Rogers, *Telegraph*, October 2, 1887; *Roster of Wisconsin Volunteers*, p. 531.

whispered response; "don't cry; am getting better; I must get well. Gen. Bragg wants me."[7]

Two months later, Rogers (and the soldiers, in their rough fashion, now called him "Bony" because of his weight loss and unhealthy pallor) joined Bragg's brigade staff despite the seeping, unknit thigh wound. After the Battle of Hatcher's Run in February, 1865, he quit the field, his boot filled with blood. A brevet to major was granted to him for his actions that day, but that had been all he could take; he resigned in March. Rogers returned home to Viroqua in Vernon County and briefly took up civilian pursuits. In 1867, he was appointed a second lieutenant in the regular army, and engaged in the Southwest Indian campaigns; but the unhealed thigh wound caused him to resign in late 1868.[8]

By 1884, Earl Rogers had become a successful merchant in Liberty Pole, Wisconsin, and would, in years to come, take important posts; first, as sergeant-at-arms in the state senate and later, as quartermaster general of the National Guard. He would also serve for nearly a decade as a district collector of internal revenue. In 1900, there would be talk of Rogers for governor, but he withdrew his name from consideration. That year, Bragg wrote of him: "ever trusty, ever ready, never growling, but always striving to attain the highest degree of excellence. . . ." His four years of service were "*sans peur, sans reproche.*" In his later years, "Bona," retired from business, spending some time traveling to Europe and throughout the United States. On one trip to Washington, D.C., he stopped at the War Department, requesting to see the old Company I muster roll; then, telling the astonished clerk to correct him, he recited every name "without an error."[9]

In 1912, a few months before shrunken Ed Bragg would die, "Bona" Rogers visited his old commander, who lay sick abed. After a brief, strained conversation, the old comrades kissed each other on the cheeks. "Good-by, my heroic and loved general," Rogers said, knowing he would never see Bragg again. "Good-by, my brave 6th Wisconsin boy and still braver aide—good-by," the Little General responded. It was another of those tantalizing little yarns that was stitched into the 6th Wisconsin lore. Eighteen

7. *Milwaukee Sunday Telegraph*, August 24, 1884; *Milwaukee Sentinel*, June 4, 1914.
8. *Evening Wisconsin*, June 3, 1914.
9. *Ibid.*; *Sentinel*, June 4, 1914; *Vernon County Censor*, June 7, 1914.

months later, on January 3, 1914, Rogers would be stricken with pneumonia and die while visiting Milwaukee; he was 74. His body would be returned to Viroqua for burial.[10]

Earl's older brother, Clayton, rarely attended the old soldier reunions; his involvement in the northern Wisconsin lumbering business was a prime focus of life, as it had been since his youth in Pennsylvania. The 51-year-old, squarely-built man was all but indefatigable in running the North Wisconsin Lumber Company mill at Hayward in Sawyer County. He had earned official plaudits during the war for his conduct at Fredericksburg while on Doubleday's staff. Joining Wadsworth's staff before Gettysburg, he had galloped about the bullet-swept battlefield that first morning, delivering orders and maintaining communication. He had also won a commendation from I Corps Commander Abner Doubleday for his action on Culp's Hill the afternoon of July 1st, when the battered I Corps rallied after the retreat through town.

Clayton had resigned July 14, 1863, but, restive out of the war, he had raised a company of volunteers, becoming a captain in the 50th Wisconsin. Assigned to the Western army, Rogers had seen service in Missouri, and served on the staff of General John Pope, the commander who had lost the Second Battle of Bull Run. Rogers's "well known fearlessness, his fiery energy and great executive ability made him notably successful. . . ," wrote a business associate after his death. He had finished his military career in January, 1866, and again returned to Wisconsin. Once widowed and twice married, the veteran had raised a family of ten. He would become a pillar of the community of Hayward in northern Wisconsin, prominent in civic as well as lumbering affairs. "Always too busy to attend soldiers' re-unions, [his] comrades are always thinking of him and his genial and kindly ways," wrote a friend. Clayton Rogers would die April 20, 1900, little more than two weeks after his 67th birthday.[11]

Aboard the rocking train, Watrous was scratching in his notebook, the piece he would publish a week later beginning to take shape. He was good at words like this, catching a mood he felt right:

10. *Milwaukee Sentinel*, January 4, 1914.
11. James G. Adams, *History of Education in Sawyer County Wisconsin*, (McIntire, Iowa, 1902), pp. 237-238; Stanley E. Lathrop, *A Brief Memorial to Captain Clayton E. Rogers*, (Hayward, Wisconsin, 1900), pp. 5-7.

It makes a glad family of gray-haired children. . . . No pen can truly and fully picture such a family reunion. How memory is refreshed. How plainly we recall the old camps, the old marches, the old hardships, the old battles, the old forces of the times. Boys—gray-haired boys —stoop-shouldered boys—bullet-riddled boys—spectacled boys—glorious old boys. . . .[12]

The late August sun slanted south as the Chicago & North Western train steamed into Dodgeville, and on the platform congregated friends and acquaintances who had come to see former Governor Lucius Fairchild off to the reunion. Tall and imposing, the politician bore an empty sleeve from the battle of Gettysburg. In command of the 2nd Wisconsin when it dashed into McPherson's Woods that morning of July 1st, Fairchild paid the price of a limb for his regiment's success. He returned to Wisconsin a hero, and became secretary of state, then rode the ballots of veterans to the governor's mansion, waving the "bloody shirt" at former rebels and suspected Southern sympathizers to retain the office for three terms. Beginning in 1872, and for the next ten years, Fairchild had served in various ministerial posts under the parade of postwar Republican presidents; but upon his return to Wisconsin, he had found the path to renewed political prominence blocked by others. Earlier, in 1884, he had been briefly touted as a favorite son, vice presidential candidate on the ticket of James G. Blaine, but the nomination had gone to another former soldier, "Black Jack" John Logan of Illinois. Fairchild, out of politics, remained a force in Grand Army affairs, and he was en route to Lancaster to renew friendships, as well as to keep his presence before fellow soldiers, and perhaps the voters as well. " I love that face and the man who owns it," said one of Fairchild's former subordinates, "and so we all do, don't we boys?" And a rousing cheer reverberated through the crowded car.[13]

Time passed quickly, the cars swaying amid the pleasant hubbub and chatter of "boys" grown gray. As the miles passed, the landforms of southwestern Wisconsin grew more rugged, and the train worried along the Military Ridge in Grant County. On the platform at Fennimore stood another of those who had paid for

12. *Telegraph*, September 7, 1884.
13. *Ibid.*; *Dictionary of American Biography*, (New York, 1946), Vol. VI. p. 254.

his service with a limb—one-legged Ed Whaley, whose brother, Bill, had won a reputation as drum major par excellence. "I can't see that man without having something crawl into my throat," confessed Watrous in print, describing the scene of Ed laboring painfully aboard with the cork and wood limb, a crutch and a helping hand or two. Whaley had almost lost that leg at South Mountain when a surgeon looked at his wound and proposed amputation; "but for Ed's nerve and a revolver, it would have been sawed off. . . ." Whaley had cocked and pointed his gun at the doctor, and his leg was saved—for a time, at least. He had been in the ranks of Company C at Gettysburg, and, in succeeding engagements, sustained three more wounds. A promotion directly from first sergeant to captain (the only such advancement in the regiment's history) had followed, and later he gained the rank of acting major of the 6th Wisconsin. He had led the regiment into the fight at Five Forks, April 1, 1865, and it was there that a gunshot shattered his leg beyond redemption. He fell, but "Rising partly up, he swung his sword and gave the command: 'Forward, Sixth, never mind me.'" It was the kind of story Watrous loved to hear and publish in his columns. Brigade Commander John Kellogg had commended Whaley for his action that day, and a brevet to major was granted by the War Department for gallant and meritorious conduct. He and a comrade had parted badly that day, but the anger would be soothed in Lancaster.

Now Ed was postmaster in Prairie du Chien, comfortable on a Federal salary and an invalid pension. The postal appointment had been made in 1869 by Fairchild—small recompense for service and loss. Ed's gray eyes brightened when his old comrades helloed him into the smoky car; hands were shaken and room was made on the nearest seat. Whaley, like Kerr and others, was a fixture at the annual brigade assemblies. He would live out the rest of his days in the Mississippi River town, his painful passage serving as a reminder of war to its citizens. When he would die on a cold, late January day in 1898, his Iron Brigade comrades published a resolution, sending a copy to Whaley's widow and children; it read in part, ". . . while we cannot fully express our sorrow at his departure, we bow our heads, and with aching hearts drop a tear in his memory."[14]

14. *Soldiers' and Citizens' Album*, Vol. II, pp. 693-694; *O.R.*, Part 1, Vol. 56, p. 886; *Milwaukee Telegraph*, February 19, 1898.

Ed's brother, Bill, the grand old drum major, was another of those whose postwar life had deteriorated into hardship. A few years before, Watrous had lamented in print that "old Whaley has no pension, no nothing; and earns a scanty living at Prairie du Chien, by ferrying with a skiff" across the Mississippi River. The newspaperman urged that comrades "chip in and make up a little fund" for the drum major. Though monetarily strapped, Bill Whaley had travelled east for the grand reunion in Milwaukee the summer of 1880, where he had "marched quietly along with a single drummer, brave Aleck Johnson" of Company C. Whaley, too, was on his way to Lancaster, some semblance of financial security abetted by his caring friends.[15]

The rail line bent south after Fennimore, on a 10-mile spur that terminated at Lancaster, a prosperous community of about 3,000, whose citizens, in 1866, had erected the nation's first Civil War monument. As the train slowed, faces pressed against the sooty windows to catch a glimpse of the town and the platform packed with welcomers. A long line of men wearing reunion ribbons, commanded by former Captain Henry F. Young of the 7th Wisconsin, stood waiting. The Lancaster Harmonica Band struck up "Marching Through Georgia," and the welcoming veterans gave an "old-fashioned cheer and a 'tiger' " as the new arrivals stepped from the cars, their faces alight with grins and smiles. "How are you, Governor?" "Give us a hand, Jim" "Hello, Bill, shake." There were scores of similar greetings, hands shaken and backs patted. More than a few eyes glistened with tears. "Would you know Dawes if you were to see him?" asked someone of Dan Alton, a Company K man who had traveled down from Martin County, Minnesota, to join the reunion. "I think so," Alton replied with a nod. "Yes, that's him." Striding toward Alton was Rufus R. Dawes, a man of modest stature, whose chest-length beard and hair had the same ashen tinge so common among the men milling on the platform. "Dan Alton," Dawes said, grasping the other man's hand firmly. "What made this scene so touching," Watrous wrote, "was that these two men had not met for twenty-two years, Alton having been wounded in 1862 and obliged to leave the service."[16]

Dawes was to be one of the featured speakers at the reunion;

15. *Milwaukee Sunday Telegraph,* August 24, 1879; July 11, 1880.
16. *Telegraph,* September 7, 1884; *Grant County Herald,* September 9, 1884.

it would be the only time he would attend an Association gathering. He had, upon hearing plans to form the organization five years earlier, written to Watrous: "If there is to be a re-union, I wish to be there, and will do all that I can to further its interests and secure its success."[17]

One of the most respected officers of the 6th Wisconsin, Rufus Dawes had commanded the regiment through most of the campaigns of 1864—the Wilderness, Laurel Hill, Spotsylvania, North Anna and Cold Harbor—and had earned promotion to full colonel. But the fatigue of campaigning had begun to seize him, and his letters home spoke fatalistically of the continued "carnival of blood." And as he had received no more than a scratch at Antietam, he worried that the next rebel ball might be meant for him. In August, 1864, his three-year enlistment having expired and being newly married, he had resigned; a brevet to brigadier general of volunteers had been dated the following March.[18]

Returning to Marietta, Dawes had suffered successes and reverses in postwar life, yet he remained, to the last, a man of integrity and rectitude who earned the respect of his community, as he had from the men of the 6th Wisconsin. Initially, he had thrown himself into business, amassing a fortune in an iron works and with other investments. But the financial panic of 1873 had demolished his resources; only the wholesale lumber business kept him modestly comfortable. In 1880, the 42-year-old veteran had received the Republican nomination for Congress, and he had defeated Judson "Silver Bill" Warner, a former Union general whose unit had fought within 200 yards of the 6th Wisconsin at Gettysburg. In the 47th Congress, Dawes had found the Republican side of the aisle packed with ex-Union soldiers; and seated opposite him, on the Democrat side, had been his former regimental comrade, Ed Bragg. Doubtless, the two had spent many an hour reminiscing about the uncounted marches, campfires and battles.[19]

17. *Milwaukee Sunday Telegraph*, November 16, 1879. Dawes' mother-in-law, Betsey Shipman Gates, in writing to her daughter, Betsey Gates Mills, August 27, 1884, noted: ". . . Rufus Pere has gone to Wisconsin to the re-union of the Iron Brigade, the first one he has ever attended." Betsey Shipman Gates, *Grandmother's Letters*, prepared by Mary Dawes Beach, privately printed by Henry M. Dawes, Christmas, 1926, p. 133.
18. *Roster of Wisconsin Volunteers*, p. 494.
19. As a legislator, Dawes had been noted for two accomplishments: he had pushed through a bill to establish diplomatic relations with Persia, and he

Dawes was defeated in his bid for reelection two years later, and returned to private life, where he had limited success in business, worked on a memoir of his war years and battled a lingering illness. One of the last public appearances of the 6th Wisconsin veteran would occur on Decoration Day, 1899. He would don his old general's uniform, and be wheeled in an invalid's chair to greet the cadet corps from Marietta High School, which had come to pay respects. His snowy hair and beard, shrunken frame and wizened visage would bespeak a man decades older than his 61 years. Yet he would be able to address the boys, speaking of patriotism and duty. Dawes would die three months later, August 1, 1899.[20]

"Was there a man at that Reunion who enjoyed himself better than Gen. Dawes did?" Watrous asked rhetorically. "I don't believe there was. It was a real feast for him from first to last, and he will be at the next, if the good Lord spares him, and every last man of the old brigade hopes he will be spared." The Lan-

---

had been among a minority who voted against the Chinese Exclusion Act. The latter stand had angered organized labor in Ohio, and he was defeated in his 1882 reelection bid by a scant 600 votes.

In 1889, strong support would arise for his nomination as Republican gubernatorial candidate, but he would decline, largely because of failing health. That year, Dawes would become critically ill from exhaustion, and never again regain the robustness that had sustained him through three years of war. During the final years of his life, he would devote much time, perhaps with the assistance of his beloved wife, Mary, and his oldest son, Charles (who would, years later, become vice president of the United States), compiling his war memoirs, which he called *Service With the Sixth Wisconsin Volunteers*. He would cull through copious war letters and comb official reports to create the book, but he would soften the imperious, sometimes boastful judgments of youth, adopting a more self-effacing tone in those pages. Within 50 years of its publication in 1890, his work would become a landmark, regarded by military historians as one of the finest war reminiscences ever produced.

20. *Memoir: Rufus R. Dawes*, (New York, 1900); Bascom N. Timmons, *Portrait of An American: Charles G. Dawes*, (New York, 1953), pp. 9-11; *Biographical Dictionary of the American Congress, 1774-1960*, (Washington, D.C., 1961), pp. 788-789. There would be a flood of sentiment from former comrades in arms at the funeral. ". . . [H]e was one of the fairest, coolest, and bravest of commanders," one former subordinate would write. Another would call him "a father to his men, but strict in his discipline." "I have seen him bearing the flag of the regiment in more than one desperate fight till some of us would force it from his hands. I have seen him, in the heat of summer and the rain and snows of winter, on the march and in camp, always and everywhere a true soldier, and gentleman," would be another encomium. Yet another would sum it all, writing, "He was my ideal commander. . . ." All the eulogizing and funeral obsequies would be gathered into a 50-page book by his son, Charles, at century's turn, and would stand as a testament to a father and veteran.

caster gathering would, of course, be the only one for the weary general; he would write often to Watrous of desires to attend the "Camp-Fires," but such wishes would never be realized.[21]

There were many reunions like that between Dawes and Alton. Ed Whaley had not seen Lewis A. Kent since the day a rebel ball had shattered Whaley's leg. Kent, a Denver newspaperman and the final field commander of the regiment, had traveled 800 miles, with his young daughter, to attend the reunion. Nineteen years before, he, and Whaley had had harsh words over whose rank took precedence, and they parted, glowering at one another south of Petersburg, Virginia, April 1, 1865.

The pair, as Watrous later wrote, caught sight of one another at the same instant. Kent rushed forward at the "double quick" while Whaley hobbled slowly on his wooden appendage. "Both hands of both men were out-stretched and the four hands clasped. They stood there for a minute and looked into each other's faces;" then they "clasped each other's arms, with tearful eyes and paralyzed tongues." Kent was the first to speak: "Ed, forgive me." "That was done long ago," Whaley replied. "Then their tongues were tied again and they wept like children."

Kent, raised in ante-bellum Virginia, was asked to speak at the Lancaster gathering, and he was effusive about his experience with his old unit. "I owe the Iron Brigade more than most of you," he began:

> My three years in Wisconsin [as a college student] removed the Southern chivalry veil from my eyes, and when the war came I had learned much of the North and its people, and knew that in the end the South would be whipped, and believed that it ought to be whipped. My residence in Wisconsin saved me from the Southern army and a service which no lover of his country could be as proud of as I am of my service with this brigade, on the right side. I cannot tell you how glad I am for having traveled 800 miles to attend this meeting.[22]

21. *Telegraph*, September 7, 1884.
22. Watrous, *Richard Epps*, pp. 113-114; *Milwaukee Sunday Telegraph*, September 14, 1884. Kent was a student at Beloit College in southern Wisconsin when war began, and in June, 1861, he enlisted in the Beloit Star Rifles, becoming a sergeant. Wounded at Petersburg in June, 1864, he won promotion to captain the next month and was transferred to the command of Company A. He had, at vari-

254

Hyde's Hall in Lancaster was filled by eight o'clock that evening. The shredded battleflags of the 6th, 2nd and 7th Wisconsin hung prominently around the room, and the men who gathered eyed with them with reverence.[23] The banners would be present for three more such annual gatherings before being retired to the state capitol. Adorning the hall's windows were the names of the brigade's commanders, each wreathed in evergreen. The stage was also "tastefully" adorned with banners and bunting, and at the right stood the Iron Brigade flag.[24]

Dapper John Gibbon, the Association's president, called the proceedings to order, pounding the podium with an empty pop bottle for attention. He had come from Fort Laramie, Wyoming Territory, where he had led the effort to pacify the Western Indians. He had gained commendation and fame for his gallant action on the third day at Gettysburg and was carried from the field, wounded that afternoon. At war's end, Gibbon had remained in the army, assigned to the West and the Indian wars. He had been in command of the infantry during the campaign against the Sioux in 1876, and there had been a temporary cloud over his career when a subordinate leveled a spurious charge of dilatory

---

ous times, been offered higher command in other units, including the 52nd Wisconsin Infantry and even a West Virginia regiment, but he remained in the 6th Wisconsin. When Whaley, his leg shattered, was taken bleeding from the field at Five Forks, Kent assumed command of the 6th Wisconsin. A few days later, he had an arresting experience at Appomattox Court House, when the black-hats received the muskets of a Virginia regiment, raised in the county in which Kent lived before the war. He recognized some of the men. "Hello, Kent! What are you doing here?" asked the regiment's colonel. "Just now I am busy taking the guns of your regiment," the fresh-faced young captain replied. That night, the 6th Wisconsin shared its rations with Kent's boyhood acquaintances. After the war, Kent relocated to Denver and got into the newspaper business. At the close of the Lancaster reunion, Kent journeyed to Virginia, where he had not visited in 27 years. *Roster of Wisconsin Volunteers*, pp. 496, 520.

23. Never present at the Wisconsin Iron Brigade Reunions were the flags of the 24th Michigan. In denying a request the flags be sent, Michigan Quartermaster General William Shakespeare noted:

It is the wish of the governor that none of the "old flags" be taken out. . . . [T]he flags are so old and rotten that but a few handlings would entirely destroy them. I trust the members of the old "Iron Brigade" will appreciate the motive and feel that the flag of the 24th Michigan should be kept in some safe place where it will be a reminder to future generations of the sacrifice that was made in behalf of a free country. [William Shakespeare, Letter, to Jerome A. Watrous, August 30, 1883].

24. *Herald*, September 9, 1884.

movement to relieve General George Custer at the Little Big Horn. But his conduct against the Nez Perces a year after the Lancaster gathering would belie the allegation and earn him a Regular Army brigadier's star.

Gibbon was beginning to rough out his reminiscences about the great Civil War for a book he intended, and he would touch upon something that resonated among Wisconsin veterans as he reviewed the spate of books being printed: there is a "great difference between battles in fact and battles in print . . . ," he wrote. His memoirs would be completed in 1885, but remain only in manuscript form until more than 30 years after his demise. He would serve as Iron Brigade Association president, unanimously reelected by his old subordinates, year after year, until his death in 1896.[25]

Gibbon's lean frame, close-cropped salt-and-pepper hair, Van Dyke beard and obvious military demeanor were well known to all assembled. But the disciplinarian of 1862 opened the meeting in uncharacteristic fashion: "This is to be a kind of bummer's meeting, a go-as-you-please Camp-Fire." As in past gatherings and most of those ahead, there was no set agenda; Iron Brigade men were called forward at random to deliver largely impromptu talks about battles and other matters of interest. The speakers played to the audience and the gallery. "It took about four minutes to warm that crowd up in good shape," Watrous recalled, "and it kept warm until the closing session." One-armed Lucius Fairchild was among the first to deliver an address Thursday evening, perhaps talking as much about current soldier concerns as about the times two decades removed. He was followed by Dawes, Tom Allen of the 2nd Wisconsin, popular 6th Wisconsin surgeon, John C. Hall, and others. Then the band played patriotic airs and a choir sang.[26] The session terminated about 11 o'clock, but the hall, as expected, did not clear immediately; some men circled around Dawes, Fairchild and Gibbon, while others clustered in small groups, exchanging information about their lives, Most, perhaps, talked about the great experience of their youth. The war seemed like only a few months past; Gettysburg occurred only last week, or so it felt to the middle-aged men.

25. Ezra J. Warner, *Generals in Blue*, (Baton Rouge, Louisiana, 1964), pp. 171-174; Gibbon, *Recollections*, p. 401.
26. *Telegraph*, September 7, 1884.

Years compressed and the fervor of youth seemed to seize them anew. Forgotten were the cold sleeps, the muddy marches, the dull and dreary camps; obscured were the fetid disease, rending wounds and the lives of promise cut short in shot and shell. Only the old camp comradeship, the impetuous charges, the grand glory remained.

However, the 21 months of war that followed Gettysburg had lacked the high drama of the earlier period. The incredible battering and loss sustained in Pennsylvania had ushered in change. Eastern regiments had been shuffled in and out of the once all-Western brigade, and its character had changed forever. Galling, too, was the dismemberment of the old I Corps and the transfer of its components to the V; no longer would the brigade be called the first unit in the Army of the Potomac. Then General U. S. Grant had taken command; certainly he was a Western man, but the manner in which he had conducted the war created more than idle talk in the ranks. From the Rapidan to the James River, over the ensuing months, almost without respite, Grant repeatedly hurled the Army of the Potomac, despite unremitting losses, against Robert E. Lee. In the horror, smoke and confusion of the Wilderness in May, 1864, the 6th Wisconsin had lost more good men, among them: popular Phil Plummer, killed; gentle Rollin Converse, mortally wounded; and John Kellogg, captured. At Laurel Hill, during the Spotsylvania campaign only days later, more casualties were added to the rolls. Cold Harbor and the initial investment of Petersburg had followed, before an early summer respite occurred while Grant decided on a course of action. Dawes, Remington, Harris, "Bona" Rogers and others had taken their discharges and gone home, creating more gaps in the leadership. But additional good men such as Tom Kerr, Charles Hyatt of Prescott and others had stepped to the fore, leading the 6th Wisconsin in its final months. Weldon Railroad in August and Boydtown Plank Road in October had been the last battles of 1864.

The flow of recruits and draftees had increased during the winter, and the regiment had almost become a stranger to itself; certainly the reinforcements had been needed, but the old veterans of 1861 exhibited stand-offishness, finding it difficult to warm to these newcomers. In the Spring campaigns of 1865, they, like as not, had dug earthworks, pulled together brushy breastworks and hunkered down instead of rushing heedlessly into the fray; let the new men take the brunt in the confused assaults and retreats south of Petersburg. Now their instinct was survive and get the thing done.

Only about 100 of the "Boys of '61" had remained that spring. The stalwart few of the 2nd Wisconsin who had reenlisted were merged into the 6th regiment, bringing much-needed bulk. And the 7th Wisconsin still slogged with them in the boggy bottoms below Lee's remaining lifeline, the South Side Railroad. But the Indiana and Michigan men were gone, and in their place was another Eastern bunch, the 91st New York. Under white-haired, emaciated John Kellogg, who had escaped rebel imprisonment and returned to fight another day, and gimpy Tom Kerr, the brigade had stumbled and stuttered through Hatcher's Run, Gravelly Run and, finally, Five Forks on April Fool's Day, 1865. There had been little sunlight, no storied charges and scant glory.

Within a score of days thereafter, the books had been closed on the Rebellion, and the Federal armies marched north to the nation's capital to be greeted by admiring throngs in May. Now, the cost of four years was beginning to be calculated. For the 6th Wisconsin, the final toll had been all but incomprehensible: one thousand and forty had been killed or wounded in battle since the baptismal fight at Gainesville in 1862. Eleven officers had been killed and 20 more carried rebel lead in their bodies. All of the shoulder straps who had remained had come up through the ranks. The price of four years had been high, indeed. But in the Summer of 1865, after the regiment had mustered from service, it had been a time to file away war memories, knit wounds and get on with the business of living.[27]

The opera house began to clear around midnight Thursday, the men moving off in twos and threes to the various hostelries they had engaged in the town. There had been an attempt to get all the participants to sign a makeshift roster; most scrawled a signature, their unit and hometown, but many did not. An accurate record of who attended the reunion that August, 1884, was never made. But there were some obvious absences, and Dawes, in the

27. William DeLoss Love, *Wisconsin in the War of the Rebellion*, (Chicago, 1866), pp. 934, 939-942, 945, 950, 952, 955, 967, 971; F. H. Dyer, *A Compendium of the War of the Rebellion*, (New York, 1959), pp. 1675-1676; Dawes, *Service*, p. 303.

waning hours of the day, may have given thought to the Kelly boys of Company B. James Kelly, whose name he had scribbled in his war journal, had fallen with a mortal wound that morning at Gettysburg, and Dawes had promised to write to his parents, telling them their son was a good soldier. While there is no record that he did, Dawes, a man of honor and conscience, more than likely fulfilled his promise to the dying lad. Kelly's body now lay in a simple grave at Gettysburg.

The other Kelly, Isaiah, (the two were not related) had carried the shot-ripped flag of the 6th Wisconsin for the remainder of the battle, but the wound he had sustained required hospitalization; he was absent from the ranks until fall. At Mine Run in November, Corporal Kelly's left arm had been horribly shattered, and amputation resulted. His days of active service ended, he had been transferred to the Veterans Reserve Corps, promoted to second lieutenant and finally discharged in June, 1866.

In war's aftermath, Kelly had a peripatetic existence, attempting to establish roots in Illinois and Nebraska; he had married in 1878, and in subsequent years fathered a son and daughter. It is unlikely Isaiah Kelly ever attended an Iron Brigade reunion. When Dawes located him, after publishing *Service With The Sixth Wisconsin Volunteers,* Kelly would be in Oklahoma Territory engaged in the real estate, insurance and pension claim business. He would thank his old commander for the book, saying he presumed Dawes had forgotten about him. While he would find the memoir generally "excellent," he did not agree with Dawes "in all respects as to what took place at the great battle" of Gettysburg; Dawes would file the letter with scores of others he had received. Isaiah Kelly would live out his days in the Southwest, and die September 23, 1910.[28]

On Friday morning, August 28th—the anniversary of Gainesville, where the Old Brigade had marched into battle for the first time—Gibbon, as he was wont to do two decades earlier in the Washington camps, called the meeting to order promptly at 10:30:

Is it necessary to remind the old gray-headed, bald-

28. U.S. Pension Office, Isaiah Kelly file, affidavit of January 2, 1867; Declaration of Invalid Pension, August 30, 1866; Kelly, Letter, to Rufus R. Dawes, August 2, 1892; Declaration of Widow's Pension, October 31, 1910.

headed "boys" here assembled, what took place 22 years ago to-day? I will not humiliate you by calling you "boys"—young "boys." Bragg, apparently because he had not got his full growth himself, seems to forget that nearly a quarter of a century has elapsed since any of us could properly be called "boys"—that is young "boys."[29]

The audience rocked with laughter at the good-natured jibing of the Little General, Ed Bragg, another of the favorites of the 6th Wisconsin, who was often the butt of jest and jape despite the fact he was a respected politician in Wisconsin. Bragg, who had from the first coveted a colonelcy or more, had risen to brigade command late in the war, and returned to Wisconsin mantled in honor. After serving in the state senate in post-war years, he had been elected to the U.S. Congress for three terms, a Democrat whose war service helped him swim in the Republican political stream; he had sat out a fourth consecutive term, but this year, 1884, he was running again. While he had been instrumental in selecting Lancaster as the site for the reunion, he could not attend; he was on the stump, garnering votes in his drive for office. He would be elected to the 49th Congress within a few months, serving one final term. He would retire from public life in 1906, after serving in ministerial posts, spending his last days in Fond du Lac, until death June 20, 1912.[30]

John Gibbon spent the opening half hour of Friday's session recalling the brigade's baptism of fire at Gainesville in August, 1862—the first time the regular army officer had led the Wisconsin and Indiana men into battle. And they had stood the test magnificently in his, and others, eyes. It was a stirring presentation. Then Jerry Watrous, the Association secretary, briefly sketched the four-year history of the organization, and expedited some prosaic business matters before the assembly was dismissed for lunch.[31]

Bill Remington was another of the 6th Wisconsin veterans whose name was not entered on the reunion roll that late sum-

29. *Telegraph*, September 7, 1884.
30. Bragg, ever the maverick, would turn against his party's presidential choice, supporting Republican William McKinley in 1896 and 1900. He would end his public life as U.S. Consul to Hong Kong, from 1902 to 1906. *American Biography*, p. 588; *Wisconsin Blue Book*, (Madison, 1885), p. 252.
31. *Telegraph*, September 7, 1884.

mer. His presence was missed. He had been among those who gathered in Milwaukee in 1880 to form the association, but he left the state for Dakota Territory shortly after; he was farming near DeSmet in 1884. Likely his Gettysburg wound still twinged 21 years after the great battle; he was also almost completely deaf from the shellburst that day. And the "tall, raw-boned, good hearted and awkward" veteran had never fully recovered from the cold that had developed on the march into Pennsylvania. It had worsened into an endemic respiratory problem which gave him little peace. After convalescing from his Gettysburg wound, Remington had attempted a return to the field, but continuing attacks of tonsilitis, diphtheria, quinsy and related maladies had prevented him from regaining his pre-Gettysburg condition. The 24-year-old officer had won promotion to captain following Gettysburg, and had earned "special and honorable mention for his conduct" in the Wilderness. Wounded again at Laurel Hill days later, he had been put out of action; and the throat and respiratory infection so dogged him that he became "generally debilitated." Leaving his sickbed, Remington had rejoined his regiment for the fight at Globe Tavern in August, 1864, leading the 6th Wisconsin when Charles Hyatt of Prescott, who was in command, went down with a shattered leg; but, when the guns had silenced, Remington was again returned to hospital. No longer physically able to keep up, the emaciated, nearly deaf captain had finally resigned in October, 1864.[32]

The frail Bill Remington, one of the original Company K boys of Juneau County, had journeyed home to his wife in Mauston, and attempted to reimmerse himself in civilian life. Unable, because of lingering maladies, to work steadily, Remington had made an initial application for disability pension in 1879, doing so reluctantly, he wrote, because his "boys were all girls"—he had two daughters. But the application was stalled because there was no one to testify about his Gettysburg wound. Dawes had been serving in Congress at the time, and a Pension Service officer told him about the case. Of course he remembered solid old Bill Remington, and recalled how he was knocked down that morning at Gettysburg in his impetuous dash for the rebel flag. Dawes

32. U.S. Pension Office, Remington file, affidavits of January 31, 1879 and September 19, 1881; Dawes, *Service*, pp. 264, 305-306.

had been delighted to assist, and, he wrote, it "did not take me long to 'call up the case,'" and file the affiidavit. Remington had been grateful for the intercession, and he wrote Dawes: "If an Angel from Heaven had appeared to help me, I could not have been more surprised." Ironically, Bill Remington would probably never receive one disability payment. He would die, at age 46, September 12, 1886.[33]

At Bill Remington's untimely demise there would be a typical outpouring of sentiment from Watrous, Dawes and others. The death of the "great-hearted, genial, brave" comrade was like the loss of a family member, the newspaperman would write. Dawes would also be moved: "His death brings back a flood of memories of one of my warmest and best of friends. . . . I have seen him knee deep in mud and loaded down with heavy knapsacks, keep the whole company in good heart by his unconquerable good spirits, and sharp sayings. . . . Our friend and comrade, hail and farewell," Dawes eulogized. Remington's body would be returned to Mauston for burial in Wisconsin soil, and his name enshrined with others in the 6th Wisconsin's heroic pantheon.[34]

There were other names, however, men who had marched with the 6th Wisconsin but not listed among the sterling legion of heroes. The bright lad Eugene Hardy, the only volunteer Ed Bragg coaxed from Weyauwega in 1861, ended his days with the regiment in lackluster fashion. He had served two years, faithfully doing his duty, "but at some real or fancied insult from one of his officers," a comrade remembered, had deserted with a pocket full of money and in civilian clothes. Hardy had traveled north through New England and finally spent time in New York City. His funds exhausted after seven weeks, Hardy had sought out a provost marshal, asking for transportation back to his regiment. He had been placed under arrest, "hustled off in disgrace" and returned to the 6th Wisconsin. In return for a pardon, the youngster, whose father had raised him as an abolitionist, had reenlisted for three years. But the star-crossed soldier's career ended in capture in 1864, and he was "confined to the shambles of Andersonville. After many months of starvation and agonizing suffering," Hardy's biographer lamented, "he died, [January 4,

33. Dawes, Service, pp. 306-307.
34. Milwaukee Sunday Telegraph, October 3, 1886; October 10, 1886.

1865] and his grave is unknown among the hundreds who gave up their lives in that modern Gehenna."[35]

The roster of those who gathered in Lancaster included only 23 names from the 6th Wisconsin, but there were many more who failed to ink their signatures. Tom, one of the Wallar brothers, signed in from Mt. Hope, Wisconsin. He had followed Frank and Sam into the 6th Wisconsin when he came of age in 1864. Frank, the only member of the regiment accorded a Medal of Honor, was not present; he was working his farm in Spink County, Dakota Territory, about a day's hard ride north of Bill Remington's place. Frank Wallar had always been seemingly modest about his great deed at Gettysburg. He had been careful to say he had only gotten a trophy that others, like Lewis Eggleston, Bodley Jones and Bill Remington, had died or been wounded attempting to capture. In battle's aftermath, Wallar had gained his third stripe, then was promoted to first sergeant; and he had veteranized with his regiment late in the year. Upon his return to the battlefield from veteran furlough in early 1865, Wallar had won his shoulder straps as second lieutenant of Company I; a promotion to first lieutenant had been made in Spring of 1865. A ceremony to award the Medal of Honor had been scheduled for early 1865, but, for unstated reasons, was postponed. "[P]resentation did not come off today," Wallar had confided in his diary; "when it will now is more than I can tell." A few days later, he noted the ceremony was "postponed indefinitely," and no further mention was ever made of the medal.[36]

Wallar had returned to Vernon County in western Wisconsin after the war, and resumed farming; he married in 1868, and three children were born in succeeding years—one son was named Loyd, after his father's old comrade, Loyd Harris. In 1880, Wallar had been elected county sheriff, but served only one term. He made an impressive-looking official—tall, stocky, bearded and balding, with a flash in his pale, deep-set eyes. Generally taciturn,

35. *Milwaukee Sunday Telegraph*, April 10, 1881; *Roster of Wisconsin Volunteers*, p. 514. The location of Hardy's grave is, in fact, known. It is grave 12586 at Andersonville, Georgia. His death was listed as due to "scorbutis."
36. *Roster of Wisconsin Volunteers*, p. 529; *O.R.*, Part 1, Vol. 27, pp. 254, 276, 278; Series III, Vol. 4, p. 816. Wallar's war diary, the property of the Vernon County Historical Society, Viroqua, Wisconsin, was stolen in May, 1977, along with his medal and other personal effects. They have not been recovered. The entries mentioned were quoted in the *Vernon County Broadcast-Censor*, June 1, 1961.

Wallar would write only once about his Gettysburg experiences in post-war years, and that to rebut what he considered an outlandish claim by Cornelius Okey about capturing the 2nd Mississippi flag. Wallar's Dakota Territory farm, some 40 miles south of Aberdeen in an area of rolling hills and glacial lakes, was modestly prosperous. But at the opening of the new decade, Wallar would find it necessary to apply for invalid pension, stating he could not work more than one-third of the time—a common claim made by applicants. Near the end of the century, Wallar would be widowed; he would leave his farm to live with an older son near Melette. Here he would die, in April, 1911, of a mastoid abscess. His remains, like those of Remington, would be returned to Wisconsin and interred near the Vernon County hamlet of Retreat. Francis Asbury Wallar, the only member of the 6th Wisconsin to receive the Medal of Honor, also took his place on the hallowed roll of honor.[37]

The breeziness and jocularity of the Friday afternoon session at the Lancaster reunion continued for some hours. Gibbon called upon representatives of each regiment to say something about their units. Gilbert Woodward gained the floor for the 2nd Wisconsin, and he carried forward a "tradition" that dated to early 1862, when the brigade regiments had been first pulled together. "[T]he 2nd Wisconsin was the seed out of which the whole brigade grew. Some pretty good old seeds in it too." There was laughter, but likely some of the 6th Wisconsin men gritted their teeth, for here it was again, that old lording by the Ragged 2nd about being first to fight. Would it never cease? Woodward suggested that the anniversary of the First Battle of Bull Run be marked as conspicuously as were the dates of the other brigade engagements. There were groans and catcalls from the old boys of the 6th and 7th over this, but they could not prevent him from making a windy recitation about the glorious exploits of his regiment that July day of 1861. Here it was, 20 years after the fact, and the 6th Wisconsin was again being bested, vanquished by the verbal assaults of their comrades.[38]

Fifteen-year-old Albert Harris, son of the 6th Wisconsin officer,

37. *History of Vernon County, Wisconsin,* (Springfield, Illinois, 1884), p. 262; U.S. Census, Dakota Territory, 1885, 1900; U.S. Pension Office, Francis A. Wallar file, affidavit of May 10, 1911.
38. *Telegraph,* September 7, 1884; *Herald,* September 9, 1884.

Loyd, perhaps fidgeted in his opera house seat as the impromptu oration dragged on. His father had brought him along from St. Louis, to attend the reunion and meet old veterans. Loyd, who would celebrate his 44th birthday within a week, was a slender, dark-eyed man who looked younger than his years; he was another of the "little fellows," barely five-foot-five. Harris was becoming one of the steady contributors to Watrous' newspaper, recalling light-hearted, humorous vignettes, particularly about the infamous 6th Wisconsin band, foraging, pretty girls and more.

After months of recuperation from his Gettysburg wound, Harris had returned to the regiment and a position of adjutant. He had participated in the sanguinary spring campaigns of 1864, and left the service upon expiration of his three-year enlistment. But military life had apparently appealed to him, and in 1865, he once again donned a uniform, enlisting in the U.S. Marines for three years. The photos which survive show him in a neat, double-breasted frock coat, left hand tucked in Napoleonic pose. But the mid-1870's, Harris had again returned to civilian life in St. Louis, and he became a manufacturing representative. Widowed early, he had remarried, and to the three children of his first marriage were added three more.[39]

Harris had also become active in veterans' activities, and been among those who had gathered in Milwaukee during the Grand Reunion of 1880 to form an association of Iron Brigade men; he had attended all of the annual gatherings since. In St. Louis, he became prominent in the Missouri Commandery of the Loyal Legion, and would, within a few years, head the unit's singing school. He penned scores of cheery and sad reminiscences using his middle name, Grayson, and Watrous was delighted to print them. Dawes, among many others, was an avid reader of Harris' "humorous pen." In his final years, Harris would serve as president of the St. Louis Lumberman's Exchange. He would die, at age 78, December 1, 1918.[40]

In addition to the speeches, socializing and friendship that pre-

39. *Roster of Wisconsin Volunteers*, p. 505; U.S. Pension Office, Loyd G. Harris file, affidavit of April 3, 1915; *Milwaukee Sunday Telegraph*, August 24, 1879.
40. *Milwaukee Sunday Telegraph*, August 19, 1888; *Milwaukee Telegraph*, May 20, 1893; Dawes, *Service*, p. 152; U.S. Pension Office, Loyd G. Harris file, affidavit of December 27, 1918.

vailed at the August gathering in Lancaster, there was also talk of those who needed aid, and collections were taken to assist them. One of the most immediate concerns was the Widow Hauser Fund, which had begun the year previous. The drive had been spearheaded by diminutive Otto Schorse, a German immigrant who had joined William Lindwurm's Citizens' Corps, Company F, in the first days of the war. He, too, had risen from the ranks of common soldier to become captain of his company and, later, regimental adjutant; he had been one of those fun-seeking officers who had joined Loyd Harris in forming a burlesque band in the Washington camps those distant days of 1861. Schorse, a modestly prosperous pharmacist and Association adjutant, was always among those who closed ranks with less fortunate comrades. Just the year before, he had been a leader in assisting destitute 6th Wisconsin veteran, John F. Hauser, working to secure a pension for the physically and emotionally ravaged old major.[41]

Trumpet-voiced John Hauser, regimental major that day at Gettysburg, was another of the tragic figures whose civilian pursuits never measured to the heights of war service. The German major, whom Dawes had officially commended for "particularly brave and efficient" service that day, had not been scathed; but he had been stricken July 6th with a relapse of remittent fever; that had triggered neuralgia and epileptic seizures, and hospitalization resulted. His condition had likely been exacerbated by the news of his daughter's death in Wisconsin. While he had participated in the abortive Mine Run campaign that fall, he was forced to submit his resignation; his wife had collapsed and was nearly comatose over the loss of her only child. As Hauser had prepared to take leave of his comrades, brother officers drafted a resolution which read in part:

Resolved, that we desire to testify to Major Hauser and the world, our confidence in him as an officer, won by coolness and bravery in the field, and his courteous and gentlemanly bearing in camp as well as our positive knowledge of his skill and efficiency as an officer.

41. [Flower], *Milwaukee*, p. 1044; Jerome A. Watrous, *Memoirs of Milwaukee County*, (Madison, Wisconsin, 1909), Vol. 1, p. 769.

The document had been unanimously adopted and signed by every officer of the regiment and presented to the departing immigrant. Hauser must have been moved by the expressions.[42]

Hauser had returned to Fountain City, Wisconsin on the Mississippi River, and his wife, Mary, recovered within months. He had engaged in post-war politics, stumping for Grant in 1868; in gratitude, he was named consul to Brindisi, but the appointment had been terminated within six months. Subsequently, he had founded a German-language newspaper, and had won a seat in the state legislature in 1871. But scandal (unsubstantiated allegations by townsmen of moral impropriety) had forced Hauser and his wife to leave Wisconsin, and they removed to Tennessee and began farming. Perhaps it had been epilepsy or the crush of failure in post-war years that had caused Hauser to become a "hopeless invalid" in 1876; he was only 45, and Mary had been forced to care for him, watching meager resources drain away. In 1880, the couple had returned to Milwaukee, where he was hospitalized in the National Soldiers Home. Former 6th Wisconsin comrades learned of his plight, and quickly closed ranks in support. Congressman Bragg had been named his attorney, and Schorse spearheaded a drive to raise funds. The outpouring of concern and support had buoyed the debilitated old soldier. Watrous had interviewed him, and asked why he had not earlier applied for a disability pension. "Well, you know I was quite independent as well as patriotic," he had responded. "So long as I could earn a living I would not think of applying . . . , and when I was broke down entirely I was unable to make the application, nor could I give friends the information on which to base a claim." He said his needs were modest. ". . . [I]f a fair pension is allowed, we can finish up our lives in comparative ease."[43]

---

42. *O.R.*, Part 1, Vol. 27, pp. 254, 276, 277. The resolution was duplicated in a handwritten testimonial at the Iron Brigade Association reunion in La Crosse, Wisconsin, September 12-13, 1883.

43. *Ibid.*; *Milwaukee Sunday Telegraph*, July 9, 1882. An interesting postscript was added to the Hauser story 60 years later, when a Pennsylvania college professor wrote to the U.S. Pension Office seeking information about the 6th Wisconsin major. He was writing on behalf of Hauser's daughter, Wilhelmina, born to her father's first wife in Germany; she was 90 and living in Switzerland. On April 12, 1940, the Veterans Administration responded, reporting Hauser had died at the National Soldier's Home, but the place of burial was not known. Tragically, it seems, Wilhelmina Hauser died not knowing the final resting place of her father. U.S. Pension Office, John F. Hauser file.

Hauser's long, dark night had appeared to be passing. His pension application was processed, old comrades visited him at the Soldiers Home, and his days were stable. He had also taken considerable pleasure in the gathering of Iron Brigade veterans during the 1882 reunion of the Army of the Cumberland in Milwaukee; scores of old comrades such as Gibbon, Bragg and even some of his former Company H "geese" were on hand to talk and reminisce. At the conclusion of activities, they had clasped hands and promised to meet at LaCrosse the following year. John Hauser, however, would not join them. He died June 8, 1883, and was among the first 6th Wisconsin soldiers to be buried at the Soldiers Home cemetery, amid the rows of white veteran markers. Watrous, Schorse and others had been there to comfort the widow. In LaCrosse later that summer, Hauser's old comrades had honored him by drafting a lengthy testimonial; it is unlikely the document was ever published. He, too, was enshrined among the storied ranks of regimental heroes.[44]

The Lancaster reunion of the Iron Brigade Association was nearing its end. Friday's spontaneous orations continued until late afternoon, when the assembly was adjourned for the evening meal. The rumpled veterans again talked casually, over the excellent fare prepared by the good women of Lancaster. Another of those who enjoyed these gatherings and would write to set the record straight about the 6th Wisconsin and the great charge on the railroad cut at Gettysburg was George Fairfield, the prosaic diarist who had recorded with fidelity the miles marched and weather conditions two decades past. The July 1st wound, caused by a ball that had ripped through his canteen and gashed his left hip, had bled freely, he had written, but he remained in the ranks with his company. The tall Crawford County sergeant had been hit again at Laurel Hill during the Spotsylvania campaign. "I was a good nurse," he wrote in a lengthy letter to the U.S. Pension Office about the first injury, "and binding [the wound] tightly I continued with my company," he attested. Later that day, he had been struck again, and, after the regiment was relieved from the battle line and halted on its rearward march, Fairfield had rested on an "empty ammunition box and fell asleep

44. Testimonial, Iron Brigade Association, September 12-13, 1883. Iron Brigade Association Papers, State Historical Society of Wisconsin.

and the Regt. went off and left me," he groused years after the event.[45]

With the termination of his three-year enlistment, Sergeant Fairfield had taken his discharge and returned to Wisconsin. He married, and five children were born to the couple in Crawford County. In the final decades of his life, he would live modestly in Prairie du Chien, perhaps visiting now and then with Ed Whaley and the old Company C boys who were still around. An avid reader of *The National Tribune*, the soldier newspaper published in Washington, D.C., Fairfield was occasionally disposed to submit rebuttals, correcting what he considered errors in fact; his war diaries were the unerring documentation for his assertions. He would be another sentinel on watch for slights against the 6th Wisconsin and the Iron Brigade. He would challenge unfair assertions by Eastern veterans, and write to set the record straight. George Fairfield would die in his hometown July 31, 1908, at age 68, of uremic poisoning.[46]

"The last evening [at Lancaster] was the best of all the meetings," Watrous penciled in a notebook growing thick with reports of the sessions—the scraps and snippets of conversations, and all those details he loved to enhance and print in his columns. This was a "Camp-Fire whose flames penetrated all of the heart's recesses," he wrote. The talks wound down, the middle-aged men perhaps wearying a bit of the rambling recitations yet warmed still by the camaraderie and memories. Watrous was one of the last to speak, but perhaps in humility, he failed to reprint the content of his presentation. His brief talk did close, however, with a reference to West Point regular army officers—and that seemed to spark something in General Gibbon's memory.

"Now we will have 'Benny Havens,'" Gibbon said, and turned to Loyd Harris, a man he knew had used music as an antidote to the rigors and boredom of camp life. "Start it, Capt. Harris," Gibbon commanded. The Company C veteran would, in years to come, be able to talk about the officer chorus of 1862 which sang together around the Virginia campfires—a fine aggregation of harmonizers composed of Ed Brown, Johnny Ticknor and Orrin Chapman—all of whom had fallen on fields of battle—Gilbert

45. U.S. Pension Office, George Fairfield file, affidavit of October 20, 1905.
46. *Ibid.*; State of Wisconsin, Certificate of Death, July 31, 1908.

Woodward, Amos Rood and himself. But something now seized Harris' throat, as he perhaps recalled the last time they had sung together—the night before Edwin Brown was killed at South Mountain in Maryland. He was stricken to silence.

"You can't?" asked Gibbon. "Woodward, you start it." More stony silence. "And you refuse, too? Well, I'll sing it myself," said Gibbon. And what followed was etched in the memories of many who attended, but especially in the mind of Watrous, who recorded the scene.

"[B]rave, prim, dignified, Johnny Gibbon . . . went to the piano and started 'Benny Havens,' and sang the whole of it in a voice that was as sweet to those ears as anything they had heard for years." Finally, Harris, Woodward and several others were able to bestir themselves to join in the chorus:

Oh, Benny Havens, oh, Benny Havens, oh.
We'll sing our reminiscences of Benny Havens, oh!

As the last words wafted through the opera house, applause burst forth for the man Watrous called the "Sweet Singer of Fort Laramie."

Then the meeting was closed with a few brief remarks by Gibbon, Fairchild and others. The gathering for 1885 was set for Madison, at the urging of Fairchild, and "orders" were issued that all now present assemble there to answer the roll. The pop bottle pounded again on the podium as Gibbon terminated the final session. The opera house emptied more slowly than the night before, the Iron Brigade men unwilling to see the end of the proceedings, to let loose of the close friendships that had cheered them for the past two days and that had helped them renew the great adventure of their youth. There were, too, unexpressed fears that some here present would not, because of circumstances, be able to make the trip to the state capital the next year; more worrisome, perhaps, others would never again attend—the capriciousness of life and death was becoming better known to these graying men who had already lost so many of their comrades. The ranks of the grand old Brigade thinned at an ever-increasing rate these days.

Around midnight Friday, after the final session, Watrous recalled another "pleasant incident." About 20 of the old Black

Hats sat around the Wright House where they boarded; the Chicago & North Western train east to Madison and Milwaukee was not scheduled until the following day. As the men chatted, smoked and tipped a glass or two, a group of young boys stopped before an open window on the balmy late summer evening and began serenading the veterans. "A number of old army tunes were rendered in the sweetest manner. How still it was in that company as the beautiful strains crept into that room and filled the night air." The serenaders were the sons of Iron Brigade men who had come to entertain their fathers' friends: they were led, appropriately, by young Albert Harris, who had more than a touch of his father in him. The Wisconsin men were moved again. Fairchild could but look at the ceiling, Tom Allen pulled out a handkerchief and wiped his nose. But Loyd Harris "faced the music, [and] two tears, large ones, broke away and escaped over his cheek." Moments of silence permeated the room before someone said, "Well, now, that was good in the boys." It was another of those vignettes Jerome Watrous would print in his newspaper, romance and milk for every cloying drop of sentiment.[47]

Watrous returned from Lancaster carrying a sheaf of notes and impressions; these he would cast into an unofficial report that consumed much of the front page and more. It was a typical report of those old soldier gatherings, and he caressed the memory of the Lancaster reunion for all to read:

> Camp-Fire [Watrous' pseudonym], though old, stoop-shouldered and bald-headed, is a lover; he loves the old brigade—loves all of its members, and when he gets to writing about it and them, he don't know when to stop. . . .[48]

Watrous' *Telegraph* continued for 14 more years, and he published ream upon ream of stories submitted by Loyd Harris, Johnny Cook, "Bona" Rogers and dozens of others, including, of course, J. P. "Mickey" Sullivan. The newspaperman rejoiced publicly when his comrades were successful, and lamented loudly when they fell on hard times or passed away. In its halcyon days,

47. *Telegraph*, September 7, 1884.
48. *Ibid.*

the newspaper printed 10,000 copies each week, and grew into one of the larger soldier papers in the Old Northwest. In 1891, Watrous took his son, Robert, into the business, and that spring, the publication's name changed to *The Milwaukee Telegraph* and its printing date moved to Saturday.

With the outbreak of the Spanish-American War in 1898, Jerry Watrous, already 60 years old, offered his services, and was assigned as paymaster, first in Washington, and, later, on the West Coast and in the Philippines. He submitted articles while he was away, descriptions of old battlefield haunts, recollections of camps, meetings with war friends. But declining subscriptions toward the end of the century forced the paper to cease in November, 1899. Ironically, one of the final issues carried the obituary of Rufus R. Dawes.

After eventual release from service, Watrous returned to Milwaukee, writing for local and other newspapers, and, in 1909, he pulled together a two-volume history of the city entitled *Memoirs of Milwaukee County.* In 1917, the agile 76-year-old writer again tendered his services for war, and he offered to forego rank and pay because, he admitted, long marches might be too much for his old legs. While the War Department gratefully declined his offer, it sent the indefatigable Watrous to deliver more than 250 recruiting speeches, trying to convince a new generation of young men to follow the example of his contemporaries. Watrous ended public life as commander of the Veterans Home in Waupaca, then returned to Milwaukee for his final years. Ever the admirer of women, he had three marriages, the last, in 1919, when he was 78 years old. Through all his days he never ceased writing and talking about his old regiment and the Iron Brigade. Watrous died June 4, 1922—one of the last of the 6th Wisconsin men—and a large funeral cortege, with full military honors, marched his remains to the final campground.[49]

J. P. "Mickey" Sullivan had begun to gather his thoughts about the war years during the reunions, but he had committed only his Gettysburg experiences to paper before Lancaster. His once boyish visage now covered with gray side whiskers, the irrepressible Irish immigrant was farming in the Vernon County town of Forest. He had met his wife, Angelina, while hospitalized in Phil-

49. Conard, *Milwaukee,* pp. 395-397; *Dictionary of Wisconsin Biography,* (Madison, 1960), p. 367; *Milwaukee Sentinel,* June 5, 1922.

adelphia with his Gettysburg wound; they had married in February, 1864, just before the 23-year-old reenlisted for three years. The plucky private had sustained another wound, his most grievous, at Globe Tavern on the Weldon Railroad in August, shell fragments cutting into his back and neck, and a shot ripping his right thigh. While he was only briefly hospitalized, he carried the shell splinters in his skull for the rest of his days; they would ultimately cause his death. "Mickey" had yet again been nicked in the right thigh, during the confused battle around Boydtown Plank Road in October. He was a sergeant by then, but still retained the same devil-may-care attitude toward soldiering that had stamped him since 1861. He and his uncle, Tommy Flynn, had overstayed passes during the late winter days of 1865, likely celebrating the birth of Sullivan's first son. That, in addition to the fact that the war was in winter's ebb, had been reason enough to miss a few roll calls. Sullivan had lost his stripes over the incident, but he had not seemed to mind overmuch; he was happy to return to the back rank as high private.[50]

"Mickey" had been in the final push against Lee the spring of 1865, and he watched the rebels stack arms and furl colors for the last time. Near the end, his stripes had been returned, the officers not wanting to send him home with a bare sleeve. After the cessation of hostilities, he had returned to Vernon County and the mundane matters of farming: he was again pitching hay, not rebels. It must have been dull for the 25-year-old veteran. By the early 1880's, the scars of war had become the ailments of middle age—he was seriously troubled with a bad back and needed to wear a special truss to carry on with plow, pitchfork and wagon. Like most of his comrades, Sullivan was in his mid-40s when the Iron Brigade Association annually gathered in Wisconsin; these meetings served as impetus for "Mickey" to begin composing his recollections of the great adventure of his youth. The first of these had appeared in Watrous' *Telegraph* in the fall of 1882, when Sullivan spun a light-hearted anecdote about the regiment's loss of a contraband cook.

He had been invited by Ed Bragg, the following year, to address the Iron Brigade Association reunion in LaCrosse, to present some of the humorous yarns of life as a common soldier. He

50. U.S. Pension Office, Sullivan file, affidavits of March 30, 1874 and April 18, 1891; Descriptive Book, Sixth Wisconsin Volunteer Infantry, March, 1864.

was the first enlisted man to be included on the docket, setting a precedent for others from the ranks who followed.[51] That fall, he had composed for Watrous a lengthy recollection of the Battle of Gainesville that was larded with prickly pronouncements about generals he deemed incompetent, inept and imperious. The piece had occasioned a written criticism from one of his old comrades.[52]

Also about that time, he had traveled to Madison and was told by the State Historical Society curator there was no written record of the 6th Wisconsin or the Iron Brigade. His Irish temper rose, and he fumed about it in print:

> It may be owing to the fact that our men were not of the hymn singing, testament-carrying kind who spent their time in camp writing home letters of "Just Before The Battle Mother" variety, but they were always ready for march or battle and when that was over they were more interested in a stag dance or penny ante than what the newspapers were saying about them. I think that a state that annually appropriated thousands of dollars wrung from poor and often needy farmers [of which he was one] to support professors of agriculture, state fairs, and to educate lawyers, might share a few dollars to prepare a record of the patriotism of those who gave health, wealth, life and limb for the honor of the state.[53]

So J. P. Sullivan, who had by then gained the fulsomeness of middle-age (old comrade Ira Butterfield would have been proud of the way he had "feathered out" since 1861), still possessed a thick shock of iron gray hair and whose family called him "Pat" or "J.P.," set about creating the record, adding to the body of his writings. Using what he claimed was his memory, a diary, and notes made on the pages of a *Casey's Tactics* drill manual 20 years before, he produced what was styled as a "correct and truthful account" of the events of July 1 to 3, 1863 as they came under his observation. "Ours was not a blundering dash, but a

51. *LaCrosse Morning Chronicle*, September 15, 1883; *LaCrosse Republican and Leader*, September 15, 1883, as cited in Richard H. Zeitlin, "Beyond the Battle: The Flags of the Iron Brigade, 1863-1918," *Wisconsin Magazine of History*, Vol. 69, No. 1, Autumn, 1985, p. 56.
52. Sullivan, *Telegraph*, November 4, 1883; Sullivan, *Telegraph*, November 11, 1883.
53. Sullivan, *Telegraph*, September 30, 1883.

steady, cool, straightforward advance against a greatly superior force . . . ," he wrote:

> No poet laureate has written about it, and no senti-
> mental young lady draped in the Stars and Stripes has
> recited it to an enthusiastic audience, as I have witnessed
> Tennyson's ["Charge of The Light Brigade"] poem. . . .[54]

Jerry Watrous obtained a copy of "Mickey's" two-part recollection of the 6th at Gettysburg, perhaps while they were together at Lancaster. The affable editor, however, took some liberties with his old comrade's prose, removing many of the more testy assertions before publishing the piece in *The Telegraph* the December after the reunion. It was the beginning of a contributor/editor relationship that would flourish for the next several years.

On New Year's Day, 1885, five months after the Lancaster gathering, an event occurred that galvanized "Mickey" further. He returned to Mauston for a gala Company K reunion. It was one of those winter days in south central Wisconsin, with the thermometer hovering at 20 below, that made the snow crunch underfoot and the air so clear it was almost brittle. Nearly 600 people, including most of the old company who survived, came in by train, sleigh and foot from the neighboring towns of Lindina, Summit and Wonewoc. One of the highlights of the affair was the public reading of a letter from an old comrade, Rufus Dawes, which had been written in November from Ohio. Regretfully, he said, because he had travelled to the Iron Brigade reunion in Lancaster just months before, he was unable to join the festivities. But he did want to send a "proper acknowledgment" to his comrades in the company and to their families. Twenty-one of the 198 men who had served with the Lemonweir Minute Men had been killed in battle and another 51 wounded, Dawes noted. Many of the living veterans, he wrote:

> . . . are now your plain fellow citizens, but they were
> heroes tried and true as ever offered life on the field of
> battle. The young generation can hardly realize that
> their modest neighbors are soldiers who fought on more

54. Sullivan, *Mauston Star*, February 13, 1883.

fields of battle than the Old Guard of Napoleon, and have stood fire with greater firmness. . . .

Sullivan and the old soldiers of the 6th Wisconsin pressed in close to catch the words, for Dawes was touching something that had festered in them for a generation—a resentment that they had been cheated of a full share of the credit for their fight at Gettysburg, and elsewhere as well. Somehow the importance of their accomplishment had been overlooked in the multitude of battle accounts rolling from the presses—mostly by Eastern writers and Eastern officers. Dawes's letter concluded: "[Your old comrades] lie scattered over the land, and their names should be gathered up around your campfires, and their character and deeds presented."[55]

Sullivan's determination to tell the story of the 6th Wisconsin was burnished anew; he would insure that the names were indeed gathered and the deeds remembered. Soon he submitted more pieces to Watrous, gaining notoriety for himself and his regiment; he wrote about campaigns—subjective but telling accounts, column after column, on South Mountain, Fitzhugh's Crossing, Laurel Hill, Weldon Railroad and others—about the raising of the Lemonweir Minute Men and other episodes of the war. His old comrades enjoyed his ofttimes iconoclastic, irreverent recollections, perhaps because "Mickey's" caustic pen spared no one; even Rufus R. Dawes was once slightly scorched. "Mickey of Company K" would never mellow or change. While refusing to mythologize or romanticize, he did treat the maiming, bloodletting and dying with almost casual indifference; a way, perhaps, to erase the grim memories.

Sometime before the century's turn, J. P. Sullivan, with characteristic impetuosity, divorced his wife of 34 years, and, as a man in his 50s, married a woman 30 years his junior. He also gave up his farm and moved into the little Vernon County hamlet of Ontario with his wife and her three young children. Here, he took up a law practice, and along with other townies, puffed through an old toot horn in the city's coronet band and carried the flag at the head of the community's Fourth of July parade. Sullivan always did what he damned well pleased, even fathering

55. Dawes, *Star*, January 8, 1885. The account contains Dawes' letter of November 23, 1884, and a December 22, 1884, letter from Jerome A. Watrous.

a son while in his 60s. But despite the springy wife and youngsters under foot, "Mickey" could not ward off the weight of his wounds and the encroaching years. A long, painful illness marked his declining years, and a photo that survives shows him white and stooped. He lived to celebrate his 65th birthday, but on October 22, 1906, he succumbed. One of the causes of his death was the shell fragments lodged near his brain 42 years before, in the muddy bottoms of Virginia. Jaunty James Patrick Sullivan ("Mickey of Company K") was buried at Ontario Cemetery with a few old veterans there to render a salute at his last roll call.[56]

With his death and that of Jerome Watrous in the 1920s, the major chroniclers of the 6th Wisconsin passed from the scene. While the words of Rufus R. Dawes in *Service With The Sixth Wisconsin Volunteers* and those of Company A men Phil Creek and Mair Pointon remained, the record of the regiment was largely consigned to brittle manuscripts and letters and in decaying volumes of *The Telegraph*.

In the century and a quarter that has passed since the 6th Wisconsin's charge at Gettysburg, the record of the regiment's accomplishment has not yet been set straight, and Dawes' admonition to gather up the names and deeds of the 6th Wisconsin men has not been completed. One can travel to the quiet National Cemetery at Gettysburg and stand before the simple stones of the Wisconsin men, or to the gravesides of J. P. Sullivan at Ontario, Wisconsin, and to those others who stood in ranks with the "Calico Boys" of 1861, but only few today remember Frank King, James Kelly, Loyd Harris, Johnny Ticknor, Pete Markle, Orrin Chapman, George Fairfield, Frank Wallar, Bodley Jones and "Mickey of Company K." And, somehow, Sullivan's bitter words of 1883, about the great deed of his regiment at Gettysburg, still echo from the 19th century. "It is forgotten by all except a few veterans and cripples and the wives and mothers who lost all they held dear."[57]

56. U.S. Pension Office, Sullivan file, affidavits of March 30, 1874 and April 18, 1891; U.S. Census, Wisconsin, 1880, 1900; *Vernon County Censor*, October 31, 1906.
57. Sullivan, *Star*, February 13, 1883.

Amos Lefler

1837 - 1911

Larry Lefler Collection

AMOS LEFLER
Shot in the Face at Gettysburg
278

APPENDIX I

Capturing a Flag

One of the old soldier controversies that divided 6th Wisconsin veterans after the war involved the capturing of the flag of the 2nd Mississippi Infantry. The dispute began during an 1880 reunion, when former Corporal Frank Hare of Company B, in casual conversation with a few friends, claimed he captured the rebel banner in the charge of the railroad cut at Gettysburg. The story circulated at the meeting and finally got back to Frank Wallar, who received a Congressional Medal of Honor for the deed. He and several others (from various companies) confronted Hare, who was forced to admit he may have captured a Confederate flag, but wasn't sure to which Confederate regiment it belonged. Wallar had several of his comrades sign a statement that it was, in fact, *he* who had captured the flag, and that appeared to settle the matter once and for all.

The controversy heated up again when Cornelius W. Okey of Company C wrote his "Echoes of Gettysburg" for the *Milwaukee Sunday Telegraph*. He claimed:

> My wound, was bleeding so profusely that I gave the flag, which was now entirely in my possession to a sergeant, I think of Co. H, and started for the rear, and finally went into the city and into the Courthouse hospital. . . . [While in Cuyler hospital. Germantown, Philadelphia, I was] surprised some days afterward to receive a visit from the sergeant to whom I had given the rebel flag on the battlefield, and about which he made the following statement: "As near as I remember I only had the flag in my possession for a few minutes when I was wounded through the thigh. I broke the staff in two, taking the butt end for a cane with which to get off the field, and gave the flag to Corporal F. Waller [sic], the

279

piece of the staff I now have with me and will give to you as the original captor." I still have the piece of flag-staff in my possession, and value it very highly as a war relic. It is of hard yellow pine, about three feet in length and one and a half inches in diameter. On the butt end there is a heavy brass ferule and the other end has the appearances of having been broken off.[1]

The account stirred Earl Rogers, Wallar's former company commander, who was always quick to protect the reputation of his boys. He sent a copy of the article to Wallar, then farming at Petonka, Dakota Territory. In a May 10, 1883, letter addressed to "Friend Bona," the Medal of Honor recipient had a blunt answer:

> You ask me to read . . . [Okey's account] and write what I know about it. I know that C. W. Okey is a damned liar, and doubt if he was in the battle of Gettysburg at all. . . . [I gave the flag to Dawes]. Just then a sergeant of Co. H. came up wounded, and was going to the rear, and the colonel told him to take it and take care of it. I then went on the skirmish line. . . . I afterwards saw the sergeant, after we came home on furlough [January, 1864], and I asked him how the staff got broken and he told me that when he went back to the city he entered a house and went to bed, and when we were driven back he thought that if the flag was left standing in the room they (the rebs) would get it, so he broke the staff in two and put the flag in bed with him, and in that way saved it. Now, if C. W. Okey has a part of the staff, there is where he got it. I thought very little of the 14th Brooklyn man who tried to steal the flag from me on the battle field, but I think less of Okey to wait almost 20 years, and then try to steal the honor of capturing the whole flag, by stealing a piece of the staff 20 years ago. . . .[2]

Rufus Dawes, always careful in what he wrote, left a number of versions. In a March 18, 1868, letter, Dawes wrote:

1. Okey, *Telegraph*, April 29, 1883.
2. Wallar, *Telegraph*, July 29. 1883.

Capt. Remington, Corporal [Frank] Ashbury Waller [sic], Corporal Lewis Eggleston and some other sprang for their colors. When skirmishing began again, Remington was shot. Eggleston was killed. Waller got the Color.

In his more dramatic account published in the *Milwaukee Sunday Telegraph* 28 years after the fact, Dawes noted:

> Before we reached the edge of the cut, First Lieutenant William N. Remington, of company K, sprang forward of the line to get the rebel colors. He was shot at once, the bullet striking his shoulder. Then Corporal Eggleston, of company H, first seized the color. For this daring feat he paid with his life. He was shot dead on the spot. Private Anderson, of company H, in fierce and desperate anger at the murder of his friend and comrade, clubbed his unloaded musket and crushed the skull of the rebel who shot Eggleston. Anderson was a rough looking man with a shaggy head of hair and was called in the regiment "Rocky Mountain Anderson." He was a noble soldier and a good man. Sergeant C. W. Okey, of company C, was shot also while holding onto the rebel colors. Corporal Asbury Waller finally captured the colors.[3]

In his *Service With The Sixth Wisconsin Volunteers*, published in 1890, and in a speech that same year in Ohio to the Military Order of the Loyal Legion, Dawes presented two additional accounts. Both were virtually identical:

> The rebel color was seen waving defiantly above the edge of the railroad cut. A heroic ambition to capture it took possession of several of our men. Corporal Eggleston, of company "H," sprang forward to seize it and was shot and mortally wounded; Private Anderson, of his company, furious at the killing of his brave young comrade, recked little for the rebel color, but he swung aloft his musket and with a terrific blow split the skull of the

3. Dawes, *Telegraph*, April 27, 1890.

rebel who had shot young Eggleston. This soldier was well known in the regiment as "Rocky Mountain Anderson." Lieutenant William N. Remington was shot and severely wounded in the shoulder, while rushing for the color. Into this deadly melee came Corporal Francis A. Waller [sic], who seized and held the rebel battle flag. His name will forever remain upon the historic record, as he received from Congress a medal for his deed.[4]

In an undated letter to Editor Jerome Watrous for the *Milwaukee Sunday Telegraph*, Earl M. Rogers wrote:

Major Blair, of the Second Mississippi, finding no way to escape, ordered his men to surrender, and springing to the ranks of the Sixth, gave his sword to Col. Dawes. In the terrible confusion of this moment, it seemed impossible for the men to hear the orders to cease firing, when Corporal Frank A. Waller [sic], of Company I, after several attempts by others to seize the flag of the Second Mississippi had failed, jumped into the Confederate ranks and seized the flag which was firm in the bearer's hands and wrenched it from him. He jumped back upon the embankment and threw the flag upon the ground and stood upon it, took his gun and again commenced firing. . . ."

From the surviving evidence, it is clear most 6th Wisconsin veterans credited Wallar with capturing the flag of the 2nd Mississippi Infantry at Gettysburg. Okey's role in the whole incident is less sure. Except for Okey's own, self-serving "Echoes of Gettysburg," Dawes' *Telegraph* dispatch is the only other mention of Okey being involved in the attempt to seize the flag. However, despite Wallar's sharp response to the claim, it would appear Okey was one of the several soldiers who rushed the Confederate colorbearer that confused morning. It would seem logical a veteran claiming credit for a false deed would not write for publication about it in the *Telegraph* (where it would be read by his comrades) and it would seem unlikely it would be reprinted sometime later by Aubery in his *Recollections*. Ex-Corporal Okey,

4. Dawes, *Service*, pp. 168-169.

however, probably claimed a bit more credit than he should have for his attempt.

Another of the unanswered questions is whether the flag of the 2nd Mississippi was still attached to its staff when carried into Gettysburg by Sergeant William Evans. In his *Service With The Sixth Wisconsin Volunteers*, Rufus R. Dawes noted:

> It is a rule in battle not to allow sound men to leave the ranks. Sergeant William Evans of Company "H," a brave and true man, had been severely wounded in the thighs. He was obliged to use two muskets as crutches. To him I intrusted the battle-flag, and I took it from the staff and wrapped it around his body.

In his "Align on the Colors," published in the *Milwaukee Sunday Telegraph*, April 27, 1890, but actually written five to seven years earlier, Dawes noted:

> I did not feel justified in sparing any sound man from the ranks and Evans was disabled by a shot, I think in his thigh. At all events he hobbled away, using two muskets as crutches. I put the flag under his coat around his body and charged him to keep it safely at all hazards. He became weak and faint and made slow progress so that when, in the afternoon, we were driven by the enemy through Gettysburg, Evans was overtaken by the crush in the streets. Determined to hide his flag from the rebels, he staggered into a house and fell fainting upon the floor. He fell into the hands of friends whose kindness was equalled by their bravery and acuteness. Two ladies raised him from the floor and placed him upon a bed. They tore open his coat to give him aid and found the flag.

However, Cornelius W. Okey, in his suspect account of how he captured the flag, "Echoes of Gettysburg," *Milwaukee Sunday Telegraph*, April 29, 1883, claimed:

> . . . My wound was bleeding so profusely that I gave the flag, which was now entirely in my possession to a sergeant, I think of Co. H, and started for the rear . . .

I was sent out with others [wounded] to the Cuyler hospital, Germantown, Philadelphia, where I was surprised some days afterward to receive a visit from the sergeant to whom I had given the rebel flag on the battlefield, and about which he made the following statement: "As near as I remember, I only had the flag in my possession for a few minutes when I was wounded through the thigh. I broke the staff in two, taking the butt end for a cane with which to get off the field and gave the flag to Corporal John F. Waller [sic]. The piece of the staff I now have with me and will give it to you as the original captor." I still have the piece of flag-staff in my possession, and value it very highly as a war relic. It is of hard yellow pine, about three feet in length and one and a half inches in diameter. On the butt end, there is a heavy brass ferule and the other end has the appearance of having been broken off.

Corporal Wallar, in his July 29, 1883, response to Okey's April 29, 1883, article in the *Milwaukee Sunday Telegraph*, wrote, however:

I afterwards saw the sergeant [William Evans of Company H] after we came home on furlough [in 1864], and I asked him how the staff got broken and he told me that when he went back to the city he entered a house and went to bed, and when we were driven back he thought that if the flag was left standing in the room, they [the rebels] would get it, so he broke the staff in two and put the flag in bed with him, and in that way saved it. Now if C. W. Okey has a part of the staff, that is where he got it. . . .

Loyd G. Harris, who was not above "romancing" an incident or two in writing of his war adventures, left two versions. The first was from his "Adventures of a Rebel Flag," *Telegraph*, February 29, 1880, and in a letter published in a footnote in Dawes' war memoir:

I regret that Miss Julia's [one of the two young ladies in the home] letter has been lost. It was addressed to me

284

in reply to a vote of thanks tendered the two sisters by our regiment for saving the flag. It described their consternation on finding it in their possession, while the rebels were in their yard seeking water; no time was lost by their father in making fire wood of the staff, and for a better place of concealment the colors that had been carried amid the smoke and carnage of many battles, was spread under the sheets of his daughter's bed. The men of the Mississippi brigade were frequently visitors during the second and third days, but little imagined how near they were to their lost flag.[5]

Acting on the advice of the surgeon, we found pleasant quarters with the family of Mr. Hollenger [sic], and while there were joined by one of our sergeants (William Evans, I think) who had the rebel flag. This was about noon. Just after our dinner, firing began in the front . . .[6]

So, what did happen to the flag staff? Dawes said clearly he took the flag from the staff in wrapping the banner around Evans' body and under the sergeant's coat. It would seem unlikely the wounded Evans would have been left to hobble toward Gettysburg dragging the staff. It would seem likely, however, that he did take the staff to use as a crutch in his long walk to the town. That would seem to explain the reports (written long afterward) by Okey, Wallar and others that the staff was in the house in Gettysburg, and it just could be that Evans, or Harris and the other wounded officers, re-attached the flag to it just before they were forced to flee the city ahead of the advancing Confederate army.

5. [Harris], *Telegraph*, February 29, 1880.
6. Harris in Dawes, *Service*, fn pp. 171-172.

LT. JOHN BEELEY
Wounded at Gettysburg
286

APPENDIX II

The Charge

In his recollection of his Civil War years, General John Gibbon, who accomplished much between 1861-65, left an observation to be considered by anyone writing on Gettysburg. There is a "great difference between battles in fact and battles in print," the old general wrote, and certainly that would draw quick agreement from anyone trying to sort out what happened on the morning of July 1, 1863.[1] The veterans themselves, at the time and in later years, were in much dispute about various events. The charge on the railroad cut was no exception.

If the men of the 6th Wisconsin Infantry were successful on the battlefield that hot morning, they always felt they lost the war of words fought in the old soldier publications over the next 50 years. There were a number of reasons for all this, and probably the main one involved distance: the Badger veterans lived hundreds of miles from the center of the old soldier activities, and what they wrote of their experiences during the Civil War was printed in newspapers and publications of less prominence. Eastern officers and writers were more active, of course, and what they produced was widely circulated and, ultimately, accepted as fact. Even Rufus R. Dawes, the regiment's most articulate spokesman, did not publish his account of the 6th Wisconsin's charge until 1890.

The confusion over credit for the successful attack on Davis' Brigade in the railroad cut resulted, in part, from the claims of the commander of the 14th Brooklyn (officially the 84th New York Infantry), and it started when Colonel Edward B. Fowler filed his report dated July 9, 1863. In it (a rather brief document for the glory he claimed), Fowler said he had ordered the 95th New York and his "Fourteenth New York State Militia" to "march

1. Gibbon, *Recollections*, p. 401.

287

in retreat until on a line with the enemy [Davis' Brigade], and then change front perpendicular to face them, the enemy also changing front to meet us." All that was correct, but Fowler added:

At this time the Sixth Wisconsin Regiment gallantly advanced to our assistance. The enemy then took possession of a railroad cut, and I gave the order to charge them, which order was carried out gallantly by all the regiments, by which the piece of artillery was recaptured. The advance was continued until near the cut, when I directed the Sixth Wisconsin to flank it by throwing forward their right, which being done, all the enemy within our reach surrendered—officers, battle-flag, and men. Those in line on the left of my line escaped by following through the railroad cut. I held this position until ordered to the rear to join the brigade.[2]

The role of the 14th Brooklyn in the charge was further enhanced in the New York unit's history, published in 1911 to commemorate the 50th anniversary of the regiment's muster into U.S. Service. In the section on July 1, 1863, compilers C. V. Tevis and D. R. Marquis wrote:

This simultaneous attack on rear and front caused the Fourteenth to fall back and toward the left a short distance. . . . Colonel Fowler ordered his command, the Ninety-fifth and Fourteenth, to change front on Tenth Company. This difficult maneuver the command executed coolly, although the men were already beginning to drop. The command retreated until on a line with the enemy, and then, changing front forward on the right, faced the Confederates in the railroad cut. At the same moment the enemy changed front, facing Colonel Fowler's line. The Fourteenth, with the Ninety-fifth on its right, then coolly advanced to a point near the Chambersburg pike, and lay down for a few minutes. The Sixth Wisconsin, at this juncture, was sent to the aid of the two New York regiments, and as the Wiscon-

2. Fowler's report, *O.R.*, Series One, Vol. 27, Part One, pp. 286-287.

sin troops joined his command on the right Colonel Fowler ordered a charge. The command by this time had warmed to the work, and was wild to do some execution that the men could see. At the Colonel's command they rushed forward with a cheer. There was an ascent of about three feet at the pike. As the troops, charging with dash and spirit, reached this little eminence, they were met with a murderous hail of musket bullets. . . . For just an instant, as the full force of this terrible fire broke along their front, the line wavered. But it was only for an instant, and then, with another cheer, louder and more determined, the men rushed on. As they met Davis's brigade, the Confederate lines wavered in their turn, for a moment. And then the Mississippians, who composed Davis's forces, stiffened again. A fierce hand to hand fight ensued, with clubbed muskets, the Confederates defending their colors and the cannon they had previously captured, with the ferocity of wild cats. But the New York regiments were not to be denied . . . Some of the hottest work went on just at the end of the railroad cut, and the Confederates were finally driven into it. As the enemy retired into the cut Colonel Fowler ordered the Sixth Wisconsin to flank him, a movement which was promptly executed. This ended the struggle. Nearly all of Davis's brigade threw down their arms, yielded up their battle flags, and passed through the ranks of the Fourteenth to the rear, as prisoners. The Fourteenth and the Ninety-fifth, besides capturing the brigade, with the help of the Wisconsin regiment, regained the cannon taken by the Confederates earlier in the day.[3]

The history also included a recollection by Colonel Fowler, supposedly written July 28, 1863, while in camp near Warrenton Junction, Virginia:

. . . The enemies' fire still continued as deadly as ever, and there seemed a strong disposition on part of our men to halt at this point, as there was a slight cover

3. [Tevis and Marquis], *Fourteenth Brooklyn*, pp. 83-84.

caused by the banks and fences of a road running parallel to the R.R. cut, but I saw that to do so would be fatal to us. I therefore commanded, urged and shouted to advance, which after some little hesitation was done, and the line advanced up to the enemies' position. When nearing the cut, I sent my Adjutant to the 6th Wisconsin, directing them to flank the enemies' position by advancing their right wing, which they did; our boys giving a tremendous cheer as they advanced up to the cut. The enemy rose up, threw down their arms and surrendered. Some on the left of our line (their line being longer than ours) escaped by following through the cut. As the prisoners came out of the cut to our right, they surrendered their colors to the Regiment there (6th Wisconsin) which Regiment, from its position, made most of the captures . . .[4]

Those accounts mistakenly left an impression Colonel Fowler and his 14th Brooklyn, assisted by the 95th New York, and, belatedly, by the 6th Wisconsin, made the successful charge on the railroad cut. But it was Fowler's official report that was widely accepted in the early accounts of Gettysburg, and, as a result, the role of the 6th Wisconsin left somewhat muddled.

In even a casual look at the body of literature on Gettysburg, it almost seems every participant, from lowly private to lofty general, wrote about it, along with a good many others (the authors included) who described the event from a further distance. Confusion over the sequence of events abounds. For example, Union artillery commander Henry J. Hunt, in his account of the first day, clearly relying on Fowler's official report, told how the commander of the 14th Brooklyn "thereupon changed his front to face Davis's brigade, which held the cut, and with Dawes's 6th Wisconsin—sent by [General Abner] Doubleday to aid the 147th New York—charged and drove Davis from the field."[5] One of Doubleday's staff officers, E. P. Halstead, in an account published at the same time, on the other hand, told of the capture of Confederate General James Archer and noted: "Very soon after this episode the 6th Wisconsin, under Lieuten-

4. *Ibid.*, pp. 133-134.
5. Henry J. Hunt, "The First Day at Gettysburg," *Battles And Leaders of hte Civil War*, Vol. 3, (New York, 1956), reprint, p. 277.

ant-Colonel Dawes, made a successful charge, resulting in the capture of a force of the enemy in the railroad cut north of the Cashtown [Chambersburg] road . . .".[6] An early history of the battle, published in 1875, gave credit to the Wisconsin regiment: "As the Sixth moved it was joined by the two regiments of Cutler [14th Brooklyn and 95th New York], which had been originally posted on the left side of the cut."[7] Another history, published in 1892, said the 147th was saved "subsequently by the movement of the 14th Brooklyn, 95th New York, and 6th Wisconsin." The author then partially refuted what he had written by inserting a long excerpt from Rufus R. Dawes outlining how that officer began and led the charge on the railroad cut.[8]

Another description of Gettysburg in *The National Tribune* in 1885 was even further afield, mistakenly identifying the 56th Pennsylvania as the "156th Pennsylvania," overlooking the 6th Wisconsin as a unit in the Iron Brigade, and crediting the 100 men in the Iron Brigade Guard to the "149th Pa." Of the charge itself, the writer almost got it right:

> Doubleday sees the Confederates under Davis north of the railroad cut rushing eastward in pursuit of Cutler's three retreating regiments. He orders the reserve under Lieut-Col. Dawes to advance. The other two regiments of Cutler's, which have fallen back, right about face and advance once more, pouring a flank fire across the excavation upon the Confederates, who for protection rush into the cut as thoughtlessly as mice into a trap. They do not mistrust that it is a trap. But suddenly the eastern end closes. Adjt. Brooks, with a company shuts the eastern end, while down upon them comes a storm so pitiless that nearest the east end thrown down their guns and lift their hands in token of surrender.[9]

6. E. P. Halstead, "Incidents of the First Day at Gettysburg," *Battles and Leaders*, Vol. 3, pp. 284-285. The account carried a footnote saying it was from a paper read before the District of Columbia Commandery of the Loyal Legion, March 2, 1887. Halstead served on Doubleday's staff during the Gettysburg campaign.
7. Samuel P. Bates, *The Battle of Gettysburg*, (Philadelphia, 1875), pp. 65-66.
8. J. H. Stine, *History of The Army of the Potomac*, (Philadelphia, 1892), pp. 462-469. The Dawes account was a slightly revised version of the address he had given the Military Order of the Loyal Legion in Ohio in 1890.
9. [Charles Carleton Coffin], "Saving The Nation," *National Tribune*, March 26, 1885. A native of New Hampshire, Coffin was a war correspondent for the

The official reports of Gettysburg, as usual, self-serving and depicting none of the confusion of the battlefield, provide some insight. General Abner Doubleday, who directed the defense of McPherson's Ridge after the death of General John Reynolds, took a good share of the credit for himself, but clearly indicated it was Dawes and the 6th Wisconsin that had led the attack:

> The moment was a critical one, involving the defeat, perhaps the utter rout of our forces. I immediately sent for one of Meredith's regiments (the Sixth Wisconsin), a gallant body of men, whom I knew could be relied upon. Forming them rapidly perpendicular to the line of battle on the enemy's flank, I directed them to attack immediately. Lieutenant-Colonel Dawes, their commander, ordered a charge, which was gallantly executed. The enemy made a hurried attempt to change front to meet the attack, and flung his troops into the railroad cut for safety. The Ninety-fifth New York Volunteers, Colonel [George H.] Biddle, and the Fourteenth Brooklyn, under Colonel Fowler, joined in the charge; the cut was carried at the point of the bayonet, and two regiments [sic] of Davis' (rebel) brigade were taken prisoners.[10]

In his short official report on Gettysburg, 1st Division Commander James S. Wadsworth, said, ". . . the Fourteenth New York State Militia, Colonel Fowler; Sixth Wisconsin Volunteers, Lieutenant-Colonel Dawes, and Ninety-fifth New York Volunteers, Colonel Biddle, gallantly charged on the advance of the

---

Boston Journal. After the war and until his death in 1896, Coffin primarily traveled and wrote. He transformed his wartime adventures into eight books. Coffin was best known for his children's books, including a history of the Civil War from Bull Run to the fall of Richmond.

10. Doubleday, *O.R.*, Series One, Vol. 27, Part One, p. 246. Rufus Dawes later claimed Doubleday "falls into the time-honored line of battle fiction, when he says that the cut was 'carried at the point of the bayonet'. Not a single bayonet was fixed for use in the regiment." Dawes, *Sketches*, p. 353. However, at least four Wisconsin men who took part in the charge clearly indicate bayonets were used by the Badgers. It may be some of the company commanders, or the individual soldiers themselves, fixed bayonets just before the charge. Sullivan, *Tribune*, May 16, 1885; Fairfield, Letter, to Watrous, undated; Marston, *Telegraph*, April 24, 1881; Rogers, Letter, to Watrous, undated.

enemy, and captured a large number of prisoners, including two entire regiments with their flags."[11] Major Edward Pye, commanding the 95th New York after the regiment's colonel was wounded, reported the 95th New York and 14th Brooklyn "retired a short distance" when the right wing of Cutler's Brigade gave way, then "formed line of battle in connection with the 6th Wisconsin Volunteers, and together charged upon and took as prisoners a large number of the enemy, being part of the same force which had previously driven back the right wing of the brigade."[12] Second Brigade Commander Lysander Cutler (the first colonel of the 6th Wisconsin) reported the 147th New York could not retire "until relieved by a charge on the enemy from the left by the 6th Wisconsin, Ninety-fifth New York and Fourteenth Brooklyn, which resulted in capturing a large body of the enemy . . ."[13]

The men of the 6th Wisconsin, obviously, left a slightly different version of events, one that was supported by at least one ex-Confederate officer who faced them in the railroad cut.

In his own official report, dated July 17, 1863, Rufus R. Dawes (who at the time had not seen Fowler's report) noted the 95th New York and 14th Brooklyn formed on his left on the Chambersburg Pike. He also outlined his meeting with Major Edward Pye of the 95th New York, and credited that regiment for joining the left of his unit, after which the "men of the whole line moved forward upon a double-quick, well closed, in face of a terribly destructive fire from the enemy."[14]

In his war memoir published in 1890, by then aware of the claims made by Fowler, Dawes tried to set the record straight in a footnote:

> Colonel E. B. Fowler fourteen Brooklyn, in his official report, has given the impression that he ordered the sixth Wisconsin regiment to make this charge. He gave us no orders whatever. I did not know he was on the field until the charge was over. I called Colonel Fowler's attention to the matter and he stated as an explanation

11. James Wadsworth report, *O.R.*, Series One, Vol. 27, Part One, p. 266.
12. Edward Pye report, *O.R.*, Series One, Vol. 27, Part One, p. 287.
13. Lysander Cutler report, *O.R.*, Series One, Vol. 27, Part One, p. 282.
14. Rufus R. Dawes report, *O.R.*, Series One, Vol. 27, Part One, pp. 275-277.

that he sent an officer to give me such an order. Colonel Fowler was retreating his regiment when we arrived at the turnpike fence. He then changed front and joined our advance. The fourteenth Brooklyn and ninety-fifth New York jointly had no more men in action than the sixth Wisconsin.[15]

In an 1868 letter to a man gathering information for a history of Gettysburg, Dawes, smarting from the claims in Fowler's Gettysburg report and becoming aware the role of his regiment was being overlooked, was more explicit. He noted:

[The 95th New York] . . . went up closely joined on my left. We were clear out in the field before the 14th Brooklyn started and that regiment came up en echelon. I do not say this with any disparagement of that gallant regiment. I have fought beside them in many battles and gladly attest their valor. I say it in evidence of what is simply the truth. That with my regiment of near *five hundred men in line* I ordered and commenced the charge and carried the weight that won success. The 95th and 14th both together did not muster three hundred men in ranks, and where the 14th reached the cut it is 10 to 30 feet deep, and the rebels were in the bottom of it, as you know they must have been."[16]

What Dawes left unsaid was that the rebels "in the bottom of the cut" were unable to fire on the advancing 14th Brooklyn. It was the careful statement of a careful man. In 1885, in another letter, Dawes also tried to get credit for his regiment:

It is due to the 6th Wisconsin Regiment for me to say that the regiment led the charge and by its dash forward substantially accomplished the results. A statement of facts is enough to show this. The 6th Wis. had about 450 muskets. The 95th N.Y. had not 100 men there. The 14th Brooklyn had not enough to exceed 250 men. The 95th N.Y. came up on my left. Major Pye was

15. Dawes, *Service*, p. 167.
16. Dawes, Letter, to Bachelder, March 18, 1863.

the only officer I saw and he appeared to be in command. I have explained this exact because Colonel Fowler has claimed to have ordered me to charge. He had no command over me, and I did not know his regiment was there until I saw them come up and pour a volley into the cut upon the rebels who had already begun to surrender. The 95th New York came promptly up with us, stood their full share of that fearful fire poured on us from the cut, and should have full credit for all that is implied in the statement. The 14th Brooklyn came gallantly up exactly as I have indicated. . . . They would doubtless have been ahead of us if they *had been* so ordered for they were splendid body of soldiers. But the truth is the 6th Wis. came on the run from a distant part of the field and their movements were without the slightest regard to the 14th Brooklyn, of whom they had no knowledge until after the colors of the 2nd Miss. were captured.[17]

A Confederate officer who faced the 6th Wisconsin, A. H. Belo of the 55th North Carolina Infantry, supported Dawes' account of the events of that morning. In a speech January 20, 1900, to the Sterling Price Camp at Dallas, Texas, Belo said about the charge on his regiment in the railroad cut:

After the repulse of Cutler's Brigade we continued our advance and soon saw another Federal force coming on the field, one regiment, which afterwards proved to be the Sixth Wisconsin, marching at right angles with us. They formed a line of battle and changed front to meet us, and at the same time were joined by the Ninety-Fifth New York and Fourteenth Brooklyn.[18]

One of the staff officers of Cutler's 2nd Brigade, John A. Kellogg (the same 6th Wisconsin officer who helped organize the Lemonweir Minute Men with Rufus R. Dawes at Mauston in 1861) also watched his old regiment from a woods on Seminary Ridge. In a November 1, 1865 letter written from Mauston, Wisconsin, to John B. Bachelder, Kellogg wrote:

17. Dawes, Letter, to Kranth, May 9, 1885.
18. Belo, *CV*, p. 165.

Prior, however, to [Cutler's Brigade] falling back the enemy threw a force of I think about three regiments across the left flank of our Brig in the RR cut. The 6th Wis and 14 [Brooklyn] and 95th [New York] at this time were between the Seminary and the RR cut, under the bank. Seeing the enemy's movement, Col. Dawes, then commanding the 6th, after consulting with Maj. Pye commanding the 95th agreed to charge the Cut the 14th at the same time agreeing to participate, and the 6th commenced the movement, supported on the left by the 95th and the 14th on left of them. The 6th reached the cut about 3 minutes before any other Regt and captured the 2nd Mississippi and the other troops being a little behind. . . .[19]

An officer in the 19th Indiana, William Dudley, also covered the charge of the 6th Wisconsin in his "Official Report" of the Iron Brigade. Published as a pamphlet in 1878, Dudley said he made "great pains to collect all the obtainable data, and all the facts within the recollection of surviving officers of the Brigade, and have found, and placed upon file, the originals of the regimental reports that are known to be in existence." On the charge itself, Dudley wrote:

Comprehending the imminent danger to his comrades of the Iron Brigade, and the threatened annihilation of Cutler's brigade, Col. Dawes ordered his men forward to the rescue *upon the run.* Forming his command south of the Chambersburg road and parallel to it, he with great impetuosity charged the thus far victorious Rebel line, which he had previously checked by a well directed

19. In a March 31, 1868 letter from La Crosse, Wisconsin, to William Bachelder, Kellogg wrote:
    At Gettysburg, I was acting AAG to Gen. Cutler and detached from my Regt—and did not participate in the charge. At the time the charge was made I had just reported to Gen. Wadsworth the fact that the cut was occupied by Rebels and that the enemy were then placing a battery in position on the right flank of Cutler's Brigade. . . . My rank at the time was that of Captain and I was mounted on a White horse which at the time had been wounded three times [,] one shot in the buttock [,] one through the ears and one through the butt of the tail. My hat had been shot from my head and my clothes cut in several places.

fire delivered from a position at the turnpike fence. The charge drove the enemy back to and into the railroad cut some two hundred yards north of the road. Here after a brief though fierce resistance, the enemy surrendered to Col. Dawes. The forces thus surrendering to him were the 2d Mississippi, Maj. Blair commanding, with fragmentary portions of other regiments belong to Davis' brigade. . . . It is but just to say that Major Pye with his regiment, the 95th New York volunteers, seeing the attack and charge of the 6th Wisconsin, while retreating turned and joined with the sixth on its left, and participated in the capture of the Rebels in the railroad cut above referred to. The 14th Brooklyn (N.Y.S.M.) [New York State Militia], under Col. Fowler seeing the change in affairs, also turned and came up rapidly upon the left of the 95th New York, but too late to materially assist in the capture of Davis' Rebel troops. To them the firm and dauntless bearing of the Iron Brigade men was an inspiration, and they assisted manfully in turning defeat into victory.[20]

Three other 6th Wisconsin men, Lieutenant Loyd Harris of the Iron Brigade Guard, Sergeant George Fairfield of Company C and Private James P. "Mickey" Sullivan of Company K, left stronger statements. "The 14th Brooklyn came up on our left just a moment after the surrender," Fairfield said flatly.[21] In his account for a Milwaukee newspaper, printed in 1884, Sullivan stated:

After the surrender and before the prisoners were marched off, the division rear guard, which contained some of the 14th Brooklyn, came up and assisted in guarding them, the prisoners greatly outnumbering what was left of the 6th Wisconsin, and that was the only way in which the 14th Brooklyn took part in that charge.[22]

In the same newspaper, in 1885, Harris, obviously bitter about

20. Dudley, *Gettysburg*, p. 8.
21. Fairfield, *Tribune*, December 14, 1905.
22. Sullivan, *Telegraph*, December 11, 1884.

the credit given the 95th New York and the 14th Brooklyn for sharing in the charge, noted:

> The 95th N.Y. did rally and re-form their regiment and deserve great praise for it, but they never joined the left of the 6th. That place was occupied by the "Iron Brigade Guard" . . . They [95th New York] failed to respond, and the "truth of history" compels me to state that the 6th, with the brigade guard, charged, singly and alone.

In 1885, responding to the article on Gettysburg by journalist Charles Carleton Coffin, Sullivan wrote the editors of *The National Tribune*:

> I have noticed in your paper various articles concerning the opening fight at Gettysburg, but not being controversially inclined, I have refrained from correcting them; but . . . [the] article in your issue of March 26 [1885] breaks the back of my patience. So far as my knowledge extends, "Carleton's" statements are a tissue of errors from beginning to end. . . .

Sullivan took a few swipes at the character and veracity of newspaper reporters in general and "Carleton" in particular, then left his own description of the charge and what he surely must have felt was the final word on the whole matter:

> We did not fire a shot until the road with a fence on each side of it was reached. In this road we halted a moment until all hands came up, when the command was again "Forward!" and from the road to the railroad cut, a distance of 150 or perhaps 200 yards, our men fired two or three rounds, loading and firing at will as we advanced. All the while the enemy kept up a deadly fire and our killed and wounded lay thick on the grass between the road and cut. Upon reaching the cut bayonets and clubbed muskets were used by the 6th Wis. and the rebs were clubbed and bayoneted into surrendering. . . . The 6th Wis. received no support morally or physically, from any New York or Pennsylvania regi-

ment, but charged alone and unaided. The 6th Wis. lost 40 killed and 82 wounded between the Seminary and the railroad cut, and if necessary I can and will furnish the name of each individual.[23]

The article was signed, no less proudly than if he had been a general of the army: "James P. Sullivan, Co. K, 6th Wis."

23. Sullivan, *Tribune*, May 16, 1885.

LT. LOYD G. HARRIS
Carried Harmonica to Gettysburg

APPENDIX III

The Uniform of the Iron Brigade at Gettysburg July 1, 1863

By
Howard Michael Madaus

INTRODUCTION

In 1961, Macmillan of New York City released the first printing (of what eventually would be three editions) of Alan T. Nolan's *The Iron Brigade: A Military History.*[1] Appendix 4 of that work concerned "The Uniform of the Iron Brigade." Much of the research for this section had also appeared during the same year as the text for a color plate entitled "2d Wisconsin Volunteer Infantry of the 'Iron Brigade,' 1862-1863," published as No. 185 of the Company of Military Historians series *Military Uniforms in America.*[2] Nolan's research was meticulous, utilizing a combination of documentary and photographic sources to advance his conclusions. In the intervening years, however, considerable heretofore undiscovered documentary and photographic data has surfaced. This new data adds new dimensions to Nolan's initial pronouncements.

A common misconception regarding the uniform of the famous "Iron Brigade of the West" (initially called during most of 1862 "The Black Hat Brigade") suggests that the distinctive dress of

1. The second edition of this work was released in 1975 by the State Historical Society of Wisconsin, Madison, Wisconsin. The third edition was released in 1983 by the Historical Society of Michigan at Ann Arbor. Each of the new editions incorporated newly discovered photographs that expanded upon the information incorporated in the appendix of the first edition.
2. A black and white rendition of this plate with its text was printed in *Military Collector & Historian*, Vol. 13, No. 2 (Summer, 1961), 46-47 and 49.

the brigade was adopted as a single occurrence shortly after Brigadier-General John Gibbon attained command of the brigade.[3] In his memoirs, Gibbon gave credulity to this idea, stating: "At Fredericksburg, in order to have the regiments of the brigade in the same uniform, I had ordered all to be equipped with regulation black felt hats."[4] In fact, what would become the distinctive uniform of the brigade evolved over a period of several months, and was the result of several developments. The first of these developments was the adoption of grey as the color of the uniforms of the initial eight regiments of Wisconsin volunteers.

THE GREY UNIFORMS OF THE WISCONSIN REGIMENTS OF KING'S BRIGADE

The State of Wisconsin uniformed and equipped the first nineteen regiments of volunteer infantry sent to the War. To the 1st through the 8th regiments, the state issued grey uniforms. With the benefit of 20/20 historical hindsight, it seems ludicrous that the state officials should have adopted and issued uniforms that were the same color as those of their enemy. In fact, when the decisions were made, there were substantial causes for their actions. These causes blended the ignorance of the actions of their opponents with a strong tradition of states' rights, a prewar tradition of grey with a reticence to change course once the decision had been instituted, and the practical considerations of availability and expense.

When the 1st Wisconsin Infantry adopted grey as the color of its uniforms on April 27, 1861, its officers and the state officials in charge of procuring the uniforms had little information regarding the similar actions of their Southern counterparts. "Official" regulations covering the grey uniform adopted for the nascent Confederate Regular Army would not be published until the last week

3. Gibbon was commissioned Brigadier-General on May 2, 1862 and was appointed to command the 3rd Brigade, King's Division, Department of the Rappahannock by virtue of Special Orders No. 46 of that Department on May 7, 1862—see U.S. War Department, *The War of the Rebellion: A Compilation of the Official Records of the Union and Confederate Armies* (Washington: Government Printing Office, 1880-1901), Series I, Vol. 51, Pt. 1., p. 605. Hereafter cited simply as *O.R.* with appropriate series, volume, part, and page data.
4. John Gibbon, *Personal Recollections of the Civil War* (New York, G. P. Putnam's Sons, 1928), p. 93.

in May, and then only in Southern newspapers.[5] In the interim between South Carolina's secession in December of 1860 and the firing upon Fort Sumter on April 12, 1861, several Southern states had independently adopted grey uniforms for their state forces. Georgia had established a grey uniform for its "Regular Army" on February 15, 1861; grey uniforms for Alabama state forces (other than the Alabama Volunteer Corps) were also announced as early as February 15; similarly the grey uniforms adopted for the Mississippi state army were publicized on the 27th of the same month. North Carolina would also take separate state action and adopted a grey uniform on May 27, 1861, only seven days after leaving the Union.[6] However, while a few Southern newspapers

5. Technically, the Confederate uniform regulations published in May of 1861 did not have the sanction of the Confederate War Department. This did not, however, prevent their widespread dissemination. They were carried by the *New Orleans Picayune* as early as May 25, 1861 under the heading "Uniform of the Confederate States Army." The *Charleston Mercury* ran the same description under the title "The Uniform of the Confederate Army" on May 29. 1861 (p. 1, col. 5), while the *Charleston Daily Courier* repeated the New Orleans heading and story on May 30, 1861 (p. 1, col. 3). There is no evidence that the Wisconsin newspapers copied any of these articles.

6. General Orders No. 4, dated February 15, 1861 from Milledgeville, establishd grey coats and trowsers trimmed respectively black and orange for infantry and artillery of the Georgia Regular Army; for full details see Sydney C. Kersis, *Plates and Buckles of the American Military 1794-1874* (Kennesaw, Ga.: The Gilgal Press, 1974), pp. 545-547. The same text was earlier submitted by Kerksis under the title "Uniform and Dress of the Army of Georgia," in *Military Collector & Historian*, Vol. 13, No. 4 (Winter, 1961), pp. 122-124.

The report of the adoption of grey uniforms trimmed in the same facing colors as the U.S. Army for the Army of Alabama appeared in the *Charleston Mercury* of February 15, 1861 (p. 4, col. 4). Evidently, however, these regulations did not cover the forces of the Alabama Volunteer Corps, for which a uniform composed of a blue coat and grey trousers was adopted by General Orders No. 1 dated March 28, 1861 from Montgomery; for full details, see Kerksis, pp. 541-542. See also Frederick P. Todd, *American Military Equipage 1851-1872, Volume II-State Forces* (New York: Chatham Square Press, 1983), pp. 616-617.

The *Charleston Mercury* reported the adoption of the grey uniform of the Army of Mississippi on February 27, 1861 (p. 3, col. 4) but incorrectly described the facing colors. These were crimson for infantry, yellow for cavalry, and orange for artillery; see Kerksis, pp. 550-552 for the complete text of the regulations.

General Order No. 1, dated May 27, 1861 from Raleigh established a grey uniform with trimming of either black, yellow, or red for respectively infantry, cavalry, and artillery for the ten regiments of "North Carolina State Troops" created by the legislature in 1861. See Kerksis, pp. 548-549 for the full text of the order. The text was earlier published by Kerksis in an article titled Regulations for the Uniform and Dress of North Carolina Troops, 1861," in *Military Collector & Mistorian*, Vol. 14, No. 1 (Spring, 1962), pp. 20-22.

carried accounts of these actions, the Northern press was either totally ignorant of, or at least silent on, these actions. Equally important, even if Wisconsin's officials had been aware of these Southern decisions to adopt grey uniforms, they were separate state actions. And, philosophically Wisconsin's decision to adopt a grey uniform was a state action that owed subservience neither to similar actions by any other state nor to the Federal government. The events of 1859-1860 (first centering upon Sherman Booth's defiance of the Fugitive Slave Law and subsequently the refusal of Captain Barry's militia company to acknowledge state authority as superior to Federal) had demonstrated Wisconsin's adherence to the principle of 'States' Rights.'[7] April of 1861 found the situation ironically reversed, but Wisconsin maintained her cherished allegiance to "States' Rights" and (like many of her Northern counterparts) adopted a uniform color that befitted her militia traditions.

During the War of 1812, a shortage of dark blue cloth had caused the officials in charge of procuring uniforms to substitute grey cloth for a number of units of the expanded U.S. Regular Army. Although the subsequent victory on the northern border by General Winfield Scott's forces so uniformed would have a significant impact on cadet uniforms and those of some eastern militia companies, those events would little influence the decision of Wisconsin's officials to adopt grey in 1861. Rather, the tradition that would affect the Wisconsin decision to adopt grey would be related to the ethnic nature of the volunteer militia movement during the 1850's.

The volunteer militia movement that expanded so dramatically in all sections of the United States during the 1850's owed much of its growth to the yearning for social acceptance. For the most part, the volunteer militia companies that gathered strength in the cities of the nation formed about ethnic nuclei. The nicknames adopted and the uniforms that the companies were permitted to adopt reflected their ethnic origin. In Wisconsin, the volunteer militia movement centered in Milwaukee, where both German and Irish companies had been formed by 1850. Conse-

7. For background on Wisconsin's flirtation with "States Rights" dogma during the 1859 and 1860 Booth and Barry affairs, see Richard N. Current, *The History of Wisconsin, Volume II—The Civil War Era, 1848-1873* (Madison: State Historical Society of Wisconsin, 1976), pp. 219-220 and 270-281.

quent to a religious riot the prior year, a "Native American" company was formed in 1855 that styled itself the "Milwaukee Light Guard" in honor of the "English" ancestry of its membership. Lacking funds to purchase the uniform of the English Guard units that had gained notoriety during the Crimean War, the company initially opted to adopt a simple uniform consisting of a single breasted grey frock coat and trowsers, trimmed in red.[8] This uniform followed the basic design that had been adopted by the English Volunteer Rifle Corps.[9] It would be copied by other Wisconsin companies that would similarly style themselves as "Light Guards," including two that would join the 2nd Wisconsin Active Militia in 1861.[10] When, during the summer of 1858, the "Milwaukee Light Guard" was finally able to afford a uniform that duplicated the cut and style (though not the color) of the English Guards, the former uniform would be retained as a fatigue uniform.[11] The retention of the grey for "fatigue" use would prove

8. Herbert C. Damon, *History of the Milwaukee Light Guard*, (Milwaukee: The Sentinel Company, 1875), pp. 24-26. See also "Company 'A', Milwaukee Light Guard 1858-1861," in *Military Collector & Historian*, Vol. 31, No. 1 (Spring, 1979), pp. 22-23.
9. Philip Katcher, "British Rifle Volunteers of the 1860's," in *Military Images Magazine*, Vol. 1, no. 1, (July-August, 1979), pp. 5-8.
10. An article, presumed to have appeared in a Madison newspaper, described the 2nd Wisconsin Active Militia at Camp Randall and indicated that:

> The La Crosse Light Guards have grey coats and pants, striped and trimmed with black, with a dark blue cap. They bore a white silk flag with blue fringe and inscribed on an oval ground in the centre: Presented by the Ladies of La Crosse, July 4th 1860, to the La Crosse Light Guards. . . .
> The Portage Light Guards wore Grey coats and caps, with dark pants, all trimmed with red. They had a superb national flag of silk presented to them by the ladies of Portage, the evening before their departure. . . .

See, Edwin B. Quiner, "Correspondence of Wisconsin Volunteers," (a scrapbook compilation of contemporary newspaper clippings organized by regiment and chronologically), Archives, State Historical Society of Wisconsin; Madison, Wisconsin; Vol. 1, p. 70. Hereafter cited simply as Quiner, "Corr. Wis. Vols." with appropriate volume and page numbers.
11. Herbert C. Damon, in his *History of the Milwaukee Light Guard*, indicates that the new uniforms of the unit were received on July 13, 1858. He described them (on p. 93), however as "of light grey, faced with black." This is thought to be an error in memory. The lithographed cover of H. N. Hempsted's "The Light Guard Quickstep" (which Damon acknowledged to have been presented for the first time on March 12, 1859, see p. 108) depicts the officers and one sergeant in the new uniform of the company, a dark blue tail coat and trowsers, trimmed with buff and gold and complemented with a fur busby. The red trimmed grey frock coat and trowsers (that became the fatigue uniform of the unit) is also depicted. Orders dated May

a significant factor in the adoption of a similar uniform for the 1st Wisconsin Active Militia when called into service in April of 1861.

The 1st Wisconsin Volunteers (3 months' service) was formed from pre-existing volunteer militia companies. The first of these to be accepted by Wisconsin's governor was the "Milwaukee Light Guard," and its former commander, John C. Starkweather, was appointed the regiment's colonel. On April 27, 1861, Colonel Starkweather issued the regimental order that established the uniform for the 1st Regiment. In part it specified that the uniform be:

> Non-commissioned officers, grey pants, with black cord or cloth inserted in the seams of pants, one-eighth of an inch in width. Grey frock coat, single-breasted, with chevrons half an inch in width of black cloth. Privates the same kind of pants as non-commissioned officers, with coats single-breasted and plain. Caps of grey cloth, with a black cord one-eighth of an inch inserted at the top of the band with patent leather strap—Seventh Regiment style.

Except for the color and location of the trim and the adoption of a different cap style, the uniform duplicated the color and style worn by the Milwaukee Light Guard as dress from 1855 to 1858 and as fatigue from 1858 to 1861. The officers were directed to wear dark blue uniforms conforming to U.S. Army regulations but with dark blue caps in lieu of hats.[12] The officers also purchased grey uniforms of the same style as the enlisted men but decorated with black outline shoulder straps for fatigue wear.[13]

Despite the fact that the Federal authorities had called upon

---

30, 1859 (see Damon, p. 109) indicate that both uniforms were taken by the unit on its New York tour. Specifically mentioned are the white epaulets that were a part of the new uniform.

12. *Milwaukee Sentinel*, April 28, 1861, p. 1, col. 6, Regimental Order No. 4. The order is identical to that appearing in the Regimental Order Book of the 1st Wisconsin Volunteers (3 months') in the collections of the Milwaukee Public Museum.

13. The surviving coat of this pattern belonging to Captain Lucius Fairchild, commander of Company K, 1st Wisconsin Volunteers (3 months'), survives in the collections of the State Historical Society of Wisconsin; see J. Phillip Langellier, *Parade Ground Soldiers: Military Uniforms and Headdress, 1837-1910 in the Collections of the State Historical Society of Wisconsin* (Madison: State Historical Society of Wisconsin, 1978), pp. 18-19, figures 28 and 29.

Wisconsin to furnish only one regiment of volunteers for three months' service, so many militia companies responded to Governor Alexander Randall's call for volunteers to revenge Fort Sumter's insult to the flag that he formed the residual companies into a second regiment. The 2nd Regiment Wisconsin Active Militia was ordered to report to Camp Randall as the companies reached the designated strengths. The inertia that had propelled the equipping of the 1st Wisconsin Volunteers determined the color and style of the uniforms of the 2nd Regiment. To guide local tailors in making these uniforms, Wisconsin's Adjutant-General William L. Utley issued orders on April 27 that defined the color and style:[14]

The following uniform is prescribed for the Wisconsin volunteers:

Commissioned officers.

Full U.S. Army Regulations of blue cloth. (Company officers will be provided with a suit of gray for active service, at the expense of the state.)

Sergeants, Corporals, Privates, Drummer and Fifer.

Coats—Grey cloth, plain—single breast, standing collar—9 buttons on front and 2 behind—pockets in skirt—hook at neck—black lasting buttons—length, ⅔ from hip to knee. Three chevrons for sergeants, and two for corporals, of black braid, ½ an inch wide.

Trowsers—Grey cloth, plain—black welt ⅛ inch wide in outside seam.

Caps.—Grey cloth—7th Regiment style—patent leather strap.

N.B. Caps will be furnished by the state for the 2d regiment immediately.

Note—Whenever practicable, it is desireable that volunteer companies provide themselves with uniforms before departing from their homes for rendezvous, as the cloth can generally be procured. No uniform shade of grey is required, but a dark shade is objectionable. Whenever sufficient cloth of one shade cannot be procured at home for both coats and trowsers, different

14. *Janesville Daily Gazette*, May 1, 1861, p. 2, col. 2.

shades may be used for the two, running uniformly through the company.

It is not intended to confine the volunteers strictly to the above uniform, as circumstances may render it impossible for some companies to conform to it; but wherever practicable it is desireable.

Except for the black buttons, the uniform coat and trowsers specified for the enlisted men and non-commissioned officers of the 2nd Wisconsin were identical to those of the 1st Regiment. The headgear of the 2nd Wisconsin, however, would be a different pattern.

On May 29, 1861, J. H. Freeman of Milwaukee offered to manufacture for Wisconsin anywhere from one to ten thousand "of my 'army caps'" of grey cloth at the rate of $15.00 per dozen or $12.00 per dozen if the state furnished the cloth. Indicative of the shortage of wool broadcloth, Freeman stated that the grey cloth for the caps would be "composed of wool & cotton and not exceeding twenty percent of cotton." Freeman noted that "If required, I will carry the visor around farther on each side for the better protection of the face, and enlarge the rain protector on the back of the caps without extra charge. All caps to be made with the patent spring top, and fully equal in all respects to sample." A photograph of Frederick Lythson of the "Randall Guards" (subsequently Company H, 2nd Wisconsin Infantry) indicates that the spring top referred to in the proposition kept the crown taught and upright like a shako. Like the caps of the 1st Wisconsin, a narrow piece of black cloth divided the band from the upper portions of the crown.[15] On the following day, the state accepted his proposition for two thousand and fifty-six of the caps at $15.50 per dozen. The extra cost was to insure that the "visor" would be "two and a half inches deep, lined with green morocco leather, and to extend back to about center of cap," and that the "back piece to be larger and to extend forward so as to nearly meet base of visor." A notation on the contract indicated that "These caps are for the Second and Sixth Regiments."[16]

15. Collection of Mr. Lance Herdegen; Milwaukee, Wisconsin.
16. Wisconsin National Guard, Quartermaster Corps, General Correspondence of the Quartermaster General (Record Group 1159), Box 1, (folder covering May 26-31, 1861), "Proposition of J. H. Freeman of Milwaukee to Manufacture 'Army Caps,'" May 29, 1861 and "Articles of agreement . . . Between

The inability of the state to locate a source of dark blue wool cloth at any price had been one of the influencing factors in the decision by the state to adopt grey for the uniforms of the Wisconsin Active Militia. Despite the efforts of the two woolen mills of the state, even grey cloth of a uniform hue and unadulterated by cotton "fill" proved difficult to find. C. K. Pier, of Company I, 1st Wisconsin Active Militia, noted in a letter that:[17]

> We have at last received our cloths, which they call uniforms, although one would think to see the company on parade, that the tailor had warranted each uniform to fit the largest man or the smallest boy. The cloth is gray, of various shades; much of it is of poor quality and will not stand hard service. The pants have a black cord down the sides, and the coats have brass buttons and stand-up collars.

When the 2nd Wisconsin Infantry received its coats, the same complaint concerning the lack of quality was heard. When Company H received their new uniforms, a Madison newspaper commented that "the Randall Guards made a fine appearance in their new uniforms, which after all are not quite uniform in color."[18] Although the state had contracted with G. H. Stewart & Company of Beaver Dam, Wisconsin for significant quantities of grey cloth, the inability to secure woolens or mixtures thereof in a uniform color for the 1st and the 2nd Regiments caused the state to temporarily look elsewhere for uniforms.[19] The result would provide a significantly different style uniform (albeit still grey) for the 6th and the 7th Regiments.

In early June of 1861, Governor Randall commissioned W. D. Bacon of Waukesha and Lysander Cutler of Milwaukee to travel to New York City in order to secure uniforms, accoutrements, and camp impedimenta to complete the equipping of the 3rd

---

J. H. Freeman . . . and State of Wisconsin," May 30, 1861. Hereafter all references to Record Group 1159 cited simply as "Wis. Q.M.G., Gen. Corr." with appropriate box and folder citations.

17. *The History of Fond Du Lac County, Wisconsin* (Chicago: Western Historical Company, 1880), p. 538.
18. Quiner, "Corr. Wis. Vols.," Vol. 1, p. 80.
19. *Milwaukee Sentinel*, May 3, 1861, p. 1, col. 2.

through the 6th Regiments Wisconsin Active Militia.[20] They were not seeking blue cloth. As Brooks Brothers had already discovered in attempting to fulfill their contract with New York State for 12,000 uniforms, the supply of dark blue cloth in the New York City market was exhausted. This had forced them to deliver slightly more than seven thousand uniforms of grey "shoddy," causing a considerable scandal.[21] Moreover, when Bacon and Cutler departed, the state had already entered into an agreement with E. D. Eaton of New York for three thousands sets consisting of coat, trowsers, and overcoats. This contract, signed on May 23 had called for:[22]

> Three thousand, more or less, Jackets (fatigue) of good substantial, all wool, grey cloth, with bands of black cloth on the sleeve and three buttons on the bands, with shoulder straps, of the style, color, and quality of the sample shown, and three thousand, more or less, pairs of trowsers of same kind of cloth with welt of black cord on the outside seam, the trowsers and Jackets to be of uniform color, for the sum of Eight dollars per suit of Jacket and Trowsers.
>
> Also three thousand, more or less, overcoats of the usual Army Style, of either grey cloth or blue pilot cloth as may be desired. Each coat to have a cape with five buttons in front, and the coat to be made thorough and lined through the back with all wool flannel, for the sum of Ten dollars (Ten) per coat, as per sample shown.

The "fatigue jacket" described was actually a "blouse." A member of the 3rd Wisconsin Infantry later described the uniform as "a blouse or frock, such as old fashioned western people call "wamuss,' and light grey trowsers, . . . The trowsers were of exceedingly tender material not suited to rough service; though it is undeniable that the boys 'had more out of them than shelter in

20. *Ibid.*, June 7, 1861, p. 1, col. 2, June 8, 1861, p. 1, col. 3, and June 14, 1861, p. 1, col. 3.
21. New York State Senate Document No. 29 of 1862, pp. 12-15, 27, 49-51, and 160-197.
22. "Wis. Q.M.G., Gen. Corr.," Box 1, (folder covering May 21-25, 1861).

them.' They were excellent for ventilation."[23] Upon arriving at New York, Messrs. Bacon and Cutler visited Eaton's establishment to examine uniforms Eaton had prepared. They were sorely disappointed. It would not, however, be the tender nature of the "tweed" fabric that caused them concern. Rather, they so disliked the pattern of the blouse and overcoat that they threatened to cancel the contract unless changed. Eaton reported their actions on 11 June, commenting that the commissioners "did not approve of the Style of garment for a Soldier" as the blouse "did not look military enough and in fact wished the whole thing changed in Style of garment, overcoat without cape and unless I would change the contract according to their views they were not disposed to accept any of them."[24] Essentially "over a barrel," Eaton was forced to accede. Commissioners Bacon and Cutler did permit him, however, to send the 1046 sets of blouses and trowsers already prepared to Colonel Hamilton's 3rd Regiment at Fond Du Lac. Those for the 4th and 5th Regiments, however, were to be in accordance with new specifications. On 10 June 1861, Bacon and Cutler submitted these specifications. The jacket was:[25]

In length to come three in. below waist, pointed before & behind—Standing collar well stuffed with canvas—arm holes to be cut in a manner to give plenty ease to wearer

23. Edwin E. Bryant, *History of the Third Regiment Wisconsin Veteran Volunteer Infantry 1861-1865* (Madison: Regimental Veterans Association, 1891), p. 14.
24. "Wis. Q.M.G., Gen. Corr.," Box 2, (folder covering June 10-12, 1861), E. D. Eaton to Q.M. Gen. W. W. Tredway, 11 June 1861.
25. *Ibid.*, Box 3 (folder July 11-15, 1861) Specifications for Jacket and Specifications for Trowsers, appended to letter from E. D. Eaton to Q.M. Gen. W. W. Tredway, July 14, 1861. The Specifications for Trowsers stated:

   All inside seams of legs & crotch seams to be sewed by hand—a welt of black cloth & corded to be sewed in each outside leg seam. Pockets to be made of brown drilling; waistbands to be lined with brown Holland drill & supported with a lining from waistband to crotch on back side. The backstrap to be trimmed with a brass or metal buckle; the fly to have four buttons, waistband one, and six suspender buttons to each pair. All button holes to be worked with black silk twist and all seams to be sewed with best quality flax thread. According to size of pants, the legs thereof are to measure from 19 to 20½ in. around the knee. In the seat there is to be a piece running downward. The whole is to be of such sizes to fit the men.

according to size. Shoulder straps to be edged with black cloth; bands of black on sleeves and three small size military buttons on each band. Eight full size military buttons in front & one on each shoulder for strap, one loop in each hip to support scabbard belt & edged with black cloth—One inside pocket in each jacket of drilling. Sleeves to be lined with corset jean. All button holes to be worked with black silk twist and all seams to be sewed with best quality flax thread. Front of Jacket to be thoroughly supported with canvas & lined with corset jean to the side seam of the Jacket, the front to be waded & quilted—buttons to be gilt with coat of arms of State of Wis.; the whole to be of such sizes as will fit the men.

In defining this pattern of jacket, Bacon and Cutler established the style of grey clothing that would be worn by Wisconsin's 4th through 8th Regiments. The black trim's location, however, would apply only to those for the 4th and 5th Regiments. The trim on those jackets provided to the other three regiments would depend on another contract, that for the uniforms of the 6th Regiment.

Lysander Cutler was not only a commissioner for the governor of Wisconsin but was also the colonel-designate for the 6th Regiment Wisconsin Active Militia. Cutler was evidently concerned that his regiment would have superior clothing to that contracted for from Eaton for the 4th and 5th Regiments. Accordingly, on June 17, 1861, he and Bacon entered into a contract with Jaraslawski & Bros. of New York for one thousand and fifty "sets of uniforms, consisting of Trowsers, Jackets, and Overcoats" at the price of $5.60 per set, the state of Wisconsin providing all of the cloth except that needed for the trimmings.[26] Specifications were not included with the contract; however, a member of the 6th Regiment later recollected with considerable accuracy the cut of the uniform and its trimmings:[27]

---

26. *Ibid.*, Box 2 (folder June 17-19, 1861), contract between Jaraslawski Bros. and Bacon and Cutler, June 17, 1861.
27. (James P. "Mickey" Sullivan), "Old Company 'K'," in *Milwaukee Sunday Telegraph*, May 23, 1886, p. 3, col. 1. The article continues:

> . . , a fatigue suit of pepper and salt gray cotton cloth, (i.e. a sack coat and trowsers with a red welt in the outside seam,) two heavy

The uniform was a short gray jacket reaching to the hips, faced with black at the ends of the collar, on the upper side of the cuffs, on the shoulders and straps on the sides

dark blue woolen shirts, two pairs drawers, two pairs socks, a pair of cowhide shoes, a linen and glazed cloth cap cover, cap, etc.

These gray "cottonade" fatigue uniforms were purchased from several manufacturers in the Mid-West. Fisher & Rohr of Watertown, Wisconsin and M.M. Merriman of Hartford, Wisconsin respectively contracted for 2,500 and 2050 pairs of the "cottonade" trowsers on June 10 and 12, 1861. S. Klauber of Madison also provided trowsers. The majority of the sack coats evidently were made by S. M. Kohner; however, S.F. White & Bros. of Chicago also had a contract for 1056 each of both jackets and trowsers, for which they were paid on July 16, 1861.

The fatigue uniforms were issued to at least the Wisconsin regiments that had assembled at Camp Randall in Madison. The 2nd Wisconsin received their fatigue uniform in early July. According to Quiner ("Corr. Wis. Vols.," Vol. 1, p. 94), on July 12 one correspondent commented "It may be well for me to remark that we have been seen strutting about for a day or two in our summer uniform; it is light and durable and is an addition to our comfort one hundred percent." Charles C. Dow of Company I, 2nd Wisconsin, provided a description of this issue in a letter dated July 10:

The regiment has been supplied with new summer uniforms, which are made of "cottonade," and are trimmed with red. The coats are of the round-a-bout pattern and I like them far better that I do the old uniform. The coat tails are not in the way, and it will cut off all such amusements of the rebels as playing marbles on them when we get on a retreat.

(quoted in Alan D. Gaff, ed., *The Second Wisconsin Infantry* (Dayton: Morningside Bookshop, 1984), pp. 135-136).

The red trim was not limited to the stripes on the trowsers. On June 1, 1861, both Amasa Cobb of the 5th Wisconsin and Lysander Cutler of the 6th Wisconsin commented to Quartermaster-General W. W. Tredway that:

We have today examined the fatigue jacket (cotton) brought to the camp by M. Kohner from the Q.M. office and we are one of opinion that our Regiments should be furnished with such clothing for summer fatigue duty if within the potency of the dept. to furnish them with the trimming changed from red to blue or black, we would fancy it very much as a fatigue uniform.

("Wis. Q.M.G., Gen. Corr.", Box 2—folder June 1-5, 1861). Although none of these fatigue uniforms survive, a photograph of Private John Luke, Company I, 6th Wisconsin Infantry, held by the G.A.R. Memorial Museum, Madison, Wisconsin, indicates that the jacket was a single breasted sack coat closed by five buttons, having a falling collar and shoulder straps, the latter colored either red or black. According to the entries in Wisconsin Quartermaster General's Military Store Inventory, 1861 (pp. 59 and 155), the 6th Wisconsin received 1,100 pairs of "cottonade pants" in five lots between June 27 and July 27, 1861 (100 on June 27, 484 on June 29, 450 on July 2, 16 on July 3, and 50 on July 27, and 1,014 "cottonade jackets" in three lots between July 25 and 30 (588 on July 25, 376 on July 26 and 50 on July 30). The same documents lists the issues of similar clothing to the 5th and 7th Regiments. Two separate guides to the prices charged for state

to hold up the waist belt, gray pants with a black welt in the outside seam, . . .

Photographs of Sergeant John W. Fonda and Private Stephen Vesper (both of Company C) as well as the surviving jacket of Corporal John Luke (Company I) confirm that the black trim included not only the vertical "band" on each cuff, but also extended to the entire shoulder strap and the front half of the collar.[28] (Other photographs of individuals of both the 7th and 8th Regiments indicate that this trim pattern would be copied by the makers of the jackets for those two regiments.) These wool uniforms were issued to the 6th Regiment between July 16 and 18, 1861.[29] Between July 16 and 18, the 6th Regiment also received 1,045 of the overcoats that had been ordered from Jaralawski Bros.

On June 19, 1861, Jaralawski Bros. in accordance with instructions from Commissioners Bacon and Cutler had sent a sam-

clothing (that of Lieutenant H. P. Clinton, Quartermaster of the 7th and James M. Perry, Company A, of the 7th) respectively indicate that the cottonade jacket and trowsers cost $4.62½ or $4.63 per set.

28. The photograph of Sergeant Fonda is held by the State Historical Society of Wisconsin; the photograph of Stephen Vesper is privately held in Jacksonville, Arkansas (see Rena M. Knight, "With Pen in Hand: The Civil War Letters of Stephen Vesper," in North South Trader's Civil War, Vol. 16, No. 4—May/June, 1989, 31-34); the uniform jacket of Corporal John Luke is held by the G.A.R. Memorial Museum; Madison, Wisconsin.

29. The Wisconsin Quartermaster General's Military Store Inventory, 1861 (pp. 80 and 95) shows the issuing of 1,042 jackets between July 16 and July 18 in six lots (288 on July 16, two lots of 100 each on July 17, and lots of 300, 143, and 100 on July 18. During the same period 1,020 pairs of "woolen pants" were issued in five lots (559 on July 16, 100 and 53 on July 17, and 89 and 249 on July 18). Another 26 pair of trowsers were issued on July 24 and 30. These were for officers, and their issue coincides with the issuance of 28 "woolen coats" during the period from July 19 to 30. (See p. 79).

Several contemporaneous sources confirm the issue of the grey uniforms to the 6th Wisconsin in this time period. In his diary entries of July 17 and July 18, Corporal Levi B. Raymond of Company G (privately held in Des Moines, Iowa), indicates that he "spent part of the day in fitting uniforms" on the 17th and on the next day "The boys got their uniforms". On July 18, Private Calvin R. Hubbard, also of Company G, wrote to his Beloit newspaper: "Yesterday morning uniforms of our regiment were distributed. They were well made and from good cloth. The uniform consists of pants, a jacket, and an overcoat. Our shoes, stockings, shirts, summer pants, caps, havelocks, cap covers, blankets, and rubber blankets were distributed when we first arrived in camp." (Quiner, "Corr. Wis. Vols.," Vol. 1, p. 236.)

ple of this coat to Quartermaster General Tredway, explaining that another overcoat had also been "given by us to Mr. Eaton of this city, who is to deliver a lot of them to your State according to this sample."[30] This was the "overcoat without cape" complained of in Eaton's letter to Treadway of June 11. Bacon and Cutler provided a glimmer of additional information on these overcoats in a preliminary report of their activities up to June 14. In reference to the contract with E. D. Eaton, the commissioners indicated that they had contracted with him for "overcoats for four Regiments of 1050 each; overcoats to be lined with red flannel."[31] In the commissioners' final report of June 20, they were more explicit, indicating the purchase from E. D. Eaton of "Suits & overcoats" for the 4th and 5th Regiments and overcoats alone for the 2nd and 3rd Regiments.[32] Hence, all five regiments (2nd through 6th) received overcoats of the same pattern, though of two different makers. These overcoats would be one of the more longer lasting items of the Wisconsin issue clothing. On 6 October 1861, Rufus R. Dawes, then captain of Company K, 6th Wisconsin Infantry, noted that "Every man in my company has one cloth uniform coat, one overcoat, some men two, . . ." With respect to the overcoats he annotated his comment: "One blue and one gray. When the men gave up the gray clothing they were disposed to keep the overcoats, because of their superior quality."[33] Like the other equipage purchased by the commissioners in New York which was not discontinued in October, it is difficult to assess the length that the overcoats remained in service.

30. Wis. Q.M.G., Gen. Corr.," Box 2 (folder covering July 17-19, 1861), Jaraslawski & Bros. to Quartermaster General W. W. Tredway, June 19, 1861.
31. Ibid., Box 2 (folder covering June 12-16, 1861), W. D. Bacon to Governor A. W. Randall and Quartermaster General W. W. Treadway.
32. Ibid., Box 2 (folder covering June 20-25, 1861), "Brief Abstract of Col. Cutler's Eastern purchases &c., &c., June 20, 1861."
33. Rufus R. Dawes, Service with the Sixth Wisconsin Volunteers (Madison: State Historical Society of Wisconsin, 1962), p. 23.
    The sky blue overcoats, however, were issued during the last week of November 1861, coincidently with those of the 7th Wisconsin. In his diary entry for November 25, 1861, Sergeant Levi B. Raymond of Company G recorded "We drew our blue overcoats." (Levi B. Raymond Diaries; private collection, Des Moines, Iowa.) Major Bragg confirmed the addition of the sky blue coats in his letter to his wife of December 7, 1861, stating: "The men never looked better with their knapsacks neatly packed and their new blue overcoats nicely rolled up and strapped on the top." (Bragg Papers; State Historical Society of Wisconsin; Madison, Wisconsin.)

Among the other equipage and apparel that the commissioners purchased were rubberized blankets at $1.00 each. Enough were purchased from the Rubber Clothing Company of New York to provide for the needs of the 2nd, 3rd, 4th, 5th, and 6th Regiments. Six thousand "Blue Woolen Shirts" were purchased from Martin & Bros. of New York at the rate of $16.50 per dozen. The 6th Regiment received a portion of these. The commissioners also purchased two thousand cartridge boxes, cap boxes and bayonet sheaths from A. Hitchcock of New York. These were intended for the 5th and 6th Regiments. For the same two regiments, the commissioners purchased two-thousand each "Knapsacks, Leather cloth—heavy" and white duck haversacks. Also secured were a number of items of headgear. Two-thousand one-hundred havelocks were procured to protect the necks of the men of the 5th and 6th Regiments from the sun. For inclement weather thirty-one hundred glazed cap covers were purchased to keep the caps dry among the men of the 2nd, 5th, and 6th Regiments. However, only one-thousand and fifty caps were actually purchased in New York, all destined for the 5th Regiment.[34] The other regiments had already been provided for by the state. The 3rd Regiment had purchased from William Dodd of Cincinnati light grey hats of the pattern worn for dress in Regular Army, and the 4th Regiment had contracted with a "Mr. Throop" for plain grey caps.[35] As already indicated, J. H. Freeman of Milwaukee had secured the contract for the patented "spring top" grey caps of the 2nd and 6th Regiments.

Although the descriptive language of the contract was vague,

34. Wis. Q.M.G., Gen. Corr.," Box 2 (folder covering June 20-25, 1861), "Brief Abstract of Col. Cutler's Eastern purchases &c., &c., June 20, 1861."
35. William Dodd reconfirmed his offer of May 22, 1861 to manufacture grey army hats in a letter to Quartermaster General Tredway on May 30, 1861, but objected to the size requested, i.e. a 4 inch high crown and 4 inch wide brim. He suggested instead the size he had recently provided for Indiana regiments, a 6¼ inch high crown and a 3 inch wide brim. What was determined upon has yet to be determined; however, Dodd acknowledged the payment of $878.86 on August 8, 1861 for the hats he had furnished to the 3rd Regiment—see "Wis. Q.M.G. Gen. Corr.," Box 2 (folder covering May 26-31, 1861), William Dodd to Quartermaster General Tredway, May 30, 1861, and Box 5 (folder covering August 6-10, 1861); the latter also acknowledges the receipt of $55.00 for 1,100 letters for the companies of the 3rd Regiment. The information regarding the caps for the 4th Regiment appears in the *Milwaukee Sentinel*, June 29, 1861, p. 1, col. 6.

one member of the 6th Wisconsin left an accurate description of the caps that Freeman provided:[36]

> Every article received from the state was of excellent quality, except the dress caps, and that was something wonderfully and fearfully made. What a carpenter would call the carcass was made of hair cloth, the frame and studding of wire and whalebone, and the siding of gray cloth; the inside finish of black alpaca, and the cornice base board, and outside trimmings of patent leather, a front vizor or porch square with front elevation and projecting on a level; a rear vizor or piazza extending downwards at one-third pitch, and the hole heavily and strongly put together according to specification.

The same individual indicated the sport that the men made with these caps:

> The caps afforded the boys an unlimited opportunity to exercise their powers of sarcasm, and they were universally named after a useful chamber utensil, and many were the theories advanced and overthrown in regard to the use of the hind vizor or tail piece; but Hugh Talty finally solved the vexed question in an undisputable manner: "That when we were fi'tin', the inimy couldn't tell win we ware advancin' or retratin'," which was accepted as the only correct and reasonable hypothesis. The caps furnished the boys an excellent substitute for footballs and considerable exercise in "hop, step and jump," the jump generally ending on top of somebody's cap, but the caps like Banquo's ghost, would not down but Anteers-like sprang up refreshed after every disaster, the hair cloth acting as an indestructible spring to restore them to the original shape after the pressure was withdrawn, and it was not till they were remodeled by taking out the hair cloth and cutting off the rear vizor that the boys took to them kindly and generally.

36. (James P. "Mickey" Sullivan), "Old Company 'K'", in the *Milwaukee Sunday Telegraph*, May 23, 1886, p. 3, col. 1.

In addition to the photographs of Private Stephen Vesper and Sergeant John W. Fonda, a group photograph of seven other members of the 6th Regiment depict them wearing this cap in its fully upright and "restored" conditions.[37]

Like the caps of the 6th Regiment, those of the 7th and the 8th Regiments were manufactured in Wisconsin. Photographs of individuals identified to both regiments indicate that the caps of the 7th were similar to those purchased in New York and worn by the 5th Regiment, i.e. the "chasseur" pattern of the 7th Regiment New York National Guard, having a wide black band below the grey low crown, while those of the 8th were plain grey fatigue caps following the pattern worn by the 4th Regiment. The jackets and trowsers of these two regiments were identical. The grey trowsers were trimmed with a narrow black welt down the outside seams, like that of the first six regiments. Except that they closed with eight buttons rather than seven, the jackets followed the pattern delivered by Jaraslawski Bros. of New York to the 6th Regiment, with black vertical bands on the cuffs decorated with three small buttons, solid black shoulder straps, and collars half faced black. The grey cloth for these uniforms was procured from G. H. Stewart of Beaver Dam, Wisconsin. Contracts were let to several firms to cut and sew the uniforms, but Zellner & Bonns of Milwaukee was reported to have received a contract for producing five hundred uniforms for the 7th Regiment.[38] By August 20, Quartermaster General Tredway indicated that nearly all of the uniforms were complete.[39] This included the contract for the overcoats for the 8th Regiment, which were sky-blue rather than grey.[40] This would prove provident, for the grey uniforms of the Wisconsin Volunteers were about to be declared obsolete.

37. J. A. Watrous, "That Group of Seven," in *Milwaukee Telegraph*, March 30, 1895, p. 8, cols. 1-2.

38. *Milwaukee Sentinel*, August 1, 1861, p. 1, col. 6.

39. *Ibid.*, August 20, 1861, p. 2, col. 1.

40. *Ibid.*, August 20, 1861, p. 2, col. 1, "Contract Let." The short article quotes the Madison *Patriot* to indicate that J. V. Robbins had completed the overcoats of the 8th Wisconsin. In regard to the 8th Regiment, Quiner (in "Corr. Wis. Vols." Vol. 2, p. 8), clipped a quote stating: "The volunteers are all supplied with handsome light blue overcoats, reaching to their knees or lower, with large capes." Presumably the 7th Regiment received grey overcoats.

THE DEMISE OF THE GREY AND THE ADOPTION
OF THE BLUE.

On September 23, 1861, the Acting Secretary of War, sent a circular to the governors of all the loyal states, stating:[41]

> The Department respectfully requests that no troops hereafter furnished by your State for the service of the government be uniformed in gray, that being the color generally worn by the enemy. The blue uniform adopted for the Army of the United States is recommended as readily distinguishable from that of the enemy.

By the Fall of 1861, the state officials of Wisconsin had already initiated a change from the grey uniforms that had proved so conducive to so much confusion. The motivation, however, was less influenced by military practicality than by utter necessity. By September, the grey wool uniforms of the 2nd Wisconsin were quite worn and tattered. One veteran glibly commented to a home paper on September 19, 1861 concerning the state of the regiment's dress:[42]

> Governor Randall was in camp yesterday and made us a short speech, in which he said that he was sorry we had not received our cloths from the Government before this, and if we did not get them soon he would do his best to furnish them for us at the expense of the state of Wisconsin, and call on or have it charged over to the Government. The Government sees plainly that we need clothes though we are not in a suffering condition. The other Wisconsin regiments have been dressed up in their blue uniforms since they arrived at Washington, and as a matter of course they crow over us some—call us the "Ragged Second" and some other names not as appropriate.

Governor Randall's efforts brought results from the U.S. Quartermaster's Department. The new uniforms arrived during the first

41. *O.R.*, Series III, Vol. 1, p. 531.
42. Quiner, "Corr. Wis. Vols.," Vol. 1, pp. 147-148.

week of October, 1861. On the 6th of that month one correspondent commented that:[43]

> The boys no longer look like beggars, with ventilated suits of clothing, but present a very neat, tidy and soldier-like appearance. Their new uniform consists of a handsome blue frock coat, pants of the same, a high felt hat, blue cord and black plume; now if we only had good rifles instead of sheet iron muskets, we should be fitted out.

Another correspondent confirmed the date the new uniforms had been received. Writing on October 10, 1861, he commented that "last week we got our new uniforms—blue frock coats, blue pants, and the regulation hat, feather etc. . . ."[44] Three days later Private John Webb, of LaCrosse's Company B, wrote home to his brother and also confirmed the arrival of the new clothing, stating simply: "The Reg't. has rec'd new Blue Uniforms (dark) and the regulation Hat. We are the gayest looking Reg't in the business."[45] Indeed, the new uniforms made a startling impression on the soldiers of the 2nd. A Madison newspaper quoted a member of Company H, who wrote home: "We now have our entire new suit, all dark blue, with army hats with plume—the handsomest uniform in the service."[46]

Photographs taken during the period confirm these descriptions. Private Antle Henry of Racine's Company F and Sergeant Charles C. Dow of Company G each stood separately before the camera wearing their new uniforms shortly after their issue.[47] These photographs confirm that the hat was the fully decorated regulation dress hat of the U.S. Army, that the trowsers were indeed the same dark blue as the coat, and that the coat was the standard infantry frock coat, single breasted with nine equally spaced buttons on its breast, and edged on the collar and cuffs with a nar-

43. *Ibid.,* Vol. 1, p. 149
44 *Ibid.,* Vol. 1, p. 150.
45. Papers of John Webb, LaCrosse Historical Society; LaCrosse, Wisconsin.
46. Quiner, "Corr. Wis. Vols.," Vol. 1, p. 148.
47. For the photograph of Antle Henry, see Eugene W. Leach, *Racine County Militant: An Illustrated Narrative of War Times, and a Soldier's Roster* (Racine: E. W. Leach, 1915), p. 64. For the photograph of Sergeant Charles C. Dow, see Robert K. Beecham, *Gettysburg: The Pivotal Battle of the Civil War* (Chicago: A. C. McClurg & Co., 1911), facing p. 66.

row sky blue trimming. Except for the dark blue trowsers, this is the uniform that Gibbon was credited with adopting for his brigade eight months later.

Dark blue trowsers had been regulation for the forces of the Regular Army of the United States (companies serving as light artillery excepted) since 1858. The constant problem in securing a uniform of sky blue had convinced the Quartermasters Department that the additional expense of the dark blue cloth offset the inconsistency in the dye lots. In 1861, with the tremendous influx of volunteers into Federal service, the situation changed. After comparing costs on the large scale, the Quartermaster General determined to revert to sky blue trowsers. Accordingly, on December 16, 1861, the Adjutant General's Office issued General Orders No. 108, which opened: "The Secretary of War directs that the following change be made in the uniform trousers of regimental officers and enlisted men: The cloth to be sky-blue mixture. The welt for officers and stripes for non-commissioned officers of infantry to be dark blue."[48] On January 2, 1862, the Quartermaster General ordered the commanding officer of the main clothing depot of the Army at Philadelphia to begin manufacturing trowsers of sky blue and discontinue general issue of the dark blue. In fact, however, sky blue trowsers had been widely issued prior to the official change. To accommodate the shortage of dark blue cloth, sky blue trowsers had been contracted for in quantity by U.S. quartermaster officials as early as August. A contract between the New York Q.M. Depot and William P. Enders of Boston, dated August 21, called for the delivery not only of twenty-thousand pairs of dark blue trowsers but also an equal number of light blue trowsers. Other contracts for sky blue trowsers followed through the Fall of 1861. The 2nd Wisconsin's timely acquisition of the dark blue trowsers seems to have been a chance circumstance rather than a deliberate attempt to conform strictly to the 1861 Revised U.S. Army Regulations. What was unusual concerning the 2nd Wisconsin's wearing dark blue trowsers was not their original acquisition but rather their retention through at least the Fall of 1862.

At least two documents as well as photographs confirm the retention of dark blue trowsers by the 2nd Wisconsin Infantry through 1862. On May 10, 1862, the 7th Wisconsin Infantry,

48. *O.R.*, Series III, Vol. 1, p. 744.

among other items requisitioned 150 "pairs Sky Blue trousers (Infantry)." In justifying the expense the Quartermaster of the 7th indicated that "The Regiment is not supplied. The last lot rec'd. was 138 prs. Dark Blue Pants which we could not use but turned over to the 2d Regt. Wis. Vols." These trousers had been received on April 22, 1862 and turned over to the 2nd Wisconsin's Quartermaster on May 5, 1862.[49] The dark blue trowsers continued to be requisitioned even after newly appointed Brigadier-General John Gibbon assumed command of the brigade to which the 2nd was attached. On August 13, 1862, the 2nd Wisconsin requisitioned a number of replacement items for those worn out in service. These included 150 haversacks and an equal number of canteens, 30 infantry blouses, and lastly "20 Inf. trowsers, dark blue."[50] The group photographs taken of the 2nd Wisconsin while at Fredericksburg in May and July of 1862 confirm the continued wearing of the dark blue trowsers.[51]

The photographs also reveal that at least two other types of upper garments were worn by the enlisted men of the 2nd Wisconsin while in the field, possibly both for fatigue purposes. A photograph of Joseph Mann, of Company F of the 2nd, depicts him wearing a dark blue sack coat. Although it has only four buttons, it is considerably longer than standard U.S. issue sack coat, coming well to mid-thigh.[52] A photograph of the band of the 2nd Wisconsin, believed to have been taken at Fredericksburg in May of 1862, also depicts the men of that organization wearing the same style coats.[53] The band had been supplied by Wisconsin

49. Papers of Lieutenant H. P. Clinton, Quartermaster, 7th Wisconsin Infantry; Milwaukee Public Museum; Milwaukee, Wisconsin, (collection no. E13391/-3772), "Civil War Papers," Vol. 3, pp. 34, 95, and 103. Of the 138 pair of dark blue trowsers received, only 134 pair were turned over to the 2nd Wisconsin. The balance were purchased by the field officers of the 7th Wisconsin on May 7, 1862; see p. 33 and 36.
50. Entry 4381, Record Group No. 393, Pt. II, National Archives.
51. The most noteable group photograph depicts Company C, 2nd Wisconsin Infantry; it is held by the State Historical Society of Wisconsin; Madison, Wisconsin; negative no. WHi (X3) 11298. This photograph is thought to be part of a set of group photographs taken at Fredericksburg in July of 1862. An enlisted man in dark blue trowsers (and wearing a U.S. Army regulation fatigue coat) appears in one of at least three group photographs of the field officers of the 2nd, also held by the State Historical Society of Wisconsin; negative no. WHi (X3) 13029.
52. State Historical Society of Wisconsin; Madison, Wisconsin; negative no. WHi (X3) 19049.
53. State Historical Society of Wisconsin; Madison, Wisconsin; negative no. WHi (X3) 11029.

with dark blue uniforms in July of 1861. Charles Dow of Company G, mentioned the new uniforms of the 2nd Wisconsin's band in a letter home on July 10: "The Band have just got a new uniform, which is made of dark blue broadcloth, trimmed with light blue, and it looks first rate. The caps are of the army regulation pattern, and made of the same material as the uniforms."[54] Neither the headgear nor the coats in the photograph conform to this description. Rather the pattern of sack coats worn by both Mann and most of the band was a common loose coat often purchased by officers for fatigue wear and was commonly available from sutlers or military purveyors in the larger cities of the North.

At the same time that the band posed for their image, a photograph was taken of five of the sergeants of Company E of the 2nd. Only one of these, 1st Sergeant Rueben Ash, wears a frock coat, G. E. Smith only wears a light colored shirt, and the other three sergeants wear short, waist length jackets or roundabouts with at least six visible buttons on the breast and three at each cuff.[55] As with the long sack coats, these were most likely privately purchased, for they were also generally available as an item of fatigue dress for officers. These same photographs also show that the band and the sergeants are wearing dark blue trousers, the latter with proper width (1½") sky blue stripes. In this respect they contrasted starkly with the other Wisconsin units of the brigade. These units had also undergone the change to Federal blue during the Fall of 1861.

On 27 August 1861, the 2nd Wisconsin Infantry, which had been separated from its comrades of Bull Run since the 4th, joined the newly formed brigade of Brigadier-General Rufus King.[56] King's Brigade had been initiated on August 5, 1861 with the assignment of King to report to Baltimore. There, on August 7, he and the 5th and the 6th Wisconsin regiments, were or-

---

54. Quoted in Alan D. Gaff (ed.), *The Second Wisconsin Infantry* (Dayton: Morningside Bookshop, 1984), pp. 135-136.
55. State Historical Society of Wisconsin; Madison, Wisconsin; negative no. WHi (X3) 11030. This photograph dates to early May, 1862. In a letter of his brother dated May 24, 1862, and enclosing a tintype of himself, Cornelius Wheeler of Company I, 2nd Wisconsin Infantry noted: "George Otis has the non-commissioned officers in groups and is going to send them to Professor Moffits at Mineral Point so you can see them there."
56. For the detaching of the 2nd Wisconsin from Sherman's Brigade, see *O.R.*, Series I, Vol. 51, Pt. 1, pp. 434-435, Special Orders No. 10, Hdqrs, Division of the Potomac, August 4, 1861.

dered to proceed to Washington. On the 9th, these two Wisconsin commands and the 19th Indiana were formed into a provisional brigade under King's command. When, on September 28, 1861, the 7th Wisconsin was ordered to replace the 5th, the nucleus of the "Iron Brigade" was formed.[57]

When the 2nd Wisconsin was added to this brigade, like it, all of the three other regiments were uniformed in grey. The new commander in the East, Major-General George McClellan was working diligently to reorganize the army assembling at Washington. This included ridding the army of the deceptive grey uniforms.[58] A member of the 6th Wisconsin hinted at the impending changes in a letter home as early as August 22:[59]

I think there will be some warm work before long; everything has that appearance. We are being issued new arms, and forty rounds of cartridges. In a few days the men will receive new uniforms of blue, the new U.S. regulation pattern; the grey is to be thrown away; it being exclusively worn by the rebels. Some of our regiments in grey were fired upon by our own men at the battle of Bull's Run, supposing them to be the enemy. Such mistakes will hereafter be prevented. . . .

The issuance of the blue uniforms to the 6th Regiment would begin in September. On September 3, Levi B. Raymond of Company G recorded in his diary: "we drew our blue coats, and at

57. For the organization of King's Brigade, see *O.R.*, Series I, Vol. 51, Pt. 2, p. 438, Special Orders No. 11, Headquarters of the Army, August 5, 1861; *O.R.*, Series I, Vol. 5, pp. 556-557, Major-General John A. Dix to Assistant Adjutant General E. D. Townsend, August 7, 1861; *O.R.*, Series I, Vol. 51, Pt. 1, p. 438, Special Orders No. 21, Hdqrs, Division of the Potomac, August 9, 1861; and *O.R.*, Series I, Vol. 51, Pt. 1, p. 489, Special Orders No. 82, Hdqrs, Army of the Potomac, September 28, 1861.

58. On August 25, 1861, Major-General McClellan had addressed a letter to the Secretary of War, suggesting:

. . . that a circular be sent from your Department to the Governors of the several States from which volunteers have been accepted, requesting that no regiment hereafter be received, whether raised under the authority of the Governors or of the Department, may be uniformed in gray, that being the color generally worn by the enemy.

O.R., Series III, Vol. 1, p. 453. This prompted the circular of September 23, 1861, already cited.

59. Quiner, "Corr. Wis. Vols.," Vol. 1, p. 246.

about 10:30 P.M. long roll beat and the regiment fell in & we marched through Georgetown up to the Chain bridge 7 miles above Washington, climbed the heights & camped down in the orchard." Despite this early beginning, the process of uniforming the 6th in blue took more than a month. Not until the 21st of September would Raymond record that "we drew our new blue pants."[60] Other companies received their blue uniforms in lots through the first week of October. For example, in a letter dated September 23, 1861, Stephen Vesper of Company C indicated that his company had obtained their new uniforms.[61]

By October 6, 1861, most of the 6th Regiment was supplied with blue. Accordingly Colonel Lysander Cutler ordered the discontinuance of the grey:[62]

> . . . The gray uniform clothing, both cotton and woolen, except for the woolen pants and overcoats, of all enlisted men who have drawn blue uniforms will be packed and boxed and delivered to the Quarter Master before One o'clock P.M. tomorrow. Of those who have not blue uniforms, a similar disposition of similar articles of their gray uniforms will be made, as soon as they may receive the blue.

Four days later, Cutler indicated what was to be done with the two grey items that were to be retained:[63]

> The knapsacks shall contain the blankets, change of shirts, drawers and stockings, the spare pantaloons, and shoes, the blacking, brushes, towels & combs of the men. and no other articles or things whatever, except by permission of their captains. The overcoats shall be rolled within the rubber blankets, and the roll strapped upon the top of the knapsack. Articles may be left out of the knapsacks sufficient time for the purpose of washing and drying, . . .

60. Diaries of Levi B. Raymond, Company G, 6th Wisconsin Infantry; private collection; Des Moines, Iowa; entries of September 3 and September 21, 1861.
61. Stephen Vesper Correspondence, letter of September 23, 1861; collection of Rena M. Knight; Jacksonville, Arkansas.
62. Regimental Order Book, 6th Wisconsin Infantry (Record Group No. 94), National Archives; General Regimental Orders No. 27 (1861).
63. Ibid.; General Regimental Orders No. 30 (1861).

Evidently, there was some reluctance on the part of some of the captains to secure the blue uniforms. The primarily German Company F of the 6th did not receive their blue coats until the 9th of October. Because its captain resisted completing the necessary paper work so that the men of his company would not be charged for the blue issue, Colonel Cutler found it necessary on November 27, 1861 to address a Special Order to the company commander:[64]

> Captain Lindwurm, Company F. You having received of Quarter Master Isaac N. Mason of the regiment Eighty one (81) Private (Infantry) coats for your Company on the 9th day of October 1861 without the usual form of a requisition and voucher therefor, will make the proper requisition and mark in the usual form of the above date for the coats as received and deliver the same to the Quarter Master at once.

Lindwurm's concern probably stemmed from the fact that his men would in effect be double charged for uniforms, the second (blue) issue being deducted from their meager monthly pay of $13.00. It would not be until July 2, 1862 that a special board of survey would be drawn up to "report the value 'to the men' of the Grey Clothing furnished by the State of Wisconsin for the time they wore the same" so that they could be credited for the difference.[65]

The second Wisconsin unit of King's newly formed brigade to receive blue uniforms was the 5th Wisconsin. On September 9, 1861, a member of the regiment wrote from "Camp Advance, Va." that "at Camp K (Kalorama) we got our blue uniforms."[66] Contemporary photographs confirm that these were dark blue frock coats, dark blue trowsers, and dark blue forage caps. The association of the 5th Regiment with King's Brigade, however, would be short. On September 28 the 5th was withdrawn and added to Hancock's Brigade; three days later on October 1, the 7th Wisconsin marched into camp to take their place, wearing the new grey uniforms that had been provided by the state.

64. *Ibid.*; Special Regimental Order No. 11 (1861).
65. *Ibid.*; Special Regimental Order No. 21 (1862).
66. Quiner, "Corr. Wis. Vols.," Vol. 1, p. 220.

The 7th Wisconsin did not begin reequipping with blue uniforms until the last week of October. A complaint from the 7th's Surgeon, Henry Palmer, to Colonel Joseph Vandor confirms the wearing of the grey jackets at least to October 23. Palmer ventured that the regiment's problems with intestinal distresses were "produced by the present method of wearing the Cartridge box. The height of the boxes and the tightness with which the belts have to be worn to keep them in place are decidedly injurious to the health of the soldiers under your command." Palmer recommended "that immediate action be taken to procure shoulder straps and that the cartridge boxes be suspended from the shoulder instead of the hips."[67] From the wording of Palmer's letter, it is evident that the enlisted men of the 7th were relying upon the cloth belt straps sewn and buttoned to the grey jackets to support the cartridge boxes affixed to the waist belt. Documentary evidence and photographs indicate a gradual adoption of the blue uniform, similar to transition that took place in the 6th Regiment.

James M. Perry, of Company A of the 7th, kept meticulous notes on his clothing draws in his diary. On October 23, 1861 he noted the receipt of one cap at 63¢ (the price listed for Federal forage caps in his comparative list of state and Federal prices). Three days later he recorded the issuing to him of "1 pr. pants" at $3.03. It would not be until November, however, that he would replace his jacket and overcoat. On the 21st, Perry recorded a charge of $7.20 for one overcoat and six days later noted the acquisition of "1 dress Coat" at the price of $6.71. [68] The date of Perry's discarding of his grey jacket was not limited to himself or Company A. Incomplete quartermaster records of the 7th Regiment for the fourth quarter of 1861 show the delivery of 103 overcoats to Company D of the 7th on November 26 and 89 coats to Company F two days later.[69] The latter issue reflects the

67. Regimental Order Book, 7th Wisconsin Infantry (Record Group No. 94), National Archives.
68. Diaries of James M. Perry; Archives, State Historical Society of Wisconsin; Madison, Wisconsin.
69. Papers of Lieutenant H. P. Clinton, Quartermaster, 7th Wisconsin Infantry; Milwaukee Public Museum; Milwaukee, Wisconsin, (collection no. E-13391/-3772), "Civil War Papers," Vol. 3, respectively pp. 80 and 82. Hereafter sited simply as "Clinton Papers" with appropriate page reference. Some of the overcoats may have been issued earlier than November 26 since at least 80 were acknowledged to have been received by Clinton on November 12, 1861; see p. 111.

receipt by the 7th's quartermaster of 838 "Infantry Frock Coats" in fourteen cases on November 27, 1861.[70] Evidently the trowsers and caps were issued earlier, as indicated by Private Perry's Diary, as issues to the regiment for the first quarter of 1862 indicate that only 244 pair of trowsers and 21 caps were received, while extant issue records for the same period account for only five of the caps.[71] Another 41 forage caps were received by the regiment on April 22, but these were turned over to the post quartermaster at Falmouth on June 12, 1862 consequent to the issue of the M1858 dress hats.[72] Two photographs taken between November of 1861 and May of 1862 confirm several details of these issues.

On November 21, 1861, 1st Sergeant George H. Brayton of Company B, 7th Wisconsin received his commission as 2nd Lieutenant of the same company. Shortly afterward, Brayton received permission to travel to Washington, probably to properly equip himself in the uniform of his new appointment. During his stay, he stopped at Brady's Washington studio to have a carte de viste made depicting him at his new rank. Evidently when he stopped he had not completed the process of obtaining his complete new uniform. Although he had acquired a new sword and sash as well as a new blue cap with embroidered infantry insignia encompassing the number "7," he had not yet acquired a regulation frock coat for his rank. Instead he still wore a private's blue frock coat with sky blue trim on the cuffs and collar to which he had attached the shoulder straps of a 2nd lieutenant for the photo. Judging from the narrow stripe, the trowsers were either the proper design for his rank or his old grey state issue.[73] The date of Brayton's commission confirms that the frock coats issued to the 7th Wisconsin at the end of November did indeed conform to federal specifications. Although it lacks a back mark, a carte de viste of Sergeant Philo C. Buckman of Company D, 7th Wis-

70. *Ibid.*, p. 116.
71. *Ibid.*, p. 117. One of the caps was issued to Company K on January 14 "to replace one lost;" one was issued to Company A on March 26, and three were issued to Company H on the same date; see pp. 2, 13, and 14. During the same quarter the 7th received 39 infantry private's coats. In the second and third quarters of 1862, the regiment respectively received 119 and 189 frock coats; see p. 124.
72. *Ibid.*, pp. 95 and 104.
73. Collection of Craig Johnson; Towson, Maryland. This photo is printed in Alan D. Gaff's *Brave Men's Tears: The Iron Brigade at Brawner Farm* (Dayton: Morningside, 1985), p. 118.

consin, was taken about the same time, also in a Washington studio. It depicts not only the style of the frock coat but confirms that the enlisted men's caps were the regulation fatigue cap adopted by the U.S. Army in 1858 and that the trowsers issued to the 7th were light blue.[74] In order to maintain uniformity, regimental requisitions for new trowsers from June through September of 1862 clearly specified that these replacements were to be sky blue.[75] Since the requisition for replacement trowsers for the 6th Regiment, dated August 9, 1862,[76] also specified light blue trowsers, it is presumed that those originally issued to that regiment paralleled those obtained by the 7th and were sky blue.

The Revised Regulations of the United States Army provided for a clothing allowance for enlisted men over a five-year period.[77] Included was a five-year allotment of eight coats, alternating at the rate of two the first year, one the second, and two the third, etc., thirteen pair of trowsers, also alternating but on a sequence of three and the two alternate years, and a single fatigue cap per annum. The government allowed fatigue clothing for mounted men and individuals on ordnance or engineer service, but made

74. *Ibid.*; Buckman's photo appears on p. 119.
75. Entry 4381, Record Group No. 393, Pt. II, National Archives. The requisition of June 27, 1862 called for 60 pair of light blue infantry trowsers. This does not appear in the original requisition in the "Clinton Papers," (p. 64), but are among the items acknowledged as received on June 28; see "Clinton Papers," p. 96. The requisition of July 5, 1862 called for 52 pairs of "Sky Blue Trowsers (foot)," and is confirmed in the "Clinton Papers" on p. 68. A requisition of August 8, 1862 called for 279 pair of sky blue trowsers. This requisition does not appear in the "Clinton Papers," but one of September 5, 1862 did request 268 pairs of "Sky Blue Trowsers;" see "Clinton Papers," p. 73.

During the 1st quarter of 1862, the 7th drew a total of 244 pairs of trowsers, the color of which was not specified but were were most likely sky blue; see "Clinton Papers," p. 117. During the 2nd quarter of 1862, the 7th found it necessary to frequently requisition new trowsers. In addition to the 60 received on June 28, the regiment had received 536 on June 2, 150 on May 16, 355 on May 2 and 138 on April 22; see "Clinton Papers," p. 118. Since the 138 pairs received on April 22 were later specified as dark blue and of no use to the regiment (accounting for their transfer to the 2nd Wisconsin on May 5), it may be assumed that all those received after that date were also sky blue.

76. Entry 4381, Record Group No. 393, Pt. II, National Archives. Earlier requisitions, dated June 19, 1862 and July 5, 1862, had respectively called for 95 and 106 pair of trowsers, but neither had specified the color.
77. *Revised United States Army Regulations of 1861. With an Appendix Containing the Changes and Laws Affecting Army Regulations and Articles of War to June 25, 1863* (Philadelphia: George W. Childs, 1863), pp. 160-170, paragraph 1150.

329

no provision for fatigue clothing for the infantry, though the regulations defining the uniforms provided for both lined and unlined "sack coats" for fatigue purposes.[78] This oversight was corrected in early November of 1861 with the issuance of a general order adding two flannel sack coats per year to the soldier's clothing allotment. Revised Regulations were suitably altered when reprinted.[79] Despite this allowance, there is no evidence that any of the three Wisconsin units of King's Brigade took advantage of the prevision during his command of the brigade. Indeed, there is a demonstrable lack of evidence to indicate that any action to obtain fatigue coats took place until late in the term of his successor, Colonel Lysander Cutler.

ADDITIONS TO THE UNIFORM UNDER COLONEL CUTLER'S COMMAND

On March 8, 1862, President Abraham Lincoln ordered the creation of five army corps in the Army of the Potomac. This order was complied with on March 13, 1862, and the divisions of Generals Franklin, McCall, and McDowell (the latter including King's Brigade) were assigned to the 1st Army Corps. On the same day, consequent to the elevation of McDowell to command the 1st Army Corps, Brigadier-General King was assigned to command his former division. As senior colonel of the four regiments of King's former brigade, Lysander Cutler took command of the brigade, now the 3rd Brigade, 3rd Division, 1st Army Corps. On April 4, 1862, McDowell's command was redesignated the Department of the Rappahannock. Although the numerical seniority of King's Division would change during the next few months as divisions were added or taken away from McDowell's command, the changes were strictly nominal, and the command structure within King's Division would remain fundamentally unaltered with Colonel Cutler in command of King's old brigade until the assignment of Brigadier-General John Gibbon to the brigade on May 7, 1862.[80] During Cutler's command of the brigade, two

78. *Ibid.*, p. 464, paragraphs 1485 and 1486.
79. *Ibid.*, p. 517, paragraph 65. The Order changing the allotment was General Orders No. 95, War Department, Adjutant-General's Office.
80. For the creation of 1st through the 5th Army Corps, see President's General War Order No. 2, March 8, 1862 and General Orders No. 151, Headquarters Army of the Potomac, March 13, 1862, both in *O.R.*, Series I, Vol. 5, p. 18. For assignment of Brigadier-General King to command McDowell's former

significant developments occurred, the issue of sack coats to one (if not more) regiments of the brigade, and the expansion of the army dress hats to at least a second regiment of the brigade.

On May 1, 1862, the quartermaster of the 7th Wisconsin Infantry submitted a special requisition to fill the regular monthly requisitions that had been submitted by the company commanders of the regiment. The requisition called for "85 Infantry Coats," "355 Pairs Pants (Sky Blue)," and a significant amount of shoes, underclothing, and accoutrements. Lastly, however, it called for "850 Blue Flannel Blouses." Quartermaster Clinton justified the requisition with the comment that the items "are needed by the 7th Regt. W.V. for the comfort of the Privates." Captain Daniel G. Thomas, military store keeper at Washington, D.C. delivered these stores for transportation to the 7th Wisconsin on May 2, including all eight-hundred and fifty of the lined sack coats.[81] These flannel sack coats were distributed to the companies during the succeeding three weeks.

Subsequent requisitions for the 7th Wisconsin during the summer of 1862 evidenced the continued issue of both replacement sack coats as well as frock coats. On July 5, 1862, the 7th requisitioned (among other items), eight sack coats and five "infantry coats." On August 8, 1862, the same regiment requested an additional thirty-nine blue flannel sack coats. One month later the regimental quartermaster of the 7th ordered "184 Infantry Coats" together with "14 Blue Sack Coats."[82] These requisitions represent

division, see Special Orders, No. 75, Headquarters Army of the Potomac, March 13, 1862, in O.R., Series I, Vol. 51, Pt. 1, p. 551. For orders creating the Department of the Shenandoah from the former 5th Army Corps and the Department of the Rappahannock from the former 1st Army Corps on 4 April 1862, see O.R., Series I, Vol. 12, Pt. 3, p. 43. Gibbon was assigned to command the 3rd (Cutler's) Brigade of King's Division by virtue of Special Orders No. 46, Headquarters Department of the Rappahannock on May 7, 1862; see O.R., Series I, Vol. 51, Pt. 1, p. 605. Another change took place on June 26, 1862 with the creation of Major-General John Pope's Army of Virginia from the Mountain Department, Department of the Shenandoah, and Department of the Rappahannock; see O.R., Series I, Vol. 12, Pt. 3, p. 435. In this change, McDowell's command was redesignated as the 3rd Corps of the new army. Although the changes were again primarily nominal, the absorption of Wadsworth's heretofore independent brigade into King's Division caused Gibbon's Brigade to be renumbered as its 4th Brigade.

81. "Clinton Papers," pp. 36 and 100.
82. For the requisitions of 5 July and 8 September 1862, see "Clinton Papers," pp. 68 and 73 respectively. For the requisition of August 8, 1862, see Entry 4381, Record Group No. 393, Pt. II, National Archives.

equipment to replace that worn out or lost in the field. Because issuances beyond the allowance permitted by regulations were charged against an individual's meager pay, the soldiers did their best to keep draws to a minimum. The diaries of James M. Perry of Company A, 7th Wisconsin show a detailed list of all clothing drawn by Perry during his enlistment. These indicate that he received a dress coat on November 27, 1861, a fatigue blouse on May 19, 1862, and two more of the latter, respectively on April 8 and April 9, 1863. He did not draw another dress coat until November 25, 1863 and then drew a new blouse on March 21, 1864.[83] The mutual use of both frock coats and sack coats by the 7th Wisconsin at Gettysburg is evident from an inspection of the brigade six weeks after the battle. Among the deficiencies noted for the 7th Wisconsin were eleven frock coats and thirty-three blouses.[84] The same report shows deficiencies among other regiments of the brigade that suggest the two other regiments of the brigade had drawn sack coats in addition to their frock coats.

According to the inspection report on the Iron Brigade of July 17, 1863, the 19th Indiana Infantry was short one frock coat and thirty sack coats, while the 2nd Wisconsin Infantry was short twelve sack coats.[85] In both cases these regiments appear to have been issued sack coats in May of 1862. In at least three photographs of the 2nd Wisconsin thought to have been taken in May of 1862 while the regiment was encamped opposite Fredericksburg, U.S. issue sack coats are in evidence.[86] The 19th Indiana probably received sack coats about the same time though

83. Diaries of James A. Perry, State Historical Society of Wisconsin; Madison, Wisconsin. Perry's service was evidently much harder on trowsers, as he drew a pair of these each on October 26, 1861, May 7, 1862, September 12, 1862, December 4, 1862, March 23, 1863, June 22, 1863 (just a week before Gettysburg), August 16, 1863, December 18, 1863, March 21, 1864, June 23, 1864, and July 4, 1864. After his transfer to regimental staff on November 4, 1864, he further drew trowsers on December 13, 1864, December 16, 1864 (for mounted use), and May 15, 1865.
84. Report of Captain H. Richardson, Acting Assistant Inspector General, 1st Division, 1st Army Corps, July 17, 1863; Papers of the War Records Office (Record Group No. 94), National Archives; Papers for O.R., Vol. 27, Box 48.
85. Ibid.
86. These include the view of the regimental band of the 2nd (State Historical Society of Wisconsin negative no. WHi (X3) 11029), wherein the individual on the far right is so attired; a view of the regimental headquarters (SHSW negative no. WHi (X3) 13029), wherein an enlisted man is visible to the far left in the picture wearing a sack coat; and the group photograph of Company C (SHSW negative no. WHi (X3) 11298), wherein the entire company appears in sack coats.

documents and photographs attributable to the period are lacking. On July 1, 1862, however, two-hundred blouses were among the items requisitioned for the 19th Indiana consequent to the regiment's disposal of much equipage during the brigade's first heavy march.[87] Subsequent clothing records for the 19th are sparse; nevertheless, a comprehensive list of receipts by Company B of that regiment survives covering the period from October 15, 1862, through October 8, 1864. This document confirms the continued issue of frock coats to the company during this period. It also shows that a few sack coats were issued: four on January 28, 1863, ten on February 24, 1863, three on April 28, 1864, one on July 8, 1864, two on August 5, 1864, and one each on September 4, October 6, and October 7, 1864.[88] Given the cycle on which Private Perry of the 7th Wisconsin replaced his coats, it is likely that the enlisted men of Company B of the 19th Indiana preserved their initial issue as long as possible.

Although the Iron Brigade inspection report of July 17, 1863, shows deficiencies of sack coats in four of the regiments (twelve in the 2nd Wisconsin, thirty-three in the 7th Wisconsin, thirty in the 19th Indiana, and seventy in the 24th Michigan), in reporting the clothing requirements of the 6th Wisconsin, the report only notes that the regiment was short thirty frock coats.[89] As evidence, this document supports two propositions: either the enlisted men of the regiment were fully supplied with the item, or the regiment had not been issued sack coats. The documentary and photographic evidence that survives tends to support the proposition that some individuals requisitioned sack coats but that the regiment did not receive them as a group as had the 7th Wisconsin.

Shortly prior to his muster-out on December 18, 1862, Philip Cheek of Company A, 6th Wisconsin Infantry posed with two of his friends. A. L. Sweet of the 12th Rhode Island Infantry and John Rothwell of the 1st Wisconsin Heavy Artillery, at Fairfax,

87. Entry 4381, Record Group No. 393, Pt. II, National Archives.
88. Manuscript copy in the possession of Mr. Alan Gaff; Fort Wayne, Indiana. Frock coats were issued as follows: forty-two on October 21, 1862, two on January 1, 1863, five on May 18, 1863, one on November 25, 1863, seven on December 12, 1863, one on February 12, 1864, two on March 21, 1864, one on April 30, 1864, one on July 8, 1864, five on October 6, 1864, and one on October 8, 1864.
89. Report of Captain H. Richardson, Acting Assistant Inspector General, 1st Division, 1st Army Corps, July 17, 1863; Papers of the War Records Office (Record Group No. 94), National Archives; Papers for O.R., Vol. 27, Box 48.

Virginia. In the picture, Cheek wears his dress hat and a four-button U.S. issue sack coat.[90] Cheek, however, had been away from his regiment since his wounding at Antietam, so the strong possibility exists that he drew it while hospitalized.

In his diary entry of May 10, 1862, Sergeant Levi B. Raymond, of Company G of the 6th Wisconsin, noted that he had "Got a Blouse."[91] Significantly, the timing of Raymond's receipt is nearly identical to the issue of the sack coats to the 7th Wisconsin, implying that Raymond's receipt may have been part of a general issue. Raymond, however, was not with the regiment when he wrote of the receipt of his "blouse." On March 21, 1862, Raymond had been severely injured in his side while playfully wrestling with Lieutenant Carpenter of his company. Because he could not carry his knapsack, on April 4, 1862, he had been left in the camp, assigned to the hospital. Hence, Raymond's receipt of his sack coat was not part of a regimental issue.

The evident lack of a regimental requirement of sack coats in the 6th Wisconsin shows in the requisitions for replacement clothing during the summer of 1862. The regimental requisition of June 19, 1862, requested seventy-two frock coats, ninety-five pairs of trowsers, and numerous other items of clothing and equipage, but no sack coats. One-hundred and six pair of trowsers were among the items requisitioned on July 5, 1862, but again no sack coats were wanted. Finally, on August 9, 1862, the regimental requisition called for another thirty-two pair of trowsers, fifteen frock coats—infantry, and two musician's coats, size No. 1 as well as many other items of clothing, but again no sack coats.[92] Until the final year of the war, sack coats seem to have been only occasionally drawn in the 6th Wisconsin.[93] And yet, the inspection report of July 17, 1863, indicates that thirty men of

90. Philip Cheek and Mair Pointon, *History of the Sauk County Riflemen, Known as Company "A," Sixth Wisconsin Veteran Volunteer Infantry 1861-1865* (Madison: Democrat Printing Company, 1909), facing p. 220.
91. Diaries of Levi B. Raymond, Company G, 6th Wisconsin Infantry; private collection; Des Moines, Iowa. On March 21, 1862, Raymond recorded: "I got pitched on to a stump and badly hurt in the side. About 5 p.m. I was carried to the Hospital where I spent a miserable night." On May 15, 1863, Raymond indicated that he "was appointed Acting Hospital Steward" at the hospital where he was quartered.
92. Entry 4381, Record Group No. 393, Pt. II, National Archives.
93. Captain Andrew Gallup, Company K, 6th Wisconsin Veteran Infantry maintained a record of the clothing requisitions for his company in 1865. These included seven infantry private's coats on February 16, 1865 (as well as ten

the 6th Wisconsin either had no frock coats or were wearing coats so sadly deteriorated as to require their replacement. Presumably, those who had no frock coats were wearing sack coats.

As inferred by the July 17 inspection report, frock coats were in the dominance among enlisted men of the 6th Wisconsin at Gettysburg. Cornelius W. Okey, a private in Company C, remembered that he was wearing a frock coat when he and Eggleston attempted to seize the flag of the 2nd Mississippi Infantry. He later recorded that a corporal in the 2nd Mississippi's color guard fired upon him and that "his charge of three buckshots and a ball passed through my frock coat."[94] Although obtaining a photographic

---

pair of trowsers, one pair of which was for mounted use), one similar frock coat and two lined "flannel sack coats on March 31, 1865 (as well as seven pair of trowsers, again including one for mounted use), twenty-one sack coats on May 31, 1865 (together with twenty eight pair of pants, again one for mounted use), and six frock coats and four lined sack coats on June 30, 1865 (and twenty pair of trowsers, two pair of which were reinforced for mounted service.)—see Papers of Captain Andrew Gallup, Company K, 6th Wisconsin Infantry; State Historical Society of Wisconsin; Madison, Wisconsin.

The use of sack coats in the 6th Wisconsin at the close of the war is also confirmed by a list of clothing, camp and garrison equipage, etc. transferred to Company G on June 30, 1865. Included among the many items received were three frock coats, three flannel sack coats, twelve pairs of infantry trowsers, and five pairs of mounted trowsers—see Papers of Lieutenant William H. Church, Company G, 6th Wisconsin Infantry; State Historical Society of Wisconsin; Madison, Wisconsin.

Evidently, the 1864 campaign wrought havoc on the uniforms of the 6th Wisconsin, the men choosing to depart from regulations and regimental practice without reprimand. With the introduction of the mass of draftees into the regiment in late 1864, measures were taken to improve discipline, including the appearance of the uniform of the regiment. Accordingly on December 6, 1864, Regimental General Orders No. 24 (of 1864) directed that "Those men having Artillery or Cavalry Jackets will take the trimming off without delay. They are forbidden to wear the Jackets on reviews or parades." This directive was followed by Regimental General Orders No. 38 (of 1864) on December 23, 1864, which required that "Company Commanders will see that each of their men have one good pair of Shoes" and that "Hereafter on the March, no enlisted man will be permitted to wear anything but the shoes furnished by the Government." As the final means to insure cleanliness and discipline, on January 9, 1865, Regimental Orders No. 6 (of 1865) instructed company commanders to "see that every gun is in order, every brass cleaned, every button bright, and the clothing perfectly neat and clean, and the shoes of the men blackened" by 10:00 a.m. each day. The order further directed that before the afternoon drill "Clothing should be again brushed and shoes cleaned." See Regimental Order Book, 6th Wisconsin Infantry; Record Group No. 94, National Archives.

94. Cornelius W. Okey, "An Echo from Gettysburg," in "Doc" Aubery, *Recollections of a Newsboy in the Army of the Potomac 1861-1865*. (Milwaukee:

image to send home was decidely a "dress" occasion, studio photographs taken during the first three years of the war confirm the preference of the men for the coats. In wearing their frock coats, those men of the 6th Wisconsin may well have given consideration to the weight they must carry in their knapsacks. Sack coats were not required by the 6th's regimental or brigade orders, but the possession of a frock coat by every enlisted man of the brigade had been.

On April 8, 1863, Brigadier-General Solomon Meredith, then commanding the 4th (Iron) Brigade, 1st Division, 1st Army Corps, issued General Orders No. 12. This order in part required:[95]

> Company Officers will inspect their respective Companies each day, weather permitting. These inspections must be thorough, the men appearing upon them with boots or shoes and belts properly blacked, brass cleaned and clothing in good order. Men failing to observe the above will be required to do the drudgery of the Company, such as policing the streets, attending sinks, &c. If this fails in accomplishing the result, more stringent measures will be taken.
>
> *Every enlisted man will be required to have at all times a Uniform Coat in good serviceable condition. Any deviation from this must not be tolerated.*
>
> The several Regiments will be required to be Uniform in their covering for the head, either the hat or cap, hats preferred if they can be procured.

Presumably those enlisted men who decided to wear sack coats, carried the required frock coat in their knapsacks.

The late reference to caps in this order reflects the fact that the 24th Michigan Infantry, which had joined the brigade in October of 1862, had yet to receive the distinctive hats worn by the remainder of the brigade. This would be rectified on May 27, 1863,

---

n.p., c. 1904), pp. 156-159. This was originally published by Okey under the title "Echoes of Gettysburg," in the *Milwaukee Sunday Telegraph* of April 29, 1883, p. 3.

95. General Orders No. 12, Headquarters, 4th Brigade (1st Division, 1st Army Corps), April 8, 1863, in Regimental Order Book, 7th Wisconsin Infantry; Record Group No. 94, National Archives, p. 225.

when the hats were finally issued to the 24th.[96] The other four regiments of the brigade had continued to wear the black felt dress hats of the regular army since Cutler and Gibbon had instituted the uniformity of that item within the brigade in May of 1862.

On August 15, 1855, the U.S. Army adopted a new item of headgear for the two newly created regiments of cavalry that had been authorized on March 3, 1855. The tall black felt hat with wide brim turned up on one side, had been recommended by a board that had met in July and which was based on a similar design worn in the Belgian Army, thought to have been adapted from the hat popularized by Hungarian revolutionary Kossuth. Because it was adopted during the regime of Jefferson Davis as Secretary of War and because Major William Hardee was the secretary of the board that made the recommendation, the hat eventually gained the erroneous sobriquet "Jeff Davis" hat or "Hardee" hat. In 1858 a slightly modified version of this style hat was adopted for the entire Regular Army except companies equipped as light artillery. The hat adopted on March 24, 1858, stood 6¼ inches high in the crown and had a brim 3¼ inches wide. For enlisted men of foot or mounted services, the brim was turned up on respectively the left or right side and fastened with a stamped brass eagle so as to avoid being bumped from the head during respectively musket or saber drill. A black ostrich plume decorated the side of the hat opposite the turn up. A twisted wool cord of the color of the branch of the service circumvented the base of the crown, and stamped brass insignia of service as well as company letter and regimental number decorated the front of the crown.[97]

As already noted, the 2nd Wisconsin Infantry had been issued and continued to wear the M1858 dress hat of the regular army since October of 1861. Photographs of members of the 2nd Wisconsin Infantry indicate that they invariably wore their hats either as specified in Army Regulations (i.e. with the left side of

---

96. O. B. Curtis, *History of the Twenty-fourth Michigan of the Iron Brigade, Known as the Detroit and Wayne County Regiment.* (Detroit: Winn & Hammond, 1891), pp. 141-142.
97. Edgar M. Howell, *United States Army Headgear 1855-1902: Catalog of United States Army Uniforms in the Collections of the Smithsonian Institution, II* (Washington: Smithsonian Institution, 1975), pp. 1-12.

the brim turned up and secured by the brass eagle), or with the brim left down completely.

The studio portraits of the members of the 2nd Wisconsin almost always depict it turned up, usually on the left side as proper, but in at least one instance on the right side. The same photographs indicate that the hat was usually worn with most of its trim. John T. Christy of Company F, sat with his hat in his lap, the left side turned up, a feather at the right, a bugle in the center, and a cord with tassels around the base of the crown. No company letter or regimental number is in evidence. Sergeant Charles C. Dow, of Company G, on the other hand, posed with his hat on a nearby table, fully decorated except for a company letter. Corporal Cornelius Wheeler of Company I, wore his hat similarly decorated but turned up on the right side when he posed for his tintype. Private Elon F. Brown of Company H, and Private Antle Henry of Company F, however, posed with their hats fully decorated with both letter and number and correctly turned up on the left side.[98]

While the indoor photographs of the 2nd Wisconsin indicate that the hat was invariably worn with its left side turned up, those outdoor photographs taken while encamped opposite Fredericksburg indicate that the hat brim was worn at the wearer's discretion while in the field. The previously mentioned view of the sergeants of Company E, taken in May of 1862, depicts them with their hat brim secured on the left side by the brass eagle.[99] The group photograph of Company C, taken near Fredericksburg, Virginia most probably in May of 1862, depicts eleven men of the rear rank with their hat brim down on both sides while the other sixteen men of the same rank and the color bearer have the left side turned up. The other two ranks are not clear but it would appear that six men of the middle rank (of nineteen individuals) and seven of the seated front rank (of twenty-three enlisted men)

98. For the photograph of Private John T. Christy, Co. F, see State Historical Society of Wisconsin negative no. WHi (X3) 19053; for the photograph of Sergeant Charles C. Dow, Co. G, see Robert K. Beecham, *Gettysburg: The Pivotal Battle of the Civil War* (Chicago: A. C. McClurg & Co., 1911), facing p. 66.; for the tintype of Corporal Cornelius C. Wheeler, Co. I, see SHSW negative no. WHi (X3) 26352; for the tintype of Private Elon F. Brown, Co. H, see SHSP negative no. WHi (X3) 43922); and for the photograph of Private Antle Henry, Co. F, see SHSP negative no. WHi (X3) 19052.

99. State Historical Society of Wisconsin, negative no. WHi X3) 11030.

wear their hats with both sides down; the balance wear their hats properly turned up on the left side. Several are missing elements of the hat brass in addition to the eagle that secured the side.[100] This, however, would be rectified on July 11, 1862. Among the items requisitioned by the quartermaster of the 2nd Wisconsin on that date were "11 hats complete: 70 eagles, 50 bugles, 40 feathers, 40 letters 'C,'" and "60 figures '2.'" Earlier requisitions from the 2nd Wisconsin had also brought the regiment new hats, including "60 Army Hats complete" on June 18, 1862, and "50 uniform hats, trimmed complete" on July 3, 1862.[101]

A view of Company I of the 7th Wisconsin, also taken opposite Fredericksburg in May or July of 1862 shows the hats turned up on either side or not at all. Surprisingly a good many of the hats in the photograph of the 7th Wisconsin are turned up on the right side, even though they are shown with their Austrian rifles at the old shoulder arms position of Scott's obsolete tactics.[102]

On May 1, 1862, a full week before Brigadier-General Gibbon was officially assigned to the command of the brigade, the Quartermaster of the 7th Wisconsin requisitioned "850 Uniform Infantry Hats," citing as the justification, that the "7th Regt. Wis. Vols. needs them for Summer use." Included with the requisition were 850 each of "cords & tassels, feathers, eagles, bugles, "shells & flames" (an erroneous reference to the plume holders used for the light artillery caps' plumes; these were not issued) and the figure "7." Also requisitioned were 1,000 "Letters, assorted."[103] These hats were shipped from Washington on the same day as the sack coats, also ordered on May 1.[104] On May 5, 1862 they would be issued to the companies of the 7th as follows:[105]

100. State Historical Society of Wisconsin, negative no. WHi (X3) 11298. A number of the enlisted men in this view are not wearing the complete brass insignia. In view of the resupply of insignia that took place on July 11, 1862, the May date seems a more likely probability.
101. Entry 4381, Record Group No. 393, Pt. II, National Archives.
102. State Historical Society of Wisconsin, negative no. WHi (X3) 1798. Often credited as having been made at Arlington, Virginia, the spires of Fredericksburg are clearly evident in the background of the photograph. The photograph is one of three taken at the same time. The other two respectively depict the line officers of the company and a company street view—see SHSP negative nos. WHi (X3) 12952 and WHi (X3) 11028. In the company view and the street view, the enlisted men definitely wear the U.S. issue sack coats that had been requisitioned on May 1, 1862.
103. "Clinton Papers," p. 35.
104. Ibid., p. 100.
105. Ibid., pp. 28-32.

```
A   B   C   D   E   F   G   H   I   K
93  95  81  86  74  94  75  85  76  77
```

This distinctive hat and its trimmings would be periodically re-issued throughout the career of the regiment. For example, on June 27, 1862, the 7th submitted a requisition for replacement uniforms and equipage that included "21 uniform hats." Again, on July 5, 1862, among the articles requisitioned by the quarter-master of the 7th were "9 Hats (uniform)." Similarly, on September 8, 1862, he would issue a request from the U.S. Quartermaster's Department on behalf of his regiment "185 Uniform Hats & Trimmings."[106] The reissue of the hats and their trimmings would extend to the other regiments of Gibbon's Brigade.

GENERAL GIBBON'S "BLACK HAT BRIGADE"

When Brigadier-General John Gibbon relieved Colonel Cutler as commander of the 3rd Brigade, 1st (King's) Division, Department of the Rappahannock consequent to orders of May 7, 1862, at least two of the four regiments of the brigade were fully equipped with the distinctive black felt regulation M1858 hats of the U.S. Army. Lack of firm documentation leaves the question open as to whether the transition to these hats by 19th Indiana and the 6th Wisconsin took place before Gibbon's assumption of command or as a result of his arrival. The meager evidence that does exist, however, seems to indicate that the headwear of the 19th Indiana and 6th Wisconsin was made uniform with the other two regiments of the brigade after Gibbon arrived. Gibbon most certainly saw to it that these two regiments, like the 2nd and the 7th Wisconsin, were periodically reequipped with the hats when lost, damaged, or worn out.

While the date that the regiment first acquired their hats is unrecorded, the 19th Indiana received replacements for them periodically thereafter throughout its career as an independent command. On July 1, 1862, consequent to the brigade's first forced march in full regalia, the regimental quartermaster of the 19th found it necessary to requisition (among other items) "50 uniform hats" for those lost or thrown away during the brief campaign. At the same time missing insignia was replaced, as the quartermaster

106. *Ibid.*, respectively pp. 64, 68, and 73.

340

separately ordered "60 feathers, 120 numbers, 60 bugles, 50 cords, & tassels," and "60 eagles for hats." Two weeks later, on July 14, additional apparel was requisitioned, including "9 uniform hats & trimmings."[107] The clothing records of Company B of the 19th Indiana indicate that the regiment maintained the quality of their hats and periodically replaced its trimmings. On October 15, 1862, the company received five new "Uniform Hats." On the same date, it also received "Six Cords & Tassels, Six Feathers, Two Eagles, Ten numbers (obviously five '1's and five '9's) Five Bugles" and "Two letters." Six days later on October 21, the company again received replacement clothing, including "Ten Letters, Ten Feathers, 10 Cords & Tassels, Twenty Numbers, Ten Bugles, Ten Eagles," and "Ten Hats." On December 5, 1862, after Gibbon's departure from the brigade, Company B once more drew new hats, acquiring "5 Hats" and "5 Cord & Tassels." Hats continued to be replaced during Brigadier-General Meredith's command of the Iron Brigade, Company B being issued "7 Felt Hats Complete" on January 1, 1863, nine of the same on February 24, 1863, "14 Hats" on March 22, 1863, and "9 Felt Hats, Cords & Eagles" on May 24, 1863.[108] After Gettysburg, the practice continued. Although the inspection report for the Iron Brigade of July 17, 1863, showed that the 19th Indiana was deficient by twenty-four hats, none of these evidently applied to Company B. Though "3 Hat Letters" and "6 Numbers" were issued to the company on November 1, 1863, its next draw of hats was not until December 19 and 20, 1863, when a single hat without adornments and five hats together with five each of the cords and tassels, eagles, bugles, and letters were drawn. Company B, continued to sporadically replace hats in 1864 until the regiment was consolidated with the 20th Indiana on October 18, 1864.[109]

Based on the entries in the Perry Diary (7th Wisconsin), it would appear that a hat lasted an average of about four to five months. Despite this average during the latter period of the war,

107. Entry 4381, Record Group No. 393, Pt. II, National Archives.
108. Manuscript copy in the possession of Mr. Alan Gaff; Fort Wayne, Indiana.
109. *Ibid.* Deliveries of hats to Company B in 1864 included "4 Hats Complete" on January 7, "2 Hats" on March 21, "2 Hats" (together with 2 bugles, 2 cords & tassels, 4 numbers, 2 letters, and 2 feathers) on April 10, "1 Hat" (together with bugle, eagle cord & tassels, and feather) on April 30, "2 Hats" (together with 2 bugles, 9 numbers, 2 letters, 2 cords & tassels, 2 feathers, and 2 corps badges) on July 19, "2 Hats" on August 11, and "2 Hats" on September 4.

Perry did not find it necessary to draw a new hat after his initial issue of May 7, 1862, until October 23, 1863, a period of over eighteen months. Evidently Perry was fastidious about preserving his equipage, as he did not draw any new brass after May 7, 1862.[110] Regardless of his fastidiousness, by Gettysburg, the hats of the 7th (and probably all of the Iron Brigade) were somewhat misshapen courtesy of the elements and the individuality of the enlisted men. Indeed, on September 14, Major Mark Finnicum, commanding the 7th Wisconsin due to Colonel W. W. Robinson's elevation to brigade commander subsequent to Gettysburg, found it necessary to announce that:[111]

> The Government has made and provided that the hats furnished & worn by enlisted men shall be worn in a certain form or shape set by regulations. Company Commanders of this Regiment are required to see that all enlisted men of their respective commands wear their hats in the form or shape as made and pointed out by the Regulations and in no other in all cases where possible.

Some of the deficiencies in the Iron Brigade reported on July 17, 1863, may well have included hats that were battered out of shape. Those deficiencies included, in addition to the twenty-four in the 19th Indiana, twelve in the 24th Michigan, forty-four in the 7th Wisconsin, twenty-five in the 2nd Wisconsin, and fifty in the 6th Wisconsin. In the last regiment, most of the deficiencies were probably losses occasioned by the charge of the regiment into the Railroad Cut on July 1.[112]

Like the other regiments of Gibbon's Brigade, the 6th Regiment drew replacement hats through the summer of 1862 and presumably afterward as well. Requisitions for replacement clothing and equipage dated June 19, July 5, and August 9, 1862, indi-

110. Papers of James Perry, Company A, 7th Wisconsin Infantry; State Historical Society of Wisconsin, Madison, Wisconsin. Perry drew hats on May 7, 1862, October 23, 1863, January 6, 1864, April 20, 1864, August 4, 1864, December 1, 1864, and May 15, 1865.
111. Regimental Order Book, 7th Wisconsin Infantry; Record Group No. 94, National Archives; Regimental General Order No. 29 (of 1863).
112. Report of Captain H. Richardson, Acting Assistant Inspector General, 1st Division, 1st Army Corps, July 17, 1863; Papers of the War Records Office (Record Group No. 94), National Archives; Papers for O.R., Vol. 27, Box 48.

cate that the 6th Wisconsin was issued respectively "8 hats complete," "15 hats complete," and "40 Hats complete."[113] These hats served as replacements for those damaged or lost after the initial issue in May of 1862.

Like that of the 19th Indiana Infantry, the definite date of the original issue of hats to the 6th Wisconsin Infantry is open to conjecture. Major Rufus Dawes of the 6th, in his history of that regiment, noted that: "On Saturday May 17th, the regiment was fully supplied with white leggings, black felt hats adorned with feathers, and white cotton gloves."[114] A letter "From the Sixth Regiment" dated May 18, 1862, and posted from the camp opposite Fredericksburg, seemingly confirmed Dawes' recollections, commenting:[115]

> . . . Since my last Col. Cutler has taken command of the regiment, and Gen. Gibbons, of the U.S.A., has taken command of the brigade. This brigade now wear the regulation hat with a black feather, with shoes and white leggings, which give it a beautiful appearance.

No out door photographs are known to exist of the 6th Wisconsin while encamped at Fredericksburg in May or July of 1862. Nevertheless, at least four individuals posed for itinerant tintype artists shortly after having been issued their hats, three also wearing their newly issued leggings. These photographs include Private Mair Pointon of Company A, Private Charles A. Keeler of Company B, Private Amos Lefler of Company E, and an unidentified corporal of Company A.[116] These photographs reveal that the 6th at least initially wore their hats fully trimmed with all appropriate brass insignia. Private Pointon (the only individual without

113. Entry 4381, Record Group No. 393, Pt. II, National Archives.
114. Rufus R. Dawes, *Service with the Sixth Wisconsin Volunteers* (Marietta, Ohio; E. R. Alderman & Son, 1890), p. 44.
115. Quiner, "Corr. Wis. Vols.," Vol. 3, p. 246.
116. The photograph of Mair Pointon appears in Philip Cheek and Mair Pointon, *History of the Sauk County Riflemen, Known as Company "A," Sixth Wisconsin Veteran Volunteer Infantry 1861-1865* (Madison: Democrat Printing Company, 1909), opposite p. 27. The photograph of Private Charles A. Keeler was held by Alan T. Nolan; Indianapolis, Indiana. The photograph of Private Amos Lefler is held by Lawrence G. Lefler; Fremont, Nebraska. The photograph of the unidentified corporal of Company A was held by Herb Peck, Jr. of Nashville, Tennessee. This last photograph was made at the same studio where Elon Brown of Company H, 2nd Wisconsin posed for his tintype.

leggings) wears his hat with both sides turned down. Upon first glance, the other three, however, appear to have their hats fastened up on the right side. Indeed, they do, but not as a permanent fixture. In all instances the photographs appear to have been tintypes or ambrotypes. Such photographs produced a reversed positive image. To compensate for the reversal, many photographic artists had their subjects rearrange their apparel so that the final portrait gave the illusion of a non-mirror image. There is evidence that the three individuals deliberately attempted to alter their equipment to obtain that result. In all likelihood, therefore, the enlisted men of the 6th Wisconsin wore their hats as prescribed by regulations, i.e., turned up on the left side.

Although Major Dawes would claim that the hats were issued to the regiment together with the leggings on May 17, a regimental order issued by Colonel Cutler the previous day would seem to infer that they had them by that date. General Regimental Order No. 32 from the Head Quarters of the 6th Regt. Wis. Vols. at its Camp opposite Fredericksburg, Va., dated May 16, 1862, read:[117]

> Men are not to be allowed to attach to their hats or any part of their uniforms any article of ornament or fancy, not prescribed as a part of the uniform.
>
> When new clothing is drawn, it is not to be worn by the men when about the ordinary duties of camp, until the old is worn out, but to be carefully preserved and worn at guard mountings, dress parades, and other parades of ceremony.
>
> Men who are negligent in the care of their clothing, arms and accoutrements, or are any way dilatory in the discharge of their duties, are, in all cases, to be selected for Police and Fatigue duty, in preference to those who are neat, prompt and faithful.

Although this order was under Colonel Cutler's signature, the second paragraph is indicative of Gibbon's fondness for the neatness of the Regular Army. That provision, as well as his insistence

---

117. Regimental Order Book, 6th Wisconsin Infantry; Record Group No. 94, National Archives; General Regimental Order No. 32 (of 1862).

on the newly issued leggings would cause him problems with his new command.

GENERAL GIBBON'S "LINNEN" LEGGINGS

If there was one element of the uniform of the Iron Brigade for which John Gibbon was responsible in completing the distinctive dress of that unit, it was the white leggings he caused to have issued from U.S. Quartermaster stocks approximately one week after assuming command of the brigade. The leggings were not well received by the men, as Gibbon discovered when he found his horse's legs decorated with two pairs shortly after they had been issued. Although Gibbon would not mention the incident in his *Memoirs*, several other members of the brigade recorded the incident after the war.

Michael H. Fitch, then serving with the 6th Wisconsin Infantry remembered.[118] "The men had issued to them, shelter tents and white leggings, for the first time. The next morning after the issue, General Gibbons found the legs of his horse ornamented with white leggings." In the same vein, Philip Cheek and Mair Pinton of Company A, of the same regiment later recollected:[119]

At the time of assuming command of the brigade, Gen. Gibbon issued an order that every man should have an extra suit of clothes, including underwear, stockings and shoes, also white leggings. There was a storm of protest as it involved large expense to each and we all knew that on the first hard march it would all be thrown away.

Col. Fairchild of the 2d Wisconsin had a man equipped as required by the order and the outfit weighed eighty-five pounds. One morning shortly after the order, Gen. Gibbon found his pet horse equipped with leggings much to the amusement of the men.

First Lieutenant William H. Harries of Company B of the 2nd

118. Michael H. Fitch, *Echoes of the Civil War As I Hear Them* (New York: R. F. Fenno & Co., 1905), p. 36.
119. Philip Cheek and Mair Pointon, *History of the Sauk County Riflemen, Known as Company "A," Sixth Wisconsin Veteran Volunteer Infantry 1861-1865* (Madison: Democrat Printing Company, 1909), p. 27.

Wisconsin provided the best anecdote relating to the event, at the same time establishing that Gibbon certainly remembered it well after the War:[120]

> . . . General Gibbon tried at one time to make us wear leggings. They were troublesome to keep clean. The Virginia mud would cling to them with a tenacity that would make the soldiers swearing mad. One day just as we were starting out for brigade drill, as the general's horse was brought out to him to mount it was found someone had enclosed his horse's legs in the leggings. When the boys saw this they raised a great shout of laughter. Gibbon tried to find out who it was that played the trick but was unable to do so. About sixteen years after the war, a reunion was held at Boscobel, Wis., of the soldiers living in Southwest Wisconsin. Gibbon in citizen's clothing hearing of it as he was passing through the State, stopped off. As soon as he got to the gathering he inquired if there were any members of the Iron Brigade present. They brought him one of the old boys of whom the general inquired if he was a member of the Iron Brigade and he said he was. "Well," said Gibbon, "I am looking for the man." "What man?" says the soldier. "Why, the man who put the leggings on my horse when we were opposite Fredericksburg."

The leggings in question were issued to the brigade during the third week of May in 1862. The Quartermaster of the 7th Wisconsin requisitioned 850 "Canvas Leggings" on May 10, 1862, and Military Store Keeper D. G. Thomas at Washington forwarded that number in two crates on May 16.[121] Of the 850 he requisitioned, however, only five-hundred were received. One crate containing three-hundred and fifty never arrived, and as a result Companies A, F, G, and H of the 7th were not fully supplied. Most of the five-hundred "Linnen Leggings" (as the distribution

120. William H. Harries, "In the Ranks at Antietam," in *Glimpses of the Nation's Struggle. Sixth Series. Papers Read Before the Minnesota Commandery of the Military Order of the Loyal Legion of the United States, January 1903-1908* (Minneapolis: Aug. Davis, 1909), p. 557.
121. "Clinton Papers," pp. 34 and 102.

records called them) were distributed to the other six companies on May 17 and 19, as follows:[122]

B	C	D	E	I	K
90	80	83	79	77	69

The meager balance (twenty-three) that remained after these six companies had been supplied was evidently distributed to the officers of several companies in the second and third weeks of June. Company F received three pairs on the 11th, Companies A, D, and H three pairs on the 17th, and Companies G and I respectively nine pairs and two pairs on the same date.[123] Judging from the three photographs taken of Company I of the 7th Wisconsin taken opposite Fredericksburg (not at Arlington as is oft stated), probably in July of 1862, the leggings were strictly for field wear and special occasions. Company I of the 7th had received 77 pairs of leggings on May 17, 1862, yet the views of camp and the photograph of the company drawn up for parade show no evidence of them.

Until the quartermaster of the 7th was absolved of responsibility for the missing three-hundred and fifty leggings, the 7th was unable to draw further leggings. This process took until July.[124] Such was not the case in other regiments of Gibbon's Brigade. The 6th Wisconsin, whom Dawes indicated received their leggings on May 17, 1862, requisitioned another twenty-three leggings on June 19, probably for the officers of that regiment. On July 5, 1862, the quartermaster of that regiment requisitioned another twenty-four pairs of leggings, and on August 9, 1862 yet another two pairs.[125] These leggings continued in use through the Fall of 1862, for Rufus Dawes recorded in a letter dated October 27, 1862 that: "Our brigade had entered the Pope campaign overloaded with clothing and abundantly supplied with everything needed, but the feathers of our hats were drooping and the white leggings, which, as a protection to the feet and ankles, were now more useful than ornamental, had become badly soiled."[126]

122. *Ibid.*, pp. 16, 17, 18 and 37.
123. *Ibid.*, pp. 52, 53, and 56. There is a discrepancy of 1 pair of leggings between the 500 received and the total issued on May 17-18 (478) and June 11 and 17 (23).
124. *Ibid.*, pp. 131 and 132.
125. Entry 4381, Record Group No. 393, Pt. II, National Archives.
126. Rufus R. Dawes, *Service with the Sixth Wisconsin Volunteers* (Marietta, Ohio: E. R. Alderman & Son, 1890), p. 104.

The leggings mentioned in these letters and reminisces were of the pattern supplied to a great number of regiments in the eastern army by the United States Quartermaster's Department. The design had been approved by Quartermaster-General Meigs, based on a French model, and was distinguished by closing the outer seam by means of a series of leather looped thongs. Each loop was attached to the inner flap of the legging. Each loop was threaded through a grommet in the outer flap to close the legging. Then beginning with the lower loop, each thong was brought up to the higher thong, which was passed through the loop of the lower thong. The procedure was repeated until the last thong was brought to the top of the legging, where a leather strap secured the highest thong. This leather strap is clearly visible in the tintype of Corporal Cornelius Wheeler of Company I of the 2nd Wisconsin. These leggings must have been surprisingly strong and well made, for at least one pair (and probably others) continued in use in the 6th Wisconsin as late as Gettysburg.

In the charge of the 6th Wisconsin upon the Railroad Cut on July 1, 1863, Private John Rader of Company F was severely wounded in the left arm by a bullet. The wound necessitated the amputation of Rader's left arm, and on August 24, 1863 he died at Cuyler General Hospital from the effects of that wound and amputation. There was little that was salvageable from what he wore that day. His personal effects consisted only of twelve dollars in cash, one comb, one hat, one pair of trowsers and one *"pr. gaiters."*[127] Evidently these were the same leggings that Rader had been issued in May of 1862. Although the revised clothing allowance permitted the drawing of one pair of "Gaiters (for foot troops)" per annum, and although the U.S. Quartermaster's Department would contract for and continue to issue many of this style legging well into 1863, the "Iron Brigade" would receive only the single issue in May of 1862. The gradual disappearance of the leggings probably had much to do with Gibbon's successor as brigade commander, Brigadier-General Solomon Meredith, formerly colonel of the 19th Indiana, and his chaffing under Gibbon's disciplinary measures in June of 1862.

Meredith's problems began during the "Black Hat Brigade's" first major campaign under Gibbon, from May 26 until June 11,

127. Records of Cuyler General Hospital (Pennsylvania Hospital Register 354, Record Group No. 94, National Archives.

1862. Remembering the twenty mile plus march of May 30, Rufus Dawes of the 6th Wisconsin noted:[128]

It was one of the hardest marches the regiment ever had. . . . The men were here absurdly overburdened. They had been required to carry each an overcoat, an extra pair of shoes, an extra pair of pants. These superfluous articles, added to the necessary hundred rounds of ball cartridges, shelter tent, gum and woolen blankets, haversack full of rations, canteen full of water, musket and accoutrements, were a load beyond the strength of ordinary men. . . . Vast numbers of new overcoats and many knapsacks were flung away by the exhausted men on the march. The men said they were "issuing overcoats to the rebel cavalry," and it is very likely that they were.

Robert K. Beecham, of Company H, 2nd Wisconsin Infantry, also recollected the incident in later years and sarcastically recorded:[129]

Gen. Gibbon was in command of our brigade. . . . Having nothing else to do in the early Summer of '62, he thought it an opportune time to make "regulars" of his brigade. So he issued an order directing that each and every soldier should be supplied with an extra uniform, to be worn on parade, and also that each soldier should have two pairs of canvas leggings. In making his requisition for these supplies for his regiment, Col. Sol Meredith, of the 19th Ind., made also a requisition for four extra mule teams to transport the extra luggage, as a gentle reminder to Gibbon that infantry marched on foot and carried their belongings; but Meredith did not get his mule teams, though we all got our leggings and extra uniforms.

For the next few days Gibbon's Brigade was the flower of the First Corps when we appeared on parade, all dressed in bran-new uniforms and neat and clean

128. Rufus R. Dawes, *Service with the Sixth Wisconsin Volunteers* (Marietta, Ohio: E. R. Alderman & Son, 1890), p. 46.
129. Robert K. Beecham, "Recollections of an Iron Brigade Man," Part II in the *National Tribune*, August 21, 1902, p. 3, cols. 1-4.

canvas leggings, and General Gibbon was greatly pleased with the success of his undertaking. Then came marching orders, and the corps moved up the Valley. Of course no volunteer would pack an extra pound in June weather, much less an extra uniform and a lot of useless canvas leggings, so each soldier donned his best and abandoned all superfluous luggage. The next time we appeared on parade, Gibbon's Brigade was only a trifle better dressed than the balance of the corps, and there was not a legging in sight. . . .

Beecham's account suffers from several inaccuracies. The men had only been issued a single pair of leggings, and as indicated by Dawes and others, not all were discarded. It is clear, nevertheless, that the greatest reluctance to the leggings as well as the extra items of uniform occurred in the 19th Indiana. The day after the return of the brigade to Fredericksburg after its first campaign, Gibbon reviewed and inspected his brigade. The next day, June 13, 1862, Gibbon published on order that chided the 19th Indiana for its slovenly appearance:[130]

The General Commanding the Brigade was much pleased with the military bearing and apperance of the Regiments on Review yesterday. But whilst commending their appearance as a body he regrets to be obliged to refer to the marked contrast between the 19th Indiana Volunteers and the other Regiments of the Brigade.

Three weeks ago when reviewed by the President every one remarked the neat and cleanly appearance of this Regiment, and the Genl. noticed with regret the contrast presented on review yesterday.

It appears that during one of the recent marches most of the men recklessly threw away the clothing just issued to them. Such foolish waste of Stores provided by the Government cannot be tolerated and would never occur in a properly disciplined body of men. The 38th Article of War provides a severe punishment for such acts. At the approaching muster of this regiment, every

130. General Orders No. 58, Head Quarters Gibbon's Brigade, Opposite Fredericksburg, June 13th, 1862, in Regimental Order Book, 7th Wisconsin Infantry, Record Group No. 94, National Archives.

man who has not now in his possession the clothing issued to him during the past month will be charged on the amount deducted from his pay. The Regimental and Company commanders will be held strictly accountable that this order is strictly enforced.

Indeed, based on the regimental requisitions of mid-June and early July, the clothing lost or thrown away by the 19th Indiana far exceeded that of the other three regiments of the brigade. The leggings suffered the most. On June 17, 1862, the quartermaster of the 19th requisitioned two-hundrerd and ninety pairs of new leggings as well as ten "tents d' abri" (shelter halves). On July 1, 1862, the impact of General Gibbon's order of June 13 was truly felt. In addition to requisitioning another two-hundred and ninety pairs of leggings, the quartermaster of the 19th found it necessary to draw for the men of the regiment four-hundred pairs of shoes, two-hundred each of sack coats, pairs of trowsers, shirts, and pairs of socks, fifty uniforms hats and supplementary hat brass, four-hundred and twenty rubber blankets, ninety shelter tents, one-hundred each canteens and haversacks, and one-hundred and eighty-five knapsacks with straps.[131] Gibbon's order of June 13 cost the 19th more than embarrassment, as these replacement items were paid for by the individuals of the regiment.

Although there is good evidence to indicate that the 2nd, 6th, and 7th Wisconsin regiments also disposed of excess clothing during the march of May 30, 1862, the laxity in appearance seems to have been confined to Meredith's 19th Indiana. The commanders of the other regiments of the brigade used several ploys to insure that their regiments met Gibbon's standards. On the day of Gibbon's review, the commanding officer of the 7th Wisconsin issued a special order to prod his men into complying to Gibbon's standards through punitive measures, stating: "If there is any man found in any Co. who does not pass a thorough inspection in arms, accoutrements or clothing or person, the entire company will be cut off from all papers until the company is brought to & passes a satisfactory & thorough inspection. No papers will be granted until after the above named inspection."[132] This inspec-

131. Entry 4381, Record Group No. 393, Pt. II, National Archives.
132. Regimental Order Book, 7th Wisconsin Infantry; Record Group No. 94, National Archives; Special Orders No. 63, Head Quarters 7th Reg. Wis. Vol.; Camp opposite Fredericksburg, June 13/62.

tion was to take place on the 14th of June. Two weeks later, the same officer reiterated his instance on neat appearance by demanding that "the commandants of Companies will see that their Companies are in proper condition with shoes, cartridge boxes & belts blacked, Arms in perfect order, persons cleaned, and clothing cleaned and mended if necessary."[133]

These measures were not limited to the 7th Wisconsin. On July 23, 1862, Colonel Cutler of the 6th Wisconsin also attempted a combination of punitive measures and rewards to discipline the appearance of his unit by instructing that:[134]

> At the evening parade each day, the Several Company Commanders of this Regiment will select from their companies the two men whose arms, accoutrements, clothing and person are in the neatest and best condition; and credit them with one turn of Guard duty. They will also select the two whose general appearance as to neatness is the poorest, and they will constitute the detail for the Police duties of the camp. The First Sergeants will keep an accurate record of said Selections and when any soldier has been Selected for neatness ten times, his name will be published at the head of the regiment and he will receive such further mark of approbation as the Regimental Commander shall deem proper. The names of such as are selected a like number of times for their slovenly habits will also be published and such further punishment inflicted as the Commanding Officer shall judge expedient.

As admitted in his memoirs, General Gibbon also learned to "dangle the carrot" rather than rely solely on the whip. Gibbon's

133. *Ibid.*; General Order No. 61, Head Quarters 7th Wis. Vol.; Opposite Fredericksburg, Virginia, June 27, '62. The disciplining of the 7th was not limited to the enlisted men. On August 3, 1862, General Orders No. 67 of the regiment required that "Non-commissioned officers who have not chevrons on their coats or blouses will immediately procure them." It further directed that "Company Commanders will inspect their non-commissioned officers & report the names & grade of those lacking chevrons to the Adjutant in writing by 10 A.M. tomorrow in order that Regimental Tailors may be detailed to get the braid and make the chevrons."

134. Regimental Order Book, 6th Wisconsin Infantry; Record Group No. 94, National Archives; General Orders No. 45, Head Quarters, 6th Regt. Wis Vols.; Camp Opposite Fredericksburg, Va, July 23d 1862.

mellowing was reflected in marching orders issued to the 7th Wisconsin on August 13, 1862. In preparation for the campaign, the regimental commander of the 7th directed that: "On the march the men must carry on their persons one of three articles under the direction of their company commandants, viz: a woolen blanket or an india rubber blanket or a tent." He further noted that "As the transportation is insufficient, company commandants will make a thorough inspection of Knapsacks and discard all unnecessary articles. They will also require the Knapsacks to be packed in the smallest possible form."[135]

Although relenting on the amount of baggage the soldiers were forced to carry on their backs, Gibbon continued to insist that the men be resupplied with requisite clothing. While on the Maryland campaign of 1862, Captain John B. Callis of Company F of the 7th, then commanding the regiment by virtue of his seniority and the wounding of all the field officers at Brawner Farm, directed that: "The Commanders of Companies will as soon as practicable make out a list of such articles of clothing as their respective commands may stand in need of and report to the Quarter Master of the regiment, who will at once take steps to furnish the required articles."[136] With the close of that campaign, on October 24, 1862 General Gibbon ordered an inspection of his regiments, insisting that "Every man with & without equipments or clothing will attend except cooks, guards and sick excused by Surgeons as unable to parade."[137] The results of that inspection are evident in the requisitions of the various regiments of October 26, 1862. Included among the various items of clothing drawn on that date were thirty-five overcoats in the 7th Wisconsin, fifty-five in the 19th Indiana, and nine in the newly added 24th Michigan.[138]

On November 4, 1862, General John Gibbon's official association with the Iron Brigade ended when he was assigned to com-

135. Regimental Order Book, 7th Wisconsin Infantry; Record Group No. 94, National Archives; General Order No. 69, Head Quarters 7th Regt. Wisconsin Vols.; August 13th 1862.
136. *Ibid.*; General Order No. 87, Head Quarters 7th Wis. Vol.; Upton's Hill, Sept. 15, 1862.
137. Special Orders No. 140, Head Quarters Gibbon's Brigade; near Bakersville, Md., Oct. 24th 1862, in Regimental Order Book, 7th Wisconsin Infantry; Record Group No. 94, National Archives.
138. Entry 4381, Record Group No. 393, Pt. II, National Archives.

mand the 2nd Division of the 1st Army Corps.[139] Lysander Cutler of the 6th Wisconsin Infantry, as senior colonel, again assumed command of the brigade. While on sick leave, Colonel Solomon Meredith, and his friends had been campaigning for a separate command and a generalcy for Meredith. The latter came on October 6, 1862 with Meredith's appointment as brigadier-general. On November 25, 1862, much to John Gibbon's chagrin, Brigadier-General Solomon Meredith was appointed to command Gibbon's old brigade, a post he would hold through Gettysburg.[140] During his tenancy, the knapsacks of the brigade would be lightened considerably, but the appearance and discipline of the units would also be allowed to deteriorate.[141]

KNAPSACKS, ACCOUTREMENTS, AND TENTAGE.

There is significant evidence to indicate that the Iron Brigade did not remove their knapsacks prior to entering combat on July 1, 1863. Given the rapidity of their entrance into action, it had long been thought that it had been impractical for the men to strip and stack their knapsacks. That presumption has been confirmed by several sources.

Robert K. Beecham was a member of Co. H of the 2nd Wisconsin on the morning of July 1, 1863. He was captured on July 1 while retreating through Gettysburg after the collapse of the 11th Corps line. He later recollected that the prisoners were not stripped of their belongings until reaching Staunton. There "we were robbed of every tent, blanket, poncho, knapsack, haversack and canteen in our possession."[142] The diary of Charles Walker,

139. *O.R.*, Series I, Vol. 51, Pt. 1, p. 922; Special Orders No. 44; Headquarters 1st Army Corps, November 4, 1862. The 3rd Corps of the Army of Virginia had been redesignated as the 1st Army Corps, Army of the Potomac on September 12, 1862. The change was merely nominal and affected neither the structure of Gibbon's Brigade nor of King's 1st Division.
140. *Ibid.*, Series I, Vol. 51, Pt. 1, p. 951; Special Orders No. 62; Headquarters, 1st Army Corps, November 25, 1862.
141. As an example of the deterioration that took place during Meredith's regime, on September 4, 1863, Colonel Bragg found it necessary to fine both Ferdinand Caesar and Joseph Schmidt of Company F, 6th Wisconsin five dollars each for "insulting language to their superior officer Christian Beltz, 1st Sergt of said Company, and for habitually neglecting their clothing and personal appearance." See Regimental Order Book, 6th Wisconsin Infantry; Record Group No. 94, National Archives; General Regimental Orders, No. 34, Head Quarters 6th Regt. Wis. Vols.; Sept. 4th 1863.
142. Robert K. Beecham, "Adventures of an Iron Brigade Man," Part X, in the *National Tribune*, October 16, 1902, p. 3, cols. 1-5.

Company B, 7th Wisconsin, provides further confirmation. Walker, who was detached to the brigade provost guard (and who would have accordingly had an even better opportunity to shed his knapsack) recorded that an artillery projectile passed through his knapsack and killed the person next to him as he was engaged on July 1, 1863.[143] Walker's earlier diary entries are revealing as to what was probably carried in the knapsacks. When detailed in light marching order in early June, the detail was to carry no more than one woolen and one rubber blanket for every two men. Very likely this was the case as the men marched to Gettysburg as well, though it is known that the Iron Brigade was also carrying their shelter halves as well, and probably the remaining portion of their rations in their knapsacks.[144] Confirming that the men of the brigade continued to wear their knapsacks at least until the night of July 1, the inspection report of July 17, 1863 indicates that the brigade was deficient only thirty knapsacks on that date. These include none in the 2nd Wisconsin, five in the 6th Wisconsin, twelve in the 7th Wisconsin, one in the 19th Indiana, and two in the 24th Michigan. The loss of haversacks, canteens, shelter tents, and rubber blankets had been much more severe, distributed accordingly:[145]

	2nd Wis.	6th Wis.	7th Wis.	19th Ind.	24th Mich.
haversacks:	50	68	98	45	60
canteens:	35	40	27	25	20
shelter tents:	50	12	11	8	10
gum blankets:	5	20	34	17	8

The higher losses among these accoutrements and items of equip-

143. Diaries of Charles Walker, Company B, 7th Wisconsin Infantry, entry of July 1, 1863; private collection, transcription courtesy of Mr. Robert Braun; Fredonia, Wisconsin.
144. *Ibid.*, entry of June 7, 1863—"Could only take 2 blankets for every two men, one rubber and one woolen, and carry our knapsacks." In his entry of June 15, 1863, Walker recorded: "Got into Centerville at 4 P.M. just about used up. I did not put my tent up for I was too tired to do that."
    1st Sergeant John O. Johnson of Company H, 6th Wisconsin Infantry remembered that on June 30, 1863, that "I had sat all night under a shelter tent in the state of Pennsylvania, making out the muster rolls. The work was completed just at reveille after which the company was mustered, and the men proceeded to get their breakfast." See "One Rebel Flag," in *Milwaukee Sunday Telegraph*, January 17, 1887, p. 3.
145. Report of Captain H. Richardson, Acting Assistant Inspector General, 1st Division, 1st Army Corps, July 17, 1863; Papers of the War Records Office (Record Group No. 94), National Archives; Papers for *O.R.*, Vol. 27, Box 48.

age probably reflects the heavy wear that these items suffered even during usual usage. The surviving quartermaster records of the brigade show a high attrition rate for these items throughout 1862 and 1863. In the Wisconsin regiments, the knapsacks in use at Gettysburg were the standard federal issue, as were the haversacks and canteens. In these units the state issues had long since been replaced.

The 2nd Wisconsin had received their initial issue of knapsacks haversacks, and canteens from state of Wisconsin. When the 2nd Wisconsin departed Madison, a reporter described the equipage carried by the men: "Every man had on his knapsack, with a couple of good blankets; each man was furnished with a tin canteen, enclosed in green flannel. In their knapsacks were two rations each."[146] These knapsacks had been made in Wisconsin under a contract with J. W. English of Racine on May 24, 1861 in accordance with his sample No. 2. The contract indicated that this pattern of knapsack had been "adopted by the State of New York." Under the same contract English delivered the haversacks for the 2nd Regiment, made of "heavy sail duck."[147]

The knapsacks of the 2nd Regiment survived the disaster at

146. Quiner, "Corr. Wis. Vols.," Vol. 1, p. 82. See also pg. 96 for a reference to the rubber blankets.
147. "Wis. Q.M.G., Gen. Corr.," Box 1 (folder covering May 21-25, 1861). The actual contract of May 24 called for only one-thousand each of the knapsacks and haversacks. The contract was periodically modified, however, to include 4,350 knapsacks and 5,000 haversacks. On June 14, 1861, it was also modified to change the size of the knapsack:

> J. W. English is to widen the flap of the knapsacks hereafter to be made for the 4th Regiment by Seven inches in width and deepened three & ¼ inches; the knapsacks are to be lettered with white oil paint giving No. of Regiment, letter of Company, and Number of the order in the same. The haversacks to be lettered the same, black, and the maker is to receive twenty five cents extra on each pair, this is to say for lettering a knapsack and haversack & for widening the flap of the latter.

On June 19, 1861, a further modification was made, specifying that: "The Straps to pass entirely around instead of being riveted on, and the flap to be wide so as to fold under on the sides and end for the 4th Regt's supply and the last lot, and the price to be twenty five cents in addition to the contract price." Under this contract one-thousand haversacks were delivered on June 6 (probably for the 1st Regiment), one-thousand and seven haversacks and five-hundred knapsacks on June 14 and thirty haversacks and five-hundred and fifty knapsacks on June 19. These deliveries of June 14 and 19 were most likely for the 2nd Regiment as the delivery of one-thousand and fifty each of knapsacks and haversacks furnished by English on July 5 were sent to Fond du Lac, where the 3rd Wisconsin was rendezvousing.

Bull Run as they were left in the Washington. On July 14, 1861 as the 2nd Wisconsin prepared to embark on its first campaign, a member of the regiment noted: "We are to carry with us our blankets, which are rolled into long close rolls and slung over our shoulders. Our knapsacks . . . are to be either sent to Alexandria or left with our tents with a guard of one-hundred men."[148] The requisition records of the 2nd Wisconsin, however, indicate that by the summer of 1862 the accoutrements and equipage had been gradually replaced by draws upon U.S. Quartermaster stocks.[149] The same was true of the rubber blankets of the regiment.

The rubber blankets provided by Wisconsin for the 2nd Regiment had been purchased in New York by state commissioners Bacon and Cutler from The Rubber Clothing Company of New York City at the price of $1.00 each. The same company furnished these "Rubber Spreads or Blankets" for the 3rd through 6th Regiments.[150] The same two commissioners had purchased knapsacks and haversacks in New York for the 5th and 6th Regiments. These were bought from the firm of Peddy & Morrison. The latter were described as made from a "heavy leather cloth" and the former from "White Duck."[151] Like the haversacks of the 2nd Regiment, those furnished by the state to the 6th Wisconsin were unpainted. Although this provided less protection of the contents from the elements and conversely to the clothing from the greasy contents, this proved a benefit in terms of longevity as it permitted the sacks to be washed. Sergeant Levi Raymond of Company G of the 6th recorded in his diary on August 28,

148. Quiner, "Corr. Wis. Vols.," Vol. 1, p. 95.
149. Entry 4381, Record Group No. 393, Pt. II, National Archives. The deliveries for the 2nd Wisconsin during the summer of 1862 include:

	June 12, 1862	July 3, 1862	July 11, 1862	August 13, 1862
Knapsacks	25	50	73	—
Haversacks	70	100	113	150
Canteens	51	100	57	150
Rubber Blankets	—	75	2	—
Shelter Tents	24	100	88	—

150. "Wis. Q.M.G., Gen. Corr.," Box 2 (folder covering June 20-25, 1861), "Brief abstract of Col. Cutler's Eastern purchases, &c., &c., June 20, 1861." See also Box 2 (folder covering June 12-16, 1861) for bills per regiment. The rubber blankets of the 2nd Regiment were shipped to Milwaukee on June 13, 1861; those for the 5th and 6th Regiments were shipped on June 20, 1861.
151. *Ibid.*

1861 that "I went . . . to the creek & washed my haversack &c."
Hence, Raymond was able to make his haversack last eight
months. Not until February 10, 1862 would he record in his diary:
"In the afternoon we received new haversacks."[152] Judging from
the frequent reissue of haversacks (as well as other accoutrements and equipage) during the summer of 1862, the new haversacks would not survive as long, especially under the duress of
campaign.[153]

As the 7th Wisconsin was not called into service until the late
Summer of 1861, it would appear that much of its state issued
accoutrements and equipage survived the Winter of 1861-1862 in
tolerable condition. An exception were the canteens, and to a
lesser degree the haversacks. Although only requisitioning two
knapsacks and thirteen rubber blankets during this three month
period, the quartermaster of the 7th Wisconsin found it necessary
to draw upon the U.S. Quartermaster Department for two-hundred and fifty-eight new haversacks and six-hundred and nine
new canteens.[154] The next quarter would see a more dramatic
deterioration of the state issued equipage. On April 22, 1862, the
7th's quartermaster would requisition four knapsacks, forty-nine
haversacks, and twenty-eight canteens. On May 1, this would be
followed by a further request for fifty-six knapsacks, one-hundred
and nine haversacks, thirty-three canteens, and seventy-eight
rubber blankets, the last not delivered. A month later, the requisitions would include seventy-six knapsacks, one-hundred and
eighteen canteens, twenty-nine rubber blankets, and fifteen shelter tents.[155] The regiment's first active campaign, however,

152. Diaries of Levi B. Raymond, Company G, 6th Wisconsin Infantry; private
    collection, Des Moines, Iowa; respectively for 1861 and 1862.
153. Entry 4381, Record Group No. 393, Pt. II, National Archives. The deliveries
    to the 6th Wisconsin during the summer of 1862 include:

	June 19, 1862	June 21, 1862	July 5, 1862	August 9, 1862
Knapsacks	20	—	12	2
Haversacks	16	—	24	41
Canteens	14	—	15	82
Rubber Blankets	—	410	—	38
Shelter Tents	27	20	40	15

154. "Clinton Papers," p. 117.
155. *Ibid.*, p. 118; for individual requisitions or receipts see also p. 95 (April 22,
    1862), p. 36 (May 1, 1862), p. 20, May 20, 1862. See also pp. 100, 102,
    and 104.

quickly reduced the amount of state issued equipage to shambles. Accordingly, on June 24, 1862, Colonel Robinson of the 7th Wisconsin convened a board of survey for the purpose of "examining into the condition of Knapsacks, Haversacks, Canteens, & Camp Kettles belonging to the 7th Wis. Vols."[156] The board accomplished its charge quickly, and three days later the quartermaster of the 7th submitted a requisition for six-hundred knapsacks, three-hundred and twenty-five haversacks, one-hundred and twenty five canteens, one-hundred and sixty-five rubber blankets, and fifty-two shelter tents. In justifying the requisition, Quartermaster Clinton observed that "a number of knapsacks, haversacks, canteens, & camp kettles have been condemned by a board of survey."[157] The haversacks were not immediately available, causing Clinton to requisition a total of four-hundred and three on July 5, together with another nineteen canteens, seventy-three rubber blankets, and five shelter tents.[158] In the interim, the new knapsacks had arrived, and only July 19, Colonel Robinson ordered:[159]

> Company Commanders will before Reveille tomorrow cause the knapsacks of their respective companies to be marked with ink or otherwise with the letter of the Co. and number of the owner corresponding with his number on the Descriptive Roll. They will see that the knapsacks are in readiness to turn over at that time to Ordnance Sergt. Cowen to be marked and will detail such assistants as he may designate.

On July 31, 1862, Robinson would again convene a board of survey, this time to "examine and report upon the condition of the Shelter tents belonging to this regiment."[160] Judging from the regimental requisitions of August 9 and September 8, 1862, Colo-

---

156. Regimental Order Book, 7th Wisconsin Infantry, Record Group No. 94, National Archives; Special Orders No. 70; Head Quarters 7th Reg. Wis. Vol.; Opposite Fredericksburg, Va., June 24, 1862.
157. "Clinton Papers," p. 64; see also p. 96.
158. Ibid., p. 68.
159. Regimental Order Book, 7th Wisconsin Infantry, Record Group No. 94, National Archives; Special Orders No. 77; Head Quarters 7th Wis. Volunteers; Camp opposite Fredericksburg, July 19, 1862.
160. Ibid., Special Orders No. 81; Head Quarters 7th Wis. Vols.; Camp Gibbon near Fredericksburg, Va., July 31, 1862.

nel Robinson would not be as successful in obtaining new tentage for his regiment. The old tents would have to serve the regiment through the summer.[161]

It is important to note that this equipage was carried upon the men themselves during the march. It was not stored in the baggage train. Indeed, in October of 1863, Colonel Bragg of the 6th Wisconsin reemphasized this practice and demanded that "No knapsacks except those belonging to the Sergeant Major, the Adjutant's Clerk, & Acting Lieutenants shall be received into the wagons, except by special permission from the officer in command of the Regiment.[162] General Meredith may have been able to lighten the load on the men's backs as they marched toward Gettysburg, but he could not eliminate it.

CORPS BADGES

As already noted, not only hats but hat trimmings were periodically replaced in the units of the Iron Brigade in both 1862 and 1863. On March 21, 1863, another decoration was ordered to be added to the hats of the men. On that date, a circular was issued from the Headquarters, Army of the Potomac that specified:[163]

For the purpose of ready recognition of corps and divisions in this army, and to prevent injustice by reports of straggling and misconduct through mistake as to its organization, the chief quartermaster will furnish without delay the following badges, to be worn by the officers and enlisted men of all the regiments of the various corps mentioned. They will be securely fastened upon the center of the top of the cap.

Inspecting officers will at all inspections see that these badges are worn as designated.

161. For the requisition of August 8, 1862, see Entry 4381, Record Group. No. 393, Pt. II, National Archives. In terms of accoutrements and equipage, this requisition only called for fifty-one canteens and twenty camp kettles. For the requisition of September 8, 1862, see "Clinton Papers," p. 73. This requisition called for (among other items) seventeen knapsacks, forty-seven haversacks, fifty-eight canteens, one-hundred and ninety-nine rubber blankets, and only twenty-two shelter tents.
162. Regimental Order Book, 6th Wisconsin Infantry, Record Group No. 94, National Archives; Regimental General Order No. 35; Head Quarters 6th Regt. Wisc. Vols.; October 22, 1863.
163. O.R., Series I, Vol. 25, Pt. 2, p. 152.

First Corps, a sphere—First Division, red, Second, white; Third blue. . . .

Contrary to popular myth, these badges were not "cut from the lining of the men's overcoats." Rather these corps badges were actually cut with metal dies by the division quartermasters upon regular requisition, the appropriate cloth being kept on hand at division or requisitioned as needed. Documentary evidence indicates that the system was finally in place by mid-April of 1863.

On April 15, 1863, Colonel Edward S. Bragg of the 6th Wisconsin Infantry created a "camp guard" who were "to remain & protect camp whenever the Regiment marches." To the five men nominally assigned to that task, Bragg added the fourteen men then on sick call and unfit for active duty. In closing these orders, Bragg instructed the company commanders "to see that these changes are effected," and "They will also see that all the men who march are provided with the badge prescribed for this division & if necessary they are hereby authorized to take them from the Guard above designated."[164] Two days earlier, Company B of the 19th Indiana had received a quantity of requisitioned replacement clothing and equipage. Among the items received on that date were also "38 Badges."[165] Clearly these were the red circular discs that had been order on March 21.

Various brigade orders issued in April of 1863 directed how several of the regiments would wear the newly issued cloth corps badges on their caps in conjunction with the other insignia. Un-

164. Regimental Order Book, 6th Wisconsin Infantry, Record Group No. 94, National Archives; Special Regimental Orders No. 11 and Special Regimental Orders No. 12; Headquarters 6th Regt. Wis. Vols.; Near Belle Plain, Va., Apl. 15, 1863.
165. Manuscript copy in the possession of Mr. Alan Gaff; Fort Wayne, Indiana. These same records show the reissue of "10 Badges" on November 24, 1863 and "2 Badges (Corps)" on July 19, 1864 (at the same time as two new hats with all trimmings were also issued.) It is important to understand, that the brigade did not give up their distinctive corps badges and designating flags when the 1st Army Corps was consolidated with the 5th Army Corps on March 24, 1864. Even after the multitude of reorganizations during the Spring and Summer of 1864, the badge continued in use. On November 2, 1864, Brigadier-General Edward S. Bragg, commanding the 1st Brigade, 3rd Division, 5th Army Corps (consolidated Iron Brigade and Pennsylvania Bucktail Brigade), reinforced this practice by noting that "All First and Third Division badges will be discarded at once. Until further orders this command will wear the badge of the old First Division, First Army Corps." See O.R., Series I, Vol. 42, Pt. 3, p. 487.

fortunately no such orders for the Iron Brigade, then the 4th Brigade, 1st Division, 1st Army Corps, survive. From surviving photographs and specimens, however, it is evident that the enlisted men in the Iron Brigade were ordered to wear the red disc (1⅜″ in diameter of red wool worsted) in the center of the front of the crown of the hat.

A photograph of Principal Musician John Vollenwieder of the 7th Wisconsin depicts the red disc so located with a brass "7" centered upon it. Although battered, the hat still bears of plume.[166] In a like manner a photograph of an unidentified member of Company E, 24th Michigan shows the corps badge worn on the front of the crown near the center with the numerals "24" directly on the badge. A commercially purchased (Schuyler, Hartley & Graham) brass "E" partly overlaps the badge above the figures.[167] Of more importance, the hat that color-sergeant Philadner B. Wright wore into the attack on the 1st of July survives. Like Vollenwieder's, it is badly battered, but still has remains of both the sky blue hat cord and the plume. The red disc is sewn to the upper center of the front of the crown, and a brass "2" is centered on it. The sergeant's company letter, "C" is set on the hat below the badge.[168]

While the enlisted men evidently wore the corps badge in the front center of the crown of the hats, the officers were allowed more discretion. A photograph of Captain Joseph N. P. Bird of Company I, 7th Wisconsin depicts him wearing the red disc (with a gold edge border) on the right side of his hat, with a brass or silver "7" on its center. Although cords and tassels are evident, no infantry insignia appears on the front of his hat.[169] The photograph is thought to date from 1864.

166. Collection of the W. H. Over Museum; Vermillion, South Dakota. Vollenwieder became principal musician of the 7th Wisconsin on July 1, 1863. The photograph, therefore, must postdate Gettysburg. The same museum also has a photograph of Private Stanley J. Morrow, Company F, 7th Wisconsin Infantry, wearing a sack coat and holding his M1858 dress hat on his lap. The faint outline of the red disc is visible on the front of the hat.
167. Collection of Michael Lauer; Wixom, Michigan. As the 24th Michigan Infantry did not receive its M1858 dress hats until May 27, 1863, the photograph most likely postdates Gettysburg.
168. Collection of the Wisconsin Veterans Historical Museum; Madison, Wisconsin. The hat has an unusual feature added; three eyelet ventilators were spaced around the crown by Wright.
169. Collection of Jerry W. Carlton; Hancock, Wisconsin.

ARMAMENT AND ACCOUTREMENTS

Federal records leave no doubt as to the armament of the Iron Brigade at Gettysburg. The summary statements of ordnance on hand in the brigade had been made out on June 30, 1863. The 19th Indiana Infantry and the 24th Michigan Infantry were armed with .58 caliber "Springfield" rifle-muskets. Nine companies of the 19th had a total of two-hundred and forty-seven arms. (Company G did not submit a report.) The five companies of the 24th Michigan that reported their arms had a total of 244 muskets; however, no reports survive for Companies C, D, E, H, and I.[170]

Among the Wisconsin regiments, the eight reporting companies of the 2nd Wisconsin claimed two-hundred and sixty-seven Austrian "Lorenz" M1854 rifle-muskets in their original .54 caliber. (Companies E and H failed to report their arms as of June 30.) These had replaced their "sheet iron" .69 caliber smoothbore altered percussion muskets during January of 1862. The 7th Wisconsin was similarly armed with a total of three-hundred and thirty-four Austrian "Lorenz" M1854 rifle-muskets. Most of these had been reamed up and re-rifled in .58 caliber; nevertheless, Companies A, D, and F claimed to have ninety-three in their original .54 caliber. These arms had replaced the .69 caliber Harpers Ferry smoothbore altered percussion muskets in March of 1862. The 6th Wisconsin on the other hand was armed with .58 caliber "Springfield" rifle-muskets. Its ten companies claimed a total of three-hundred and twenty-two muskets.[171] Six weeks after the battle, the various regiments listed the arms that they had lost during the engagement. Left on the field with the killed, wounded, and captured on July 1 were two-hundred and six .58 caliber Springfields of the 19th Indiana, three-hundred and forty-six similar arms of the 24th Michigan, two-hundred and twenty-two .54 caliber Austrian rifle-muskets of the 2nd Wisconsin, one-hundred and sixty-two Austrian rifle-muskets of the 7th Wisconsin, and one-hundred and sixty-three Springfield .58 caliber

170. Quarterly Summary Statements of Ordnance and Ordnance Stores-Infantry, Record Group No. 156, National Archives; Vol. 5 (quarter ending June 30, 1863), pp. 43 and 98, respectively for the 19th Indiana and the 24th Michigan.
171. *Ibid.*, Vol. 6 (quarter ending June 30, 1863), pp. 59 and 60.

rifle-muskets of the 6th Wisconsin.[172] The last arms had been received at the end of January or the beginning of February, 1862, depending on the source consulted.

On September 28, 1863, Captain George T. Balch of the U.S. Ordnance Department wrote to Colonel E. S. Bragg, commanding the 6th Wisconsin Infantry in response to the latter's letter of September 23. Therein he indicates that the "Returns for your Regt. may commence from Jany, 1862, the date they received the Springfield Rifles.[173] January of 1862 may well have been when the Ordnance Department shipped the M1861 Springfield rifle-muskets to the 6th Wisconsin, but there is substantive evidence to indicate that they were not issued until February.

In his entry of February 15, 1862, Sergeant Levi Raymond, Company G, 6th Wisconsin, indicated that: "We got new guns, Springfield Rifles."[174] Corroborating the February issue of the new arms, an inspection report for McDowell's Division dated January 26, 1862, indicates that the 6th Wisconsin was at that time still armed with "Belgian rifled muskets."[175] Several sources agree that these weapons had been issued to the regiment on the first day of September, 1861.

In his diary entry for Friday, August 30, 1861, Levi Raymond noted that: "The Col. got an order for new guns." Two days later on September 1, he acknowledged the actual receipt of these arms, simply stating: "We received our new guns, Belgian Rifles."[176] A correspondent to a Wisconsin newspaper provided more details concerning the acquisition of these arms by the 6th when he wrote home on September 2:[177]

172. Report of Colonel W. W. Robinson, 7th Wisconsin Infantry, commanding 1st Brigade, 1st Division, 1st Army Corps, September 13, 1863; Papers of the War Records Office (Record Group No. 94), National Archives; Papers for O.R., Vol.. 27, Box 48.
173. Bragg Papers, State Historical Society of Wisconsin; Madison, Wisconsin.
174. Diaries of Levi B. Raymond, Company G, 6th Wisconsin Infantry; private collection, Des Moines, Iowa.
175. O.R., Series I, Vol. 5, pp. 708-709. The same document indicates that the 19th Indiana was already armed with "Springfield rifled muskets," the 2nd Wisconsin with "Austrian rifled muskets," and the 7th Wisconsin with "Springfield altered smooth bore" muskets. Of the last, the report notes: "The muskets of the Seventh are reported as bad, and that the men lack confidence in them."
176. Diaries of Levi B. Raymond, Company G, 6th Wisconsin Infantry; private collection, Des Moines, Iowa.
177. Quiner, "Corr. Wis. Vols.," Vol. 1, p. 250.

Last Tuesday our brigade was reviewed by him (General McClellan), when he rode through our lines and examining several muskets remarked that for altered flintlocks, they were kept in better order than any in the service, and that we desired and should have better arms.

Accordingly on Saturday evening we received Belgian rifles which were distributed yesterday. If you remember this is the arm which attracted Fremont's attention during his recent visit to Europe and which he succeeded in obtaining for our government. . . .

Today our boys are practicing at target firing with the new guns. In appearance they are clumsy, and seem to have been made for service than show. I cannot state their exact range, but I think it is one thousand yards. . . .

About a week earlier, a member of Company A of the 6th, who signed his correspondence "Saukee," provided further confirmation about these weapons, stating: "At present companies "A" and "B" are armed with the Springfield rifle, the remainder of the regiment have old muskets. These arms will be exchanged for the Belgian Rifle next Saturday or Monday, the Colonel not being able to procure enough of the Springfield pattern to arm the Regiment."[178] On August 25, 1861, another correspondent of the 6th Wisconsin confirmed that the two flank companies briefly carried either Springfield M1855 or M1861 Springfield rifle-muskets, noting that: "Companies A & B have received Springfield rifles of the same pattern as those formerly used by the Governors Guard, and we are in hopes that the whole regiment will soon be supplied."[179] As indicated by the report of September 2, however, the rest of the regiment was armed with the .69 caliber U.S. M1822 smoothbore musket, altered from flintlock to percussion. If Sergeant Raymond's diary is accurate, these "cap lock muskets" had been issued to the companies of the 6th on Wednesday, August 7, 1861. Three days later, Raymond's company was also issued "our cartridge boxes, bayonet sheaths, belts

178. *Ibid.*, Vol. 1, p. 248
179. *Ibid.*, Vol. 1, p. 247.

&c, also 40 rounds of ammunition to each man."[180] This is a curious receipt, since Quartermaster records of the state indicate that accoutrements had also been issued in Madison.

During the Wisconsin state commissioners' visit to New York in June of 1861, they contracted with Alexander Hitchcock of that city for two-thousand each of cartridge boxes, cap boxes, and bayonet scabbards. These were specifically destined for the 5th and 6th Regiments.[181] These were received, and state records indicate the issue to the 6th Wisconsin of one-thousand cartridge boxes on July 6, 1861, one thousand and twenty-five belt plates on July 8, and one-thousand and twenty five each of bayonet scabbards, waist belts (presumably with cap boxes) and shoulder belts on July 9, 1861.[182] Evidently these items of state ordnance were left in Madison when the 6th departed for the east, accounting for the drawing of federal accoutrements at Baltimore.

CONCLUSIONS

When the five regiments of the Iron Brigade adjusted their knapsacks (or in a few instances bedrolls) and filed off the Emmitsburg Pike on the morning of July 1, 1863, to meet their destiny on McPherson's and Seminary Ridges and the Railroad Cut paralleling the Chambersburg Pike, they wore a common uniform that included a number of regimental differences. What distinguished them as a group were the "damned black hats" each man wore with pride. The dust and rain during the march from Virginia had combined to cause their brims to sag and their feathers droop. Not all of the men had complete brass trimmings, though it would appear that nearly all had at least the regimental number and company letter affixed to the fronts of the hats in conjunction with the universally worn red woolen discs that distinguished them as members of the 1st Division, 1st Army Corps.

In the vanguard, marched the 2nd Wisconsin, the first regiment of the brigade to be issued these distinctive hats. Some of the men may still have worn the dark blue trowsers that had dis-

180. Diaries of Levi B. Raymond, Company G, 6th Wisconsin Infantry; private collection, Des Moines, Iowa; entries of August 7 and 10, 1861.
181. "Wis. Q.M.G., Gen. Corr.," Box 2 (folder covering June 20-25, 1861), "Brief abstract of Col. Cutler's Eastern purchases, &c., &c., June 20, 1861."
182. Wisconsin Quartermaster General, Military Store Inventory, 1861 (Record Group No. 1173), Archives, State Historical Society of Wisconsin; Madison, Wisconsin, p. 166.

tinguished this command from the other elements of the brigade in 1862. Rubbing across the shoulders of their frock coats and fatigue coats were their .54 caliber Austrian rifle-muskets. The same arm, but mainly in .58 caliber, graced the shoulders of the next regiment to the turn off the road, the 7th Wisconsin, the second regiment of the brigade to have adopted the famous black hat. More of its men wore sack coats but frock coats were also in evidence above their sky blue trowsers. The next three units, respectively the 19th Indiana, the 24th Michigan, and the 6th Wisconsin all carried American made arms, the .58 caliber U.S. M1861 rifle-musket. The hats among the 19th Indiana and the 6th Wisconsin varied in quality depending on when they had been replaced during the interval between their first receipt in May of 1862 and the beginning of the campaign. Those of the 24th Michigan were relatively new, having only been received at the end of May. Like the 7th Wisconsin, all wore sky blue trowsers. The first two regiments wore a mixture of sack coats and frock coats. In the trailing 6th Regiment, however, frock coats clearly predominated. To protect their legs from dust, many of the men undoubtedly had tucked their trowsers into the cuffs of their socks, but a few, certainly at least one, still wore his old white canvas leggings that had been instituted under John Gibbon's reign as brigade commander. The knapsacks on the brigade's back had been lightened as much as possible but still bore either a rubber or a woolen blanket, while the straps above the knapsack normally reserved for overcoats bore a shelter half that could be joined with that of a "pard" to form a "tent de abri" with the two "pards'" muskets serving as its poles. Many of the brigade would not need those tents on the night of July 1. Of those who would survive, many would have to find a new "pard" with whom to bunk.

FRANK A. HASKELL
Helped Shape the Black Hat Brigade

BIBLIOGRAPHY

1. General

Annual Reports of the Adjutant General of the State of Wisconsin, 1860-1864. Madison, Wis., Democrat Printing Co., 1912.

Aubery, Doc [Cullen B.], *Recollections of a Newsboy in the Army of the Potomac.* Milwaukee, Wis., 1900. [Contains the monograph, *Echoes of the Marches of the Famous Iron Brigade, 1861-1865.*]

Bates, Samuel P., *The Battle of Gettysburg.* Philadelphia, T. H. David & Co., 1875.

Beaudot, Wm. J. K. comp., "Index to Civil War 'Soldier News' of *The Milwaukee Sunday Telegraph* and *The Milwaukee Telegraph,* 1878-1899." Milwaukee, Wis., Unpublished database, 1988.

Beaudot, Wm. J. K., comp., "Sixth Wisconsin Database, Based Upon the *Roster of Wisconsin Volunteers* and Other Sources." Milwaukee, Wis., Unpublished database, 1989.

Beecham, R[obert] K., *Gettysburg, The Pivotal Battle of the Civil War.* Chicago, A. C. McClurg & Co., 1911.

Beecham, R[obert] K., "Adventures of an Iron Brigade Man." [Paste-up of a series of articles appearing in *The National Tribune*], 1902.

Berryman, John, *History of the Bench and Bar of Wisconsin.* (2 vols.) Chicago, H. C. Cooper, Jr. & Co., 1898.

Buell, Augustus, *The Cannoneer; Recollections of Service in the Army of the Potomac.* Washington, D.C., *The National Tribune,* 1897.

Burton, William L., *Melting Pot Soldiers: The Union's Ethnic Regiments.* Ames, Iowa, Iowa State University Press, 1988.

Byrne, Frank L. and Andrew T. Weaver, eds., *Haskell of Gettysburg, His Life and Civil War Papers.* Madison, Wis., State Historical Society of Wisconsin, 1970.

Cheek, Philip and Mair Pointon, *History of the Sauk County Riflemen, Known as Company "A" Sixth Wisconsin Veteran Volunteer Infantry 1861-1865.* [n.p.], 1909.

Coddington, Edwin B., *The Gettysburg Campaign.* New York, Charles Scribner's Sons, 1968. [Revised and reprinted, Morningside Bookshop, 1979.]

Cook, John H., "Cook's Time in the Army." Unpublished manuscript. Cook Papers, Madison, Wis., State Historical Society of Wisconsin.

Curtis, O[rson] B., *History of the Twenty-Fourth Michigan of the Iron Brigade.* Detroit, Winn & Hammond, 1891.

369

Dawes, Rufus R., *Service with the Sixth Wisconsin Volunteers*. Marietta, Ohio, E. R. Alderman & Sons, 1890. [Reprinted, Morningside Bookshop, 1984.]

Dawes, Rufus R., "Sketches of War History." Military Order of the Loyal Legion of the United States, Commandery of the State of Ohio, *War Papers*, Vol. III. [Reprinted in: *Service with the Sixth Wisconsin Volunteers*. Dayton, Ohio, Morningside Books, 1984].

Dudley, William W., *The Iron Brigade at Gettysburg, 1878 Official Report of the Part Borne by the 1st Brigade, 1st Division, 1st Army Corps*. Cincinnati, Ohio, 1879.

Dyer, F. H., *A Compendium of the War of the Rebellion*. Des Moines, Iowa, 1908. [Reprinted, Morningside Bookshop, 1987.]

Ferris, Mary Walton, *Dawes-Gates Ancestral Lives; A Memorial Volume Containing the American Ancestry of Rufus R. Dawes*. (2 vols.) Chicago, Privately Printed, 1943.

Freeman, Douglas S., *Lee's Lieutenants*. (3 vols.) New York, Charles Scribner's Sons, 1942-1944.

Gates, Betsey Shipman, *Grandma's Letters*, prepared by Mary Dawes Beach. Chicago, Privately Printed, 1926.

Gibbon, John, *Personal Recollections of the Civil War*. New York, G. P. Putnam's Sons, 1928. [Reprinted, Morningside Bookshop, 1988.]

Haskell, Frank Aretas, *The Battle of Gettysburg*. Madison, Wis., Wisconsin History Commission, 1908.

Hassler, Warren W., *Crisis at the Crossroads: The First Day at Gettysburg*. Tuscaloosa, Ala., University of Alabama Press, 1970.

Hurn, Ethel Alice, *Wisconsin Women in the War Between the States*. Madison, Wis., Wisconsin History Commission, 1911.

Indiana at Antietam; Report of the Indiana Antietam Monument Commission and Ceremonies at the Dedication of the Monument. Indianapolis, Ind., Indiana Monument Commission, 1911.

Johnson, Robert U. and Clarence C. Buel, eds., *Battles and Leaders of the Civil War*. (4 vols.) New York, The Century Co., 1884-1887.

Kellogg, John A., *Capture and Escape; A Narrative of Army and Prison Life*. Madison, Wis., Wisconsin History Commission, 1908.

Lathrop, Stanley E., *A Brief Memorial to Captain Clayton E. Rogers*. ... [n.p.], 1900.

Linderman, Gerald F., *Embattled Courage; The Experience of Combat in the American Civil War*. New York, The Free Press, 1987.

Love, William D., *Wisconsin in the War of the Rebellion*. Chicago, Church & Goodman, 1866.

McClellan, George B., *McClellan's Own Story*. Philadelphia, J. B. Lippincott & Co., 1887.

McLean, James L., *Cutler's Brigade at Gettysburg*. Baltimore, Butternut and Blue Press, 1987.

Mattern, Carolyn J., *Soldiers When They Go: The Story of Camp Randall, 1861-1865*. Madison, Wis., State Historical Society of Wisconsin, 1981.

A *Memoir, Rufus R. Dawes.* New York, DeVinne Press, 1900.

Military Order of the Loyal Legion of the United States, Commandery of the State of Wisconsin, *War Papers.* Vol. I. Milwaukee, Wis., Armitage & Allen, 1891.

Military Order of the Loyal Legion of the United States, Commandery of the State of Wisconsin, *War Papers.* Vol. II. Milwaukee, Wis., Armitage & Allen, 1896.

Military Order of the Loyal Legion of the United States, Commandery of the State of Wisconsin, *War Papers.* Vol. III. Milwaukee, Wis., Burdick & Allen, 1903.

Nichols, Edward J., *Toward Gettysburg: A Biography of John F. Reynolds.* University Park, Pa., Pennsylvania State University Press, 1958.

Nolan, Alan T., *The Iron Brigade.* New York, Macmillan, 1961.

Otis, George H., *The Second Wisconsin Infantry,* with letters and recollections by other members of the regiment, ed. by Alan D. Gaff. Dayton, Ohio, Morningside Press, 1984. [Originally serialized in *The Milwaukee Sunday Telegraph* in 11 parts between July and December, 1880.]

Pier, C. K., comp. *Wisconsin Soldiers and Sailors Reunion Roster.* Fond du Lac, Wis., Wisconsin Soldiers and Sailors Reunion Association, 1880.

Quiner, E[dwin] B., *The Military History of Wisconsin.* Chicago, Clarke & Co., 1866.

Reed, Parker M., *The Bench and Bar of Wisconsin.* Milwaukee, Wis., P. M. Reed, 1882.

Smith, Donald, *The Twenty-Fourth Michigan of the Iron Brigade.* Harrisburg, Pa., Stackpole Co., 1962.

Soldiers' and Citizens' Album of Biographical Record. (2 vols.) Chicago, Grand Army Publishing Company, 1888.

Stine, J. H., *History of the Army of the Potomac.* Philadelphia, J. B. Rogers Printing Co., 1892.

Stribling, Robert M., *Gettysburg Campaign, and the Campaigns of 1864 and 1865 in Virginia.* Petersburg, Va., The Franklin Press, 1905.

[Tevis, C. V. and D. R. Marquis], *The History of the Fighting Fourteenth* [Brooklyn]. New York, 1911.

Thwaites, Reuben G., ed., *Civil War Messages and Proclamations of Wisconsin War Governors.* Madison, Wis., Wisconsin History Commission, 1912.

Thwaites, Reuben Gold, ed., *Collections of the State Historical Society of Wisconsin.* Vol. X. Madison, Wis., Wisconsin History Commission, 1888.

Timmons, Bascom N., *Portrait of an American: Charles G. Dawes.* New York, Henry Holt & Co., 1953.

War of the Rebellion, Official Records of the Union and Confederate Armies. Washington, D.C., United States Government Printing Office, 1889-1900.

Washburn, William H., "Jerome A. Watrous: The Civil War Years." Madison, Wis., Grand Army of the Republic Memorial Hall Museum, Unpublished manuscript.

Watrous, J[erome] A., *Richard Epps and Other Stories.* Milwaukee, Wis., 1906.

2. Ordnance and Technical Manuals

Coggins, Jack, *Arms and Equipment of the Civil War.* Garden City, N.Y., Doubleday & Co., 1962.

Coppee, Henry, *Field Manual of Evolutions of the Line.* Philadelphia, J. B. Lippincott & Co., 1862.

Fuller, Claud E., *Springfield Muzzle-Loading Shoulder Arms.* New York, Francis Bannerman Sons, 1930.

Hardee, W. J., *Rifle and Light Infantry Tactics.* (2 vols.) Philadelphia, J. B. Lippincott & Co., 1861.

McClellan, George B., *Manual of Bayonet Exercise.* Philadelphia, J. B. Lippincott & Co., 1862.

Reilly, Robert M., *United States Military Small Arms, 1816-1865.* Eagle Press, 1970.

Revised United States Army Regulations of 1861. Washington, D.C., United States Government Printing Office, 1863.

Thomas, Dean S., *Ready . . . Aim . . . Fire.* Bilgerville, Pa., Osborn Printing Co., 1981.

U. S. Infantry Tactics. Philadelphia, J. B. Lippincott & Co., 1863.

C. S. Ordnance Bureau, *Field Manual.* Richmond, Va., Ritchie & Dunnavant, 1862.

3. General Biographical Sources

Biographical Directory of the American Congress, 1774-1960. Washington, D.C., United States Government Printing Office, 1961.

Dictionary of American Biography. (10 vols.) New York, Charles Scribners's Sons, 1946.

Dictionary of Wisconsin Biography. Madison, Wis., State Historical Society of Wisconsin, 1960.

Warner, Ezra J., *Generals in Blue; Lives of Union Commanders.* Baton Rouge, La., Louisiana State University Press, 1964.

Warner, Ezra J., *Generals in Gray; Lives of Confederate Commanders.* Baton Rouge, La., Louisiana State University Press, 1959.

4. State, County and Local Histories

Adams, James G., *History of Education in Sawyer County, Wisconsin.* McIntire, Iowa, M. E. Granger, 1902.

Aderman, Ralph M., ed., *Trading Post to Metropolis.* Milwaukee, Wis., Milwaukee County Historical Society, 1987.

Bruce, William G., *History of Milwaukee, City and County.* (3 vols.) Chicago, S. J. Clarke Publishing Co., 1922.

Conard, Howard L., *History of Milwaukee From Its First Settlement to the Year 1895*. (3 vols.) Chicago, American Biographical Publishing Co., [1895].

Cozen, Kathleen Neils, *Immigrant Milwaukee, 1836-1860*. Cambridge, Mass., Harvard University Press, 1976.

Current, Richard N., *The History of Wisconsin . . . The Civil War Era, 1848-1873*. Madison, Wis., State Historical Society of Wisconsin, 1976.

[Flower, Frank A.], *History of Milwaukee, Wisconsin*. Chicago, Western Historical Co., 1881.

Gregory, John B., *History of Milwaukee, Wisconsin*. (4 vols.) Chicago, S. J. Clarke Publishing Co., 1931.

History of Crawford and Richland Counties, Wisconsin. Springfield, Ill., Union Publishing Co., 1884.

History of Vernon County, Wisconsin. Springfield, Ill., Union Publishing Co., 1884.

Kessinger, L[awrence], *History of Buffalo County, Wisconsin*. Alma, Wis., 1888.

Koss, Rud[olf] A., *Milwaukee*. Milwaukee, Wis., The Milwaukee Herold, 1871. [English translation for the Federal Writer's Project by Hans Ibsen.]

Krog, Carl E., *Marinette: Biography of a Nineteenth Century Lumbering Town, 1850-1910*. Madison, Wis., University of Wisconsin PhD. Dissertation, 1971.

Nesbit, Robert C., *The History of Wisconsin . . . Urbanization and Industrialization, 1873-1893*. Madison, Wis., State Historical Society of Wisconsin, 1985.

Portrait and Biographical Record of Sheyboygan County, Wisconsin. Chicago, Excelsior Publishing Company, 1894.

Smith, Alice E., *The History of Wisconsin . . . From Exploration to Statehood*. Madison, Wis., State Historical Society of Wisconsin, 1973.

Still, Bayrd, *Milwaukee, The History of a City*. Madison, Wis., State Historical Society of Wisconsin, 1948.

Watrous, Jerome A., *Memoirs of Milwaukee County*. (2 vols.) Madison, Wis., 1909.

5. Newspapers and Periodicals

Baraboo News-Republic, Baraboo, Wis.
Baraboo Republic, Baraboo, Wis.
Beloit Free Press, Beloit, Wis.
Beloit Journal, Beloit, Wis.
The Blackhat, Occasional Newsletter of the 6th Wisconsin Vols.
Chicago Chronicle
Chippewa Herald, Chippewa, Wis.
Christian Science Monitor

Civil War Times Illustrated
Confederate Veteran Magazine
Evening Wisconsin, Milwaukee
Fond du Lac Reporter, Fond du Lac, Wis.
Grant County Herald, Lancaster, Wis.
LaCrosse Morning Chronicle, LaCrosse, Wis.
LaCrosse Republican and Leader, LaCrosse, Wis.
Mauston Star, Mauston, Wis.
Milwaukee Daily News
Milwaukee Free Press
Milwaukee History, Milwaukee County Historical Society
Milwaukee Journal
Milwaukee Sentinel
Milwaukee Sunday Telegraph/Milwaukee Telegraph
Mineral Point Tribune, Mineral Point, Wis.
Missouri Republican, St. Louis, Mo.
The National Tribune, Washington, D.C.
Prescott Journal, Prescott, Wis.
Prairie du Chien Courier, Prairie du Chien, Wis.
Vernon County Censor, Viroqua, Wis.
Wisconsin Magazine of History.
Wisconsin Necrology. [51 volumes of newspaper and similar obituaries.] State Historical Society of Wisconsin.
Wisconsin Newspaper Volumes. [Clippings from various Civil War era Wisconsin newspapers.] State Historical Society of Wisconsin.

6. Census and Related

Alphabetical List of Soldiers and Sailors of the Late War Residing in the State of Wisconsin, June 20, 1885. Madison, Wis., Secretary of State, 1886.

The Blue Book of the State of Wisconsin, 1879, 1880, 1881, 1882, 1883, 1885, 1887, 1889, 1891, 1893, 1895, 1897, 1899. Madison, Wis., Democrat Printing Co., 1879-1899.

Estabrook, Charles E., *Wisconsin Losses in the Civil War.* Madison, Wis., Commission on Civil War Records, 1915.

Fox, William F., *Regimental Losses in the American Civil War.* Albany, N.Y., Albany Publishing Co., 1889. [Reprinted, Morningside Bookshop, 1985.]

Milwaukee City Directories, 1846 to 1910. Milwaukee, Wis., [Various Publishers], 1846-1910.

Roster of Wisconsin Volunteers, War of the Rebellion, 1861-1865. (2 vols.) Madison, Wis., 1886.

State of Wisconsin Census, 1875, 1885, 1895, 1905.

U.S. Census, Wisconsin, 1850, 1860, 1870, 1880, 1900, 1910.

Wisconsin Census Enumeration, 1895: Names of Ex-Soldiers and Sailors Residing in Wisconsin, June 20, 1895. . . . Madison, Wis., Democrat Printing Co., 1896.

Wisconsin Census Enumeration, 1905: Names of Ex-Soldiers and Sailors Residing in Wisconsin, June 1, 1905. Madison, Wis., Democrat Printing Co., 1906.

7. Manuscripts and Records

Bachelder, John B., Papers, New Hampshire Historical Society.

Bragg, Edward S., Papers, State Historical Society of Wisconsin.

Brown, Edwin A., Letters, Private Collection.

Cook, John H., Papers, State Historical Society of Wisconsin.

Dawes, Rufus R., Papers, State Historical Society of Wisconsin.

Descriptive Book, 6th Wisconsin Infantry, U.S. National Archives & Records Administration.

Fairfield, George, Diaries, State Historical Society of Wisconsin.

Iron Brigade Association, Miscellaneous papers, rosters, etc. State Historical Society of Wisconsin.

Morning Reports, 6th Wisconsin Infantry, U.S. National Archives & Records Administration.

Order Book, 1st Brigade, 1st Division, 1st Army Corps, U.S. National Archives & Records Administration.

Order Book, Sixth Wisconsin Infantry, U.S. National Archives & Records Administration.

Raymond, Levi B., Diary, Private Collection.

Tongue, Levi, Letters, Private Collection.

Walker, Charles, Diary, Private Collection.

Watrous, Jerome A., Papers, State Historical Society of Wisconsin.

Military and Pension records of James P. Sullivan, William N. Remington, George Fairfield, Loyd G. Harris, Thomas Plummer, Edward Whaley, Cornelius Okey, Francis A. Wallar, John F. Hauser, etc., U.S. National Archives & Records Service.

INDEX

377

378

ground, 158; mortally wounded, 190, 202

Chase, Joseph A., 79

Cheek, Philip, 38, 38n, 67, 84, 95, 167, 277; leggings, 345; uniform, 333-334

Chicago, Illinois, 313n

Chippewa Herald, 226n

Christmas, 1861, 125-126

Christy, John T., hat, 338

Citizens Corps. *See* Company F

Clinton, Henry P., 313, 314n, 359

Cobb, Amasa, 313n

Cold Harbor, battle, 257

color company, 164, 165

colors. *See* flags

Company A, 38, 57, 84, 91, 94, 95, 103, 140, 157, 166, 211, 345; hats, 343; muskets issued, 365; muster, June 30, 1863, 157n; officer purged, 120; recruited, 66-67

Company B, 85, 95, 98, 157, 164-165, 165n, 199, 208-209, 279; hats, 343; muskets issued, 365; muster, June 30, 1863, 157n; recruited, 63-64

Company C, 30, 84, 109, 116, 150, 151, 153, 155, 164, 165n, 178, 179, 186, 190, 202, 211, 224n, 227, 250, 269, 281, 297, 314; muster, June 30, 1863, 157n; nickname, 61; recruited, 59-61; songs and singing, 110; uniforms, 325, 335

Company D, 62, 74, 82, 104, 166, 243; and Milwaukee disturbance, 56; casualties, 193; departs Milwaukee, 57; muster, June 30, 1863, 157n; officers purged, 120; reaction to new officers, 123; recalcitrant recruit, 55; recruited, 53-54.

Company E, 40, 80, 81, 91, 98, 106, 108, 109, 110, 117, 120, 125, 164, 165n, 178, 182, 184, 189, 190, 193, 203, 211, 232, 237, 245; attacked by "Pug Uglies," 95; hats, 343; muster, June 30, 1863, 157n; recruited, 47-51

Company F, 54, 84, 106, 122-123, 153, 165-166, 165n, 207, 224n, 239, 266, 354n; departs Milwaukee, 56, 57; muster, June 30, 1863, 157n; protest over rations, 57-58; recruited, 52-53; songs and singing, 110-111, 163; uniforms, 326

Company G, 41n, 164, 208, 212, 314n, 315n, 357-358; muskets issued, 364-365; muster, June 30, 1863, 157n; new officers, 123; officers purged, 120, 121; recruited, 64-66; uniforms, 324-325, 334

Company H, 85, 165, 166, 195, 208, 211, 221, 237, 245, 268, 279, 280, 281, 283, 355n; muster, June 30, 1863, 157n; recruited, 61-63

Company I, 94, 101, 110, 129, 157, 165n, 166, 169, 179, 183, 201n, 205, 209, 211, 227, 247, 263, 282, 314; casualties, 192, 192n, 230; muster, June 30, 1863, 157n; new officers, 123; officers purged, 120; recruited, 44-47; retrieves artillery, 207

Company K, 25, 26, 29, 28, 30, 35, 37, 86, 93, 94, 95, 109, 110, 113, 129, 149, 158, 164, 165n, 184, 204, 211, 233, 245, 251, 261, 277, 281, 297, 315; after Gettysburg, 237; arrives at Camp Randall, 73-76; casualties, 192-193, 237, 275; muster, June 30, 1863, 157n; new officers, 123; officers purged, 120; recruited, 67-71; reunion, 1885, 275-276; songs and singing, 163; wounded at Gettysburg, 215-216; uniforms, 334n-335n

Confederate States, uniforms, 302-304, 303n

Conger, John, 229

Converse, Rollin P., 134n, 217-218, 225; background, 64; mortally wounded, 257; promoted to lieutenant, 123; retrieves artillery, 207

Cook, John H., 55, 56, 83n, 107, 271; characterizes E. Bragg, 106; confronted by Gen. Gibbon, 130-131; confronted by J. Marsh, 130-131; escapes from Camp Randall, 82-84; on J. Marsh appointment, 124; runs camp guard, 103-104; transferred to Battery B, 136

Coon Slough, Wisconsin, 46, 129, 166, 245, 246

Cornish, Ephraim B., 29, 34; wounded at South Mountain, 30

corps badges, 360-362

Cowen, George W., 359

Crane, John, 70, 120, 124

Crawford, Charles A., 189, 216; leg amputated, 233

Crimean War, 305

Culp's Hill, 224, 230, 234, 239n, 243, 248; attack of July 2, 1863, 234-235; 6th Wisconsin forms, 225-227

Curtis, Orson B., 41n

Custer, Gen. George A., 256

Cutler, Lysander, 73, 75, 80, 82, 84, 90, 91, 94, 95, 99, 100, 101, 103, 104, 114, 115, 117, 121, 123, 128, 134, 177n, 205, 239, 293, 337, 343, 357; and Dawes-Haskell rivalry, 135-136; assigned brigade command, 137, 330;

assigned 2nd Brigade command, 140;
background, 118-119; backs F. Haskell, 133, 134; confronted by W. Lindwurm, 57; contracts for uniforms, 309-
310, 311-312, 314; controversy with
B. Sweet, 128-129; criticized by E.
Bragg, 126; discontinuance of gray
uniforms, 325-326; foraging incident,
107-109; orders hats, 131; regimental
order on uniforms, 344, 352; purges
officers, 119-120, 122; reassigned brigade command, 354

Cutler's Brigade, 158, 161, 162, 163-164,
168, 168n, 171, 175-176, 177n, 179,
180, 184, 186n, 210, 217, 224n, 291,
293, 295, 296, 296n; retreats, 182;
strength, 180n

D

Dane County, Wisconsin, 35, 128
Davis, Christopher C., 200, 201n-202n
Davis, Gen. Joseph R., 180, 291
Davis, Rescun W., 68
Davis' Brigade, 180, 182, 203, 210, 287,
288, 289, 290, 292, 297; strength,
180n
Dawes, Charles, 87n
Dawes, Edward, 85
Dawes, Ephraim, 85, 86
Dawes, Henry, 67, 85, 86, 87
Dawes, Rufus R., 25, 29, 33, 35, 62, 64,
67, 70, 71, 78, 84, 91, 94, 95, 110, 115,
120, 122, 124, 144, 152, 157, 161, 162,
166-167, 169, 176, 178, 185, 199n,
202, 206, 209, 233, 237, 254, 257,
258-259, 272, 277, 280, 282, 285, 287,
291, 292, 350; accepts J. Blair surrender, 196, 198-199; aids W. Remington with pension, 261-262; aligns
6th Wisconsin, 171; aligns 6th Wisconsin for charge, 186-188; ancestry,
85, 85n; arrives at Camp Randall, 73-
76; appointed major, 136; at Iron Brigade Association reunion, 251-252,
256; background, 85-87; carries flag,
190-192; characterized, 87-90; characterizes L. Cutler, 118; characterizes
J. Marston, 193; comforts J. Kelly,
192; corresponds with W. Murphy,
201n-202n; Culp's Hill action, 230;
elected major, 134; entrusts 2nd Mississippi flag to W. Evans, 208, 283;
eulogized, 253n; eulogizes W. Remington, 262; Gettysburg report, 293;
hats, 343, 344; horse shot, 182-183,
183n; leads 6th Wisconsin through
Gettysburg, 224-225; leggings, 343,
344, 347; letter on battle, 238; letter
to Co. K reunion, 275-276; letters on
charge, 204, 295; letters on the march
to Gettysburg, 144, 144n; military career, 252; on Battery B, 217; on capture of 2nd Mississippi flag, 280-282;
on J. Kelly, 212-213; on July 2nd action, 234; on Mary B. Gates, 146; on
officer purge, 120, 121, 123-124; on
rivalry with F. Haskell, 135-136; on
6th Wisconsin band, 113; on sleeping
sentry, 150-151; on uniforms, 315,
349; on W. Whaley, 112; ordered to
the right, 178-179; orders band to
play, 164; orders charge on railroad
cut, 296-297; postwar life and death,
252-253; prepares for charge, 182;
reflects on battle, 227; removes
wounded, 210; responds to E. Fowler
report, 293-294; "servant," 90; with-
draws 6th Wisconsin, 218
Dawes, Sarah Cutler, 86, 87n
Day, William, 165n
Dearborn, F. A., 201n
Deep Run, Virginia, 144
Deiner, Jacob, 51
Delafield, Wisconsin, 165n
Deleglise, Francis A., 50, 165n; hos-
pitalized in Gettysburg, 217; on Get-
tysburg incident, 232; wounded, 189
Department of the Rappahannock, 330,
331n, 340
Department of the Shenandoah, 331n
deserter executed, 141-143
deserters, 94, 262
DeSoto, Wisconsin, 45, 192n
Dill, Daniel J., 63, 64
Dillon, John J., 80
Dillon, William A., 80
Dodd, William (Co.), 316, 316n
Dodgeville, Wisconsin, 249
Donglis, Jasper, 194
Doubleday, Abner, 176, 177n, 178, 248,
290; on July 1, 1863 situation, 182,
183n; Gettysburg report, 292
Dow, Charles C., 320; hat, 338;
uniform, 313n, 323
drill, 69, 98-99, 107, 132-133
drumming from service, 35-36
Dudley, William, Gettysburg report,
296-297
Dunn, Harry, 50, 190, 207, 231-232;
background, 190n; in Gettysburg, 216
Dunn, Henry G. See Dunn, Harry
Dunn, Patrick, drummed from service,
35-36

hospitals, 31; Gettysburg, 219-220, 221
Howard, Gen. Oliver O., 228; criticized
    by J. Sullivan, 231
Howe, Julia Ward, 111
Hubbard, Calvin R., on uniforms, 314n
Hunt, Henry J., on charge, 290
Huntington, Henry H., account of exe-
    cution, 143n
Huntley, Reuben, 34, 34n, 160, 245
Hyatt, Charles P., 209, 227, 257, 261

I

Indiana, 7th Infantry, 162, 230; 19th
    Infantry, 38, 97, 108, 114, 115, 128,
    140, 147, 147n, 162, 168, 180, 296,
    348, 349; assigned to King's Brigade,
    324; band, 114, 115; corps badges,
    361, 361n; deserter executed, 141-
    143; equipage, 355; hats, 131, 340-
    341, 341n, 342, 343; leggings, 349;
    muskets, 363, 364n, 367; nickname,
    102; uniforms, 331-333, 349-350, 353;
    20th Infantry, 341
inspections, 336, 351-352
Iowa County, Wisconsin, 57
Irish, 53-54, 56, 110, 123, 304; officers
    purged, 120, 122
Iron Brigade, 33, 99, 140, 143n, 145,
    146, 152, 160, 164, 169, 175, 176,
    177n, 180, 210, 227, 238, 242, 296,
    297, 301, 330-332, 340, 341; corps
    badges, 362; hats, 342; inspection,
    333; leggings, 345-350; march to Get-
    tysburg, 162; name acquired, 39-42,
    40n-42n; reputation, 39; uniforms,
    131-132, 301-302; order of march
    to Gettysburg, 168. See also Kings'
    Brigade
Iron Brigade Association, 127, 250, 255,
    273; formed, 265; reunion of 1880,
    242; reunion of 1883, 244; reunion of
    1884, 87n, 241
Iron Brigade Guard. See Brigade Guard

J

Jackson, Gen. Thomas J., 26, 41n, 133,
    136
James River, 257
Jaraslawski & Brothers (Co.), 312, 314,
    318
Jeff Davis Hat. See hats
Johnson, Amos S., 120
Johnson, Jerome B., 134n
Johnson, John O., 355n; on capture of
    2nd Mississippi flag, 195-196;
    wounded, 199
Johnston, Alexander, 60, 251

Jones, Bodley, 157, 166, 245, 263, 277;
    characterized, 66; killed, 199, 199n
Jones, C. L., 165n
Jones, Charles O., wounded, 192
Jones, Edwin C., 51; confronted by
    L. Cutler, 108-109
Jones, Enoch, kills rebel, 209
Jones, George, 66
Jones, Reuben, 66
Juneau, Solomon, 59
Juneau County, Wisconsin, 67, 68, 74,
    75, 76, 77, 79, 85, 87, 87n, 129, 163,
    164

K

Kalorama Heights. See Camp Kalorama
Kanouse, Theodore D., 113
Keeler, Charles A., 157; hat, 343;
    wounded, 192
Kelley, James. See Kelly, James
Kellogg, A. N., 67
Kellogg, Edward, 44n
Kellogg, John A., 67, 76, 134n, 205,
    244n, 250; "casualty" at Patterson
    Park, 95-96; commands Iron Brigade,
    258; letter on charge, 295-296, 296n;
    letter on Gettysburg, 239-240; pro-
    moted to captain, 123; wounded and
    captured in Wilderness, 257
Kelly, Isaiah F., 64, 88, 164-165, 199,
    208-209, 217, 227; carries flag, 209,
    235; military career, 259; postwar life
    and death, 259; wounded, 192
Kelly, James, 64, 157, 165, 212-213,
    259, 277; mortally wounded, 192
Kenosha, Wisconsin, 105
Kent, Lewis A., 41n; addresses Iron Bri-
    gade Association reunion, 254; meets
    E. Whaley at 1884 reunion, 254; mili-
    tary career, 254n-255n.
Kerr, Thomas, 59, 124, 250, 257, 258;
    background, 55; military career, 243-
    244, 244n; postwar life and death,
    244, 244n; wounded, 193, 243
Keyt, George M., witnesses F. King's
    death, 212
Kidd, Alphonso D., 230
Kildare, Wisconsin, 189
Killmartin, John, kills rebel, 208
King, Frank, 51, 81, 165, 245, 277;
    death, 211-212; mortally wounded,
    190; premonition of death, 178
King, Rufus, 26, 59, 102, 103, 113, 323;
    backs Haskell promotion, 133
King's Brigade, 323-324, 330; uniforms,
    326. See also Iron Brigade
King's Division, 330, 331n, 340
Klauber, S. (Co.), 313n

Philadelphia, Pennsylvania, 237, 272, 279, 284
photographs, 80, 133, 328-329, 335-336, 337-338, 344
Pickett's Charge, 235-236
Pier, Colwert K., 309
Platche, Professor, 47
Plummer, Philip W., 59, 134n; background, 60; killed in Wilderness, 257; promoted to captain, 123
Plummer, Thomas W., 59, 134n; background, 60
Plymouth, Wisconsin, 45, 192n
Pointon, Mair, 67, 84, 95, 165, 165n, 167, 277; hat, 343-344; leggings, 345
Pope, Gen. John, 136, 167n, 248, 330n
Portage, Wisconsin, 209, 305n
Portage County, Wisconsin, 32
Portage Light Guards, uniforms, 305n
Potomac River, 97, 151
Prairie du Chien, Wisconsin, 44, 59, 60, 105, 109, 158, 166, 171, 190, 224n, 229, 250, 269
Prairie du Chien Courier, 61
Prairie du Chien Volunteers. *See* Company C
pranks. *See* amusements and pranks
Pratt, Lorenzo, 216; wounded, 193
Prescott, Wisconsin, 257, 261
Prescott Guards. *See* Company B
Prescott Journal, 64
Preston, Abram W., 208
Pruyn, Howard F., wounded, 211
"Pug Uglies," 95-96
Pye, Edward, 186, 186n, 293, 294, 296, 297

Q

Quaw, David L., promoted to 1st lieutenant, 123
Quincy, Wisconsin, 30

R

Racine, Wisconsin, 320, 356
Raeder, John, 166; leggings, 348; mortally wounded, 193, 348
Randall, Gov. Alexander, 44, 68, 93, 165, 307, 309, 319; war proclamation, 43
Randall Guards, 309
Rapidan River, 257
Rappahannock River, 139
rations, 77, 84, 93, 106
Rau, Charles, 229
Raymond, Levi B., injured, 127, 334n; on equipage, 357-358; on muskets, 354-365; on officer purge, 121; on uniforms, 315n, 324-325; promoted to lieutenant, 123; uniform, 314n, 334

Reader, William A., 123
Reed, Elisha R., 143n
Reedsburg, Wisconsin, 67
Remington, William N., 166, 169, 199, 211, 223, 230, 257, 263, 264, 281; catches cold, 157; characterized, 67; escapes from Gettysburg, 223; hospitalized in Gettysburg, 220, 221; military career, 261; postwar life and death, 261-262; rushes for 2nd Mississippi flag, 194-195; travels to Baltimore, 228-230; wounded, 282
Retreat, Wisconsin, 264
Reynolds, John, 143n, 157, 182, 202n, 292; characterized, 161-162; killed, 179-180.
Rhode Island, 12th Infantry, 333
Ripon, Wisconsin, 85
Robbins, J. V. (Co.), 318n
Robinson, William W., 359-360; order on equipment, 342
Rock County, Wisconsin, 64
Rock Creek, 234
Rogers, Clayton E., 134n, 168n, 179, 217-218, 225, 245; arrests Gen. Rowley, 226; deserter executed, 141-143; postwar life and death, 248; promoted to 2nd lieutenant, 123; retreat to Gettysburg, 219
Rogers, Earl A., 44, 45, 87, 134n, 177n, 179, 190, 257, 271; encounters rebel cavalry 145; military career, 246-247; on capture of 2nd Mississippi flag, 200, 282; on charge on railroad cut, 196; postwar life and death, 247-248; remembers P. Markle, 245-246; retreat to Gettysburg, 219; visits E. Bragg, 247; writes to F. Wallar, 280
Rood, Amos, 156, 270
Rose, Eugene P., 216; wounded, 193
Rothwell, John, 333
Rowley, Gen. Thomas A., 225-226; career, 226n
Rubber Clothing Company, 316, 357

S

sack coats. *See* uniforms
Sage, Milo G., 165n
St. Clair, John, 68, 71
Salomon, Gov. Edward, 122; and Dawes-Haskell rivalry, 134
Sauk County, Wisconsin, 66, 245
Sauk County Riflemen. *See* Company A
Schildt, Henry, wounded, 193
Schmidt, Joseph, 354n
Schorse, Otto, 266, 267, 268
Schreiber, Gottlieb. *See* Schroeber, Gottfried

388